Managing
Careers

We work with leading authors to develop the strongest educational materials in business, bringing cutting-edge thinking and best learning practice to a global market.

Under a range of well-known imprints, including Financial Times Prentice Hall, we craft high quality print and electronic publications which help readers to understand and apply their content, whether studying or at work.

To find out more about the complete range of our publishing, please visit us on the World Wide Web at: www.pearsoned.co.uk

Managing Careers
Theory and Practice

Yehuda Baruch

 Prentice Hall
FINANCIAL TIMES

An imprint of Pearson Education

Harlow, England • London • New York • Boston • San Francisco • Toronto • Sydney • Singapore • Hong Kong
Tokyo • Seoul • Taipei • New Delhi • Cape Town • Madrid • Mexico City • Amsterdam • Munich • Paris • Milan

Pearson Education Limited

Edinburgh Gate
Harlow
Essex CM20 2JE
England

and Associated Companies throughout the world.

Visit us on the World Wide Web at:
www.pearsoned.co.uk

First published in 2004

© Pearson Education Limited 2004

ISBN 0 273 67800 0

British Library Cataloguing-in-Publication Data
A catalogue record for this book is available from the British Library

10 9 8 7 6 5 4 3 2 1
08 07 06 05 04

Typeset in 9.5/12.5 pt Stone Serif by 3
Printed and bound by Bell & Bain Limited, Glasgow

The publisher's policy is to use paper manufactured from sustainable forests.

In Memoriam: Eliezer Rosenstein and Gedaliahu (Gadi) H. Harel
who have guided me in my academic career

Contents

List of figures

List of tables

Abbreviations

CAST: Career Active System Triad

CNC: Computer numerical control

CPM: Career Planning and Management

EEO: Equal Employment Opportunities

EU (EC): European Union (European Community)

HR: Human Resource

HRM: Human Resource Management

IHRM: International Human Resource Management

ILM: Internal Labour Market

MNC: Multinational company

MPT: Multiple Part-Time

PA: Performance appraisal

PRP: Performance related pay

RIASEC: Realistic, Investigative, Artistic, Social, Enterprising, Conventional

SHRM: Strategic Human Resource Management

SMT: Spectral Management Theory

TCN: Third-country national

UK: United Kingdom

USA: United States of America

Preface

One slogan that for me represents an organizational truism is, 'Our people are our most important assets'. It has become the most cited motto for a multitude of organizations; many enterprises adopt it as their credo. I believe that the difference between using it simply as a slogan and genuinely adopting it as an organizational philosophy will be manifested in how organizations treat their employees, at all hierarchical levels. This, in turn, will be reflected in both individual and organizational success.

Career management clearly reveals the bond between the organization and its employees. The practice of career planning and management is concerned with one of the two primary roles of Human Resource Management (HRM) in any organization, which are to obtain and to retain employees. This book is dedicated to the second role, retaining the human talent, utilizing career systems that fit contemporary trends.

In my years of teaching HRM and careers I have found a growth of interest among students in taking a course or an elective in the careers area, and both they and those who teach them should benefit from a textbook dedicated to this field. I could not find a similar book to use for my own teaching, and it was this lack that served as the initial impetus for the writing of this book. The careers area is increasingly gaining recognition as a crucial part of HRM, but one to which the standard HRM textbooks usually devote no more than a single chapter.

The purpose of the book is to present the reader with the concepts and principles of career planning and management in light of current developments. Many concepts suggested by present-day scholars and management gurus are relevant and have important implications for career systems. In contrast, many of the reading materials for the area still refer to the traditional type of career. This book focuses on career systems and the way they are managed by organizations, reflecting the diversity that exists in management studies – both in practice and in theory. Each chapter ends with a list of thought-provoking questions for students and managers alike.

This book presents the emergence of new career systems, which is very much different from the rigid structure of climbing hierarchy ladders or relying on chance for career success, as implied by the metaphor of Snakes and Ladders portrayed on the cover of the book. Nevertheless, luck will always play role for each career, and organizational structures, be they subtle or observable, are the playing field for careers.

Apart from that, it was also marketing advice – and as in career counselling, we should learn to listen to the expert's advice!

An instructor's Manual and Powerpoint slides are available for lecturers to download from http://www.booksites.net/baruch

I have attempted to integrate traditional concepts and modern (or post-modern) innovative inspirations. The book is intended for both practising managers and the academic community in the management area – both students and scholars. The most prominent qualities of the book are:

- a focus on the organizational, managerial viewpoint
- the incorporation of innovative concepts on the future of careers
- an international perspective.

I hope the reader, whether student or scholar, consultant, HR manager or other professional, and anyone who has a career and wishes to develop it further, will benefit from the book.

Yehuda Baruch

1 Introduction: career perspectives

LEARNING OBJECTIVES

After reading this chapter you should be able to:

- Define career.

- Distinguish between individual and organizational career perspectives.

- Identify the new types of careers.

- Understand the impact of environmental factors on careers.

- Explain how organizations can work alongside individuals to match their mutual needs.

- Understand career system management within the general HRM framework.

CHAPTER CONTENTS

■ *From strategic HRM to strategic career systems*

■ *Summarizing exercise*

■ *Summary*

■ *Key terms*

■ *Discussion questions*

■ *Notes*

Introduction

In the past, careers have taken various forms. However, the present generation is witnessing a sea change in the shape of careers. From the lifelong career as an archetypal model, quite often fulfilled, we are moving to a world of work where stable employment with the same organization is not only the exception, but also not even the ideal type aspired to. Within organizations we are seeing a fluidity of structures and a continuous re-shaping of configurations, which are reflected in dynamic career systems. Both people's and organization's perspectives on career planning and management have changed.

The change in the shape of careers has not occurred in isolation. It is just one aspect of changes that are taking place, at a seemingly ever-accelerating pace, in society in general, and in management in particular. Businesses and public organizations are experiencing rapid developments in many areas – the economy, technology, society, politics and relationships – that have wide implications for the planning and management of careers.

The development of people has always been considered to be an organizational role. Organizations must invest in and develop their assets, and the statement that 'people are the most important asset of the organization' may now be a cliché, but any cliché was once a novelty. With concurrent changes in individual perspectives, the management of organizations and society generally, the notion of *career* and consequently its management, has been transformed.

Career perspectives: individual v. organizational

The meaning of career planning and management depends very much on whether an individual or organizational perspective is taken. Many observers have viewed career management as a process by which individuals develop, implement and monitor career goals and strategies.[1] Much of the literature on careers has indeed focused on the individual view. However, in the early 1990s Gutteridge *et al.* stated 'The focus of career development has shifted radically, from the individual to the organization'[2]. Still the pendulum seems to be shifting back to an individual orientation of managing careers, which follows a general trend of the modern age that emphasizes individualism rather than collectivism, in particular in Western societies.[3] This book takes a more balanced approach, arguing that organizations can, and perhaps should take a lead role in planning and managing careers, but also that this role will be different from that prescribed in the past by those who have studied the area of careers. Much of this book examines the organizational side of career systems.

What is a career?

The answer depends on the viewpoint of the questioner. A career belongs to the individual but in much, if not most, employment, the career will be planned and managed for the individual by the organization. The organizational structure forms the (internal) 'road map', providing identifiable positions, interrelationships between these positions, the qualities necessary to fill them, and moreover, mechanisms to enable people navigate this road map. This way organizations can take a leading role and have control over career planning and management.

Psychologists define career as, 'The pattern of work-related experience that span the course of a person's life'.[4] Arthur, Hall and Lawrence from the USA regard career as 'an evolving sequence of a person's work experience over time'.[5] On the other side of the ocean, Arnold defines career as 'the sequence of employment-related positions, roles, activities and experiences encountered by a person'.[6] Careers can indeed be seen as a sequencing of an individual's life, work roles and experiences, if one limits one's perspective to that of the individual. Nevertheless, careers take place in specified social environments, and in particular in organizations – a crucial point missed by many scholars who analyse careers from psychological perspective only. The normal or typical professional career usually follows a sequence of developmental phases, each of which is delineated by a distinct shift in the individual's sense of self, but each is shaped and influenced by the organization in which the person works.

The variety of definitions, only a few of which are presented here, re-emphasizes that *career* involves a process of progress and development of individuals, which is sometimes described as the life stories of people. Nevertheless there is in the careers domain a substantial overlap between individual and organizational roles.

What is the area of study?

The concept of a career builds on several theoretical disciplines, but as the formulation of career theory was quite individually focused, its development was traditionally dominated by psychologists. However, careers are, to a certain extent, a 'property' of organizations, and managed by them as part of HRM.[7] An approach that takes into account an organizational orientation may provide a more balanced definition: 'a process of development by [an] employee along a path of experience and roles in one or more organizations'.[8] Career management is part of HRM. The basic roles of HRM are to obtain and retain employees, and career systems deal with the latter role, of retaining (and sometimes releasing an excess of) employees.

Recent studies have put into focus the changing meaning of careers. Many have examined the shift from long-term relationships to transactional, short-termism.[9] At one time people would have expected to serve an organization for their entire working life. Now people expect the organization to serve them, and over a timespan that could easily be only two to three years. Planning horizons have shortened, the future needs of organizations have become less clear, and subsequently both individuals and organizations struggle to re-define careers and the mutual role each side should play in their management. The main shift is from careers that offer secure employment for all, to careers that provide 'opportunities for development'. The development has ceased to be merely an organizational obligation, and rather rests with the individual. Similarly, in a recent review of the literature on career writing during the last century, Sullivan[10] has identified two prominent streams of research in career studies: developmental stage theories and the boundaryless career, emerging at the end of the 1990s. Another core stream in the study of careers is career choice theories.

Another distinction that is sometimes made in the study of careers is between the concepts of the individual focus and those of the organizational/cultural focus. However, convergence is better than distinction as a way of understanding careers. Balancing individual and organizational needs is the goal of many career models and writing about them.[11] The need to satisfy and comply with individual and organizational requirements has long been established,[12] and individual aspirations are developed within organizational contexts and career systems.[13] A broader perspective would treat the wider environment – professional, organizational and cultural – as the reference point for individual career aspirations.

Balancing individual and organizational needs

Herriot and Pemberton[14] offer the model presented in Figure 1.1. They outline four properties they feel an established career model should possess. These are:

(a) Conceptualization (i.e. taking into account not merely the organization, but also the business, political and economic environment)
(b) Cyclical and processual nature of the model
(c) Subjectivity (rather than normativity) for the meaning of career success

and

(d) Interactive nature in the sense of relationship between the organization and the individual.

Let us examine the model from both the organizational and individual perspectives.

The first proposition of the model associates the business environment with the organization in terms of strategy, structure and processes. As will be shown later (Chapter 4), these correspond with philosophy, policy and practice. This conceptualization means that factors such as sector of operation, national culture, business activity or prosperity of the market influence the strategic goals set by organizations, how organizations are designed and structured and the prac-

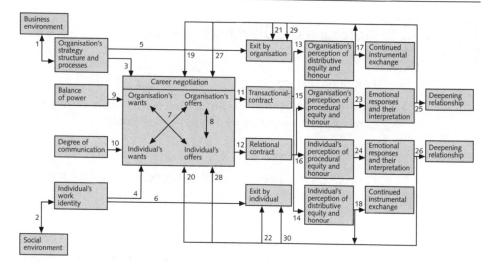

Figure 1.1 A contractual model of careers

Source: P. Herriot and C. Pemberton (1966) 'Contracting careers', *Human Relations*, 49(6) p. 760.

tices they apply for managing people and processes. The model argues that the Internal Labour Market (ILM) is an ideal archetype, i.e. that promoting from within is the best approach to career management, but that absolute ILM never occurs in practice.

From the individual perspective, proposition 2 suggests that the social context in which people grow and develop influences their values, norms and beliefs. These, in turn, influence their career aspirations, career choice, and progress.

Propositions 3 and 4, respectively, argue that organizational strategy, structure and processes will determine what organizations need from people and their careers, whereas people's identities will determine what they wish to gain from the organization. Similarly propositions 5 and 6 reflect the ways in which organizations and people conclude their contractual relationships.

At the core of the Herriot and Pemberton model lies the element of mutual recognition, negotiation and agreement about the 'give and take', the psychological and contractual agreement organizations and individuals consent to (or believe they have agreed upon). It is the point of equilibrium between what people offer to the organization and what they expect in return, and vice versa. Other influential factors on this core process are the balance of power (proposition 9) and communication between the parties (proposition 10).

The intermediate outcomes of the core process are manifested in two types of relationship between the individual and the organization. These can be transactional, calculated 'deals', on the one hand (proposition 11), and relational, even emotional, bond relationships (proposition 12) on the other. The transactional relationship is instrumental (in that services are provided in exchange for compensation). The relational relationship reflects mutual commitment. In practice both types exist in any employment relationship. There is then the perception of distributive justice (propositions 13 and 14) and of procedural justice (proposition 15 and 16). (On distributive and procedural justice, *see* Exhibit 1.1.)

<table>
<tr><td>

**EXHIBIT
1.1**

</td><td>

Procedural and distributive justice[15]

</td></tr>
</table>

Procedural justice

Perception about justice or fairness that occurs when the process utilized to set work outcomes and benefits is seen as fair and reasonable.

Distributive justice

Perception about justice or fairness that occurs when the actual work outcomes and benefits are seen as fair and reasonable.

As a result of the perception of organizational justice, people and organizations will continue to exercise instrumental exchange if they perceive that there is adequate distributive equality (propositions 17 and 18). They will not do so if they believe there has been a breach of the 'contract' – in such a case they will try to re-negotiate the contract (propositions 19 and 20) or leave the organization (propositions 21 and 22). In a primarily relational contract, the impact of organizational justice will be mainly on the emotional element, and if the contract is perceived as fair the positive interpretation (propositions 23 and 24) will be reflected in a deepening relationship (propositions 25 and 26). Breach of a contract would similarly lead to an attempt to try to renegotiate the contract (propositions 27 and 28) or to leave the organization (propositions 29 and 30).

Question

> Think about your latest career move (this can be your first job search, an internal move within an organization, a move to another organization or starting your own enterprise). How can you analyse that move in light of Herriot and Pemberton's model? How significant was your perception of both procedural and distributive justice as an input in making your decision?

Herriot and Pemberton's model places at its core the traditional conception of requiring a match between individual and organization in terms of needs, wants and provisions. It is a dynamic model in the sense that, in line with the Open Systems approach,[16] events are cyclical. The model views an organizational career as a continuous sequence of renegotiations of psychological contracts (see later chapters for a more detailed discussion). The contracts are 'signed' between the employee and the organization. This leads to the question of whether a psychological contract can exist with an entity that is not a person. In practice the 'contract' is agreed with people that represent the organization (managers, HR department).

All in all, the model is reinforced by evidential support suggested by Herriot and Pemberton, and fits well with the evolving nature of organizational careers.

Labour markets

Employers' requirements from the labour market are complex. They face a highly competitive, global market, in which flexibility is essential to cope with continually changing trends and positions. As a result, when seeking staff, they look for people with multiple competencies, high skills levels and capable of high performance. At the same time they also need a highly flexible workforce. Commitment is still important, as is loyalty, but such sentiments now tend to be towards the profession, the team or the project, and not necessarily to the organization. Non-traditional workers – people who work in alternative arrangements such as on-call workers, independent contractors, temporary workers or agency workers, as well as contingent workers called in to work in emergencies – form an increasing proportion of the workforce. Some may opt for the non-traditional career route from choice whereas others are forced into this path by the lack of other opportunities. One phenomenon that is beginning to emerge is that people who wish to work full time but cannot find a single full-time job are opting instead for multiple part-time jobs. All of these alternative contractual work arrangements are part of the general flexibility that companies need to apply in their operational practices.

In addition to the acquisition and maintenance of knowledge and capabilities, one element crucial for organizational competitiveness is 'to know what you know' – whom these competencies reside with. For example, in a large project, different people will be needed at different stages. The organization should be able to detect where these people are, what they are occupied with, and further, how to utilize the newly gained knowledge. If there is a lack of resources, the organization needs to know where they can buy them; or how to outsource these activities. Networking relationships with the wider business environment are necessary in such a case.

EXHIBIT 1.2	The temptation of temping...

In October 1946, with an office in Detroit, Michigan, and two employees, William Russell Kelly started a new company to meet the office and clerical needs of Detroit-area businesses. The company was staffed by housewives and students – people who had flexible schedules. Growth was fast, and involved lending employees to customers. Kelly's development of this new type of service – creating a pool of people with a variety of office skills to provide temporary help for offices – marked the beginning of the modern temporary staffing services industry.

Companies realized that using reliable temporary employees made good business sense. Temporary employees, especially women, discovered a good way to find work for short periods of time. Soon it became apparent that the relationships with the 'mother company' can be long term, and that the services need not be restricted to low-level skills jobs. The next stage was internationalization.

The business community recognized that such temp companies offer flexibility, diversity, quality, and above all – delivery of performance.

Exhibit 1.2 continued

Some comparisons...

Kelly Services entered the *Fortune 500* in the late 1990s (ranked 384 in 2001). The company employs more than 800 000 employees annually. Let us compare it with another Detroit-based company, General Motors. General Motors is currently *Fortune* No. 3 (and by 2001 had held the No. 1 position for 32 of the 44 years in which the list has been in existence). General Motors employed only 355 000 people in 2001 in 44 countries (395 000 people in 1998). Both Kelly and GM are dwarfed by Manpower's 1.9 million staff (2001 data), operating in 61 countries. Manpower, a leading company, was ranked 182 in the 2001 *Fortune 500* list.

Both Manpower and Kelly Services started their business in the late 1940s (1948 and 1946 respectively). At the time GM had many more employees than it has today. Both became international in the mid-1950s. Today, a curious fact is that Manpower's largest market is France, followed by the USA.

Business growth is a characteristic of the temp service sector. Good news for these companies. But what about their staff? Generally temporary employees tend to have less training, lower payment, no stability, and ambiguous job security as compared with permanent employees. (That is, they have no secure role, implied from their status, and only a low level of job security from their employing temp agency.)

Since the Industrial Revolution the organizational career has evolved as the norm. Of course, the traditional organizational career was never applicable to all: redundancies were not invented in the late 1980s, though that was when they became so frequent and on such a large scale. Small businesses and sole traders have always existed. Even in Japan, lifelong employment was promised and provided only by large firms, which employed just one-third of the workforce. However, this was the role model for a 'proper' and desired career. Career success has been defined in terms of progression up the hierarchy. Derived from this definition is expectations – what each person would expect from their career, and in particular, from the employing organization, in relation to their career. If individuals see it as solely their own role to manage their career, the organization is neutralized from its role as partner in the management of careers.

The level of involvement is diverse, ranging from irrelevant, through to a supporting role, a directive role, and up to a controlling or managerial role. Two cases illustrate the extremes of involvement. The first is the portfolio career person, who manages his or her own career, and who has no need of organizational mechanisms to manage, direct or support their career development.[17] The other extreme can still be found in large bureaucracies (e.g. army systems), where new recruits are set on a clear career path, planned and designed, at least for their first few years of service, and managed from the top until they reach the higher ranks (e.g. when they become officers). In most organizations, however, there is a certain degree of freedom, but the amount depends very much on the sector, the profession, the size of the organization and the state of the economy. Medical doctors still have to invest some seven years in their basic training, and further time in their specialization. To change career, even within the profession, would mean a further investment in time and effort, and is neither popular nor usual – one rarely finds medical specialists changing to another specialism, e.g. a general practitioner or a heart surgeon becoming an orthopaedic surgeon or an anaesthetist, etc. Moreover, people from outside the profession cannot embark on a career in the medical field. The same is true in any chartered profession, but even for others long-term investment is needed to start making a living in a new career. However, the opposite route is available. Many medical doctors can opt to leave the role of active practitioner, and become managers in the health service, combine consultancy with other activities (this is a form of portfolio career), or move to academia or politics, etc. Other professions, especially in the information technology sector, are more likely to witness career transitions.

The changing nature of careers

Arthur *et al.*[18] have indicated that the concept of a career is not the property of any one theoretical or disciplinary view. They present eight viewpoints on the career concept (those of psychology, social psychology, sociology, anthropology, economics, political science, history and geography), mostly within the boundaries of the behavioural sciences. New trends in this framework are manifested in the need to fit contemporary changes in culture and economic conditions. These lead to different shapes of career. The theoretical framework encompassing them started with the boundaryless career.[19] This was followed by individual perspectives such as the Protean career (a concept of individual-focused career, introduced in 1976 and gained wide recognition in the 1990s; *see* Chapter 3 for elaboration)[20] and the perspectives of the organization and the wider society such as the post-corporate career (*see* Chapter 4 for elaboration).[21] These approaches to the management of careers have developed as a result of the deterioration of order and the relative simplicity associated with clear and open organizational structures and procedures. To understand the new career systems scholars may benefit from utilizing non-conventional approaches. One recent such exercise was an attempt to build on the New Science as a source for understanding careers. With the turbulence and lack of structure and order evident in the realm of careers, even Chaos Theory may well prove useful in this regard.[22]

Organizational careers: the rumours of their death have been premature

However, there is a change, a transformation, and a transition. The notion of career and the meaning of career success have moved, perhaps been upgraded. Mounting the hierarchy is no longer the sole criterion. Inner satisfaction, life balance, autonomy and freedom have entered the formula (for further elaboration *see* Chapter 3). Many would recognize the true nature of the situation as being analogous to the following statement:

Growth for the sake of growth is the ideology of the cancer cell. (Edward Abbey)

Similarly, climbing up the organizational ladder, just for the sake of being higher in the hierarchy, does not make sense. Realization of this notion has enabled significant changes to the meaning of career advancement. Many contemporary scholars[23] view the changes in structure (and restructuring) of organizations, together with economic turbulence, as the factors which have forced significant shifts in the paradigm of careers. The traditional career has dominated industrial employment for decades, because most organizational structures supported it. Such structures were bureaucracy based, and the many managerial layers created a metaphorical ladder for climbing up the organization.[24] With the flattening of organizations and the elimination of entire managerial layers, career paths have become blurred since the 1980s and the 1990s.[25] Nevertheless, there may be other factors, probably a combination of economic forces and the way in which people perceive their career, that enable the flattening of organizations.

Whether it be cause or effect, these changes mean that a different approach to the management of careers should be sought, one that would cope with and fit the new reality of work, and the new characteristics are derived from the nature of change in the working life. The transformation of careers in general, and of psychological contracts specifically, is due to large economic, demographic and cultural forces, combined with business globalization and competitiveness. One aspect is the short horizons of career planning. 'Just-in-time' and business process re-engineering (mostly in manufacturing), and the privatization of many services are translated into limited options for long-term career plans at organizational level.

An example of transformation in both the social and economic realms is the decreasing level of involvement of the state in life. There is less support for the deprived in society, and Socialism has ceased to be the ideal. Governments have reduced subsidies for lagging sectors (see the cases of the steel and textile industries in the UK or the car industry in Sweden, for example). A free-market, individualistic oriented approach has come to dominate capitalist governments. This free-market economy has also contributed to the transformation of careers.

New psychological contracts: the evolution of employment relationships

Today's organizational structures and hence, career systems, are characterized by continual change. To keep the right people, organizations and employees need to develop new psychological contracts in line with contemporary business culture.[26] The idea of the psychological contract was originally suggested by Levinson and his colleagues in the early 1960s.[27] It was re-introduced to organizational studies and developed later by Kotter and others. It is still very topical, in particular within the context of its transition into the new psychological contract.[28] In lay terms, the psychological contract is 'The unspoken promise, not present in the small print of the employment contract, of what [the] employer gives, and what employees give in return'. Such a contract is fundamentally different from the formal, legal employment contracts in their context and expected impact.[29]

The evolution of the new psychological contracts led to a situation where there are no long-term contracts of loyalty and no mutual commitment. Organizational commitment was commonly accepted as the desired norm, for both organizations and employees. As a result the downsizing process has had very negative outcomes.[30] It is not only a common belief, but also a widely veri-fied conjecture, that organizational commitment, motivational levels and satis-faction are associated with each other, and a high level of these will lead to improved performance and a tendency to remain in an organization.[31] However, since mutual commitment has diminished or ceased to exist and the trust-based relationship has deteriorated in the industrial world, the relevance of the con-struct of organizational commitment has declined.[32] Others argue for the need to maintain organizational commitment even in such times for the benefits it gen-erates to organizations.[33] Moreover, it is argued, proper HRM management improves employees' organizational commitment.[34]

Instead of the traditional concept of developing and gaining commitment, new ideas need to be introduced to compensate for the loss of balance in the relationship equation. We can now find ideas based on employability, with the organization being expected to invest in the training and development of its employees, and the employee being expected to exert effort and be flexible. Through the concept of employability, employees will be able to find either good jobs if the company has no further need for their services, and the company will be released from a lifelong obligation to employees.[35] This means a new deal, which is different from that of mutual commitment, and is not necessarily the one employees would prefer, nor the one that organizations would easily adopt.[36]

The organization seems to have abandoned traditional thinking. Let us look at the roots of career theory.[37] Hughes argues for the importance of ordering work experience and logic to the linkages between successive positions occupied over time. Thus his 'moving perspective of time' means, for organizational career man-agement, that the career concept implies a relationship between employer and employee over time. A career is more than a single job, a single position or a single role. It is a developmental process of progression. The individual and the organiz-ation share duties and responsibilities, both are equal partners in the game.

The beginning of the 1990s saw a significant change in the nature and notion of the psychological contract (e.g. Hiltrop, 1995), as these contracts are based on the interactive process of an exchange relationship.[38] Robinson and Morrison[39] studied the impact of such changes to discover the role of trust in mediating the adverse impact of breaking former psychological contracts. In the new deal, it is difficult to create trust in the traditional sense.

Employees do not always welcome such a transformation. It means no more lifetime employment (or a promise of such), no more mutual loyalty. The typical traditional deal was: employees offer loyalty, conformity, commitment; employ-ers offer security of employment, career prospects, training and development and care in trouble. The archetype was a full-time career with a single employer. Both sides based the relationship on 'trust'. To a certain extent employees can easily understand and accept this type of relationship.

Under the new deal, employees offer long hours, assume added responsibility, provide broader skills and tolerate change and ambiguity, whereas employers offer high pay, reward for performance and above all, the fact of having a job.[40] There is no single archetype model that fits all – diversity and flexibility are the new rules. When there is readiness for changes and adjusted expectations there will not be a process of disillusionment and a feeling of betrayal on the part of employees, as suggested by Brockner and his colleagues.[41]

The new psychological contracts fit well with concepts and terminology that emerged in the 1990s. DeFillippi and Arthur[42] were among the first to use the term 'boundaryless career', an idea that developed alongside the concept of the boundaryless organization (*see* Exhibit 1.3).

EXHIBIT 1.3

The boundaryless organization[43]

Ashkenas *et al.* present a framework for better understanding the ways in which organizations undergo both structural and mental transitions. Even traditional bureaucracies try to adjust to a rapidly changing business environment. Flexibility is a key to gaining competitive advantage, including adaptation to the change, leading change, being both responsive and proactive. Ashkenas *et al.* suggest that breaking down barriers is one of the ways in which organizations can struggle to survive and flourish.

According to Ashkenas *et al.* there are different types of barriers to be overcome. These are: vertical, horizontal, external and geographical.

Breaking down vertical barriers is crucial since hierarchical bureaucracies tend to restrict the flow of information, are reluctant to respond to changing environments and are inflexible in both their thinking and their actions. The question, of course, is how to break down these barriers and maintain established procedures, stability and organizational memory.

Breaking down horizontal barriers means, according to Ashkenas *et al.*, eliminating the traditional barriers between the conventional functions and operations of organizations.

Breaking down the barriers between the organization and the environment or other organizations is complex, but working with joint ventures, suppliers, customers, government agencies, etc. blurs the boundaries.

Lastly, breaking down geographical boundaries is reflected at both the national level (in terms of alternative work arrangements and 'virtual organizations') and the international level (in terms of globalization).

From our point of view, the boundaryless organization is the site of the boundaryless career. These four 'deviations' from the traditional type of organization have a direct impact on individuals and, in particular, on organizational career systems. The breaking down of hierarchical bureaucracies demolishes the old-style system of a career ladder, strict rules for promotion and upward movement. The elimination of the barriers between organizational functions opens up new career paths that cross boundary lines within organizations. High levels of interactivity with the environment, including competitors, enable new practices (e.g. secondments), and finally, the global realm offers a wide range of opportunities to grow and develop anywhere, from home to the other side of the world.

The blurring of boundaries will be dealt with further in Chapters 4 and 5. Terms other than boundaryless career have been used. Examples include Arthur, Claman and DeFillippi[44], who suggested the phrase 'intelligent careers' (which will be further elaborated in Chapter 3). Waterman et al.[45] spoke of the 'career resilient workforce', while Peiperl and Baruch[46], with the 'post-corporate career', used different wording, but all these terms reflect a trend. There has been a change from what we knew in the past. The concept of a rigid ladder which people move up, as long as they do the right thing, was the basic building-stone of the management of people. (Of course, certain moves have always depended on one's social background: for example, slaves had very limited opportunities for promotion; aristocrats frequently filled top managerial positions.) These days have passed. It will take less than a generation for people to get used to the 'new deal'[47] and the new psychological contracts. At the turn of the century the industrial world is in the middle of a transition process, and the question is how organizations should handle the transformation to cause as little harm as possible. How can such new contracts be agreed upon and be 'signed'?

There are exceptions to and deviations from Table 1.1. It appears that scholars arguing for the existence and the changed meaning of the psychological contract have ignored certain facts. While many, in particular managers, work longer hours, the overall tendency in Europe is to shorten the legal weekly working hours. Investment in employability has always been present, but new types of training mean *less* employability. Organizations' claims to promote employability via the new deal are perhaps exaggerated.[48] For the individual, of course, having employability is very positive. Perhaps this is one reason for the increased

Table 1.1 Traditional v. transformed deals

Aspect	Traditional deal	Transformed deal
Environmental characteristic	Stability	Dynamism
Career choice made	Once, at early age in career	Series, at different age stages
Main career responsibility lies with:	Organization	Individual
Career horizon (workplace)	Single organization	Several organizations
Career horizon (time)	Long	Short
Employer expects/Employee gives:	Loyalty and commitment	Long-time working hours
Employer gives/Employee expects:	Job security	Investment in employability
Progress criteria	Advancement according to tenure	Advancement according to results and knowledge
Success means	Winning the tournament, i.e. progress on the hierarchy ladder	Inner feeling of achievement
Training	Formal programmes, generalist	On-the-job, company specific, sometimes ad hoc

level of cynicism amongst workers when they are presented with what they may perceive as fads.[49]

Full-time employment in one organization was never the rule for many, but it usually represented the desired option. Nevertheless, there are certain occupations and organizations where this was and is still the norm. Money (income) was and continues to be a definite criterion for career success evaluation, as are other extrinsic outcomes, but success is not measured merely in terms of money or other extrinsic outputs. Among the desired extrinsic outcomes was usually advancing up the ladder. Of course, fewer options were available when organizations became flatter. At the same time, the inner feelings of achievement and satisfaction were always important and they are even more so now. All in all, the new deal does not represent a full revolution, but a widespread evolution.

Changing the rules of the game

The massive restructuring of the economy has a fundamental effect upon peoples' careers. There is not merely a new psychological contract. There is also a shift from a skill-based to a knowledge-based labour market. The portfolio of competencies needed for success continues to evolve.

The fact that these major changes have occurred within one generation time has left us with insufficient time to adapt easily to all the changes involved.[50] In terms of the economy, the hyper-turbulent environment as reflected in the labour markets does not allow the conventional process of supply and demand to dictate the rules of the game for the economy. Sometimes the behaviour of the market (and also career opportunities as reflected in the labour market) resembles Chaos theory[51] rather than traditional processes. Reaching a 'steady state' in terms of balance, stress and performance, for example, may require more time than modern conditions allow.

The pace and the magnitude of change are accelerating continually, and have a profound global impact in many areas of change. It is not just that there are specific changes in the areas of technology, the economy, politics, demography, society and psychology, the family, and knowledge, but the fact that all of these changes happen simultaneously.

There is not space here to look at developments in each of these areas, so we shall consider just some of them.

We look first at demographic change. After the baby boom generation that followed the Second World War, a decline in the birth rate characterized the industrial world. At the same time developing countries enjoyed the benefits of improved medical treatment, lower death rates, and a substantial increase in their population. One result of these changes is that the most sought-after jobs tend to be primarily in the industrialized societies, mainly the USA, Europe and Japan. Another outcome is that more and more people live longer in retirement age, and deserve to enjoy this stage of life. A person's career does not need to end at formal retirement. Many work after retirement, sometimes in part-time jobs, while many choose to engage in voluntary work in the community (such as for charitable bodies). This is a career change from which organizations can benefit, for example by using former employees, now retired, when extra personnel are needed.

However, the more fundamental demographic change is within the working population, and is concerned with massive moves across sectors. If we use three categories – primary (agriculture, mining, utilities), secondary (manufacturing and construction) and tertiary (services, business and professionals), we can analyse historical trends and their relevance for the creation of new career opportunities alongside a decline in traditional ones (Figure 1.2). In the past the primary sector accounted for some 80–90 per cent of the population, but since the Industrial Revolution the share of this sector has declined sharply, and it is now less than 4 per cent of the population. At the same time the secondary sector has grown rapidly, encompassing over 50 per cent of the workforce by the middle of the twentieth century. Since then the tertiary sector has flourished, causing the manufacturing sector to decline to about a quarter of the workforce by the 1990s. The health and the education sectors alone now comprise some 20 per cent of the workforce in the industrial world. The retail and transport sectors comprise an additional 20 per cent and business and public and professional services the remaining 30 per cent. Data from Europe (Sweden) manifest a shift in labour engagement in the three main sectors of agriculture, industry and services. In 1870, 72 per cent were employed in agriculture, 15 per cent in industry and 13 per cent in services. In 1980 the distribution was 5 per cent in agriculture, 36 per cent in industry and 59 per cent in services.[52] These shifts in labour market constituencies mean that there are far more professions and career options available than in the past. Moreover, such change processes are still taking place, and it is likely that in future people will have to be prepared to change career and adapt to new circumstances. A second career was the exception even in the 1970s. A series of careers had become the new norm by the beginning of the twenty-first century.

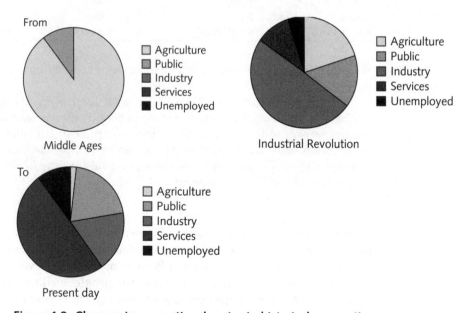

Figure 1.2 Changes in occupational sector in historical perspective

EXHIBIT
1.4

Can we learn from history?

The only thing we learn from history is that we don't learn from history (Woody Allen).

Western Europe's population almost doubled in the second half of the eighteenth century, mostly as a result of the use of new food crops (such as the potato) and a decline in epidemic diseases. A population growth of this magnitude compelled change: peasants and craftsmen now had too many descendants for the former system of inheritance, which formerly ensured continuity, to work. They had to seek new forms of labour to survive. Similarly, the families of businessmen and landlords had to innovate to provide for their families, more of whom were now surviving. These demographic pressures, coupled with the fact that both industry and trade were developing rapidly, and on a global scale, resulted in the availability of human resources for the Industrial Revolution. The other two elements that enabled the Industrial Revolution to take place were technological developments and an increase in the available capital (partly due to access to global markets as a result of colonialism).

The same triad, of people, technology and capital, is operating in the present revolution. The technology involved is IT (Information Technology). Through IT, coupled with still easier access to overseas markets, the Internet provides a non-territorial, global market. And the HR, people, emerge from the competitive forces that have ended the employment of so many people. Table 1.2 indicates the contribution of these factors in the major eras of the history of mankind.

Table 1.2 The roles of people, technology and capital over time

Historical era	Human added value	Technology	Dominant capital
Hunter-gatherer	Instinct	Primitive	Wild animals
Agriculture	Tradition	Simple	Land
Industry	Process	Heavy	Finance
Knowledge	Knowledge	Knowledge	Knowledge

We now look at an example from a totally different careers era – the project-based industry:

DeFillippi & Arthur[53] describe a sector in which careers development is not associated with an organization, but involves floating from project to project. Such an environment is not restricted to the case they present – the film industry – and more sectors may move to this type of employment relationship and career progress. The construction industry also operates in this way for those involved in the lower echelons of the workforce.

Different career patterns have been created throughout history. Probably the first profound change was from the prehistoric hunter-gatherer to an almost fully agriculture-based society (it should be remembered that even in ancient Rome and early China, less than 10 per cent of the people lived in urban areas).[54] This status was stable for generations, until the growth of mostly manufacturing societies in the industrial world following the Industrial Revolution in the eighteenth and nineteenth centuries, and in turn the move to mostly services-based economies in the twentieth century. Note that the pace of change has accelerated. Drucker (1999) discusses the most recent change, to a knowledge-based society, a change that we are experiencing at present. Sociological, psychological and technological factors are likely in the future to further reshape the face of employment.[55] Early signs indicate that we may expect a considerable level of permanent unemployment or under-employment.

The future will see more knowledge-related work and knowledge-based careers. Organizations require rapid diffusion of knowledge to those with an immediate need for information.[56] Some knowledge acquisition and knowledge maintenance is technology led, some via system-embedded knowledge, but much is knowledge that resides within people. Data and information are highly valued, not for their intrinsic worth, but via human capital which enables their effective use.

Knowledge management is being constantly revolutionized through innovation by inspired and inventive human beings utilizing state of the art technologies. The knowledge industry creates innovative types of careers. Knowledge can now be captured through Internet connections, and shared through cellular telephones, video-conferences and e-mail. Networking has become more crucial than ever for personal progress. Within traditional industries too, the growing need for knowledge management requires the establishment of specialist positions. Employees in these positions seek out the information necessary for effective decision making and then transmit it to those who must implement organizational policies. IT support as a specific organizational unit has been incorporated in the organizational structure of most enterprises. These new occupations have emerged and gained recognition and remuneration while other vocations have been declining, some becoming obsolete.

Intelligent careers

Following these major shifts, different qualities have served as key factors for a successful career. In particular career resilience and openness to new experiences are considered indispensable. Different career competencies are required under the new psychological contract. The concept of 'intelligent careers', for example, introduced the mid-1990s, focuses on the three types of knowledge – know-how, know-why and know-whom[57] (*see* Chapter 2 for elaboration).

The new psychological contract has changed the way people and organizations are associated with each other. The typical traditional deal was: employees offer loyalty, conformity, commitment; employers offer security of employment, career prospects in terms of a ladder to climb, training and development and care in time of trouble. Both sides based the relationship on mutual trust. Under the new deal, employees offer long hours, assume added responsibility, provide broader skills and tolerate change and ambiguity, whereas employers offer high pay, reward for performance, lateral moves as a norm, and above all, having a job at all. Indeed, there exist a long time frame and extreme conceptual differences between the sociological contract of J.-J. Rousseau and the new psychological contracts of D. Rousseau.[58]

J.-J. Rousseau coined the term social contract, to reconcile what rights permit us to do and what our interest prescribes. His famous phrase, 'Man is born free, and everywhere he is in chains', relates to the rule of laws, regulations and customs. For the purpose of this book, these can be reflected in organizational realities. Within an organizational context these would be the strategy, policy and practices that will generate what Rousseau called 'conventions', which serve as the basis of all legitimate authority. Each participant in society gives trust to that society and its consensus, and receives in return the right and obligation to participate in, and contribute to, that general consensus or general will, by which each is governed. In an organizational setting the consensus of career progress is the trust and commitment to the role, the profession and the organization, which will be reflected in the way people develop within the organization. If this trust is breached people will leave, to start a career elsewhere, where they feel a better fit exists between their needs and aspirations and the opportunities that the organization offers.

Career systems and their multi-constituencies: who brings what, who does what

The main four constituencies of careers are the individual (and his/her family), the organization, society, and public bodies (which range from local bodies and professional associations to national governments and international organizations such as the United Nations).

Figure 1.3 depicts the different elements each participant brings into the system and participants' responsibilities (with Figure 1.3a examining who *brings in* what and Figure 1.3b looking at who *does* what).

The following section will discuss both figures and the system they represent in career management. Each segment of the figure will be accompanied by a Box, in which a case example will illustrate the way the system works. The example focuses on the issue of women in the workplace and in management, and the role of the various constituencies.

Public bodies

The government is responsible for employment legislation (e.g. that on equal employment opportunities (EEO)), and also is involved with behavioural norms (mostly through the education system).

One example of the areas covered is the reduction in working hours for employees. In Europe the average working hours per week have declined sharply in the last few decades. By the end of the twentieth century, the average was below 40 hours per week in most of Western Europe. Indeed, Germany aims to have a 30-hour week, in order to keep unemployment low.

Another aspect of working life is the trend towards the 'litigious society'. This global trend follows the American lead in increasing the involvement of the legal system in employment (as well as in other facets of life), moving the boundaries

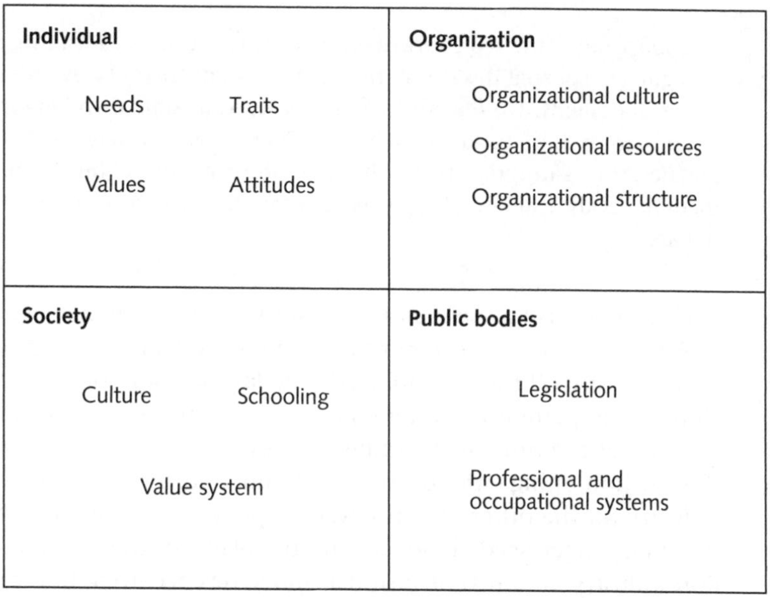

Individual	Organization
Needs Traits Values Attitudes	Organizational culture Organizational resources Organizational structure
Society	**Public bodies**
Culture Schooling Value system	Legislation Professional and occupational systems

(a) Who *brings in* what

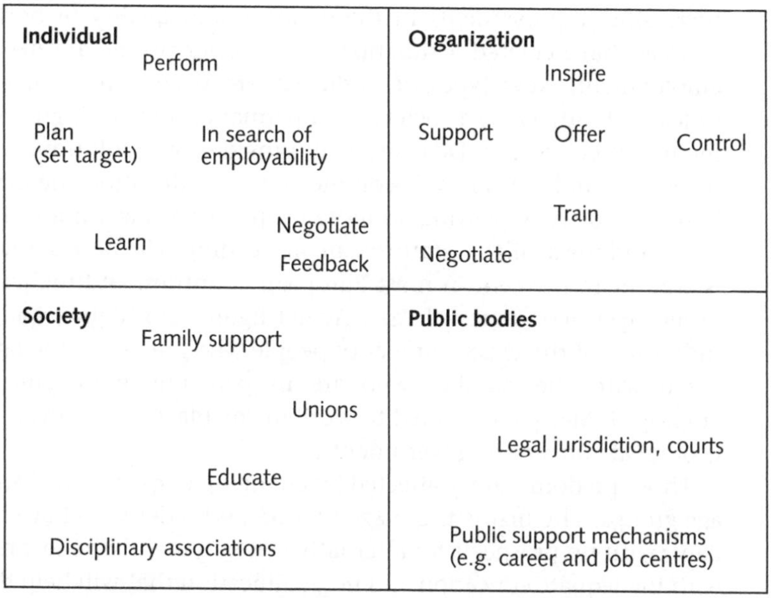

Individual	Organization

Perform
 	
Plan   In search of
(set target)   employability
 	
                        Negotiate
Learn
                        Feedback
	Inspire
	
	Support Offer Control
	
	                        Train
	Negotiate

Society	**Public bodies**
Family support Unions Educate Disciplinary associations	Legal jurisdiction, courts Public support mechanisms (e.g. career and job centres)

(b) Who *does* what

Figure 1.3 Who brings in what, who does what

of what conventional thinking regarded as a management prerogative. Employers are increasingly seen as liable for any ill-treatment their employees might suffer during their work. Many relate to discrimination, harassment and occupational health (especially stress related), all are concerned with career management and development. (*See* Exhibit 1.5.)

EXHIBIT 1.5	In 2000 a San Francisco court ruled that United Airlines, a leading American airline, was guilty of sexual discrimination against some 16 000 stewardesses, reversing an earlier judgment. United Airlines stipulated that staff members must maintain an 'attractive' weight to keep their job. There was a difference between males and females, the assumption being that men were of a heavy build whereas females had medium body frames. This decision cost the company hundreds of millions of dollars.

Governments have a major interest in the maintenance of a stable progressive society in a flourishing economy. The new model economy does not enable full-time work for all the unemployed. The last occasion on which there was such a shift in the pattern of employment was the massive move from agriculture to industry at the time of the Industrial Revolution. The salvation in that case was the creation of big cities on the one hand, and the emergence of manufacturing industry on the other. When fewer people were needed to produce food for all, those no longer needed moved, and the place for them to go to was the production industry. In our time a similar move has occurred: fewer people are needed to produce goods for all, and the surplus of producers transfer to service industries. Now, the impact of system and information technology, coupled with ever-increasing improvements in the quantity and quality of both production and services, have created a situation where fewer people are needed in traditional employment. New types of 'industry' are needed to make use of the talent unleashed, otherwise a society with permanently very high levels of unemployment will be created. Diversity may provide some solution, with the Internet a big player, and e-business, e-commerce and e-education the new buzzwords. The leisure industry is growing, as more people work fewer hours. But many have no work, and the available statistics are misleading. The official unemployment level is around 10 per cent in most European countries, and higher in Japan and the other Tiger Economies of Asia. Actual figures are higher, and there is no clear indication of the exact number of people who are out of the labour market compared with the number who are in part-time employment or are under-employed. Many have opted to work in the black economy, a development that is of great concern to governments.

Those predominantly affected by changing employment patterns fall into two age groups. The first is those aged 50–55 and older who have been made redundant, with no prospects for alternative employment. The second is young people with inadequate education and no qualification that will help them gain employment. For the young people governments have been establishing new initiatives. In the UK there is the 'New Deal' programme, under which the government pays employers a subsidy for a certain period at the start of the young person's employment. Germany has developed a programme to encourage young unemployed people to join business start-up projects. For the older age group, much work may be done in non-traditional areas (e.g. volunteering). However, to make such work a viable alternative, governments should provide a proper budget for such initiatives that would yield further career options. Other people can opt for part-time, or multi-part-time employment arrangements.

EXHIBIT
1.6

The government deals with both EEO legislation, and setting the norms in education. For example, books for teaching in primary school may portray a woman working in the kitchen and a man driving a lorry. However, books for older children may show how, while the woman bakes a cake, the man cooks the dinner, and while a man can do office work, a woman can be a postman (note the role of language in shaping career options – the job title is postman, not postwoman) or a lawyer.

Moving beyond legislation, the government's role in shaping future careers for women can be manifested via a benefit system that treats women working as a norm. This would mean, for example, encouraging the development of full child-care facilities and other activities to give males and females equal opportunities in the labour market.

Society

The role of society is wider than that of government, and is concerned with setting and establishing the values and attitudes that provide norms for behaviour (and inhibit deviations from the norm). Values towards work can be associated with education – as indicated earlier, and at home, in the community or in religious institutions. Values such as power distance or collectivism versus individualism,[59] have their impact on work attitudes and career perspectives.

A variety of clusters of work attitudes have been identified[60] in different geographical regions, and the implications of these are relevant to career systems. For example, in an individualistic and a high achievement-oriented society we should expect an environment of career tournaments (e.g. the archetype American model of career success – see Chapter 3) while in collectivistic-oriented societies slow career progress coupled with the ability to reach consensus may be the preferred choice.

Another realm with an impact on values is that of religion. Max Weber's article, 'The Protestant Ethic and the Spirit of Capitalism' cited the Protestant work ethics as an example of how religion can encourage people to invest effort in work.[61] In contrast, a fatalistic approach to life would not encourage great investment in work and career, and is associated with an external locus of control.[62]

EXHIBIT
1.7

Women in management[*]

In women's careers, the role of society is strongly associated with values attached to and attitudes towards working women. These values, attitudes and norms are affected by how working women are portrayed in the media – in newspapers, films and advertisements. The education system also may offer mechanisms for combating discrimination, and in this context one may note the professionalization of management via the MBA degree and the effect this has had on helping to reduce discrimination. Lastly, the family, as the part of society which is closest to the individual, has a crucial role in enabling women to work. For example, even if the government provides the option for fathers to take paternity leave, it is up to the family to decide whether he will or will not take this option.

* *See* Chapter 8 for a full discussion of diversity.

The individual

The individual's characteristics and values strongly determine a person's career choice and means of progress and the way that person manages their career. Most people work in organizations, whereas certain individuals would prefer to start their own business, or simply wish to be self-employed. Career systems in organizations require people to be able to manage their careers, and in most cases encourage them to help others (subordinates, and sometimes colleagues too) to manage theirs. People negotiate career options, and actively progress towards their career goals. Of course, the other extreme can be found too, of people who are indifferent, such as those who leave their career to chance, and some who are prepared to remain unemployed for a long time.

Individuals bring into the career world their inner needs and values. Maslow's hierarchy of needs can still provide a strong, though somewhat simplistic, explanation for people's career choices. A career can fulfil needs for recognition, self-esteem and self-actualization. A complementary need theory, that of McClelland, focus on people's need for power, achievement and affiliation.[63] It is clear that different combinations of needs determine whether people seek a managerial role, a professional occupation or work in the supportive services, as these choices are subject to individual preferences and dominant needs. (The issue of career choice will be elaborated upon in Chapter 2.)

Values

> Value in the sense of *good* is inherently connected with that which promotes, furthers, assists, a course of activity, and ... value in the sense of *right* is inherently connected with that which is needed, required, in the maintenance of a course of activity.
>
> (Dewey, 1939: 57)[64]

Rokeach has pointed out that values, whether at the individual, organizational or national level, form the base for attitudes and behaviours.[65] Rokeach's empirical work shows that values may also be measured. This adds a practical dimension to the management of careers: the ability to fit systems to match not only the inner needs, but also the values of employees. Values form the foundation stone for company philosophy and hence must be useful in developing a strategy for career systems.

Question

What would you consider your main values, and how are they reflected in your career aspiration?

How has your local culture influenced your values (e.g. in what way would your values be different if you had been raised in another place. For example, if you are from New York, what if you had been born in Utah, or in another US state? Or what differences are possible between people from a village in Sussex and people from Newcastle (in the UK)?

Many of the values and perceptions of the career world are learned through observation, and the first impact is largely due to experience within the family. Individual family background affects children's values, attitudes and behaviours, and as a result, will influence the future career choices of children.[66]

Traits

Many traits, most obviously the physical ones, are due to inheritance. Our genes determine our bodily dimensions and appearance, which are important for career choice and success at work. More important (for most jobs), however, are our intellectual capacities, and again, these are determined by our genes as well as by environmental influences and educational inputs. Studies of leadership have not been conclusive about the impact of traits on leadership,[67] but they certainly are associated with the career choice, the career aims and the career strategy people follow. However, if we look beyond demographic and inheritance traits, we observe that personality traits have much to do with career choice and career success. Judge and colleagues[68] have noted the role of personality factors (in particular the 'Big Five') on career success (*see* Chapter 2 for an elaboration of the 'Big Five' personality traits).

Attitudes

Fishbein and Ajzen provided a model that is based on the general behavioural approach, which ascertains that values, norms and beliefs are antecedents to attitudes that subsequently lead to intentions, inclinations and tendencies, which in turn, generate actions.[69] In addition, attitudes (as well as values and norms and beliefs) are affected by individual personality (and demography) and by culture and environment. Fishbein and Ajzen's theory of planned action can serve to explain the 'why' of career choices (*see* Figure 1.4).

People's attitudes towards different career patterns can be affected by the general culture of their society, the media to which they are exposed, the education system they experienced, and of course, the career advice and direction provided by the organization for which they work.

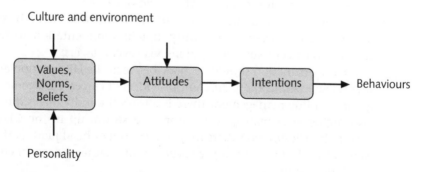

Figure 1.4 Fishbein and Ajzen model

Source: Adapted from M. Fishbein and I. Ajzen (1975) *Belief, attitude, intention, and behavior: An introduction to theory and research*, Reading, MA: Addison-Wesley.

EXHIBIT 1.8	The careers of many women differ from those of men. For example, career breaks after the birth of a child are not uncommon, and do not necessarily indicate a lower level of commitment on the part of women. The great importance attached to having a career means that a growing number of women in Western societies choose now to delay the arrival of children as long as possible, or not to have children at all. Nevertheless, modern developments and lifestyles enable women to shorten significantly the length of their career breaks, with minimal interruption to their careers. Another trend, observed by Healy (1999),[70] is that some women, when they reach the higher ranks of organizations, leave to start their own businesses.

Kolb's framework of individual experiential learning[71] is applicable to career management. His stages of experience, reflection, conceptualization and experimental loop can be translated to the steps of career development. The later addition of a retention stage (which follows the conceptualization phase) by Popper and Lipshitz[72] makes sense in this perspective.

EXHIBIT 1.9	Individual values towards women's equality have a mostly implicit rather than explicit impact, in a litigious society where people are obliged to behave in a politically correct manner. Nevertheless, different people and different cultures pose a wide range of approaches to women's work. At one extreme is the total exclusion of women from the workforce (e.g. no female expatriate can work as a manager in Saudi Arabia); at the opposite extreme we find full equality, as in Scandinavia. The attitudes people hold – for or against women in managerial positions – dictate the spectrum for women's career choices, the types of organizations and professions they try to enter and their career aspirations.

Organizations

Organizations are where careers occur and develop. Moreover, organizations ARE career systems. Organizations plan careers and manage them. In this sense organizations have multiple roles in the world of careers.

In view of the organizational focus of this book it should be emphasized that an organization may be an entity, but its representation to the employee in relation to career issues can be done via several layers.

A basic distinction should be made between the HR function and line management. Even within these different providers of career management there are subgroups. In line management there is always the individual's direct manager, but also higher-level managers, mentors and so on, up to the CEO or MD, while within the HR function there may be a central or headquarters HR department as well as the HR function of the specific unit – either a departmental, a plant or a divisional HR unit.

The organization sets the scene for the career system. The metaphors of 'battlefield' or 'career tournament'[73] will probably deter certain people from 'enjoying the game' of career development in such organizations. The structure of such organizations, and the procedures for developing within them can support or hinder women's advancement. The organizational culture is of extreme importance. In a chauvinist culture women will face the glass ceiling.[74] The resources and policies of organizations' investment in people will determine the degree of equality in their developmental programmes. Moore and Buttner[75] found that an increasing number of women over 40 are choosing self-employment as their second career.

The impact of technology

Breakthroughs in mechanical technology and the energy-generation methods that followed preceded the Industrial Revolution. Another technological breakthrough has had a significant impact on the creation of our information age – the IT revolution.

Technological innovation can end in de-skilling for many, as happened in the car industry at the beginning of the twentieth century. The trend towards efficiency at the time meant a division of labour. This concept originated with the thinking of Adam Smith and was further developed with the 'discovery' of *scientific management*.[76] Scientific management and Fordism stripped employees of their knowledge and de-skilled work in the conveyer-belt industries. A further development in this direction came when robots started to replace employees in mundane areas of work. Simultaneously the service sector grew enormously. By 1983 'white-collar' knowledge jobs had overtaken 'blue-collar' jobs, and the gap continues to widen.[77]

Advanced technology was the decisive factor in reducing the number of blue-collar workers in a variety of industries. Computer numerical control (CNC) machines in metal etching and robotics in the automotive industry are just two prominent examples of the direct impact of technology in this trend. Computers and advanced IT have had similar effects on layers of clerical workers (e.g. bank tellers) and later, of middle management.

These require the replacement of their lost career options, in the same way as did the agriculture labourers who moved into industry, and later the jobless industrial labourers who moved into services. Modern service industries, however, include both extremely challenging intellectual work in the areas of research and development, innovation and marketing, but also a multitude of mundane roles such as those in call centres, which can be seen as the sweatshops of the modern age.

Call centres, the sweatshops of the modern age

Many call centres operate along the lines of the plant conveyor belt. Employees have prescribed messages that they are expected to read from their computer screens. Each answer will lead to the following question the computer tells them to ask, using prescribed wording. There is no room for variation or initiative, and the work is usually conducted under tightly controlled conditions, with continuous monitoring.

Technology can affect or enable the creation of a different culture. This can be due to the opportunities opened up by new technology. Just as the technology of shipbuilding enabled European countries to become explorers and colonists, new frontiers have been opened in the cyberspace. Technology can influence individual characteristics too: Tapscott[78] suggests that the present generation of young people has the following qualities: curiosity, self-reliance, contrariness, smartness, focus, ability to adapt, high self-esteem, and possessed of a global orientation. They are also at ease with digital tools. Cultures characterized by openness, immediacy and an emphasis on results suit them well. They use the e-mail for communication. They prefer flat organizations, and would not hesitate to become entrepreneurs. Companies need to harness these qualities, otherwise they will lose this pool of talent.

The so-called Generation X are believed to be obsessed with the electronic media. For them, e-business poses a positive challenge, not only as customers or to fill their leisure time, but also as an employment domain. On the labour market front, the Net industry generates a variety of new jobs and roles. Some are totally new and innovative (such as the design of Web pages). Others represent a retreat in type of skills and abilities required: Alongside those who initiate new sales points on the Net there is the return of what might be termed milk-round drivers – after all, even if goods are sold virtually, someone needs to pack and deliver them to the customer's home or office. The competencies of others are upgraded too: in August 2000 the first Internet bank robbery was reported in the UK: organized criminals raided Egg (the first UK online bank) using false accounts.

As a result there are new challenges: what alternatives are there for people in the middle levels? Technology can help them to move up, to use their other higher skills, but more frequently, to get down, to the ordinary, simple and not so challenging jobs.

Successful career systems

Successful career systems depend on the process that takes place between the individual and the organization. Later in this book we will consider what we mean by individual career success, and the role of the organization in this. At this point it is sufficient to indicate that the essence of what a career is has changed, and with it the meaning of career success. The meaning of career success differs, of course, according to various dimensions:

- internal – how a person sees the development of their own career in terms of inner values, goals, aspirations;
- external – how career success is perceived by the external environment, such as in terms of status, hierarchy, income and power;
- organizational – in terms of organizational power and influence; these were once measured by position on the career ladder, and now in different, more subtle ways;
- society – the labour market, professional development, globalization.

From the organizational viewpoint, much of the substance of career management is reflected in the career practices for planning and management of careers. The importance and prominence of organizational career practices as part of HRM has been recognized by many scholars, as will be discussed and elaborated in Chapter 6.

Various approaches exist to the study of careers, and much attention is paid to the changing nature and context of careers. As mentioned earlier in this chapter, Arthur *et al.*[79] have indicated that the concept of a career is not the property of any one theoretical or disciplinary view. Later contributions, many of which have been presented in this chapter, refer to the transition in the world of work, offering new models of careers in transition.

In this book the emphasis is directed towards the organizational level, and in particular to ways by which organizations plan, develop and manage employees' careers. To better understand organizational context let us look at Figure 1.5.

Vertical integration is the basis of integrating HRM into the strategic management of the organization, rather than holding the minor supportive role of an administrative function. At its 'highest' level it comprises strategic alignment.[80] Vertical integration starts with an organization's business strategy (or its general strategy, for non-business organizations). Out of this strategy are derived the requirements of resources, and in particular of human resources – human capital. To achieve this strategy the HR function has to apply career practices, the vehicle through which the actual, practical management of people is conducted. These, in turn, should target individual needs, values and behaviours.

Horizontal coherence refers to a more specific, professional aspect of HRM, the integration within the organization of all HRM practices, which starts with acquiring the right people, and continues up to the time of their release. Recruitment and selection is only the first stage in the management of people. Once the people are selected, the process to make them effective organizational members begins. For the HRM function this requires putting into operation a

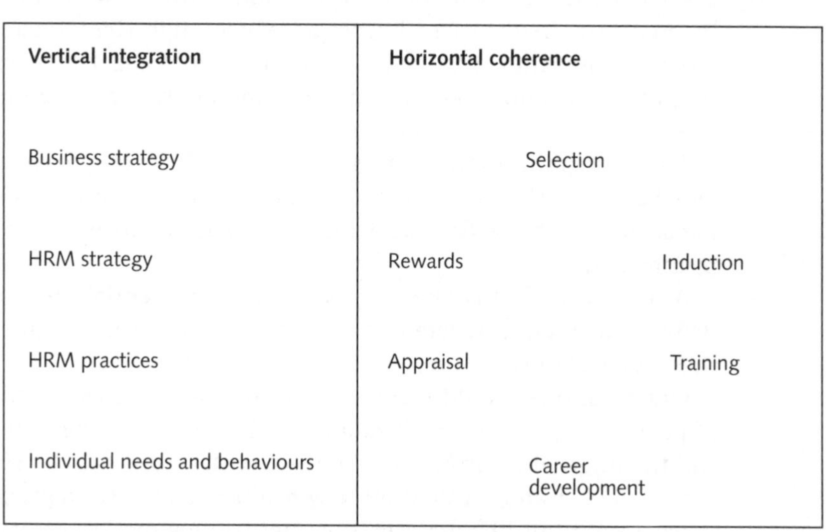

Vertical integration	Horizontal coherence		
		Selection	
Business strategy			
HRM strategy	Rewards		Induction
HRM practices	Appraisal		Training
Individual needs and behaviours		Career development	

Figure 1.5 Vertical integration v. horizontal coherence

comprehensive array of career practices to plan and manage the retention of the members of an organization. Moreover, as will be presented in Chapter 6, there is a need to integrate the practices to achieve a harmony of operations, which I term horizontal coherence.

The art of career management requires the combining of vertical integration and horizontal coherence.

The HR matrix

The HR matrix reflects two aspects of HRM: the practical aspect, which is manifested through the operational element of HRM practices, and the level of strategic alignment, which is expected to form the base for SHRM.[81] Highly strategic management of HRM is important for the overall competitive advantage of an organization. Aligning HRM and organizational strategy is important to the attainment of organizational goals. The HRM function can utilize practices very professionally, or not at all professionally. At the same time the level of strategic alignment with other business or operational units of the organization may be low, even abandoned altogether, or consequential. The quality of the HRM function can be evaluated in terms of the strength of its operational practices.[82]

In the Low-Low quadrant of the HR Matrix figure (Figure 1.6) there are organizations with poor HRM practices, and those which lack strategic planning and management. In the High-Low quadrant there are organizations which manage to apply best practices (and later in the book we will deal with the option of outsourcing some or all of these practices). In the Low-High quadrant there are organizations that have developed strategic thinking and aligned HRM with business planning and management. These organizations achieve high strategic vision, but lack the practical ability to apply this in day-to-day activities, the building stones of HRM. These organizations are more inclined to outsource HRM activities, and later on we will examine the common pitfalls they can meet in doing so. Lastly there is the archetype High-High organization, the ideal model organization that achieves what I would call HR excellence. This is the type of organization that manages to combine strategic alignment and best practice.

Thus, if organizations apply best-practice HRM, they have achieved only half of what they should achieve. Similarly, applying highly integrated strategic management at the top tier without backing it up with the right practices is insufficient.

As represented in Figure 1.6, a schematic differentiation can be made, using a two-by-two matrix, where organizations can be either high or low on each of these dimensions.

Organizations should incorporate a strategic approach into the management of people. At present, organizations are subject to changes in both the external and the internal environment. These alter the conventional HR systems and call for different strategic thinking. New realities require strategic direction, such as a move away from hierarchical structures to new models of organizational architecture (e.g. flexibility, core versus peripheral employees, outsourcing business

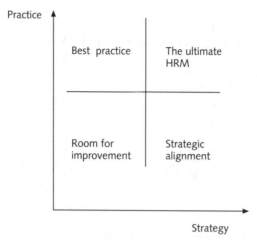

Figure 1.6 The HR matrix

functions and the 'virtual organization'). Special attention needs to be devoted to the issues of globalization and the international management of people (e.g. expatriation). Accordingly, new practices should be applied to transform the strategic vision into practical management issues, finding new ways to maintain the relationship between individuals and their organizations.

From strategic HRM to strategic career systems

Taking a further step, from general HR management to career planning and management, the rest of this book focuses on career issues. It takes a strategic approach to the management of careers, in line with the conceptual framework of Sonnenfeld and Peiperl, which refers to career management as a strategic response and requires a fit with strategic organizational management (their model being based on the Miles and Snow (1978) framework).[83] On the other dimension of the HR matrix, the practical level, best practice should be applied[84] for the creation and maintenance of a career practices portfolio to match the operational needs of the organization in terms of people management. Organizational and national level benchmarking can be useful for the latter.

While the emphasis in this book is on the organizational perspective, it is recognized that individuals play a crucial role in the careers process. Thus the following two chapters will investigate and analyse the individual perspective, and the remainder of the book will be organization oriented.

Summarizing exercise

What positive and negative practices applied by managers to retain people have you encountered in the past? Write down at least one example of a positive and one example of a negative approach. (If you have no work experience yet you may interview a family member or a friend.) Compare the approaches with

Figure 1.7 How to retain people – as seen in DilbertZone

Figure 1.7, taken from DilbertZone, which depicts a cynical approach to retaining people.

Summary

This chapter defined, compared and contrasted several career perspectives, in particular the individual v. the organizational, the balance between them, and the environment in which they take place (such as labour markets). The chapter focused on the changing nature of careers, employment relationships (and the new psychological contract) and career systems and their multi-constituencies: who brings what and who does what, with emphasis on the impact of technology. Lastly we looked at the strategic role of careers within the wider HR context.

Key terms

- Career
- Boundaryless career
- Labour market
- Internal labour market
- Procedural and distributive justice
- Temporary work
- New psychological contracts
- New deals
- Intelligent careers
- Career constituencies
- Values, attitudes and behaviours
- Vertical integration and horizontal coherence
- The HR matrix

DISCUSSION QUESTIONS

Lessons and food for thought

1 *For the student*: What do you make of this chapter when planning your own career strategy for the future? Look at Figure 1.3b – what does 'In search of employability' mean for you?

2 *For students in part-time or full-time employment*: How have changes in the external environment – economic, social, technological and political – influenced the management of people in your organization? How did your HRM department react to them in terms of its organizational career system? Do you think the HRM department was also proactive in anticipating changes and preparing for the future?

3 *For the student wishing to serve as a consultant*: What would be your advice to your employer about ways to satisfy the need for updated career systems? What would be the main points and issues you would discuss with HR managers when asked to advise on developing a career system for an organization? What would be the impact of geography, sector and demography on your advice?

Review questions

1 Which individual characteristics would provide an advantage for 'the new careerist'?

2 Show how the Fishbein and Ajzen model translates into actions in terms of career related behaviours for you.

3 In what ways does new technology influence your career aspirations? Your practical job search?

Critical thinking and ideas probing

1 How would you create your own web page in a way that will get you job offers? What would you change if you wish to have an international career rather than a career in your own country?

2 Is 'fluidity' or perceptual motion in the realm of careers 'good' or 'bad'? In what sense?

Group exercise

Exercise 1 – for MBA or other students in employment, groups of 2–4 students: Plan your next two career moves: (a) assuming these will take place within the boundaries of your employing organization; and (b) assuming these will be external to the present employer. Compare and contrast your aspirations with those of your group members.

Exercise 2 – for undergraduate students: Which would be the more beneficial first step to your career – starting in a small organization or in a large one? Debates within the group can lead to further debates between groups with different views.

Notes

1 *See*, for example, Gutteridge, T.G. (1986) 'Organizational Career Development Systems: The State of the Practice', in D.T. Hall, *Career Development in Organizations*, San Francisco: Jossey-Bass, pp. 50–94.

2 Gutteridge, T.G., Leibowitz, Z.B. and Shore, J.E. (1993) *Organizational Career Development*, San Francisco: Jossey-Bass.

3 Pervin, L. A. and John, O. P. (1999) *Handbook of Personality*, 2nd edn, NY: Guilford Press.

4 Greenhaus, J.H. and Callanan, G.A. (1994) *Career Management*, Forth Worth: The Dryden Press; Greenhaus, J.H., Callanan, G.A. and Godshalk, V.M. (2000) *Career Management*, 3rd edn, Forth Worth: The Dryden Press.

5 Arthur, M.B., Hall, D.T. and Lawrence, B.S. (1989) 'Generating New Directions in Career Theory: The Case for a Transdisciplinary Approach', in M.B. Arthur, D.T. Hall and B.S. Lawrence (eds), *Handbook of Career Theory*, Cambridge: Cambridge University Press, pp. 7–25.

6 Arnold, J. (1997) *Managing Careers into the 21st Century*, London: Paul Chapman.

7 Campbell, R.J. and Moses, J.L. (1986) 'Careers for organizational perspective', in D.T. Hall & Assoc., *Career Development in Organizations*, San Francisco: Jossey-Bass.

8 Baruch, Y. and Rosenstein, E. (1992) 'Career planning and managing in high tech organizations', *International Journal of Human Resource Management*, 3(3), 477–96.

9 Adamson, S.J., Doherty, N. and Viney, C. (1998) 'The meaning of career revisited: Implications for theory and practice', *British Journal of Management*, 9(4), 251–9.

10 Sullivan, S.E. (1999) 'The changing nature of careers: A review and research agenda', *Journal of Management*, 25(3), 457–84.

11 *See* Herriot, P. (1992) *The Career Management Challenge*, London: Sage.

12 cf. Herriot, P. and Pemberton, C. (1996) 'Contracting Careers', *Human Relations*, 49(6), 757–90; Schein, E.H. (1978) *Career Dynamics: Matching Individual and Organizational Needs*, Reading, MA: Addison-Wesley.

13 Gunz, H. (1989) 'The dual meaning of managerial careers: organizational and individual levels of analysis', *Journal of Management Studies*, 26(3), 225–50.

14 Herriot and Pemberton (1996), *see* note 12 above.

15 For updated elaboration of procedural and distributive justice, *see* Greenberg, J. and Cropanzano, R. (2001) (eds) *Advances in Organizational Justice*, Stanford CA: Stanford University Press.

16 Katz, D. and Kahn, R.L. (1966) *The Social Psychology of Organizations*, NY: Wiley.

17 Comfort, M. (1997), *Portfolio People*, London: Century.

18 Arthur *et al.* (1989), *see* note 5 above.

19 Arthur, M.B. (1994) 'The boundaryless career: A new perspective for organizational inquiry', *Journal of Organizational Behavior*, 15(4), 295–306; Arthur, M.B., Claman, P.H. and DeFillippi, R.J. (1995) 'Intelligent enterprise, intelligent careers', *Academy of Management Executive*, 9(4), 7–22; Arthur, M.B. and Rousseau, D.M. (1996) (eds) *The Boundaryless Career: A New Employment Principle for a New Organizational Era*, New York: Oxford University Press.

20 The Protean career was introduced by D.T. Hall (1976) *Careers in Organizations*, Glenview, IL: Scott, Foresman, and was recognized widely following Hall, D.T. (1996) *The Career is Dead – Long Live the Career*, San Francisco: Jossey-Bass; Hall, D.T. and Moss, J.E. (1998) 'The New Protean Career Contract: helping organizations and employees adapt', *Organizational Dynamics*, Winter, 22–37.

[21] Peiperl, M.A. and Baruch, Y. (1997) 'Back to square zero: The post-corporate career', *Organizational Dynamics*, 25(4), 7–22.

[22] See special issue on Careers and the New Science (2002), *M@n@gement*, 5(1).

[23] cf. Adamson, Doherty and Viney (1998), *see* note 9 above, Herriot and Pemberton (1995), *see* note 12 above.

[24] Traditional systems were suited to bureaucracy: Wilensky, H.L. (1964) 'The professionalization of everyone?', *American Journal of Sociology*, 70: 137–58. This claim was made again by Miles, R.E. and Snow, C.C. (1978) *Organizational Structure, Strategy, and Process*, NY: McGraw-Hill; Sullivan, S.E. (1999) 'The changing nature of careers: A review and research agenda', *Journal of Management*, 25(3), 457–84.

[25] Nicholson, N. and West, M.A. (1988) *Managerial Job Change; Men and Women in Transition*, Cambridge: Cambridge University Press; Drucker, P.F. (1999) *Management Challenges for the 21st Century*, Oxford: Butterworth Heinemann.

[26] Baruch, Y. and Hind, P. (1999) 'Perpetual Motion in Organizations: Effective Management and the impact of the new psychological contracts on "Survivor Syndrome"', *European Journal of Work and Organizational Psychology*, 8(2), 295–306.

[27] Levinson, H., Price, C., Munden, K., Mandl, H. and Solley, C. (1962) *Men, Management, and Mental Health*, Cambridge, MA: Harvard University Press.

[28] Kotter, J. (1973) 'The psychological contract: Managing the joining-up process', *California Management Review*, 15(3), 91–9; Schein, E.H. (1980) *Organizational Psychology*, 3rd edn, Englewood Cliffs, NJ: Prentice-Hall. Rousseau, D.M. (1995) *Psychological Contracts in Organizations*, Thousand Oaks: Sage; Nicholson, N. and Johns, G. (1985) 'The absence culture and the psychological contract – who's in control of absence', *Academy of Management Review*, 10, 397–407; Robinson, S.L., Kraatz, M.S. and Rousseau, D.M. (1994) 'Changing obligations and the psychological contract: A longitudinal study', *Academy of Management Journal*, 37(1), 137–52; Robinson, S.L. and Morrison, E.W. (1995) 'Psychological contracts and OCB: The effect of unfulfilled obligation on civic virtue behavior', *Journal of Organizational Behavior*, 16(3), 289–98.

[29] Spindler, G.S. (1994) 'Psychological contracts in the workplace – a lawyer's view', *Human Resource Management*, 33(3), 325–33.

[30] Kets de Vries, M.F.R. and Balazs, K. (1997) 'The downsize of downsizing', *Human Relations*, 50(1), 11–50.

[31] Sullivan, S.E. (1999), *see* note 24 above.

[32] Baruch, Y. (1998) 'The Rise and Fall of Organizational Commitment', *Human System Management*, 17(2), 135–43; Mowday, R.T. (1999) 'Reflections on the study and relevance of organizational commitment', *Human Resource Management Review*, 8(3), 387–401.

[33] Watson Wyatt (1999) *WorkUSA 2000: employee commitment and the bottom line*, Bethesda, MD: Watson Wyatt.

[34] Whitener, E.M. (2001) 'Do "high commitment" human resource practices affect employee commitment? A cross-level analysis using hierarchical linear modeling', *Journal of Management*, 27(5), 515–35.

[35] Handy, C. (1989) *The Age of Unreason*, London: Hutchinson; Waterman, R.H. Jr, Waterman, J.A. and Collard, B.A. (1994) 'Toward a career-resilient workforce', *Harvard Business Review*, 72(4), 87–95.

[36] Baruch, Y. (2001) 'Employability: A substitute for loyalty?', *Human Resource Development International*, 4(4), 543–66.

[37] Hughes, E.C. (1937) 'Institutional office and the person', *American Journal of Sociology*, 43, 404–43; cited by Adamson, Doherty and Viney (1998), *see* note 9 above.

[38] Hiltrop, J.-M. (1995) 'The changing psychological contract: The human resource challenge of the 1990s', *European Management Journal*, 13(3), 286–94; Shore, L.M. and Tetrick, L.E. (1994) 'The psychological contract as an explanatory framework in the employment relationship', *Journal of Organizational Behavior*, 1, Trends in OB supplement, 91–109.

[39] Robinson and Morrison (1995), *see* note 28 above.

[40] Herriot, P. and Pemberton, C. (1995) *New Deals*, Chichester: John Wiley.

[41] Brockner, J., Tyler, T.R. and Cooper-Schieder, R. (1992) 'The influence of prior commitment to institution on reactions to perceived unfairness: The higher they are, the harder they fall', *Administrative Science Quarterly*, 37, 241–61.

[42] DeFillippi, R.J. and Arthur, M.B. (1994) 'The boundaryless career: A competency-based perspective, *Journal of Organizational Behavior*, 15(4), 307–24.

[43] Ashkenas, R., Ulrich, D., Jick, T. and Kerr, S. (1995) *The Boundaryless Organization*, San Francisco: Jossey-Bass.

[44] Arthur, M.B., Claman, P.H. and DeFillippi, R.J. (1995) 'Intelligent enterprise, intelligent careers', *Academy of Management Executive*, 9(4), 7–22.

[45] Waterman, Waterman and Collard (1994), *see* note 35 above.

[46] Peiperl and Baruch (1997), *see* note 21 above.

[47] Herriot and Pemberton (1995), *see* note 40 above.

[48] Baruch (2001), *see* note 36 above.

[49] Kanter, D.L. and Mirvis, P.H. (1989) *The Cynical Americans*, San Francisco: Jossey-Bass.

[50] Lea, K. (1997) *Careers Encyclopedia*, 14th edn, London: Cassell.

[51] Glieck, J. (1988) *Chaos: Making a New Science*, London: Heinemann; Bailyn, L. (1993) 'Patterned Chaos in Human Resource Management', *Sloan Management Review*, 34(2), 77–84.

[52] Swedish Institute (1984) *Fact Sheets on Sweden*, Stockholm: Swedish Institute.

[53] DeFillippi, R.J. and Arthur, M.B. (1998) 'Paradox in project-based enterprise: The case of film making', *California Management Review*, 40(2), 125–39.

[54] Giddens, A. (1997) *Sociology*, 3rd edn, Cambridge: Polity Press.

[55] Drucker, P.F. (1999) *Management Challenges for the 21st Century*, Oxford: Butterworth-Heinemann.

[56] Scarbrough, H. (1999) 'Knowledge as work: conflicts in the management of knowledge workers', *Technology Analysis & Strategic Management*, 11(1), 5–16.

[57] Arthur, Claman and DeFillippi (1995), *see* note 19 above; DeFillippi, R.J. and Arthur, M.B. (1994) 'The boundaryless career: A competency-based prospective', *Journal of Organizational Behavior*, 15(4), 307–24; Jones, C. and DeFillippi, R.J. (1996) 'Back to the future in film: Combining industry and self-knowledge to meet the career challenges of the 21st century', *Academy of Management Executive*, 10(4), 89–103; Arthur, M.B., Inkson, K. and Pringle, J.K. (1999) *The New Careers: Individual Action and Economic Change*, London: Sage.

[58] Rousseau, D.M. (1995) *Psychological Contracts in Organizations*, Thousand Oaks: Sage; Rousseau, Jean-Jacques (1762) *The Social Contract or Principles of Political Right*, NY: New American Library (revised translation in 1974 with notes by C. M. Sheover).

[59] Hofstede, G. (1980) *Culture's consequences: international differences in work-related values*, NJ: Sage Publications; Triandis, H.C. (1995) *Individualism and Collectivism*, Boulder, CO: Westview Press.

[60] Ronen, S. and Shenkar, O. (1985) 'Clustering countries on attitudinal dimensions: a review and synthesis', *Academy of Management Review*, 10, 435–54.

[61] Weber, M. (1905) 'The Protestant Ethic', *Archiv fur Sozialwissenschaft und Sozialpolitic*, Vols 20 and 21. Cited in Giddens, A. (1971) *Capitalism and Modern Social Theory*, Cambridge: Cambridge University Press, p. 124.

[62] Rotter, J.B. (1966) Generalized expectancies for internal versus external control of reinforcement, *Psychological Monographs*, 1(609), 80.

[63] Maslow, A.H. (1943) 'A Theory of Human Motivation', *Psychological Review*, July, 370–96; McClelland, D. (1961) *The Achieving Society*, NY: Free Press.

[64] Dewey, J. (1939) *Theory of Valuation*, Chicago: University of Chicago Press.

[65] Rokeach, M. (1973) *The Nature of Human Values*, NY: Free Press.

[66] Stewart, W. and Barling, J. (1996) 'Fathers' work experiences affect children's behavior via job-related affect and parenting behaviors', *Journal of Organizational Behavior*, 17(3), 221–32.

[67] Lord, R.G., De Vader, C.L. and Alliger, G.M. (1986) 'A Meta Analysis of Relation Between Personality Traits and Leadership Perceptions: An Application of Validity Generalization Procedures', *Journal of Applied Psychology*, 71(3), 402–10.

[68] Judge, T.A., Cable, D.M., Boudreau, J. W. and Bretz, R.D. Jr. (1995) 'An empirical investigation of the predictors of executive career success', *Personnel Psychology*, 48, 485–519; Judge, T.A., Higgins, C.A., Thoresen, C.J. and Barrick, M.R. (1999) 'The big five personality traits, general mental ability, and career success across the life span', *Personnel Psychology*, 52, 621–52.

[69] Ajzen, I. and Fishbein, M. (1980) *Understanding attitudes and predicting social behavior*, Englewood Cliffs, NJ: Prentice-Hall; Fishbein, M. and Ajzen, I. (1975) *Belief, attitude, intention, and behavior: An introduction to theory and research*, Reading, MA: Addison-Wesley.

[70] Healy, G. (1999) 'Structuring commitments in interrupted careers: Career breaks, commitment and the life cycle in teaching', *Gender, Work and Organization*, 6(4), 185–201.

[71] Kolb, D.A. (1984) *Experiential Learning*, Englewood Cliffs, NJ: Prentice-Hall.

[72] Popper, M. and Lipshitz, R. (2000) 'Organizational learning: Mechanisms, culture and feasibility', *Management Learning*, 31(2), 181–96.

[73] Rosenbaum, J.L. (1979) 'Tournament mobility: career patterns in a corporation', *Administrative Science Quarterly*, 24, 221–41.

[74] Marshall, J. (1984) *Women managers: Travellers in a male world*, Chichester: Wiley; Morrison, A. (1992) *Breaking the Glass Ceiling*, Reading, MA: Addison Wesley.

[75] Moore, D.P. and Buttner, E.H. (1997) *Women Entrepreneurs: Moving beyond the glass ceiling*, Thousand Oaks: Sage.

[76] Smith, A. (1776, 1982) *The Wealth of Nations*, London: Penguin; Taylor, F.W. (1911) *The Principles of Scientific Management*, NY: Harper.

[77] Lea, K. (1997) *Careers Encyclopedia*, 14th edn, London: Cassell.

[78] Tapscott, D. (1998) *Growing Up Digital: The Rise of the Net Generation*, NY: McGraw-Hill.

[79] Arthur *et al.* (1989), *see* note 5 above.

[80] Gratton, L., Hope Hailey, V., Stiles, P. and Truss, C. (1999) *Strategic Human Resource Management*, New York: Oxford University Press; Holbeche, L. (1999) *Aligning Human Resource and Business Strategy*, Oxford: Butterworth-Heinemann.

[81] Fombrun, C.J., Tichy, N.M. and Devanna, M.A. (1984) *Strategic Human Resource Management*, NY: John Wiley & Sons, pp. 19–31; Hendry, C. (1995) *Human Resource Management, A strategic approach to employment*, Oxford: Butterworth-Heinemann.

[82] Baruch, Y. (1997) 'Evaluating quality and reputation of Human Resource Management', *Personnel Review*, 27(5), 377–94.

[83] Sonnenfeld, J.A. and Peiperl, M.A. (1988) 'Staffing policy as a strategic response: A typology of career systems', *Academy of Management Review*, 13(4), 568–600. Miles and Snow (1978), *see* note 24 above.

[84] Baruch, Y. (1999) 'Integrated Career systems for the 2000s', *International Journal of Manpower*, 20(7), 432–57.

2 Individual careers: career choice and career stages

LEARNING OBJECTIVES

After reading this chapter you should be able to:

- Define individual career.
- Identify the meaning of career choice.
- Understand how individual properties influence career choice.
- Recognize a variety of career stage models.

CHAPTER CONTENTS

- *Introduction: career – the individual perspective*
- *Career choice*
- *Internal, external and organizational careers*
- *Individual models of career choice*
- *Individual models of career stage and development*
- *Personality and career*
- *Summary*
- *Key terms*
- *Discussion questions*
- *Notes*
- *Appendix 2.1 The SMT Inventory: type description*
- *Appendix 2.2 Description of Belbin's team roles*

Introduction: career – the individual perspective

While the main focus of this book concerns managing career systems and how organizations manage individual careers, it is important to start with an understanding of individual careers. Without understanding the antecedents, processes and outcomes of careers for individuals we will not be able to develop an appropriate organizational system to deal with them. Another significant factor to be recognized is that major changes are taking place in the environment, in society and in organizations. The second half of the twentieth century witnessed a shift from career systems relying on a bureaucracy, in which careers were seen as a process of climbing a clear organizational hierarchy, to a new, dynamic and apparently boundaryless system. The traditional system was depicted by academics[1] and practitioners alike[2] as upward oriented, bounded and rigid, taking place within an organizational structure. On a different dimension, that of diversity, the labour market and the world of careers were homogeneous – careers were for white males only. Females were allowed to work as secretaries or as support staff, and in manufacturing, to perform repetitive work requiring low skill levels. People of colour were restricted to unskilled jobs.

The desired career was one that ran its course in the same workplace, with the individual working for a single employer. Although performance was assumed to decline with age, in particular in production roles, it was expected that experience would compensate for such deficiencies. Thus, experience and tenure were the principal factors considered in promotion decisions. Most people worked till they reached retirement age. This type of environment and culture lends itself to strong organizational control of careers.

However, even the traditional literature on careers views the individual as the main 'owner' of the career. Some go to the extreme of suggesting that the individual is the *only* one in charge. This might be true of a few cases, albeit increasing in number in recent years, such as those working as independent consultants, portfolio career people,[3] the self-employed, interim managers,[4] etc. Nevertheless, most people work in and for organizations. As a result, the majority share responsibility for their career with their employing organization.

This chapter does not deal solely with the individual, but also looks at other aspects of individuals' careers. Apart from the employing organization and the individual, other people and bodies play crucial roles in people's careers. The family, the partner, close friends, professional bodies and trade unions – all are important. Moreover, in both career choice and career development, much is subject to chance. In many cases it seems that the direction careers take has much to do with luck and random choice, and many career choices are at least partially unintentional. Unplanned events at certain critical points in one's life and career can lead to an unexpected change of direction. Such incidents include meeting a member of a particular profession, reading a book or seeing a film that glorifies a specific type of job or role, or even accidental browsing through the 'Appointments' section of a local newspaper while unemployed or when on a boring train journey.

The two major career issues for the individual that are covered in this chapter are 'career choice' and 'career development'. Amongst the topics covered are theoretical frameworks of career choice, the early career, the career plateau, obsolescence, leaving the labour market, career and other life interests, quality of working life, stress and careers, demography, including individual and gender differences (though diversity will be fully covered in Chapter 8), dual-career couples, international careers, career aspirations, the new psychological contracts, and innovative career concepts such as the Protean career.

In the 1920s and 1930s, the Chicago School of Sociology studied the life histories of the local communities in an attempt to understand how people viewed their lives.[5] When the Chicago sociologists used the term career, therefore, they were referring to a heuristic concept, applicable to a wider range of situations than contemporary usage in management circles would imply. Only later was the concept of careers restricted to the organizational domain. Present-day approaches have returned to the original wider framework embracing all aspects of a person's life, not just the individual's organizational and professional life.

Career choice

Work is an essential and mostly a desired part of our lives. Its role goes far beyond the need to provide food, shelter and other essentials for life. Work provides people with a sense of purpose, challenges, self-fulfilment and development, as well as the essential income to enable them to participate in other spheres of life. Work is a source of identity as well as of creativity and mastery.[6] Work provides us with status and offer opportunities for social networking. Many find love and affection and meet their partners during and through work. Work helps us to pass the time and gives our lives structure. A different, 'positive', aspect of work is that for many, work may even serve as a shelter and sanctuary from home and family.[7] Hochschild agued that in order to avoid home-related issues and challenges such as relationship matters people absorb themselves in work, sometimes for long hours. In sum, in terms of the 'hierarchy of needs' suggested by Maslow,[8] work provides the basic needs as well as opportunities for achieving the higher needs.

Many of the outcomes of work and career that people face will depend on why they do what they do; this is not merely a matter of which vocation, profession, job or career they choose. It is how important work is for them, as a facet of their lives. The 'acid test' for the centrality of work and career choice can be found in 'the lottery dilemma': What would you do about work if you had won a lottery or inherited a large sum of money that would enable you to quit working and still enjoy a comfortable lifestyle.

Before turning to Table 2.1 on the next page, try to answer the question honestly. As a student you may not be working now, but if you were faced with the lottery dilemma after working for a year or two in a job, what would you choose?

■ Stop working.
■ Continue working in the same job.
■ Continue working but under different conditions.

Another question to consider is where will your fellow citizens be placed on the scale, in comparison with other nations? Now compare your answer with the data presented in Table 2.1, which ranks the answer of an international sample in the 'Meaning of Working' Survey[9] to the question 'What would you do if you were financially secure?'

Table 2.1 The lottery dilemma in various countries

Stop working		Continue working in the same job		Continue working but under different conditions	
Country	%	Country	%	Country	%
Britain	31	Japan	66	Britain	53
West Germany	30	Yugoslavia	62	USA	49
Belgium	16	Israel	50	Belgium	47
Netherlands	14	Netherlands	42	Netherlands	44
USA	12	USA	39	West Germany	39
Israel	12	Belgium	37	Israel	37
Japan	7	West Germany	31	Yugoslavia	34
Yugoslavia	4	Britain	16	Japan	27

Table 2.1 clearly indicates that people are committed to work and employment, although not necessarily to their current job or their original career choice. The level of commitment is influenced by several factors. Clearly the status and type of present job have an impact, as well as individual characteristics, but to these we need to add national and cultural background. In Britain, for example, less than one in six would stay in the same job, compared with two out of six in Japan. Noon and Blyton[10] elucidate this phenomenon, giving a variety of explanations, the first of which is the moral necessity to work. This may be the case where work is seen as a 'duty', where work is viewed as an activity central to one's life,[11] where the role of work is conscientious endeavour or disciplined compliance.[12]

Some people make their career choice at a very young age, but of these, not all achieve their aim. Other people choose a career later, while some never really make a definite choice of career. Many have to modify their career aspirations due to changes in the environment, recognition of their own limitations, changes in their values and attitudes, and in the realities of life. The choice of a career may be unintended, but even when planned people do not necessarily achieve their goals.

EXHIBIT 2.1

Unintended careers

JK was the branch manager for a national retail chain in the food sector. When he was made redundant in 1993, he was told of openings for taxi drivers. Needing to maintain his mortgage repayments, he obtained a job as a driver to provide him with a temporary source of income. He found that the job suited his needs: it gave him a lot of autonomy (e.g. determining his own working hours and holidays), there was no boss to report to, it provided a reasonable income, and was not too demanding on his skills. He is now just over 50, and may continue with cab-driving for the foreseeable future.

In the early 1980s, ML had just finished high school, and before taking on further studies she wanted to earn some money in order to travel. She opened the newspaper and saw an advertisement for a job in an insurance company where they promised training and fair working conditions and terms. Following an interview she accepted the offer of a job, and now, 20 years later, is a middle-level manager in that same large insurance company. Although she had not previously envisaged a career in insurance, and had planned just short-term employment, it seems to suit her well.

These real-life examples show extreme cases of unintended careers. Nevertheless, one must assume that unless JK had liked driving, and ML had preferred job security, they would not have ended up in their present careers. In many other instances there is certain amount of luck or an unintentional element in career choice,[13] but there is also a set of individual propensities and qualities that are required for particular vocations and professions.

Question	When did you choose the university where you are now studying? Was it a rational choice? Was it your first choice, the one you wished for and had planned for over a period of a few years? Or did you choose it on the advice of a friend, or because you read about it in a newspaper?

To what extent are people prepared for their future career? What motivates people to choose a specific career direction? In what ways do experience and individual background influence decisions? How and why are different choices made at different stages of life? To better understand these issues let us start by looking at some cases.

Exhibit 2.2 presents two typical cases of career choice dilemmas.

EXHIBIT 2.2

Trevor

Trevor studied for a first degree in Mechanical Engineering at a well-known university. Soon after graduation he started his first job in industry, working on a research and development project for a high-technology firm, part of a larger company. After he had been working for two years on the project the manager of his department left the company and Trevor was asked to take over his role. In his new position he had responsibility for three technicians, one young engineer and several support staff. He did well, but felt he was 'wasting' his time managing the department rather than being involved in engineering work. A year later the project was completed, and the mother-company decided to produce the subject of the project on a commercial basis. Trevor was asked to move to another subsidiary of the company, which focused on production.

At this point he felt that such a managerial role required further training in management. He completed an in-house course in management, and started working as deputy to the head of the production department. The most difficult area for him in his new role was the financial management of projects. After discussions with his wife and friends he enrolled in an evening course in financial management at the local business school.

Trevor found the course very interesting, and in due course undertook a Master's degree. This proved a great success, and after two years, now with two children, and with the prospect of replacing his own manager and head of the production unit, Trevor was supposed to be happy. However, he felt he might have chosen the wrong career. Even his subsequent promotion did not satisfy him. After only one year as head of department, Trevor decided he wished to embark on an academic career in the area of financial management.

Exhibit 2.2 continued

His strong mathematical competence and enthusiasm for his studies convinced a well-known professor in a prestigious university to accept him as a PhD student. He left his fairly well-paid job for a student bursary and embarked on the programme. During his three years of study his wife was supportive, and Trevor enjoyed his studies immensely. He even managed to get few consultancy projects that helped him financially. Publishing parts of his dissertation in a top management journal helped him to gain a post as a lecturer in a good university, the only disadvantage being that he had to relocate to a different city.

One of his research projects required him to work with one of the Big Five consultancy firms. He enjoyed working on two research ideas and developed a model that was adopted by the company. However, one thing bothered him. He was now in his early forties, and realized that his partners in the research projects earned about twice as much as he did. He had a mortgage to pay, three children, and the combined salaries of himself and his wife were not enough to enable them to have the lifestyle they desired. At this point one of his research projects on financial models took him to a company that asked him to undertake some consultancy work concurrently with his academic work. The benefits were enormous compared to what he earned from his salaried work. He knew there were good prospects for him to earn much more in consultancy, and he thought carefully about ending his academic career. If he were to do so, should he opt to work for a large company such as one of the Big Five, or open his own start-up consultancy?

Lynne

Lynne studied for a first degree in art and languages. At the end of her studies she took a year off to travel, and while in Australia met a girlfriend, Terry, who had graduated in art and business management. Together they started to talk about their dreams and realized they had a common wish – to design clothes and fashion items. On their return to the UK via India and Hungary they established contacts with several local textile manufacturers.

Back home they applied for a start-up loan from the Department of Trade and Industry (DTI), and received a moderate sum that enabled them to open a small boutique in Brighton. Within three years Lynne and Terry expanded the business, and then opened another branch and enjoyed a fair income. However, Lynne realized that much of her work involved either dealing with financial matters or communicating with suppliers, tax collectors and a few unhappy customers. The artistic element in her work had been reduced to a minor fraction and she felt frustrated. She took an evening class in pottery where her distinctive decorative style was highly appreciated. In fact, at the end of the course she managed to sell more of her work than any other student. As a result Lynne persuaded her business partner to open a new section in one of the shops, for pottery and other artistic objects. This success planted new ideas in her mind. She was 30 by now, and had a partner with whom she wanted to share her life.

Both Trevor and Lynne faced a career choice dilemma. Today such career and life stories are quite common, but this was not the case before the last few decades of the twentieth century. Before that there would usually be one point in life when a person would choose a career, a certain specific career, that is (and up to some 50 years ago it would be *his* career rather than 'his or hers'). Before the eighteenth century life was even simpler, of course. A man's career was usually determined by the career of his father. Females had no occupational career (with a few exceptions such as nuns). For most of the twentieth century career choices similar to those faced by Trevor and Lynne were very unusual. Even after the Second World War only a minority of people studied for a university degree. Most people did not hop from job to job, and certainly second or third careers were the exception. By the turn of the last century, about a third of the population of the relevant age group in industrial nations have studied for a first degree, and this trend continues – the UK government has set a target of 50 per cent of high-school leavers to study for a university degree by 2010. Moreover, people are expected to continue learning, not merely while of university age, but through-out their working life. People have second and third careers. The fourth career change Trevor was contemplating was unheard of even as recently as the 1970s. Starting up a business would not have been an option for Lynne's mother or aunt.

Question	What is the best career advice for Trevor? For Lynne? Does 'best advice' exist at all? What is the purpose of career counselling and what is it based on? There is more on career counselling in Chapter 3.

Question	Think about your own career pattern up to the present. Have you known from an early age what you wanted to do? Are you still following that original aspiration? Have you changed your career path? What caused the change – internal motives or external circumstances?

Let us try to gain a better understanding of the needs of individuals and the requirements of organizations and their roles in career planning and management.

Internal, external and organizational careers

In defining what career is, we should distinguish between internal, external and organizational careers.

The **internal career** is a person's self-perception about his or her own career: its development, advancement and fulfilment of goals. This self-perception involves setting subjective career goals and evaluating one's own achievement in reaching them. An internal career is subjective, and thus the definition of internal career success depends on the inner feelings and values of the person, and is relative to the career aims set by the self for the self.

The **external career** concerns how other people and organizations perceive a person's career – the development, advancement and fulfilment of the person's goals. Evaluating career success by means of external evaluation it is more objective than internal career measurement, but it still depends on the particular observer's viewpoint. Success in an external career is assessed mainly in terms of hierarchy level and pace of progress on such a ladder, social status (e.g. occupational status), professional qualifications and financial success (i.e. income and other monetary rewards).

The **organizational career** is a path people move along, in terms of the positions and the roles they fill during their working life. Career progress or advancement can be quite objective and measurable within a single organization or between organizations with equivalent promotion scales (e.g. army v. navy). However, such comparisons are less clear or may even be meaningless for dynamic careers, as moves involve multiple transitions. Here comparisons might be impractical or irrelevant. (For example is the CEO of an organization employing 1000 people 'higher' than a Vice President who manages 3000 employees in a company of 10 000?)

While organizations retain career systems through which they plan and manage people's careers, it is people who *have* careers. People will plan and manage their careers, not always according to an organization's plans and schemes. It may be most appropriate to consider careers as being under 'mutual ownership' – that of people and organizations. We now look at individual career choice models.

Individual models of career choice

Many of the career theories dealing with the individual refer to career choice. Osipow (1990) summarized the leading theories of career choice and development, and concluded that the most prominent career choice theories are Holland's RIASEC model and Social learning.[14] Let us explore these theories in turn.

Holland's RIASEC model

One of the most widely used and academically validated models of career choice is Holland's RIASEC.[15] Developed more than forty years ago, Holland's model identifies people's vocational or occupational preferences, and helps also in determining a fit between a person's choices and organizational characteristics (and sometimes even team characteristics) that can be expressed in similar terms. RIASEC stands for *Realistic, Investigative, Artistic, Social, Enterprising* and *Conventional*. These types refer to six categories of people and six models of occupational environment. There is an association among the six types, most commonly depicted as a hexagon (*see* Figure 2.1 and Table 2.2 for Holland's Personality-Job Fit theory).

Holland's theory follows the three basic elements of Parsons' (1909) concept of career choice – the person, the occupation and the fit between the two. It has

Occupational personality types

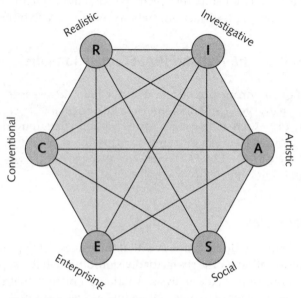

Figure 2.1 The Holland hexagon

Source: © Prentice Hall, 2001.

Table 2.2 Holland's Personality-Job Fit theory

Type	Personality	Occupations
Realistic	Shy, Stable, Practical	Mechanic, Farmer, Assembly-Line Worker
Investigative	Analytical, Independent	Biologist, Economist, Mathematician
Social	Sociable, Cooperative	Social Worker, Teacher, Counselor
Conventional	Practical, Efficient	Accountant, Manager, Bank Teller
Enterprising	Ambitious, Energetic	Lawyer, Salesperson
Artistic	Imaginative, Idealistic	Painter, Writer, Musician

the advantage of good face validity and years of corroborative empirical evidence for the theory and its practical derivatives.[16] Consistent though moderate correlation (ranging from $r = .15$ to $r = .54$) was found between person-environment fit (to use Holland's term) and job satisfaction. (However more work needs to be done to investigate the association with measures of performance or career satisfaction.) Such a fit means that there is a certain level of similarity or a match between individual vocational preferences and the characteristics of the work environment in which the person works, using the RIASEC terminology.

The *Holland Dictionary of Occupational Codes: A comprehensive Cross-Index of Holland's RIASEC Codes with 12,000 DOT Occupations* (1989) contains a vast variety of occupations and vocations, many of which did not exist in the past. The person-environment congruence has been the subject of much recent research. Even though the person-environment fit is a fundamental issue in the behavioural sciences, its prescription cannot be accurate.[17] The above-mentioned findings about the Holland theory fit well with earlier work such as a meta-analysis that found a close relationship between person-environment congruence and measures of well-being (satisfaction, stability, etc.).[18] (*See* Exhibit 2.3.)

EXHIBIT 2.3	**Test yourself on the Holland RIASEC questionnaire**

The Holland questionnaire can be found on the following websites: www.self-directed-search.com/ has John Holland's original test, which can be taken for less than £10. Alternatively, an updated version containing new occupations (but costing more to take) can be found on http://career-planning.com. Free sites related to the RIASEC model are http://www.ncsu.edu/careerkey/ and http://www.missouri.edu/~cppcwww/holland.shtml.

Managerial styles

One problem with the Holland theory is that there does not appear to be any strong theoretical justification for the six-factor division, although it is supported by empirical investigation using factor analysis. Another problem is that the theory relates mostly to the entry stage of a career. Other inventories focus on later stages, and on managerial aspects. Two UK-based and one USA-based theories which offer updated inventories are Belbin's team roles,[19] Lessem's Spectral Management Theory (SMT),[20] and Quinn's Eight Managerial Roles model. Belbin's inventory is widely used, but suffers from low academic validation whereas the SMT has received wider empirical support for its validation. All of these concepts are presented at the end of this chapter for the benefit of the reader (*see* Exhibit 2.6 and Appendices 2.1 and 2.2).

New frontiers

Since the Industrial Revolution, the number of areas of knowledge and associated jobs and vocations has expanded enormously, and large numbers of new specialties have developed. This expansion accelerated even further in the last years of the twentieth century. Basic education has become mandatory in most developed societies. More and more occupations require specific qualifications, hence extended periods of formal training. Institutions of higher education have arisen that provide the training called for by the higher levels of knowledge work. Totally new vocational areas have emerged (most notably Internet-related jobs such as web-page designing). Even in relatively traditional occupations there is divergence: Sternberg[21] describes how, within one occupation – that of psychologist – there are several sub-disciplines, each quite distinct and requiring different knowledge: academic, clinical, counselling, engineering or human factors, industrial or organizational, marketing, military, psychometric, school, or consulting. Even this list can be expanded by adding occupational psychologist, social psychologist and other sub-professions. Each of these has a different focus, and requires different academic training.

As a result, the academic sector has grown substantially in most industrial societies, and has become a career field for more than just the elite few of the past. Many embark on an academic career while others who study for a PhD have to accept underemployment due to the competitiveness of this area.[22] Williams,

Blackstone and Metcalf (1974) focused on the British academic labour market of the early 1970s, at which time it comprised only 33 000 employees. They claimed that there was a high similarity between the UK and American academic labour markets. However, unlike the US academic labour market, that of the UK is tightly regulated (e.g. all universities have fixed salary scales, and there is a high level of unionism). In 1994 the number of employees was 114 700.[23] The basis for the calculation varies according to the definition of 'higher education'. Metzger (1987) argues that the 1980 data for higher educational institutions in the USA, which at the time comprised some 850 000 instructional staff, could vary according to the definition. The exclusion of part-time staff or the inclusion of researchers could mean a variation from less than 500 000 to more than 1 250 000. Metzger (1987) pointed out the extensive growth of the academic sector in the USA, and the trend has continued in this direction. Moreover, the academic career system is becoming a role model for many occupations due to its knowledge-based and boundaryless nature.[24]

Social learning

Social learning[25] is concerned with feedback from the environment, in particular from career counselling and the development of self-efficacy[26] as a result of reinforcement. External intervention can help to facilitate high self-efficacy via learning that affects people's attitudes and behaviours. Self-efficacy has repeatedly been shown to be an antecedent of performance in organizational settings.[27] In general, the literature provides strong evidence of a high degree of correlation between efficacy perceptions and subsequent performance.[28] Both feedback from the wider environment (i.e. not just from the parents) and reinforcement of successful performance help people in choosing professions and careers that would suit them best.

To make a 'proper' choice, i.e. to optimize their career prospects, people need first to realize their own vocational inclination, and second to acquire knowledge of the occupational environment associated with various professional options. In the example above, of academic roles, to succeed one needs either to be keen to create new knowledge (i.e. research) or to educate and develop future generations of graduates (i.e. teaching), or both. Vocational inclination depends on the motivation, knowledge, personality and competence of a person. Occupation is much more than a collection of activities and functions. It is the culture, the reputation, the status, and the associated lifestyle of a particular discipline.

Entrepreneurship

Many do not wish to follow the organizational career route, but are inspired to create their own venture, perhaps a small company, sometimes just a one-person entity, or they wish to build a large company from scratch. Such people are entrepreneurs, and their careers mostly involve a struggle, and sometimes deep frustration – for every one that has 'made it', there are many who have had to give up their dreams or accept that their business will never grow as they had hoped.

One characteristic that distinguishes entrepreneurs from managers is their risk propensity.[29] Using a psychometric meta-analytic review of literature concerning the comparative risk propensities, Stewart and Roth pointed out the importance of the role personality plays in entrepreneurial career choice. The McClelland (1985) theory of needs (e.g. the need for achievement, the need for control) also provides a relevant basis for understanding entrepreneurs' careers. Many biographies of entrepreneurs (*see*, for example, the Dyson biography by Coren, 2001) account for such differences.[30]

Individual models of career stage and development

Many view career as a developmental process that comprises several stages. Most notable is Super's developmental theory (1957), one of the well-known career stage models.[31] Some maintain there are distinct stages, and have argued for specific boundaries between them. Each stage influences the next, and together they form a continuum.

The first impressions people have about careers, career roles and the world of work emerge from the individual family background. According to the Social Identity theory presented above, this will affect children's behaviour, and as a result, will influence their future career choice.[32]

Several scholars have developed career stage theories. Two of the eminent theories are those developed by Super and by Levinson. Super's (1957) theory of career stages reflects how, during the lifespan of a person, individuals implement their inner being and self-concept in one or more career (or vocational) choices. Levinson (1978, 1986) distinguishes between transition stages (each lasting for a period of five years) and stability stages, each of which may last some five to seven years. Later in this chapter we will examine both Super's and Levinson's frameworks. One problem with suggesting a specific timespan for either the chronological age or the duration of a stage is that there is no empirical support for any of the suggested figures.[33]

Levinson's (1978) theory of the 'seasons of man's life' suffers from the notion of determinism, almost fatalism, inherent in the title of the concept. That is, the use of the seasons metaphor implies that these career stages are fixed, unchangeable, and that each person has to experience the same sequence throughout life. Another criticism concerns the title of the theory, namely the gendered element. However, at the time of Levinson's earlier writing, managerial careers were mostly male dominated. Even now managerial careers, in particular at the most senior levels, still are. Hakim asserts that only 20 per cent of women are 'work-centered' against 60 per cent of men.[34] Levinson and Levinson (1996) similarly differentiate between two female career streams: the 'homemaker' and the 'work career'. (There is more about the gendered side of careers in Chapter 8.)

In the past, after a turbulent period in their early career – a period of discovery and exploration – individuals would arrive at a point at which both their own self-concept and the organization's concept of them had reached harmony. At this point they would typically have achieved a balance between work and family/social life, and their employers would begin to reap a return on their investment in the individual. In the twenty-first century that equilibrium has ceased to exist. Both individuals and organizations are creating new cycles. These can be either vicious or victorious cycles, i.e. sometimes such a cycle represents a spiral of ongoing development and achievements for both individuals and their employers, but in other cases there are cycles of deterioration in self-perception, self-esteem, and contribution, ending in long-term unemployment or poor performance, usually coupled with a poor quality of life.

<table>
<tr><td>Question</td><td>What can and should organizations do to help and prompt positive development, and at the same time to identify and prevent negative deterioration? Later on in the book we will examine the phenomenon from the organizational point of view and see what practices may be useful for such treatment.</td></tr>
</table>

Super's lifespan, life-space theory combines the psychology of individual development during life and social role theory in order to understand multiple-role careers via the Life-Career Rainbow (*see* Figure 2.2).

Chronological age and career age

Super indicated the parallelism between people's chronological age and state of development and their career stage.[35] Super's stages are: (a) childhood growth (up to the age of 14); (b) search and inquiry (up to the age of 25); (c) establishment (up to age 45); (d) continuity or maintenance (up to age 56); and (e) decline or disengagement. The other dimension of the Rainbow is concerned with life space, and the social roles of: the child, the student, the leisure seeker, the citizen, the worker and the home-maker. It is of interest to note that working life comprises just one part of the career, as was shown in early studies of the Chicago School mentioned earlier. These roles interact, and can benefit from each other, but they also create conflicts of commitments.

The following description of Super's stages is based on Super, Savickas and

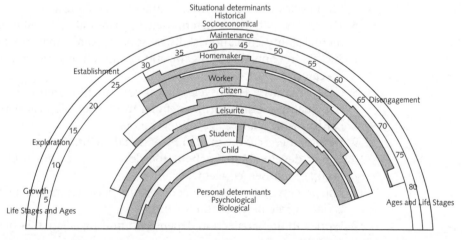

Figure 2.2 The life-career rainbow: six life roles in schematic life space

Source: D.E. Super, M.L. Savickas and C.M. Super (1996) 'The life-span, life space approach to careers', in D. Brown and L. Brooks (eds) *Career Choice and Development*, 3rd edn, San Francisco: Jossey-Bass, p. 127, © John Wiley & Sons, Inc., reproduced with permission.

Super (1996). The growth stage includes dealing with the tasks associated with becoming concerned about the future, increasing control over one's own life, committing to school and work, and acquiring competent work habits and attitudes. During the exploration stage individuals encounter crystallizing, specifying and implementing occupational choice. The establishment stage occurs at the beginning of one's career and the tasks are stabilizing, consolidating and advancing in one's occupational position. Maintenance is concerned mainly with the issue of midlife crisis and includes the tasks of holding on, keeping up and innovating. This stage can be associated with a career plateau. It can involve becoming more firmly entrenched in one's chosen occupation, or transition to a different occupation. The last career stage of disengagement is all about phasing out – deceleration and retirement.

The description fits well the stable type of career people experienced in the years between the beginning of the Industrial Revolution and the late twentieth century. The changes elaborated upon in Chapter 1 have changed the framework of reference for Super's concept, although much of it is still relevant. Let us look at the 14 major propositions of the theory, as summarized by Super, Savickas and Super (1996):

1 People differ in abilities, personalities, needs, values, interests, traits and their self-concept.
2 People are qualified, by virtue of these characteristics, for a number of occupations.
3 Each occupation requires a characteristic pattern of personal abilities, traits, etc., with a certain degree of tolerance to allow varieties of occupations for each individual and a variety of individuals for each occupation.
4 Vocational preferences and competencies and life and work situations change with time and experience, but the self-concept is relatively stable since it derives from social learning.
5 The change processes come in the time frame of the stages described above. Mini-cycles will occur when a career is destabilized.
6 The career pattern is determined by parental socio-economic background, mental ability, education, skills, personality, career maturity and opportunities.
7 Success in coping with organizational and environmental demands depends on career maturity.
8 Career maturity is a psychological construct, related to cognitive and affective qualities, but it can be defined from a sociological perspective via comparison with relative age achievements.
9 Development can be guided by external facilitation.
10 Career development is about the development and implementation of an occupational self-concept.
11 The process of synthesis or compromise between individual and social factors is one of role playing and learning.
12 Work and life satisfaction depends on finding adequate outlets for one's own qualities.
13 Work satisfaction is proportional to ability for the implementation of the self-concept.

14 Work and occupation provide a focus for personality organization for most people. Social traditions, opportunities and individual differences determine performance in the role taken by individuals in all their life-spaces.

The 14 propositions – critical perspective

Some of the propositions might be perceived as no more than simplistic trivialities (e.g. 1, 9, 12), others are outdated (e.g. 5, 8), but the majority are relevant and applicable to the understanding of individual careers. For example (4) is a strong proposition that calls for further study. All in all together they comprise a comprehensive approach to the study of individual careers.

Question

Which of these 14 propositions would you find most relevant to your own career?

The Levinson model

Daniel Levinson's work was based on American men (women being added to his analysis later), and identified four basic career stages – childhood and adolescence, which is really a pre-career stage; early adulthood; middle adulthood and late adulthood. Within each stage there is an inner stage of transition.

Early adulthood starts with entry to the labour market. At the time of Levinson's study the typical age for starting work was 17, while in the first half of the twentieth century it was even lower, age 14, as few people continued on to higher education. The early years (up to the age of 28, according to Levinson) are the time for a person to establish a direction and try to gain a certain stability. At about the age of 30, though, people may reappraise their life, moving on to a stable stage of identifying what they are seeking from life and work, establishing a role in society, in the organization and in the family.

The early adulthood stage ends with midlife transition or crisis, which takes place at around the age of 40–45. This is the time when people tend to reflect on their life so far, and contemplate the future. Levinson identified three factors that contribute to the fact that most people have such a crisis or re-evaluation of their career in their early 40s. First, by the age of 40, people have enough feedback to contemplate their achievements, their fulfilment of their childhood dreams or their failure to do so. This is coupled with a feeling of becoming 'older': the age of 40 seems something of a threshold. Lastly, people might begin to feel a decline in their physical strength even if it is only minor.

Then, according to Levinson, when they reach middle adulthood, people come to terms with their career and their inner feelings, and have a stable stage between about the ages of 50 and 55. This stage is followed, again, by an unstable phase of transition, in which they set new goals. Then comes the last career stage of late adulthood, when a combination of bodily decline and sometimes illness, and rapidly approaching retirement causes people to end their working career, and prepare themselves for retirement.

Several major changes make the Levinson model in need of re-definition and restructuring. His model is based on and was established within the context of the American economy. Moreover, in general, there have been major changes in the nature of careers, elaborated in Chapter 1 (e.g. that many have second, third or more careers, that people sometimes have to take early retirement at the age of 55 to 60, etc.). To this we must add other developments, such as general improvements in health care and the fact that people at the age of 65 should no longer feel that they should prepare for decline and death, but to a long period of active enjoyment of leisure.

Other career stage models

Several other models offer a similar idea of association between age or life stage and career development, usually in terms of career progress. There are minor variations in the ages of the groups or the names of the stages in these models such as those of Hall and Nougaim (1968), Greenhaus (1987) and Form and Miller (1949). Schein's (1978) model is also similar, but offers eight stages: growth and search (up to 21); entry to the world of work (16–25); basic training (16–25); starting full-time career (17–30); mid-career (25+); late career (40+); decline (40+); and retirement. Here there is an overlap in the age groups, but there is still an attempt to retain age boundaries. A different type of career stage model is offered by Evans (1986), who argued that there are fluctuations in the early working stage (15–35/40), then stable growth, followed by the last stage, which starts at the age of 50. This last stage can be either further growth, plateau or decline.[36]

Others wisely refrained from attaching specific ages to the stages. Such are the Baird and Kram (1983) and Dalton, Thompson and Price (1977) models. The latter focuses on professional growth and managerial development (and was validated by Thompson *et al.* in 1986).[37] Dalton *et al.* suggested a four-stage model of career development. Their model is based upon a longitudinal study of academic scholars and professional engineers, which aimed to find out why some individuals continued to contribute and be productive throughout their careers, while others' productivity and contributions diminished over time. According to Dalton *et al.*, a career can be conceptualized as a progression through developmental stages that are independent of organizational structure or hierarchy. In the first stage, the individuals or protégés take on the role of apprentices, learning to perform fairly routine tasks and taking direction from more experienced mentors. In the second stage, the protégés have developed specific competences and start to demonstrate their own initiative and creativity. By the time the individuals have reached the third stage, they have become mentors to others and have broadened their interests by contributing through others. Finally, in the last stage, the individuals have been able to shape the practices, policies and even the culture and direction of the entire organization. They guide and represent the organization, either as a senior manager, or an expert, or via resource acquisition. The employee follows an individual route and makes an autonomous search for self-responsibility. The problem with this model is that many never develop into the third stage, and even fewer reach the fourth.

Most researchers refer to career stages as a given. However, several characteristics influence the number and sequence of stages. Most notable is gender. In a further variation of his own 1957 model, Super revised it, distinguishing between males and females.[38] Four types of career path were suggested for males – stable, conventional (with some advances till stability is reached), unstable and multiple paths. For females, seven options were presented – housewife, stable (usually in

Table 2.3 Several well-known career stage models

Scholar	No. of stages	Use of age	Names of stages
Baird and Kram (1983)[40]	4	No	Establishment Progress Maintenance Retirement
Dalton, Thompson and Price (1977)[41]	4	No	Work under guidance (apprentices) Autonomous work Mentoring others Direction, representation, sponsoring
Form and Miller (1949)[42]	5	Yes	0–15: Orientation to the world of work 15–18: Beginning stage, sometimes part-time work 18–34: Entry to labour market 34–60: Stable stage 60–65: Retirement
Greenhaus (1987)[43]	5	Yes	0–25: Entry to labour world 18–25: Entry to organization world 25–40: Establishment and achievements 40–55: Plateau career 55–retirement: Late career
Hall and Nougaim (1968)[44]	5	Yes	0–25: Pre-work 26–30: Establishment 31–45: Progress 46–65: Maintenance 65+: Retirement
Levinson (1978)[45]	4 + 3/5*	Yes	0–17: Childhood and adolescence 17–22: Transitional: early adult 23–40: up to 28, entering; up to 40, settling down (with age 30 transition) 40–45: Transition: mid-life 45–60: Middle adulthood and culmination (with age 50 transition) 60–65: Transition: late adult 65+: Late adulthood
Schein (1978)[46]	8	Yes	0–21: Growth and search 16–25: Entry to the world of work 16–25: Basic training 17–30: Starting full-time employment 25+: Mid-career 40+: Late career 40+: Decline ?: Retirement
Super (1957, 1980)[47]	5	Yes	0–14: Childhood growth 0–25: Search and inquiry 25–45: Establishment 45–56: Continuity or maintenance 56+: Decline or disengagement

* Five transitional stages, three of them major between childhood, adulthood and late adulthood.

low-skilled labour), stable, dual (alongside the housewife role, sometimes via part-time jobs), disrupted (due to giving births), unstable and multiple paths.

Such gender differences were also identified by Ciabattari and by Sullivan.[39] Other differentiating characteristics include profession, culture, size of organization and type of employment, to mention just a few. Table 2.3 summarizes the major career stage models.

Using specific age groupings is inadequate in today's dynamic environment, and when people have multiple careers. Even in the past such rigidity would not fit variations among professions and their disciplinary accreditation (the training period can be very long – e.g. in medicine or accountancy), nations (if a period of military service is compulsory, the starting age of a career moves accordingly) and educational background. At the beginning of the twenty-first century we have witnessed a hyper-turbulent business environment, which has meant changes in the norms of behaviour, and even in value systems, and has reduced the relevance of age as a measure of career stage.

Similarly, to use a specific number of career stages is inadequate. People with multiple careers or who experience career break(s) will have different number of stages. Some professions have no stages (e.g. class teacher). Others have multiple career paths with different stages (e.g. military careers). What is important is the qualities associated with the different career stages people find themselves in. Amongst other aspects, career stage is important for understanding and interpreting job satisfaction. Feldman[48] argued that there is ample empirical evidence

Table 2.4 Integrated model

Stage	Description
(a) Foundation	Childhood and adolescent experience and education help in planting the seeds of career aspiration.
(b) Career entry	Usually through attainment of a profession. Can be done via apprenticeship, training on the job or attending college, university or other professional training. Even for qualified people, the first stage of work will usually include further professional establishment.
(c) Advancement	Both professional and hierarchical development within organization(s) or expanding one's own business. This stage can be characterized by either continuous advancement or reaching a plateau. In today's career environment and concepts, this stage will typically be associated with several changes of employer.
(d) Re-evaluation	Checking match between aspiration and fulfilment; re-thinking job/role/career. Can emerge from internal feelings or needs (e.g. bored due to lack of challenge, life crisis), or external forces (redundancy, obsolescence of the profession). May end with decision to remain on the same path or to change career direction, returning to stage (b).
(e) Reinforcement	After making the decision, reinforcement of present career or returning to learning stage (b) for establishment of new career.
(f) Decline	Most (except the few who have a full life of advancement till the very last moment) will start at a certain stage to envisage a withdrawal from working life, which can be swift or long term, spread over few years.
(g) Retirement	Leaving the labour market (not necessarily at age 65).

that young workers are somewhat dissatisfied with pay and relationships with supervisors, but happy with learning opportunities. Satisfaction increased later in life, and then reduced towards the 'mid-life crisis' in the early forties, which is usually overcome by a proper approach, and rectified in the final stages of the career.

Table 2.4 offers an integrated model, which has neither a definite number of stages, nor specific age boundaries. Still it encompasses and captures the common nature and notion of the various career stage models.

While the basic model comprises seven stages, stages (b) to (e) can, and in most cases will, be repeated several times. And similarly, while no specific ages are suggested, some indications can be given for most stages. The first stage will usually end with the completion of formal school education, which is about 18 in most industrial nations. The entry and acquiring a profession stage can be very short: if one decides at the age of 16 or 18 to deliver mail, within a few weeks one can start working. If one wishes to become a lawyer it takes about five years to complete the basic training. Certain life crises tend to come at a similar age (such as the mid-life crisis, which, for women, can be associated with the biological menopause stage). The age of retirement is, at the latest 65, but for many who are made redundant at a mature age, typically after 50, it may be too difficult to find an alternative job at the same status, thus early retirement is more commonplace.

Personality and career

From the individual viewpoint, career has much to do with psychology. To understand careers – career targets and aspirations, career satisfaction, career perception, etc. – we need to recognize psychological issues such as motivational and behavioural theories, e.g. the 'self-fulfilling prophecy',[49] 'Cognitive Dissonance'[50] frameworks, and new concepts in the psychology of individual traits, in particular 'the Big Five'.[51] (These frameworks are presented in most Organizational Behaviour textbooks.) These measures are more sophisticated than the traditional Myers–Briggs Type indicator, which builds on Cattell's 16PF.[52] Nevertheless, Cattell's 16PF is quite a basic tool, and the exercise in Exhibit 2.4 is a useful aid to understanding the role personality plays in shaping career.

EXHIBIT 2.4	**Personality profiling exercise: How can your personality be described and characterized?**

Stage 1

Use Figure 2.3 as a rapid self-assessment of your own 16 personality factors. Evaluate, for each question, for each pair – where, on the continuum, you lie. Mark it with a pen. (Be honest – there is no such thing as a good or bad profile.)

Exhibit 2.4 continued

Join up the 'dots' to construct your 'profile'.

	1 2 3 4 5 6 7 8 9	
Reserved, detached	* * * * * * * * *	Outgoing, easygoing
Concrete thinker	* * * * * * * * *	Abstract thinker
Emotional	* * * * * * * * *	Emotionally stable
Mild, accommodating	* * * * * * * * *	Assertive, aggressive
Serious, reflective	* * * * * * * * *	Lively, happy-go-lucky
Flexible, rule-breaker	* * * * * * * * *	Conscientious, preserving
Shy, restrained	* * * * * * * * *	Venturesome, bold
Tough-minded	* * * * * * * * *	Tender-minded
Trusting, adaptable	* * * * * * * * *	Suspicious, self-opinionated
Practical, conventional	* * * * * * * * *	Imaginative, creative
Forthright, unpretentious	* * * * * * * * *	Astute, wordly
Confident, complacent	* * * * * * * * *	Worrying, insecure
Conservative, traditional	* * * * * * * * *	Experimenting, free-thinking
Group-dependent 'joiner'	* * * * * * * * *	Self-sufficient, resourceful
Less controlled	* * * * * * * * *	Controlled, exacting
Relaxed, tranquil	* * * * * * * * *	Tense, frustrated

Figure 2.3 Personality profiling: Cattell's 16PF

Stage 2 (if done as a class or group exercise):

Compare with one or two students who sit next to you – note and discuss differences.

Stage 3

Choose three (3) factors where you gave yourself 'extreme' ranks (i.e. 1 or 2 or 6 or 7).

Think of a recent event, case or incident in which you have recently been involved. Did your behaviour on that occasion offer a good illustration of these personality characteristics?

Again, if this is done as a class or group exercise, compare your case with that of a fellow student. Look at his/her profile. Will s/he make a good policeman? A good copywriter?

Can you try and draw the profile for the present prime minister/president/head of state? How different it is from the profile you would draw for the ideal candidate for this job (of leading and managing your country)?

Exhibit 2.4 continued

Stage 4

Critical thinking – don't take anything for granted.

While the 16PF measures look valid, they have their specific problems:
1 Are all the pairs mutually exclusive or might it be that the extreme options represent two different dimensions?
2 What happens when a person behaves differently under different circumstances?
3 How does one's evaluation compare with another's, for these relative terms? (That is, some people tend to give moderate ratings whereas others would tend to vote for the extreme.)
4 What would your resulting profile be if you re-evaluated yourself next week? Next month? (Test-retest fit.)
5 Are these measures objective? What will happen if you compare your self-rating to a rating done by a group of people who know you well?

Many inventories of personality exist, but the Big Five framework is updated and comprehensive, and will be discussed here not as a representative concept but as a leading current approach to the study of personality in the context of work. The Big Five factors were introduced to the literature of personality and careers by Goldberg in 1990.[53] Measures for the Big Five factors were developed later,[54] and their implications for practice in both psychology and HRM started to receive wide attention.[55] Can the Big Five produce a profile of what is needed for a successful career? Like the Cattell 16PF they are presented as a set of pairs of opposite characteristics and qualities.

The five factors are: (a) neuroticism v. stability, (b) extroversion v. introversion, (c) openness to experience, (d) agreeableness and (e) conscientiousness. Whereas there is empirical evidence for association between some of these factors and performance,[56] more knowledge of their relevance to careers and career success is needed. For example, in international careers, the impact of certain factors will depend on the culture of operation. In Western culture, extroversion is positive and considered an important characteristic for managers. Conversely, such a quality will be less highly valued in Eastern culture. Openness to experience may be the one factor that can help in the identification of suitable candidates for global managers. However, both agreeableness and conscientiousness (or a tendency to be efficient, organized and prudent) are commonly considered desirable traits, essential to the success of any manager. All in all, the Big Five can help to explain career success, but attention must be given to the environment of operation as a contingent variable.[57]

While the Big Five factors are considered very important, their use can be problematic, not only for their simplicity (five dimensions compared to Cattell's 16), but especially since they are mostly perceived as 'positive'. For this reason, direct measurement will not reveal wide differentiation among respondents (e.g. the majority of people will tend to describe themselves as positive – i.e. stable, somewhat extrovert, open to experience, agreeable and highly conscientious).

Another stream of work about the essential ingredients for career success stems from the ideas of Howard Gardner, as expressed in his book *Frames of Mind*, on multiple intelligence,[58] which was taken further by Goleman's 'Emotional Intelligence'.[59] Empirical studies provide some support for the notion that it is the combination of competencies that is needed for success: Dulewicz identified the crucial roles of combining the three Qs – Emotional Intelligence (EQ), IQ and management competencies (MQ) – to explain successful careers.[60] He identified that IQ (27%) + EQ (36%) + MQ (16%) explains advancement or career success (*see* Chapter 3 for an elaboration of the idea of career success). Although statistics can never be accurate when people's minds and the perception of advancement are under evaluation, these findings lend support to the importance of multiple intelligences in studying individuals' careers. Along the same lines, Kanfer and Heggestad coined the term 'motivational fit', which indicates that there are outcomes in the form of either anxiety or achievement when using both emotional and motivational perspectives.[61] Exhibit 2.5 presents us with three inventories of career-related characteristics and their measurement.

To conclude, in the past, when most jobs and careers were highly dependent on physical properties, the physical attributes of people were a decisive factor in career choice and development. As most jobs and careers now depend on mental and personality factors, these have become the most crucial factors in determining career.

One possible difficulty with such inventories is their tendency towards a quantitative approach, with numbers blurring the portrayal of a person's real qualities. Antoine de Saint-Exupery encapsulates this in the following quotation:

> Grown-ups love figures ... they never ask you any question of essential matters ... Instead they demand: 'How old is he? How many brothers has he?... Only from these figures do they think they have learned anything about him.
>
> (Antoine de Saint-Exupery, *The Little Prince*)

However, such inventories and self-assessment exercises can provide individuals with better self-awareness, insight and indications of possible future directions in their search for a career. These exercises can be done via self-administered tools, but are usually carried out as a part of counselling processes.

The following chapter, then, takes us further into the understanding of career and the meaning of career success.

EXHIBIT 2.5	**Lessem's Spectral Management Theory, Belbin's team roles and Quinn's Eight Managerial Roles model**

The SMT

In today's career environments and organizational structures it may be relevant to study the Spectral Management Theory (SMT), offered by Lessem (1990) and validated by Baruch and Lessem (1997), which is an analytical instrument designed to enable people to identify their personal management style. For organizations it can help in several ways such as matching people and positions or team development.[62]

Exhibit 2.5 continued

The SMT approach leads to **eight** different kinds of management style. What is the theoretical justification for eight types? First, a two-dimensional model, quite typical in leadership studies, is inadequate and too simplistic. People are much more complicated. On the other hand, using too many dimensions would be impractical. The eight dimensions of the SMT stem from three dimensions or components suggested by the German philosopher Steiner (1966) at the beginning of the twentieth century. These dimensions, which may form a basis for understanding human being are: Thinking (T), Feeling (F) and Willing or doing (W). Later Kingsland (1985) used the terms Cognitive (C), Affective (A) and Behavioural (B).[63] Sometimes a component is dominant and is represented by an upper case letter A, B or C; sometimes a component is recessive and is represented by a lower case a, b or c. Thus an eight-category model emerges:

- Innovative manager   CAB
- Developmental manager   CAb
- Analytical manager   CaB
- Enterprising manager   cAB
- Manager of change   Cab
- People manager   cAb
- Action manager   caB
- Adoptive manager   cab

Belbin's Team Roles

Meredith Belbin, working in Britain from the mid-1980s, came up with his nine different team roles, which have been adapted by many a manager since (1983, 1991). The Belbin team-role inventory is a well-known and established measure for the identification of individual team roles.[64] In Britain specifically, if not in Western Europe more generally, his approach to team building has become perhaps the most often used amongst managers. Belbin's particular focus is on the establishment of roles within a team, where the assumption of duties and responsibilities depends on a measure of self-discovery combined with a perception of the needs of the team as a whole.

Belbin's nine team roles are: Plant, Resource Investigator, Co-ordinator, Shaper, Monitor Evaluator, Team Worker, Implementor, Completer and Specialist.

Belbin postulates that within a team particular individuals take on specific roles. The blend of these roles has a crucial influence on the effectiveness of the team. A poor blend will usually produce a poor outcome. A team needs able people in order to succeed. Yet, if the blend of people is wrong, it will produce poor results. The composition of the team therefore is of crucial importance. Belbin sets out a list of potential 'Roles' within management teams. Although it is essentially based on Cattell's 16PF,[65] which has been fairly well validated, when Belbin's team roles inventory is subject to academic scrutiny, the findings do not provide evidence for acceptable reliability and validity.[66]

The Quinn model

Around the same time that these theories were developed in the UK, Robert E. Quinn came up with his Eight Managerial Roles model,[67] which later included competencies.[68]

Exhibit 2.5 continued

The Eight Managerial Roles model introduces the roles shown in Table 2.5, along with their key competencies.

Table 2.5 Quinn's Eight Managerial Roles model

Mentor role	Understanding staff and others Communicating effectively Developing employees
Facilitator role	Building teams Using participative decision making Managing conflict
Monitor role	Monitoring individual performance Managing collective performance and processes Analyzing information and critical thinking
Coordinator role	Managing projects Designing work Managing across functions
Director role	Developing and communicating a vision Setting goals and objectives Designing and organizing
Producer role	Working productively Fostering a productive work environment Managing time and stress
Broker role	Building and maintaining a power base Negotiating agreement and commitment Presenting ideas
Innovator role	Living with change Thinking creatively Managing change

Source: R.E. Quinn, S.R. Faerman, M.P. Thompson and M.R. McGrath (2003) *Becoming a Master Manager*, 3rd edition, New York: Wiley, p. 23.

Quinn went further to present his roles in an integrative two-dimensional model, the dimensions being flexibility v. control and internal v. external focus (Figure 2.4).

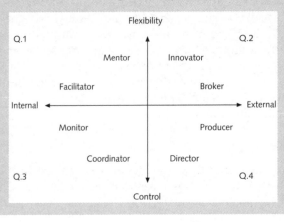

Figure 2.4 The Eight Managerial Roles model in an integrative two-dimensional plan

Source: R.E. Quinn (1988) *Beyond Rational Management*, San Francisco: Jossey-Bass, p. 48.

Summary

This chapter summarized the concept of career as perceived from the individual perspective. It covered several aspects and research directions, in particular career choice, career stages and the role personality plays in making career choices and in interpreting careers. This prepares the reader for the next chapter, where the focus will be on innovative career concepts (such as intelligent careers, the post-corporate career and boundaryless careers).

Key terms

- Internal career
- External career
- Organizational career
- Career choice
- Career stage
- Personality factors
- The Big Five

DISCUSSION QUESTIONS

Lessons and food for thought

1 *For the working student:* Does your present career fully or partially match your original career choice?
  Does your organization offer a career system that recognizes the different career choices of people? That offers diverse options for people at different stages of their career?
2 *If you aim to become an HR consultant:* What career advice could you, as a consultant, offer organizations or individual people, managers and executives, about associating their present career stage with their future prospects?
  How prepared are you to provide advice, based on career choice models, to people seeking to change their career?
3 *For the student:* At what career stage are you at present? Analyse this stage according to at least two different models. In what ways have your parents influenced your needs, aspirations, competencies? In what way have your student colleagues influenced you?

Notes

[1] Wilensky, H.L. (1961) 'Careers, life-styles, and social integration', *International Social Science Journal*, 12, 553–8.
[2] Townsend, R. (1970) *Up The Organization*, London: Coronet Books.
[3] Comfort, M. (1997) *Portfolio People*, London: Century.
[4] Clutterbuck, D. and Dearlove, D. (1999) *The Interim Manager*, London: Pitman.

[5] Barley, S.R. (1989) 'Careers, identities and institutions: The legacy of the Chicago School of Sociology', in M.B. Arthur, T. Hall and B.S. Lawrence (eds) *Handbook of Career Theory*, Cambridge: Cambridge University Press, pp. 41–65.

[6] Jahoda, M. (1982) *Employment and Unemployment: A Social Psychology Analysis*, Cambridge: Cambridge University Press.

[7] Hochschild, A. (1997) *Time Bind*, NY: Metropolitan Books, Holt.

[8] Maslow, A.H. (1943) 'A theory of human motivation', *Psychological Review*, July, 370–96.

[9] MOW (1987) *'Meaning of Working' Survey*, London: Academic Press.

[10] Noon, M. and Blyton, P. (1997) *The Realities of Work*, Basingstoke, Hampshire: Macmillan.

[11] Mannheim, B. and Cohen, A. (1978) 'Multivariate analysis of factors affecting WRC of occupational categories', *Human Relations*, 31, 525–53; Mannheim, B. and Dubin, R. (1986) 'Work role centrality of industrial workers as related to organizational conditions, task autonomy, managerial orientations and personal characteristics', *Journal of Occupational Behavior*, 7, 107–24.

[12] Noon and Blyton (1997), *see* note 10 above.

[13] But a more spiritual approach may see it in another way: 'Luck is God's way to stay anonymous' (thanks to Tim D. Hall for this observation).

[14] Osipow, S.H. (1990) 'Convergence in theory of career choice and development: review and prospect', *Journal of Vocational Behavior*, 36, 122–31; Mitchell, A.M., Jones, G.B. and Krumboltz, J.D. (eds) (1979) *Social Learning Theory and Career Decision Making*, Cranston, RI: Carroll.

[15] Holland, J.L. (1958) 'A personality inventory employing occupational titles', *Journal of Applied Psychology*, 42, 336–42; Holland, J.L. (1959) 'A theory of vocational choice', *Journal of Counseling Psychology*, 6, 35–45; Holland, J.L. (1985) *Manual for the Vocational Preference Inventory*, Odessa, FL: Psychological Assessment Resources.

[16] Parsons, F. (1909) *Choosing a Vocation*, Boston: Houghton Mifflin; Spokane, A.R. (1996) 'Holland's theory', in D. Brown and L. Brooks (eds) *Career Choice and Development*, 3rd edn, San Francisco: Jossey-Bass, pp. 33–74.

[17] Osipow, S.H. (1987) 'Applying person-environment theory to vocational behavior', *Journal of Vocational Behavior*, 31(3), 333–6.

[18] Assouline, M. and Meir, E.I. (1987) 'Meta-analysis of the relationships between congruence and well-being measures', *Journal of Vocational Behavior*, 31(3), 319–32.

[19] Belbin, R.M. (1983) *Team Roles at Work*, Oxford: Butterworths; Belbin, R.M. (1991) *Management Teams: Why They Succeed or Fail*, Oxford: Butterworths.

[20] Lessem, R. (1990) *Developmental Management*, Oxford: Basil Blackwell; Baruch, Y. and Lessem, R. (1995) 'Managerial Development Through Self and Group Evaluation of Managerial Style', *Journal of Management Development*, 1(14), 34–9; Baruch, Y. and Lessem, R. (1997) 'The Spectral Management Type Inventory – A validation study', *Journal of Managerial Psychology*, 12(6), 365–82.

[21] Sternberg, R.J. (1998) *In Search of the Human Mind*, 2nd edn, Fort Worth: Harcourt Brace.

[22] Solmon, L.C., Kent, L., Ochsner, N.L. and Hurwicz, M.L. (1981) *Underemployed Ph.D.'s*, Lexington, MA: Lexington Books.

[23] Williams, G., Blackstone, T. and Metcalf, D. (1974) *The Academic Labour Market: Economic and Social Aspects of a Profession*, Amsterdam: Elsevier; Blaxter, L., Hughes, C. and Tight, M. (1998) *The Academic Career Handbook*, Buckingham: Open University Press.

24 Metzger, W.P. (1987) 'Academic Profession in the United States', in B.R. Clark (ed.) *The Academic Profession, National, Disciplinary and Institutional Settings*, Berkeley: University of California Press, pp. 123–208; Baruch, Y. and Hall, D.T. (2004) 'The academic career system', *Journal of Vocational Behavior*, Special issue, in press.

25 Mitchell, A.M., Jones, G.B. and Krumboltz, J.D. (eds) (1979) *Social Learning Theory and Career Decision Making*, Cranston, RI: Carroll.

26 Bandura, A. (1977) *Social Learning Theory*, Englewood Cliffs, NJ: Prentice-Hall; Bandura, A. (1997) *Self Efficacy*, NY: WH Freeman.

27 Earley, P.C. (1994) 'Self or group? Cultural effects of training on self efficacy and performance', *Administrative Science Quarterly*, 39(1), 89–117; London, M. and Smither, J.W. (1995) 'Can multi-source feedback change perceptions of goal accomplishment, self-evaluations, and performance-related outcomes? Theory-based applications and directions for research', *Personnel Psychology*, 48(4), 803–39.

28 Gist, M.E. (1987) 'Self efficacy: Implications for organizational behavior and human resource management', *Academy of Management Review*, 12(3), 472–85.

29 Stewart Jr., W.H. and Roth, P.L. (2001) 'Risk Propensity Differences Between Entrepreneurs and Managers: A Meta-Analytic Review', *Journal of Applied Psychology*, 86(1), 145–52.

30 Coren, G. (2001) *James Dyson: Against the Odds*, London: Texere.

31 Super, D.E. (1957) *The Psychology of Careers*, NY: Harper & Row.

32 Stewart, W. and Barling, J. (1996) 'Fathers' work experiences affect children's behavior via job-related affect and parenting behaviors', *Journal of Organizational Behavior*, 17(3), 221–32.

33 Levinson, D. (1978) *Seasons of Man's Life*, NY: Knopf; Levinson, D. (1986) 'Conception of adult development', *American Psychologist*, 41, 3–13; Ornstein, S. and Isabella, L. (1990) 'Age vs. stage models of career attitudes of women: A partial replication and extension', *Journal of Vocational Behavior*, 36(1), 1–19; Sullivan, S.E. (1999) 'The changing nature of careers: A review and research agenda', *Journal of Management*, 25(3), 457–84.

34 Hakim, C. (2000) *Work-Lifestyle Choices in the 21st Century: Preference Theory*, Oxford: OUP; Levinson, D.J. and Levinson, J.D. (1996) *The Season of a Woman's Life*, NY: Alfred A. Knopf.

35 Super, D.E. (1957) *The Psychology of Careers*, NY: Harper & Row, pp. 71–80; Super, D.E., Savickas, M.L. and Super, C.M. (1996) 'The life-span, life space approach to careers', in D. Brown and L. Brooks (eds) *Career Choice and Development*, 3rd edn, San Francisco: Jossey-Bass, pp. 121–78.

36 Hall, D.T. and Nougaim, K. (1968) 'An examination of Maslow's need hierarchy in an organizational setting', *Organizational Behavior and Human Performance*, 3, 12–35; Greenhaus, J.H. (1987) *Career Management*, Forth Worth: Dryden press; Form, W.H. and Miller, D.C. (1949) 'Occupational career path as a sociological instrument', *American Journal of Sociology*, 54, 317–29; Schein, E.H. (1985) *Career Anchors: Discovering your Real Values*, San Francisco, CA: University Associates Inc.; Evans P. (1986) 'New directions in career management', *Personnel Management*, December, 26–9.

37 Baird, L. and Kram, K. (1983) 'Career dynamics: managing the supervisor/subordinate relationship', *Organizational Dynamics*, 11, Spring, 46–64; Dalton, G., Thompson, M.P. and Price, P. (1977) 'The four stages of professional careers: A new look at performance by professionals', *Organizational Dynamics*, 6, 23; Thompson, P.H., Baker, R.Z. and Smallwood, N. (1986) 'Improving professional development by applying the four-stages career model', *Organizational Dynamics*, 15(2), 49–62.

[38] Super, D.E. (1980) 'A life-span, life space approach to career development', *Journal of Vocational Behavior*, 16, 282–98.

[39] Feldman, D.C. (1988) *Managing Careers in Organizations*, Glenview, IL: Scott Foresman, p. 24.

[40] Baird and Kram (1983), *see* note 37 above.

[41] Dalton, Thompson and Price (1977), *see* note 37 above.

[42] Form and Miller (1949), *see* note 36 above.

[43] Greenhaus (1987), *see* note 36 above.

[44] Hall and Nougiam (1968), *see* note 36 above.

[45] Levinson (1978), *see* note 33 above.

[46] Schein, E.H. (1978) *Career Dynamics: Matching Individual and Organizational Needs*, Reading, MA: Addison-Wesley.

[47] Super, D.E. (1957) *The Psychology of Careers*, NY: Harper & Row; Super, D.E. (1980) 'A life-span, life space approach to career development', *Journal of Vocational Behavior*, 16, 282–98.

[48] Feldman, D.C. (1988) *Managing Careers in Organizations*, Glenview, IL: Scott-Foresman, p. 24.

[49] Merton, R.K. (1957) *Social Theory and Social Structure*, Glencoew IL: Free Press; Eden, D. (1984) 'Self-Fulfilling Prophecy as a Management Tool: Harnessing Pygmalion', *Academy of Management Review*, 9(1), 64–73.

[50] Festinger, L. (1957) *A Theory of Cognitive Dissonance*, Stanford CA: Stanford University Press.

[51] Goldberg, L.R. (1990) 'An alternative "description of personality": The Big Five factor structure', *Journal of Personality and Social Psychology*, 59, 1216–29; Goldberg, L.R. (1993) 'The structure of personality', *American Psychologist*, 48, 26–34; Digman, J.M. (1990) 'Personality structure: Emergence of a five-factor model', *Annual Review of Psychology*, 41, 417–40.

[52] Cattell, R.B. and Kline, P. (1977) *The Scientific Analysis of Personality and Motivation*, NY: Academic Press.

[53] Goldberg, L.R. (1990) 'An alternative "description of personality": The Big Five factor structure', *Journal of Personality and Social Psychology*, 59, 1216–29; Goldberg, L.R. (1993) 'The structure of personality', *American Psychologist*, 48, 26–34.

[54] Costa, P.T. and McCrae, R.R. (1992) *Revised NEO Personality Inventory and NEO Five-factor Inventory*, Odessa, FL: Psychological Assessment Resources Inc.

[55] Mount, M.K. and Barrick, M.R. (1995) 'The big five personality dimensions: implications for research and practice in human resource management', in G.R. Ferris (ed.) *Research in Personnel and Human Resource Management*, 13, 153–200, Greenwich, Conn: JAI.

[56] Barrick, M.R. and Mount, M.K. (1991) 'The Big Five personality dimensions: meta-analysis', *Personnel Psychology*, 44, 1–26.

[57] Judge, T.A., Higgins, C.A., Thoresen, C.J. and Barrick, M.R. (1999) 'The Big Five personality traits, general mental ability, and career success across the life span', *Personnel Psychology*, 52, 621–51.

[58] Gardner, H. (1983) *Frames of Mind: The Theory of Multiple Intelligence*, London: Heinemann.

[59] Goleman, D. (1994) *Emotional Intelligence*, Bantam Books.

[60] Dulewicz, V. (2000) 'Emotional Intelligence: the key to future successful corporate leadership?', *Journal of General Management*, 25(3), 1–14.

[61] Kanfer, R. and Heggestad, E.D. (1997) 'Motivational traits and skills: A person-centered approach to work motivation', *Research in Organizational Behavior*, 19, 1–56.

[62] Lessem, R. (1990) *Developmental Management*, Oxford: Basil Blackwell; Baruch, Y. and Lessem, R. (1995) 'Managerial Development Through Self and Group Evaluation of Managerial Style', *Journal of Management Development*, 1(14), 34–9; Baruch and Lessem (1997), *see* note 20 above.

[63] Steiner, R. (1966) *Study of Man*, London: Rudolf Steiner Press; Kingsland, K. (1985) *The Personality Spectrum*, Working paper, Centre for Leadership Studies, Sussex.

[64] Belbin, R.M. (1983) *Team Roles at Work*, Oxford: Butterworths; Belbin, R.M. (1991) *Management Teams: Why They Succeed or Fail*, Oxford: Butterworths; Senior, B. and Swailes, S. (1998) 'A comparison of the Belbin self perception inventory and observer assessment sheet as measures of individual team roles', *International Journal of Selection and Assessment*, 6(1), 1–8.

[65] Cattell, R.B. and Kline, P. (1977) *The Scientific Analysis of Personality and Motivation*, NY: Academic Press.

[66] Furnham, A., Steele, H. and Pendleton, D. (1993) 'A psychometric assessment of the Belbin Team-Role Self Perception Inventory', *Journal of Occupational and Organizational Psychology*, 66, 245–57; Dulewicz, V. (1995) 'A Validation of Belbin's Team Roles from 16PF and OPQ Using Bosses' Ratings of Competence', *Journal of Occupational and Organizational Psychology*, 68, 81–99; Senior, B. (1998) 'An Empirically-based assessment of Belbin's Team Roles', *Human Resource Management Journal*, 8(3), 54–60; Senior, B. and Swailes, S. (1998) 'A comparison of the Belbin self perception inventory and observer assessment sheet as measures of individual team roles', *International Journal of Selection and Assessment*, 6(1), 1–8.

[67] Quinn, R.E. (1988) *Beyond Rational Management*, San Francisco: Jossey-Bass.

[68] Quinn, R.E., Faermans, S.R., Thompson, M.P. and McGrath, M.R. (2003) *Becoming a Master Manager*, 3rd edition, NY: Wiley.

Appendix 2.1
The SMT Inventory: type description

Innovator manager

Innovative, creative and driven by an inner compulsion. In a group the 'innovator' will emerge as an inspired team member. The innovator is inventive and forward looking.

Developmental manager

Able to recognize and harness the forces of diversity. The developmental manager will be co-operative and a team player. In team situations the developmental manager will be a natural facilitator and learner and will like to ensure harmony, and will be able to integrate diverse concepts, people and situations.

Analytical manager

Analytical, impersonal, objective and honest. In teams the analytical manager will be a natural organizer and learner, and will be methodical, purposeful and deliberative.

Enterprising manager

Enjoys the rough and tumble of business life. The enterprising manager loves a good scrap, and responds immediately to a challenge, especially if it involves some personal and financial risk. The enterprising manager can be ruthless and unscrupulous but also fun loving. As a team member, is inclined to take a lead.

Change manager

Intellectual, needs to work in a mentally stimulating environment, and will seek professional advancement rather than promotion, necessarily, within a particular organization. As a team member a change manager serves as a networker.

People manager

Naturally gregarious, sociable and warm. In teams such a person is a natural animator, and as a learner responds to 'warm' people and non-threatening situations.

Action manager

Works hard, plays hard, has an ability to act fast, to react to situations. As a team member such a person is a 'doer', and as a learner is inclined to react immediately to people and situations.

Adoptive manager

Virtually non-existent in Western Europe and North America. An adoptive manager has faith in the company and seeks minimal individual identity. As team members such people are reflective in their orientation.

Appendix 2.2
Description of Belbin's team roles

Plant

Creative, imaginative, unorthodox. Solves difficult problems; but might ignore details or be too preoccupied to communicate effectively.

Resource investigator

Extrovert, enthusiastic, communicative. Explores opportunities. Develops contacts; but might be over-optimistic, and might tend to lose interest once initial enthusiasm has passed.

Co-ordinator

Mature, confident, a good chairperson. Clarifies goals, promotes decision making, delegates well; but can be seen as manipulative. Might delegate personal work.

Shaper

Challenging, dynamic, thrives on pressure. Has the drive and courage to overcome obstacles; but can provoke others. Might hurt people's feelings.

Monitor evaluator

Sober, strategic and discerning. Sees all options. Judges accurately; but lacks drive and ability to inspire others and can be overly critical.

Team worker

Co-operative, mild, perceptive and diplomatic. Listens, builds, averts friction, calms the waters; might be indecisive in crunch situations and can be easily influenced.

Implementor

Disciplined, reliable, conservative and efficient. Turns ideas into practical actions; but might be somewhat inflexible and slow to respond to new possibilities.

Completer

Painstaking, conscientious, anxious. Searches out errors and omissions. Delivers on time; but inclined to worry unduly. May be reluctant to delegate. Can be a nit-picker.

Specialist

Single-minded, self-starting, dedicated. Provides knowledge and skills in rare supply; but contributes on only a narrow front. Sometimes dwells on technicalities. Might overlook the 'big picture'.

3 Individual careers and career models

LEARNING OBJECTIVES

After reading this chapter you should be able to:

- Identify the meaning of career success.

- Critically analyse individual career models.

- Understand how individual properties influence career choice.

- Recognize future directions and paths available to careers.

CHAPTER CONTENTS

- *Models of individual career development and the protean career*

- *Studying individual careers*

- *Career success*

- *The Desert Generation phenomenon*

- *Intelligent, boundaryless and post-corporate careers*

- *How to reinvent and resurrect one's own career*

- *Summary*

- *Key terms*

- *Discussion questions*

- *Notes*

Models of individual career development and the protean career

There are several individual career models. Most notable are the individual development stages and career choice models (discussed in Chapter 2), and general models of individual career planning and management. One innovative model of individual career management sees it as a problem-solving process (the Greenhaus *et al.* model – *see* Figure 3.1).[1]

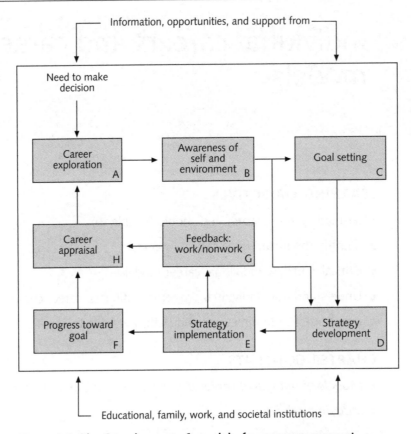

Figure 3.1 The Greenhaus *et al.* model of career management

Source: J.H. Greenhaus, G.A. Callanan and V.M. Godshalk (2000) *Career Management*, 3rd edn, Fort Worth: Dryden Press, p. 24.

The Greenhaus *et al.* model focuses on the individual as the one who needs to make a decision, a need that leads to a career search and into a process of setting career goals, developing strategies and tactics to fulfil them, making progress, and all these form a process that requires career evaluation. The organization is only an external player in the system, according to this model, along with environmental influences. The major criticism of this framework is that it undermines the role organizations play in planning and managing careers. (There is further discussion of this issue in the following chapters.)

One problem with most of the individual career models is that they derive from a psychological perspective rather than having management science in view. To rectify that, Gunz (1989)[2] offered a model of individuals' perceptions of their careers within an organizational context. Gunz described the organizational context as generating a 'career climbing-frame', but his model, unlike earlier hierarchical models, has an optional orientation form (*see* Figure 3.2).

Gunz proposed a theoretical framework, which recognizes the duality of managerial careers by distinguishing between organizational and individual levels of analysis. For Gunz, at the organizational level, careers can be seen as part of a process of social reproduction, by inducting newcomers into the internal cul-

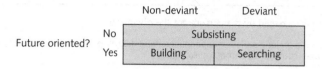

Figure 3.2 Gunz's model of orientation to organizational career climbing-frame

Source: Reprinted from H. Gunz (1989) 'The dual meaning of managerial careers: organizational and individual levels of analysis', *Journal of Management Studies*, 26(3), p. 241, with permission from Blackwell Publishing.

ture, norms and behaviours. This process links organizational forms and behaviour with comparatively stable career patterns that characterize particular firms or certain type of firms. At the individual level Gunz perceive careers as a sequence of work role transitions, representing choices between opportunities offered by organizations. Each level of analysis illuminates a different aspect of managerial careers, but it is equally important that each should be seen in the light of the other levels.

Among theories focused on the individual, one innovative approach is the **Protean career**. The idea of the protean career was first offered by Hall (1976), but it was not until the 1990s that it was recognized on reflecting real-life experiences.[3] Hall and Mirvis (1996)[4] describe the protean career as a new form, in which the individual, rather than the organization, takes responsibility for transforming their career path, in taking responsibility for their career. Moreover, the individual changes himself or herself according to need. The term protean is taken from the name of the Greek god Proteus, who could change his shape at will. Hall describes the process as follows:

> The protean career is a process which the person, not the organization, is managing. It consists of all the person's varied experience in education, training, work in several organizations, changes in occupational field, etc ... The protean person's own personal career choices and search for self-fulfillment are the unifying or integrative elements in his or her life. (1976: p. 201)

The protean career is essentially a contract with oneself, rather than with the organization. Hall used the metaphor of the career fingerprint to describe the individual nature of the protean career, which is outside the structures and traditional boundaries of the organizational hierarchy, professional progress or a stable direction. It is not restricted to the realm of paid work or work and non-work domains. The protean concept alters the relationship between the organization and the employee. The person takes on the role of his or her own agent, instead of leaving that to the organization (where either the line manager or the HR department has traditionally served as 'agent' for employees' careers).

Taking such personal responsibility for their career may be difficult for people who have spent a considerable part of their working life in the traditional organizational career system (see the discussion later in this chapter of the concept of the desert generation). Hall and Mirvis (1996) describe the changes in the careers cycle in the new model of career stages: people will have several careers, each of which will comprise the inner stages of exploration, trial, establishment and mastery. However, following mastery will come a new cycle of exploration, ending with the discovery of a new path, a different profession, role or organization. This

1. The career is managed by the person, not the organization.

2. The career is a lifelong series of experiences, skills, learning, transitions, and identity changes. ('Career age' counts, not chronological age.)

3. Development is:

   • Continuous learning

   • Self-directed

   • Relational, and

   • Found in work challenges

4. Development is not (necessarily):

   • Formal training

   • Retraining, or

   • Upward mobility

5. The ingredients for success change:

   • From know-how to learn-how

   • From job security to employability

   • From organizational careers to protean careers, and

   • From 'work self' to 'whole self'

6. The organization provides:

   • Challenging assignments

   • Developmental relationships

   • Information and other developmental resource

7. The goal: Psychological success.

Figure 3.3 Elements of the new 'protean' career contract

Source: Reprinted from D.T. Hall and J.E. Moss (1998) 'The new protean career contract: helping organizations and employees adapt', *Organizational Dynamics*, 26(3), p. 26, copyright 1998, with permission from Elsevier Science.

cycle corresponds to that identified by Cascio, i.e. that people now have several careers and thus have to manage several career cycles.[5]

In practice, when millions of jobs are lost in the industrial world, mostly from large firms, the individual has no option but to take responsibility, to manage their own career and, at best, to make good use of organizational support mechanisms and career facilities. This was the background against which ideas such as the protean career and the post-corporate career (see below) developed. Under such circumstances the protean career and career resilience[6] are fully explicable.

Individuals and career counselling

Telling people they are in charge may be easier said than done. People need support, and do not always have the knowledge or the mental strength to direct themselves without advice and guidance. This is where career counselling comes in.

Career counselling may help people to identify a suitable vocation and career path. It can identify the environment in which a person is most likely to flourish. It is typically taken at an early stage in a person's career, by school leavers, sometimes alongside 'self-managed' counselling based on books providing practical guidance (particularly popular and useful is *'What Color is your Parachute?*, by Bolles, of which a new edition is published every year).[7] However, many take career counselling at different stages of their lives. People at a crossroads in their career, people who encounter a career crisis, people who realize that they have made a poor career choice, all may find career counselling useful. Adding an objective perspective, career counselling can reveal the full picture, and may show people their 'blind spots' and thus can provide fresh insights and new directions, unleash hitherto unknown properties, competencies that can be developed and unveil hidden qualities. (Career counselling is discussed in more detail in Chapter 6.)

Individual careers counselling

Career Development International (UK)

Career Development International (CDI) provides a personalized career counselling service. It is tailor made, as the company is keen to advise each person according to their needs, and first and foremost, their personality.

CDI believes that personality drives careers, in as much as a good person-career fit will, in the longer run, produce the best performance and satisfaction all round. In addition to one-to-one counselling, CDI typically conducts some form of psychometric or psychological assessment, to guide clients through career choices. Although a small company, CDI operates worldwide, contracting local work psychologists to service their clients.

More about CDI can be found on their web-page: www.careerdi.com.

Careers Partnership (UK)

Careers Partnership offers services to both individuals and companies.

Services for individuals include: career guidance and career development programmes for all ages; self-marketing support for people seeking their next job; coaching in jobsearch techniques; and workshops to increase personal effectiveness.

Services for employers comprise: recruitment support (psychometric assessment services, staffing interviewing teams, etc.); career development, personal development, coaching and mentoring programmes; solutions for 'square peg in round hole' situations; support during organizational restructuring; redundancy counselling and outplacement programmes for individuals or groups.

More about Careers Partnership can be found on their web-page: www.careers-partnership-uk.com/.

For Students

For the student, an easy (and probably cheaper) choice of career counselling would be the local university career centre: most universities today have career centres, with options for career counselling and advice.

Studying individual careers

By the end of the 1990s, new career systems had appeared: boundaryless, multi-directional and flexible.[8] Osterman (1994) said it all in the title of his book: *Broken Ladders*. New psychological contracts have been agreed or forced upon employees.[9] Psychological contracts concerning the career one may expect to aspire to are agreed upon between organizations and employees. Diversity has ceased to be a slogan and has become a reality. Women have entered all types of jobs, but very soon discovered a glass ceiling.[10] By the end of the last century, however, that ceiling was showing signs of cracking, but only that. Similarly, there is much greater racial and ethnic diversity in the white-collar labour market than in the past. This change has occurred against a background of increased awareness of political correctness and equality issues, legislative sanctions and legal challenges to discrimination. On the other hand age discrimination is still prevalent in many professional and occupational areas. Chapter 8 of this book provides an in-depth exploration of these issues.

Much of the current research on individual careers focuses on identifying what is a career from the individual viewpoint and how people approach their careers in the wider context of life. Each person has a career, a life story, a continuum of work and non-work experiences. Work experience is interwoven with other facets of life. Developmental processes take place along this road. People look for advancement, development and progress. The simplest and the most visible way is still via promotion through the organizational ranks.

The model proposed by Greenhaus *et al.* (*see* Figure 3.1) offered a career management model, an individual-oriented approach. Greenhaus *et al.* put the individual at the centre of the model. They see the individual as needing to make a career choice (influenced mainly by family, and by educational and social institutions) and to conduct a career search, which presumably includes formal training. This stage is followed by the development of self-awareness, setting career goals and developing a strategy to reach these goals. Employing the strategy and a feedback loop provides the person with an evaluation of the suitability of the goal for their own needs and aspirations, and the level to which they can achieve the goals. As a consequence people may revise their career goals, embark on an entirely new career, or even abandon a career completely. In the model the organizational role is very limited, and is restricted to the provision of information and support systems. An essential element for individuals is the career goals – the terms in which they are set, the values they represent and the means to reach them. An old-style classical approach to careers focused on external measures, such as status and financial reward.

However, by the 1970s it was felt that career goals and the meaning of career success were much wider. Tranowieski (1973) suggested that a good manager is one who can balance role, home and personal needs. Renwich and Lawler (1978) offered five role characteristics of significance to individual careers: (a) conducting meaningful assignments, which would result in better inner feelings; (b) achieving something of worth; (c) learning new skills; (d) developing competencies; and (e) freedom in the job. Along the same lines Boerlijst (1984) offered the innovative contention that career development may be lateral, and may not necessarily lead to higher authority and control.[11] In this respect, the academic career model was one of the first to enable people to develop in their profession, gain recognition, reputation and general career success, irrespective of their hierarchical progress. The academic hierarchy scale is flat. Moreover career progress does not comprise of a series of 'upward' movements. In a typical career progression in academia we may find a professor or a senior lecturer becoming a Dean, Research Director or Head of an Examination Board, and then returning to his or her research and teaching role after few years in the position.

Continuous learning

Learning and development at the individual level will have implications for and will be reflected at the organizational level. However, there is a difference between individual learning and organizational learning, where the latter is mediated by the former. In this respect, Kolb's work as well as criticism of it is useful for understanding the learning process.[12] Organizational learning is not simply the aggregate learning of the individuals. In organizational terms it is what is left in the 'organizational memory' and reflected later in practices and policies as a result.

Career success

There are two tragedies in life. One is to lose your heart's desire. The other one is to gain it. (G.B. Shaw)

There are two things to aim at in this life; first to get what you want; and, after that, to enjoy it. Only the wisest of mankind achieve the second. (Logan Pearsall Smith)

We all want to achieve success, but the meaning of success is different for different people, and varies according to the circumstances. This section discusses the nature of career success, how it can have different meanings, and how it can be evaluated and measured.

To evaluate career success from the personal viewpoint one can refer either to objective, 'hard' measures (rank, income), or to subjective, 'soft' measures, mostly concerned with personal feelings of achievement and values. The meaning of success will always be associated with personal, professional and organizational objectives, and how far these have been accomplished. Following Marx's contention that the social circumstances in which the activity of individuals occurs condition their perception of the world in which they live, it is clear why career success will never be similar for all.

Objectives are derived also from the choice of career and the assumed progress in a particular vocation. As shown earlier, this starts with the general selection of the individual's life interests.[13] Making vocational choices depends on individual inclinations, aspirations, interests and competencies, but this choice is also influenced by the family, education and social institutions.[14] The criteria for evaluating success can be, first, reaching what you aimed for, and second, how far doing so helped to fulfil your needs. This takes us back to Shaw again: obtaining entrance to the profession, organization or specific job you have always dreamed of does not necessarily mean that you will be happy or even satisfied with your career once you have achieved it. This sobering process is most apparent in jobs such as nursing (with high proportion of nurses leaving the profession).

Question	**Objective or subjective career achievement** Think of two young men opting for a career in the army. One has set himself the goal of becoming a Captain. In the end he manages to reach the rank of Major. His friend set himself the target to become a Lieutenant-General. In the end he is promoted to Colonel. The rank of the first is lower than that of the second, but the first one has exceeded his target whereas his friend has failed to achieve his. Who has the greater success – the one who reached the higher rank or the one who surpassed his goal? Should success be measured externally or internally?

Derr's (1986) framework identified five measures for career success, contrasting with, or at least adding to, the traditional measures of career success.[15] The three traditional measures are formal education, lifelong employment with job security and hierarchical progress. Derr's five dimensions are getting ahead, getting secure, getting high, getting free and getting balanced.

Derr's dimensions may be illustrated as follows:

(a) Getting ahead: Motivation derives from the need to advance both in professional standing and up the organizational ladder.
(b) Getting secure: Having a solid position within the organization.
(c) Getting high: Being inspired by the nature and content of the work performed.
(d) Getting free: Being motivated by a need for autonomy and the ability to create one's own work environment.
(e) Getting balanced: Attaching equal or greater value to non-work interests.

Question	How important is each of Derr's dimensions for you? Try to put them in order of relevance for you. How will this preference manifest itself in the career you have chosen to pursue?

Novel contemporary careers frameworks presented later in this chapter, such as the **boundaryless**, the **intelligent** and the **post-corporate**, distinguish between individual and organizational elements, putting more emphasis on the individual role (and the **protean career** concept takes this trend to the extreme of imposing the entire responsibility of career management on the individual).

The individual, as well as having the traditional need to be promoted, can perceive career success as a multi-level set of self-development targets: gaining employability (replacing the security of the traditional 'job for life' concept); making lateral transitions for enrichment, rather than following the traditional route 'up the ladder'; undertaking self-management and entrepreneurship for those who wish to try new ventures outside the organization; and achieving a better and richer quality of life, reflected in the availability of alternative work arrangements and improved work-family balance. When the new psychological contract is 'signed', it reassures the mutual expectations of individual and organization, and enables people to look for higher meaning in life and employment.

For the organization, indications of an appropriate career system include the empowerment of people to become active participants in managing their careers. These indications are relevant in terms of career management (though not to the extreme where the organization withdraws from its roles – see Baruch's work[16]), investment in people (e.g. training, developmental processes), new career paths to replace the traditional pyramid type, flexibility in the management of people and, lastly, providing a better quality of life at work and in the wider context, reflected in work-family policies, a shorter working week, flexible working hours, etc. The new psychological contract establishes the transition. Under such conditions a new partnership arises, based on a mature trust relationship.

Table 3.1 presents the traditional, the 'New Careerist', and the contemporary concepts for both individuals and organizations, against the related indicators of career success.

> All men seek one: success or happiness. The only way to achieve true success is to express yourself completely in service to society. First have a definite, clear, practical ideal – a goal, objective. Second, have the necessary means to achieve your ends – wisdom, money materials, and methods. Third, adjust your means to that end. (Aristotle, 384–322 BC (cited in Handy 1993: 30))

Contemporary changes in individual thinking have caused many to distance themselves from this sociological, altruistic approach. Individual consciousness rather than belonging to the collective whole rules people's search in life.[17]

Table 3.1 Measures of career success

Traditional concepts	The 'New Careerist'	Contemporary – Individual	Contemporary – Organization
Formal education	Getting ahead	Self-development competencies	Empowerment
Lifelong employment, job security	Getting secure	Employability	Investment in people
Up the ladder	Getting high	Lateral transitions; spiral movements	New or no career paths
	Getting free	Self-management; entrepreneurship	Flexibility
	Getting balanced	Quality of life; work-family balance	Alternative working arrangements* and work-family policies
		New psychological contracts	
		Search for spiritual meaning based on individual consciousness	True, open partnership

*Alternative working arrangements: shorter working week, shared jobs, telecommuting, flexi-time.

Career success is a desired outcome for most individuals. However, for each individual the outcomes desired are different. In addition people develop a set of desired outcomes, not a single aim. The measures that can be used to assess such desired outcomes and the extent to which they are reached are complex.

Commonly accepted measures are:

- *Advancement*: hierarchy, power; professionalism, reputation (status), but also autonomy, entrepreneurship, self-control.
- *Learning*: gaining new skills, abilities, competencies.
- *Physiological and survival*: money making (buying power); employability.
- *Psychological*: satisfaction, recognition, self-esteem and self-actualization. To these we may add career resilience, in both meanings of resilience – toughness of spirit in confronting career crisis, and flexibility or pliability in adapting to ever-changing labour markets.

The reader will probably now recall the chapter on motivation in their organizational behaviour textbook. Indeed, the need to succeed in a career is a great motivator. The relative importance of motivators depends also on a variety of antecedents, such as demography (e.g. gender, religion) and attitudes (e.g. work role centrality).

To evaluate an individual's progress or advancement within organizational boundaries, one starts from their first role in the organization. In analysing career success it was recognized that the entry stage has a strong impact on further career progress – in terms of time in the job, in the organization, and the highest position the individual is expected to reach.[18] The first role is, however, only the first step in a long and winding road.

Ideal versus reality

To reach effective career resilience and employability, people need to acquire and maintain over time a set of competencies (abilities, know-how, skills) required for finding a job when necessary, wherever it may be. Boundaries such as the firm, the profession, and international borders should play no significant role in the job search. Nevertheless, in practice, the idea is quite illusive. Much occurs in internal markets, i.e. lateral job moves within organizations are much easier to manage than cross-organizational moves, and organizations do not view job hopping favourably. Changing one's profession takes time and effort, and the formalization of qualifications means that it is not simple to swap jobs that require specific qualifications. (The litigious society in which we live forces organizations to hire people with the right qualifications, even though such qualifications do not necessarily guarantee that those who possess them have the right qualities). And lastly national borders pose real problem for people. Whereas some borders have become less crucial (the most vivid example is the EC/EU borderless employment region), people from outside such larger communities, in particular those from less developed countries, face severe barriers to finding a job outside their own country. For example, a person from outside the EC, even from the USA or

Canada, has no automatic right to a work permit in European countries, and vice versa. People from less developed countries may find their national qualifications are worthless or irrelevant in Europe. Thus the boundaryless ideal can rarely be utilized, being in parts an oversimplification of a nice idea, replete with impractical terms.

Individual career concepts

Whyte's concept of an 'Organization Man' (1956),[19] although outdated, is still relevant, for both men and women. This is the perspective that sees people as parts of the system in organizations, where they act like cogs in a machine, and strive to climb up the ladder. However, many new forms of this concept have evolved, some of which even contradict organization man as the prevailing concept. Arthur, Inkson and Pringle (1999) depicted the new type of careers in their book, *The New Careers*. It seems that unaccustomed qualities are needed to sustain a post-modern career. There is less emphasis on stability, more on dynamism and openness. Career resilience is appreciated, and actually desired;[20] people look for 'employability'[21] rather than lifelong commitment to one organization.[22] *See* Chapter 5 for criticism of the employability concept.

Career anchors (Schein): the development of a concept

The idea of career anchors was suggested by Edgar Schein from MIT.[23] Career anchors are the perceived abilities, values, attitudes and motives people have, which determine their career aspirations and direction. These self-perceived talents and qualities serve to guide, constrain, stabilize, reinforce and develop people's careers.

It should be remembered, though, that in many instances the career path people follow does not necessarily derive from their initial aspirations. As indicated earlier, unexpected events may force people to make unintended career moves. March and March (1977)[24] went so far as to claim that career progress is (almost) random, i.e. people progress according to opportunities which happen to be placed in their way (using the metaphor of career as a journey – *see* Chapter 5 for the use of metaphors in career studies).

While serendipity does occur in life, it would be hard to base a theory solely on this factor. While luck plays a certain role in career progress, the 'snakes and ladders' metaphor (as shown on the cover of the book) rarely reflects the true nature of careers. Nevertheless, in some occupations there may be a significant role for luck and chance.

The concept itself, and in particular its constituents, the anchors, have developed with time. Originally, Schein (1978) suggested five anchors. One problem with the initial set concerned the original sample from which the concept was developed: all were MBA graduates of a top US university (MIT). Schein increased the number of career anchors to eight by the 1980s, as presented in Table 3.2. In my view, new anchors have emerged in the twenty-first century, and they should be added to the framework. Some may even replace some of the original anchors: among these new anchors I would include employability; work v. family balance and Spiritual purpose.

Table 3.2 Career anchors

	Original five (Schein, 1978)	Additional three (Schein, 1985)	New (early 21st century, suggested by Baruch)
Career anchors	Technical competencies Managerial competencies Security and stability Entrepreneurship/Creativity Autonomy/independence	Dedication to a Cause (e.g. service) Pure challenge Life style	Employability Work/family balance Spiritual purpose

Question

Your career anchors

Can you identify your most prominent career anchor? Which of Schein's anchors does not really represent you or appeal to you? Can you list the eight anchors in descending order of importance for you?

Commitment and loyalty

The early work of Gouldner[25] in the 1950s distinguished between 'cosmopolitans', people with a strong identification and with commitment to their profession, and 'locals', with strong identification with and commitment to their organizations. Gouldner went further to suggest that these commitments are orthogonal, i.e. not necessarily associated or excluding each other. One person may be high 'cosmopolitan' and low 'local' (or vice versa), but people can also be high (or low) on both.

Multiple commitments

People need relationship, partnerships to rely upon, other parties to develop mutual commitment with. In the past, apart from the obvious spouse and family, the organization was the major entity people could identify with, feel part of, be loyal to, and in particular be committed to. The developments discussed in Chapter 1 show the destruction of people's ability to build on such relationships with organizations. From the individual's point of view, these developments may be associated with the rise of 'individual consciousness' mentioned earlier. Organizationally, they are associated with the competitiveness and financial orientation that changed secure relationships to bounded transactional relationships. Thus it is not surprising that there has been a clear decline in the level and importance of organizational commitment.[26] Organizational commitment is lower in relation to new modes of work and new employment relationships, e.g. part-time employment, and has almost lost its meaning where multiple part-time work is involved.

Nevertheless, people need a certain degree of commitment, and as a result we are witnessing the creation of multiple commitments to replace the traditional organizational commitment.

The multiple commitments people may have relate to the many domains of life that each person has, each comprising of multiple constituencies.

1 **Work-related commitments**
   (a) Workplace commitments: to the organization; leader; team; department/unit; project (product); peers/colleagues and so on.
   (b) Commitments outside the workplace: to the union; profession, occupational association and so on.
2 **Family-related commitments**: to spouse; children; parents (care of the elderly); mistress/lover (if relevant).
3 **Commitments in other life domains**: to country, friend, pet (and usually higher for a dog than a cat, and even less for a rabbit – according to the mutuality of the commitment), club, church (or any other religious institution), community, political involvement (e.g. political party), even to a house (as was vividly presented in the film, *War of the Roses*).
4 **Commitment to self**: time for self, hobbies/leisure activities.

In this book we focus on work-related commitments, but the reader should be aware of the limited perspective of this approach.

About half a century after Gouldner's work, the focus of commitment and loyalty has moved from the organization to other constituencies. Such commitments may be to the work group, the leader, the business unit, the profession, the union, or generally the career. Further support for the idea that people have different set of commitments was presented in a study of nurses' commitments. This identified four distinct commitments of nurses: commitment to the general NHS (National Health Service), to the organization (usually the specific hospital), to the work group and, lastly, occupational commitment.[27] Even career commitment is not necessarily a single construct. Another study, which constructed a measure for career commitment, identified a three-dimensional model of career commitment: career identity, career planning and career resilience.[28] A positive association was found between occupational prestige (or professional standing) and career commitment. Similarly, in examining the relationship between the construct of emotional intelligence and commitment constructs, a positive correlation ($r = .51$) was found with career commitment, but no correlation with organizational commitment (although a positive correlation of $r = .30$ was found between these two commitments).[29]

The theory behind multiple commitments emerges from the theory of Social Identity, which offers applicable insights into why individuals seek to identify with and long to participate in something meaningful, as partaking enhances their personal worth and self-belief. Members of an organization tend to apply the sociological categorization of the group or organization to define or transform the individual self. Thus membership is linked to a deeper psychological process, and such processes end with feelings of commitment, loyalty and trust.[30]

For the professional, commitment may be to the profession: an academic lecturer can move to another institution or university, but will stay within his or her scientific discipline; or a doctor can easily move to another hospital, but will remain a surgeon or an anaesthetist. For individuals, self-fulfilment can be achieved outside the organization or the realm of work, and within this realm, entrepreneurship may be more highly desired than being a good organizational citizen.

EXHIBIT 3.2	**Self-rating exercise**

Where does your commitment lie?

Even as a student, you have several commitments, which it is hoped are developing. You can be committed to your university, to the school or department in which you are studying, to your lecturers and of course to the discipline you have chosen. You will also have some commitment to the students union, to your student clubs, etc. Are these all mutually exclusive? Can you identify a multiple commitments profile for yourself?

Constituency*	Low commitment						high commitment
The university	1	2	3	4	5	6	7
The school/department	1	2	3	4	5	6	7
The lecturers	1	2	3	4	5	6	7
The discipline	1	2	3	4	5	6	7
The students union	1	2	3	4	5	6	7
The club	1	2	3	4	5	6	7
Other:	1	2	3	4	5	6	7
Other:	1	2	3	4	5	6	7

* Note that these are all 'studying-related' constituencies, whereas your main commitment may lie with your family or partner, of course.

Where will your commitment lie in future?

This question is much harder to answer. As a graduate who will work in a particular profession, employed by one (or more) unique organizations, you will have many and varied commitments.

Now that it is realized that the nature of the employment relationship has changed significantly, a job-hopper is perceived as a transitional developer whereas changing jobs frequently was at one time regarded very negatively.[31] One of the strongest criticisms of MBA graduates was their tendency to leave organizations after a relatively short time, a tendency labelled job-hopping. Today such moves are recognized as a source of possible advantage for both individuals and their employers – wide experience can be gained from such diversity.

At one time a person who had been made redundant would have carried the stigma of being made jobless for the rest of his/her (working) life. Today it is quite a common experience, and can be considered one of development and learning. It becomes a clearly negative phenomenon when a person is unemployed for a long time. Such a person could become permanently jobless. (It is quite common for a person over 50 or 55 who has been made redundant to be unable to find an alternative, and to simply stay out of the labour market.)

The Desert Generation phenomenon

The discussion that follows is based on Baruch, 2003.[32]

One of the most amazing qualities of human beings is the ability to change, to develop and to transform themselves. People learn – from their success, their failures, and even more important, from the experience of others. Such is the nature of individual development. However, we are also limited in our ability to adapt and respond to external changes, as much depends on the pace and depth of change. It is relatively easy to alter behaviour, more difficult to change beliefs and almost impossible to swap values and mental frameworks. Some go so far as to claim that this limited ability is subject to the genetic make-up of human beings.[33]

When their environment changes occur at a manageable pace, most people are able to adapt to the change or cope with it effectively. However, if what is needed is an all-encompassing change, requiring a totally new direction, with severe time restrictions, it is unlikely to be achieved without casualties. An example of such a change is that in the nature of the 'rules of the game' in the management of people. This affects both individuals and organizations. This shift has left many 'lost generation' employees behind and bewildered, in a situation analogous to that of the Israelites of the 'Desert Generation' in the Old Testament.

The Bible tells us that the members of the ancient Israelite tribe were held in Egypt as slaves for about four hundred years. The story goes that their leader, Moses, delivered a message of freedom to them. They were liberated by an act of God and left Egypt to return and conquer the Holy Land.

Such a task requires motivation, determination and the fighting spirit of sovereign, independent people. However, the behaviour of the Israelites, trapped in the mental attitudes of their former life, was very disappointing. They did not trust God and some even wanted to return to a life of slavery. The outcome was that they were left to perish in the desert while a selected few went on to educate the next generation so that they would have the qualities required to establish a free nation. Within forty years, God assumed that a different political and control system, a different culture and above all, education, would generate a totally different spirit, based on a changed set of values and beliefs. It worked. The people who perished were called 'Generation of the Desert', or the 'Desert Generation'.

Modern management created a similar situation for a generation of employees. Those who were good employees and followed the traditional career pattern in the 1960s, 1970s, and perhaps the beginning of the 1980s, often do not fit the present business situation. From about mid-1980s and certainly in the 1990s, distinct concepts, new deals and different psychological contracts have emerged. Subsequently, the 1990s created another 'Desert Generation', people who were born, grew, and developed personally and professionally in a world where loyalty and commitment to the organization were the prevailing norm. Stable, long-term employment relationships with established career patterns were the rule. Now these are the exception. For many, the new career concept was unimaginable.

And here ends the metaphor. The present generation has committed no moral wrong. Change has emerged due to a combination of technological, economic and political developments. As far as business practice is concerned, these days there is no time to set affairs aside for forty years. It should be pointed out, of course, that not everyone has to change – today's labour markets are diverse and there are places, occupations and professions, which enable the 'good old days' framework to function still.

Figure 3.4 exhibits three groups. The first is the youngest – those who grew into this situation. Most of them entered the labour market in the 1980s and later, and experienced the new era of industrial relations. They do not expect too much commitment or loyalty from their employer. With such a background and psychological attitude, these people are supposedly better equipped to cope with a labour market in a state of perpetual change, and with ongoing job insecurity. Since they have not experienced organizational and environmental stability, they will not wish to return to those 'good old days'. For them the present realities of working life do not represent a new concept but just the way things are and always have been, in a similar way that the new generation of the Israelites experienced freedom. They were looking forward: born and educated as free people, with the clear goal of reaching the promised land, they would not long for the past or try to revive it.

A totally different group consists of the old generation. Like the younger group, they are not very likely to suffer, but for entirely different reasons. For them the new situation does not really apply. Some are senior managers and are, in fact, leading these changes, cutting down other people's jobs. Others have been or are due to be offered early retirement. Many organizations offer such a career exit option for older employees. And some will just manage to 'drag it out' for further few years, till retirement age or till early retirement is available.

The middle group comprises the modern Desert Generation. The special difficulties of this group are manifested in several studies on both sides of the Atlantic. Thomas and Dunkerley (1999)[34] examined middle managers in 50 UK organizations in a longitudinal study. They found that delayering, coupled with tighter demands on middle managers, deprive them of what they see as a justified reward in terms of traditional progress. They expect other middle-level managers to be more bitter and jaundiced in the future.

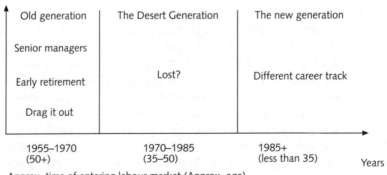

Figure 3.4 **A variety of alternatives**

Solutions

The advantage of our age over the original Desert Generation is that this metaphor, like most metaphors, is only partially true. It is revealing, but the situations are not identical. Two major differences that help to point the way to possible solutions are, first, the diversity of the population and, second, that they are not subject to a single ruler. A contingency approach will identify different types of people and organizations, thus a variety of solutions will emerge to fit each case.

Let us look at possible sub-groups (Figure 3.5).

The ostriches

The first sub-group comprises of those who cannot or are not willing to change mentally. They will perish, not necessarily literally, but as working people. They will cease to contribute to the society and the economy. Some of them will try to stick to old norms and paradigms – saying, 'it won't happen to me' – hiding their heads in the sand. People in this sub-group could become permanently unemployed, others may move around, in a constant search for alternatives. In our metaphoric concept, they will form the new Desert Generation.

The lions

The lions are those who can adapt and recuperate. They are the new breed of corporate middle managers, people with a real readiness and willingness for change, innovation, transformation. This sub-group is the source of the future generation of top managers: within some 10–15 years the older age group will retire and a new layer of executives will emerge from these people.

The bulls

Others will move into jobs and roles which retain some of the old norms, if not in competition in a different market, at least with the old-style career systems structure. Occupations such as teaching, even academia, some areas of the civil service, the army (a male-dominated environment) and nursing (a female-dominated environment) can still offer those former career structures, although not in all cases: recent research indicates that the competitive age has reached even some of the old ivory towers and fortresses.

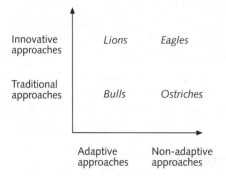

Figure 3.5 The four options

The eagles

Lastly, at the other extreme of the range, there are the entrepreneurs. They will prefer to establish their own enterprises, to exploit new markets, through recognizing and grasping new opportunities. They will generally enjoy the rough and tumble of business life, and could encounter adventures as either entrepreneurs, creating new organizations, or intrapreneurs, developing new ventures within their own organization.

Lessons

What is the proper approach for organizations, how should they advance the variety of sub-groups, in order to avoid losing the energy and motivation of a vast number of employees? How will organizations ensure that most will reach the promised land – a land of productive, satisfactory work? And what may enable people to cope effectively with the changing environment, the new era of employment relationships?

Implications for individuals

To borrow a Freudian concept, people can adopt several ways to deal with crises and threats. Withdrawal or denial may lead people to a track similar to that of the Biblical Desert Generation, though, in this era of the welfare state, not literally. Transference and sublimation can help people to 'fly high', to use the wings of their imagination and create their own promised land.

Those wishing to keep their present job should try to become indispensable to their organization, to build knowledge and skills, and excel in their performance. For example, they may make sure that they are occupied in more than one activity, thus will always be engaged in one project or another. If, however, they are ready and willing to keep an eye on outside opportunities, they should develop networks, keep and nourish contacts with other organizations, suppliers, customers, etc. – these may turn out to be their next employer or contractor who hires their services.

For others the advice could be to develop a career portfolio, to be involved in a range of activities, perhaps to be part of a virtual organization. People should be prepared to act within a wider range of opportunities and boundaries and see the globe rather than their local environment as their field of operation. Of great importance is the ability to utilize technology, especially information technology (by, for example, getting on the Web, to start with). Above all, the advice for the future careerist is – be brave and face reality.

Question | What can and should organizations do to help and prompt positive development, and at the same time to identify and prevent negative deterioration?

Implications for organizations

Turbulence and turmoil characterize many processes of organizational change.

Firms around the world try to reinvent their structures, processes and strategies. Successful transformation is not guaranteed. Many firms became disabled rather than better. It is inappropriate to refer to all redundant people as a coherent group. The four sub-groups depicted above call for a strategic contingency approach that bears in mind the key factor too often neglected in such changes – the human aspect of attitudes, beliefs and values, which are the building stones of organizational culture. Revolutions have always left casualties, and many have failed. What can be done then, on the organizational side? What advice may be offered?

Organizational HRM should be able to distinguish those more likely to perish and those who possess the qualities needed to survive. Different people have different career aspirations and 'motivational fit', and the use of the right approach may draw the line between anxiety and achievement when using both emotional and motivational control mechanisms.[35]

Organizations should encourage organizational learning and enable options for intrapreneurship. There are different ways to get the best out of people. Sometimes it may be necessary to outsource activities and operations, using former employees. If an organization has to make people redundant, it should apply best practice, to keep face with both those who have to leave and the survivors. Above all – organizations must be fair and realistic with their people. Cliché or not, people are still the most important and valuable asset of any organization. There is further discussion of the organizational implications in the following chapters.

Intelligent, boundaryless and post-corporate careers

DeFillippi and Arthur (1994) were the first to use the 'know why, know how, and know whom' classification as a set of career competencies, introducing these as the three elements of the intelligent career.[36] Know why relates to aspirations and underpinning values, including ethical values (or lack of them). Knowing how is the skills, abilities and competencies (e.g. mathematical competencies) that enable people to perform well. Knowing whom relates to the contacts and

---

EXHIBIT 3.3

Intelligent careers

- Know why – values, attitudes, internal needs (motivation), identity; what motivates people to choose (and remain in) a certain career, job and life style.
- Knowing how – what comprises career competencies: skills, expertise, capabilities; tacit and explicit knowledge, and experience that enables high-quality performance.
- Knowing whom – networking, connections, relationships.

Source: Based on M.B. Arthur, P.H. Claman and R.J. DeFillippi (1995) 'Intelligent enterprise, intelligent careers', *Academy of Management Executive*, 9(4), 7–22; and R.J. DeFillippi and M.B. Arthur (1994) 'The boundaryless career: a competency-based career perspective', *Journal of Organizational Behavior*, 15(4), 307–24.

relationship that people develop with others, in particular networking. The ability to collaborate with a prominent leader, businessman, thinker, or politician can be crucial in making an impact. Mentoring is a different way of networking. (For more on mentoring *see* Chapter 6.)

The idea of career signalling derives from the intelligent careers framework. How do individuals indicate to their immediate and wider environments their career aspirations, intentions and directions? To use another metaphor, which feathers do you place in your rooster's tail?

In making themselves visible in the wider community that may have an interest in them or in which they may have a possible impact, people choose which element/s to promote. There is never space to include everything. For example, when a person sends a memo to a decision maker, or submits their CV for a position, they should bear in mind that the decision maker has no time to read a long account of a person's past achievements. Thus, people need to be very selective in what they signal to the external environment. In terms of the job hunt, the CV and the covering letter are the basic tools. They will be followed or supported by a selection interview, a meeting with leading people, a conference, a performance review, etc. The aim of the signals is to show others what the person has achieved in the past (as an indicator of their abilities in the future), what they are doing now and most important, their aspirations, what they wish and intend to do.

The Intelligent career framework was later elaborated by Jones and DeFillippi (1996),[37] and this enlarged framework is presented in Table 3.3.

Table 3.3 enhances Arthur and DeFillippi's original framework of know why, how, and whom by anchoring a person's career in its context. Why, how and whom are primarily individual assets of motivation, skills and relationships. Yet, individual careers evolve in specific contexts – which have spatial, temporal and historical dimensions. Knowing where, when and what are important in placing careers in their geographic, temporal and historical contexts. As for 'knowing where', it is tough to succeed in the film world if one is not located in Hollywood, just as it is harder to succeed in high technology if one is not co-located with a group of firms in Silicon Valley or Route 128 in the USA or in Slough in the UK. 'Knowing when' taps into industry life cycles that shape career moves – the dot.com bubble and its bursting had substantial effects on programming careers and career moves. 'Knowing what' defines the larger institutional rules by which careers are shaped. The rules of the game are more distinct in banking than they are in high technology – from the people dress code and a variety of interactional norms to the different criteria of success and how it should be measured.

A general perception of the current labour market is that this is the era of the post-corporate career, with both the individual and the organization being in a time of transition. Peiperl and Baruch (1997)[38] have considered past and current career models and set out a vision of future careers that differs from the past in one primary way: the existence of horizontal links that transcend geographic and organizational boundaries. As these links continue to grow, they will provide more opportunity and flexibility than were ever available under the previous systems – for those who have the knowledge and skills to take

Table 3.3 Boundaryless career competencies, strategies and challenges

Competencies	Strategies	Challenges
Knowing what: opportunities, threats, and requirements.	* Know the industry and its criteria for success * Cultivate your reputation: quick but quality work, excellent technical skills and good work attitude * Use industry savvy to win opportunities	* Remain 'employed' and reduce variability in income * Adapt to bouts of frenetic activity and involuntary unemployment * Leverage your reputation to gain jobs
Knowing why: meaning, motives, and values.	* Pursue your passion * Commit to your craft * Know what you value	* Maintain passion and commitment without burning out * Balance career and family
Knowing where: entering, training and advancing.	* Enter, train and advance to the industry core	* Spot and cultivate opportunities that improve your skills and propel your career forward *Avoid 'dead-end' projects
Knowing whom: relationships based on social capital and attraction.	* Use social capital and personal charm	* Be both strategic and genuine in relationships
Knowing how: technical and collaborative skills.	* Hone your technical skills * Train cross-functionally * Develop and articulate your vision	* Evade commodity status by creating idiosyncratic value * Avoid obsolescence in a rapidly changing market
Knowing when: timing of choices and activities.	* Move on before you're trapped in a role or status * Break the other's frame of reference to move on * Get ready to get lucky	* Extend versus exploit skills * Synchronize projects and passion

Source: Adapted from C. Jones and R.J. DeFillippi (1996) 'Back to the future in film: Combining industry and self-knowledge to meet career challenges of the 21st century', *Academy of Management Executive*, 10(4), p. 91.

advantage of them. There is further discussion of the post-corporate career in Chapter 4.

How to reinvent and resurrect one's own career

Investment in the self, improving one's employability, acquiring updated competencies and good networking are the key for successful transition to a new career direction. Training and formal education are one clear route. Other life and job experiences will be essential to enable the transition.

Strategies

Which strategies can people utilize to gain career success, in particular external career success such as higher income and progress towards a better position?

Greenhaus, Callanan and Godshalk (2000: 85) offered a framework for analysing individual career strategies, i.e. the strategies people utilize to enhance their careers, to develop and make progress. The listed the following strategies.

1 Competent in current job
2 Extended work involvement
3 Skill development
4 Opportunity development
5 Development of mentor and other supportive alliances
6 Image building
7 Organizational politics

As will be demonstrated in Chapter 7, this framework is US biased. In other countries different strategies will have different relevance or impact.

Let us examine each strategy in turn.

1 **Competent in current job** This strategy emphasizes efficiency and effectiveness in job performance. A person who gets results will be successful, be promoted and will gain more income. The practice of performance-related payment is based on this concept.

It is clear that delivering results will be a prerequisite for promotion and success, but not necessarily sufficient in all cases. Such a strategy will certainly help in the lower echelons of the organization, but later will have to be supported by further strategies.

2 **Extended work involvement** Investment in the job, such as energy, long working hours and emotions shows commitment and loyalty to the organization or the project, and can improve performance. Thus it may help also in getting better career results. Such a strategy, warned Greenhaus *et al.*, may backfire as a person might lose their work–life balance.

3 **Skill development** This strategy focuses on acquiring new skills, competences and abilities, thus enhancing the know-how component of the intelligent career (Arthur *et al.*, presented earlier). Again, this is an indirect way to improve job performance, as well as generating a portfolio that will enable the individual to gain further appointments (i.e. jobs that require certain knowledge, skills and qualifications).

4 **Opportunity development** A set of strategies designed to increase career options, mostly concerned with creating contact with organizational decision makers. Such strategies can be visibility and exposure. Visibility is being able to approach top management, thus gaining an understanding of the requirements for promotion; exposure is being seen by top management, thus gaining recognition and sponsorship.

5 **Development of mentor and other supportive alliances** Finding (or having the organization appoint for you) a mentor can be a great career move – as long as the mentor is indeed successful in both coaching and promoting the protégé. Such a relationship can be beneficial also to the mentor, but contains some risk for both individuals and organizations (*see further* in Chapter 6), if the relationship does not develop in the right direction.

6 **Image building** Conveying an image of and reputation for success, by exter-

nal 'public relations' and appearance. This strategy resembles the idea of career signalling – *see* the discussion earlier in this chapter for elaboration.

7 **Organizational politics**   Being very positive towards bosses and organizational representatives. This can take the form of flattering, supporting organizational policy and practice and backing organizational rules rather than complaining. Forming coalitions and cliques as part of opportunistic networking is also political. An example of the extreme opposite to such an approach is whistleblowing.

In choosing a strategy, one should bear in mind several points. First, the strategy should match one's own personality, for example, a very introverted person may be better to focus on competence in the job and skill development, whereas an extrovert may be better off working on image building. Also, it is rarely efficient to apply a single strategy: a combination should be sought.

Seibert, Kraimer and Crant (2001) added a proactive behaviour aspect to the Greenhaus, Callanan and Dodshalk (2000) framework while Crant (2000) provided an integrated review of the research on proactive behaviour in organizations.[39] Crant defined proactive behaviour as 'taking [the] initiative in improving current circumstances or creating new ones; it involves challenging the status quo rather than passively adapting to present conditions' (p. 436). Seibert *et al.* also provided a further detailed classification of career proactive behaviour, identifying four career-related proactive behaviours: voice, innovation, political initiative and career initiative. Thus there is a certain overlap with the Greenhaus *et al.* framework. In fact, all seven strategies are concerned with proactivity on the person side. Organizations need to make sure that the right people, not necessarily the outspoken people, are those promoted.

Education

Associated with the second strategy is wider skill development, i.e. not merely a short training course to acquire specific competencies, but the wider context of education. Education is perhaps the single most important factor in determining whether a person will obtain a managerial position. In some countries (*see* Chapter 7) the degree obtained and, even more, the type of university attended, will have an overwhelming impact on a person's future career. A first degree is common requirement for any substantial position, in particular as the percentage of university graduates is constantly growing. Furthermore, to gain access to the higher echelons of organizations, a degree in management, in particular an MBA, is increasingly becoming the norm. A masters level degree can help graduates in changing direction (*see* Exhibit 3.4 for the impact of an MBA). It is not just the MBA which yields positive career outcomes for graduates. Many now choose to study for a specialized management degree, such as an MSc or MA in marketing, accountancy, HRM, etc.

People with no formal education may undertake professional training or even as a 'mature student' may enrol on a first-degree course. Other options are apprenticeship programmes (quite often used in Germany), on-the-job training, and government programmes to provide vocational qualifications.

EXHIBIT 3.4	**Education and career: to MBA or not to MBA?**

Good question.

What would an MBA degree contribute to the career prospects of the graduate? Studying for an MBA requires a huge investment – in terms of time, money and dedication. The question is – is it worth it? What are the possible benefits of an MBA in terms of career development? Should employers encourage their managers to embark on this route? Should they look to recruit from the pool of MBA graduates?

An MBA helps individuals to gain better competencies and greater self-efficacy from their studies,[40] and self-efficacy is commonly perceived to lead to higher performance. An MBA is directed at improving managerial competencies. In part, an MBA is becoming almost a prerequisite for managerial roles in certain industries. However, the costs are substantial, in time and money invested, in additional stress levels and loss in terms of work (either because one leaves the labour market for a full-time study programme, or because one has to divide one's time and show marked dedication by combining work with a part-time MBA). For managerial roles in some professional sectors an MBA would not be an advantage, and the same is true for those who have already studied for a management first degree. In some organizations, an MBA graduate might become a job hopper,[41] although recent evidence indicates that this is not necessarily the case.[42]

When considering whether or not to undertake an MBA, people should bear in mind the cost, and the prospective benefits for their career. Evidence suggests there are positive outcomes, but there are also possible pitfalls and the investment required of individuals and organizations must be evaluated.

Inspiration

The banal question usually addressed to children, 'What do you want to be when you grow up?' is replaced in the job interview with, 'What are your long-term plans?' As depicted in Exhibit 3.5, without a clear direction we will not reach our aim. Of course having a clear aim and direction does not mean people will manage to reach them. These are conditional, but not sufficient.

A key question in job interviews is, 'What would you wish to be known for ten years from now?' The answer could make or break the prospects of a candidate hoping to embark on a promising career in a top institution, even if the other signals indicate the existence of other essential ingredients (e.g. competencies). Perhaps signalling demonstrates both the level and the direction of motivation. If the organization needs these, all that is left to see is the person's prospects of fulfilling the promise. The next stage in the selection process is to see whether the person is capable of fulfilling this via personal qualities and competencies (see the parallel with know why and know how). Finally, the political issues of whom you know and what can you bring in will prove to be decisive.

As a self-exercise, analyse yourself on these three issues: when you prepare for a job interview, can you demonstrate your level on the three 'Knows' in the intelligent career? Remember – the organization will look at all of these, as well as at your fit with their culture.

A sense of direction

- Alice: Would you tell me, please, which way I ought to walk from here?
- The cat: That depends a good deal on where you want to get to
- Alice: I don't much care where—
- The cat: Then it doesn't matter which way you walk

Lewis Carroll, *Alice in Wonderland*.

Source: © Copyright the British Museum.

Summary

This chapter summarized the concept of individual careers and career models. It covered models of individual career development, such as the protean career, and innovative career concepts (such as intelligent careers, post-corporate careers, and boundaryless careers). The chapter critically analyses the notion of career success and introduced the metaphoric Desert Generation phenomenon. The chapter ended with advice on reinventing and resurrecting one's own career.

Key terms

- Career success
- The Desert Generation
- Intelligent careers
- Post-corporate career
- Boundaryless careers

DISCUSSION QUESTIONS

Lessons and food for thought

1 *For the working student*: Is there a career system in your organization? Does this career system match the individual needs presented in this chapter?
Does this career system recognize the variety of contingencies, the variety within the labour market? Does it permit flexibility in the management of people?

2 *If you aim to become an HR consultant*: What career advice could you, a consultant, offer organizations or individual people, managers, and executives?
How prepared are you to provide advice to people seeking career counselling? Which career models do you use to realize people's needs?
What would be your advice for individuals wishing to embark on a new career (a second career, a career break, a career change)?
How do you identify people's career anchors, how do you point out a fruitful direction in life for bewildered people going astray in the modern work environment?

3 *For the student*: What were your career aspirations at the age of... 5... 15... now? Are you proactive or reactive in reaching your career goals? Where would you place yourself, in terms of Schein's career anchors? What kind of career would best fit your needs, aspirations and competencies?

Notes

1 Greenhaus, J.H., Callanan, G.A. and Godshalh, V.M. (2000) *Career Management*, 3rd edn, Forth Worth: Dryden Press.

2 Gunz, H. (1989) 'The dual meaning of managerial careers: organizational and individual levels of analysis', *Journal of Management Sudies*, 26(3), 225–50.

3 Hall, D.T. (1996) *The Career is Dead – Long Live the Career*, San Francisco: Jossey-Bass; Hall, D.T. and Moss, J.E. (1998) 'The New Protean Career Contract: helping organizations and employees adapt', *Organizational Dynamics*, 26(3), 22–37; Hall, D.T. (1976) *Careers in Organizations*, Glenview, IL: Scott, Foresman.

4 Hall, D.T. and Mirvis, P.H. (1996) 'The new protean career: psychological

success and the path with a heart', in Hall D.T. (ed.) *The Career is Dead – Long Live the Career*, San Francisco: Jossey-Bass, pp. 15–45.

[5] Cascio, W.F. (2000) 'New Workplaces', in J.M. Kummerow (ed.) *New Directions in Career Planning and the Workplace* (2nd edn), Palo Alto, CA: Davies-Black Publishing.

[6] Waterman, R.H. Jr, Waterman, J.A. and Collard, B.A. (1994) 'Toward a career-resilient workforce', *Harvard Business Review*, 72(4), 87–95.

[7] Bolles, R.N. (2000) *The 2000 What Color is Your Parachute?*, Berkeley, CA: Ten Speed Press.

[8] Arnold, J. (1997) *Managing Careers into the 21st Century*, London: Paul Chapman; Hall, D.T. (1996) *The Career is Dead – Long Live the Career*, San Francisco: Jossey-Bass; Peiperl, M.A. and Baruch, Y. (1997) 'Back to square zero: the post-corporate career', *Organizational Dynamics*, 25(4), 7–22.

[9] Rousseau, D.M. (1996) 'Changing the deal while keeping the people', *Academy of Management Executive*, 10(1), 50–9.

[10] Morrison, A.M. (1992) *Breaking the Glass Ceiling*, Reading, MA: Addison Wesley; Morrison, A.M. and Von Glinow, M.A. (1990) 'Women and minorities in management', *American Psychologist*, 45, 200–8; Morrison, A.M., White, R.P. and Van Velsor, E. (1987) *Breaking the Glass Ceiling: Can Women Reach the Top of America's Largest Corporations?* Reading, MA: Addison-Wesley.

[11] Tranowieski, D. (1973) *The Changing Success Ethic*, NY: AMACON; Renwich, P.A. and Lawler, E.E. (1978) 'What you really want from your job', *Psychology Today*, 2, May, 53–65; Boerlijst, J.G. (1984) 'Career development and career guidance', in P.J.D. Drenth, H. Thierry, P.J. Willems and C.J. de Wollf (eds) *Handbook of Work and Organizational Psychology*, NY: Wiley, pp. 313–43.

[12] Popper, M. and Lipshitz, R. (2000) 'Organizational learning: Mechanisms, culture and feasibility', *Management Learning*, 31(2), 181–96; Kolb, D.A. (1984) *Experiential Learning*, Englewood Cliffs, NJ: Prentice-Hall.

[13] Holland, J.L. (1973) *Making Vocational Choices*, Englewood Cliffs, NJ: Prentice-Hall.

[14] Greenhaus, J.H. (1987) *Career Management*, Forth Worth: Dryden.

[15] Derr, B.C. (1986) *Managing the New Careerists: The Diverse Career Success Orientation of Today's Workers*, San Francisco, Jossey-Bass.

[16] Baruch, Y. (1998) 'Empowerment Models in Organizations', *Career Development International*, 3(2), 82–7; Baruch, Y. (1999) 'Integrated Career systems for the 2000s', *International Journal of Manpower*, 20(7), 432–57; Baruch, Y. (2001) 'Employability: A substitute for loyalty?', *Human Resource Development International*, 4(4), 543–66.

[17] Wolfe, A. (1998) *One Nation, After All: What Middle-Class Americans Really Think about God, Country, Family, Poverty, Racism, Welfare, Homosexuality, Immigration, the Left, the Right, and Each Other*, NY: Viking.

[18] Kakabadse, A. and Margerison, C. (1988) 'Top executives: addressing their management development needs', *Leadership & Organization Development Journal*, 9(4), 17–21; Forbes, J.B. (1987) 'Early intraorganizational mobility: patterns and influences', *Academy of Management Journal*, 30(1), 110–35.

[19] Whyte, W.H. (1956) *The Organization Man*, NY: Simon & Schuster.

[20] Arthur, M.B., Inkson, K. and Pringle, J.K. (1999) *The New Careers: Individual*

Action and Economic Change, London: Sage; Waterman, R.H. Jr, Waterman, J.A. and Collard, B.A. (1994) 'Toward a career-resilient workforce', *Harvard Business Review*, 72(4), 87–95.

[21] Ghoshal, S., Bartlett, C.A. and Moran, P. (1999) 'A new manifesto for management', *Sloan Management Review*, 40(3), 9–22.

[22] Baruch, Y. (1998) 'The Rise and Fall of Organizational Commitment', *Human System Management*, 17(2), 135–43.

[23] Schein, E.H. (1978) *Career Dynamics: Matching Individual and Organizational Needs*, Reading, MA: Addison-Wesley; Schein, E.H. (1985) *Career Anchors: Discovering your Real Values*, San Francisco, CA: University Associate Inc.

[24] March, J.C. and March, J.G. (1979) 'Almost random careers: The Wisconsin school superintendency 1940–1972', *Administrative Science Quarterly*, 22, 377–409.

[25] Gouldner, A. (1957) 'Cosmopolitans and locals: Toward an analysis of latent social roles', *Administrative Science Quarterly*, 2, 281–306.

[26] Baruch, Y. (1998) 'The Rise and Fall of Organizational Commitment', *Human System Management*, 17(2), 135–43.

[27] Baruch, Y. and Winkelmann-Gleed, A. (2002) 'Multiple commitments: conceptual framework and empirical investigation in the health services', *British Journal of Management*, 13(4): 337–57.

[28] Carson, K.D. and Bedeian, A.G. (1994) 'Career commitment: construction of a measure and examination of its psychometric properties', *Journal of Vocational Behavior*, 44, 237–62.

[29] Carson, K.D. and Carson, P.P. (1998) 'Career commitment, competencies, and citizenship', *Journal of Career Assessment*, 6(2), 195–208.

[30] Ashforth, B.E. and Mael, F. (1989) 'Social Identity Theory and the Organization', *Academy of Management Review*, 14(1), 20–39; Tajfel, H. and Turner, J.C. (1985) 'The social identity theory of intergroup behavior', in S. Worchel and W.G. Austin (eds) *Psychology of intergroup relations*, 2nd edn, Chicago: Nelson-Hall, pp. 7–24.

[31] De Pasquale, J.A. and Lange, R.A. (1971) 'Job Hopping and the MBA', *Harvard Business Review*, Nov/Dec, 4–12, 151.

[32] Baruch, Y. (2003) 'The Desert Generation', *Personnel Review* (in press, 32 (5/6)).

[33] Nicholson, N. (2000) 'Motivation-selection-connection: An evolutionary model of career development', in M. Peiperl, M. Arthur, R. Goffee and T. Morris (eds) *Career Frontiers*, Oxford: Oxford University Press.

[34] Thomas, R. and Dunkerley, D. (1999) 'Careering downwards? Middle managers' experience in the downsized organization', *British Journal of Management*, 10(2), 157–69.

[35] Kanfer, R. and Heggestad, E.D. (1997) 'Motivational traits and skills: A person-centered approach to work motivation', *Research in Organizational Behavior*, 19, 1–56.

[36] DeFillippi, R.J. and Arthur, M.B. (1994) 'The Boundaryless Career: A Competency-Based Career Perspective', *Journal of Organizational Behavior*, 15(4), 307–24; Arthur, M.B., Claman, P.H. and DeFillippi, R.J. (1995) 'Intelligent enterprise, intelligent careers', *Academy of Management Executive*, 9(4), 7–22.

[37] Jones, C. and DeFillippi, R.J. (1996) 'Back to the future in film: Combining

industry and self-knowledge to meet career challenges of the 21st century', *Academy of Management Executive*, 10(4), 89–104.

[38] Peiperl, M.A. and Baruch, Y. (1997) 'Back to square zero: The post-corporate career', *Organizational Dynamics*, 25(4), 7–22.

[39] Seibert, S.E., Kraimer, M.L. and Crant, J.M. (2001) 'What do proactive people do? A longitudinal model linking proactive personality and career success', *Personnel Psychology*, 54(4), 845–74; Crant, J.M. (2000) 'Proactive behavior in organizations', *Journal of Management*, 26, 435–62.

[40] Boyatzis, R.E. and Renio, A. (1989) 'Research Article: The Impact of an MBA on Managerial Abilities', *Journal of Management Development*, 8(5), 66–77; Baruch, Y. and Peiperl, M.A. (2000) 'The Impact of an MBA on Graduates' Career', *Human Resource Management Journal*, 10(2), 69–90; Baruch, Y. and Leeming, A. (2001, in press) 'The Added Value of MBA Studies – Graduates' Perceptions', *Personnel Review*, 30(2).

[41] De Pasquale, J.A. and Lange, R.A. (1971) 'Job Hopping and the MBA', *Harvard Business Review*, Nov/Dec, 4–12, 151.

[42] Dougherty, T.W., Dreher, G.F. and Whitely, W. (1993) 'The MBA as careerist: An analysis of early-career job change', *Journal of Management*, 19(3), 535–48.

4 Organizational career systems

LEARNING OBJECTIVES

After reading this chapter you should be able to:

- Understand organizational careers.

- Be acquainted with the CAST concept.

- Critically analyse organizational career models.

- Understand how organizational characteristics influence career systems.

- Recognize future directions of organizational career management from a three-levels perspective – strategy, policy and operative.

CHAPTER CONTENTS

- *Empowerment*

- *Evaluating career systems*

- *Summary*

- *Key terms*

- *Discussion questions*

- *Notes*

- *Appendix 4.1 Psychological contract exercise*

Question	Think of two identical twins, who grew up together, studied at the same university, taking the same degree (say business and management), and upon finishing (with quite similar grades), explored the labour market. They had two different job offers. One was accepted by a large, established corporation, whereas the other joined a new venture, a business start-up.

Although they shared the same demographic background, environment, education (and a similar genetic system), it will be clear to the reader that their careers will take quite different trajectories. Why?

The major reason would be that different organizations provide different career systems, leading to different career path options. Even if such identical twins were to work for organizations of similar size, in the same industrial sector, they would face different career systems, and this is due to the variety of ways by which organizations choose to manage careers.

From an individual-focused to an organizational perspective

The core asset for the vast majority of existing organizations is not the building, the equipment, or the money pertaining to it, but the people who comprise it. And there are several similarities at the conceptual and the metaphorical level between people and organizations. Both possess identity and 'personality' (*see* below), both plan ahead and manage their future according to explicit and implicit goals.

However, when dealing with an individual career perspective, our discussion, analysis and understanding derive from the behavioural sciences – psychology and sociology in particular. An organizational career perspective focuses on managerial issues, in particular the HRM aspect. Whereas each individual 'owns' his or her unique career, organizations, as a collective, plan, direct and manage systems wherein careers develop.

An organization is a combination of brains, bodies and behaviours. That is the source for the parallelism between individuals and organizations: organizations have identity, they hold values;[1] they even possess 'personality'.[2] These, of course, are developed by the collective community and, more particularly, by the leaders who founded the organization, who manage, inspire, control and direct it. Dutton and Dukerich (1991)[3] argued that any organization has an image and an identity, which may guide and activate individuals' interpretations of certain issues and generate motivations. Such interpretations and motivations affect patterns of organizational action over time. In addition, organizations have life cycles that can resemble the seasons of life.[4] Lipman-Blumen and Leavitt (1999)[5] speak of an organizational 'state of mind', and Roth and Kleiner (1998)[6] elaborate on organizational memory in the context of the 'learning organization'. Finally, organizations may face 'death' (Sutton, 1983).[7] All in all there are quite a few similarities (and of course, many differences) between the individual and the organization.

To maintain these life cycles, to survive and thrive, organizations need not only to recruit the right people, but also to retain them. **Organizational career management** is the comprehensive system that organizations apply to manage people's careers. This chapter will provide a systematic view of the underlying basics of such a system, Chapter 5 will discuss its dynamism, and Chapter 6 will focus on the activities undertaken by organizations that comprise the building stones of such a system. Chapters 7 and 8 will deal respectively with two prominent issues of career systems – global careers and diversity.

This chapter introduces the *Career Active System Triad*, a multi-level conceptual framework developed to help in understanding the human side of career management.

The Career Active System Triad

The components forming the *Career Active System Triad* (CAST) perspective that I offer here can be set at three levels of analysis (*see* Table 4.1): values, approaches and behaviours. The basic underlying level of values – the principles, morals and culture – forms the roots from which the other levels emerge. The second level is that of transformation – approaches and assumptions that translate those values into the third level, that of action, behaviour and practice. The values convey the aspirations (for individuals) and strategy (for organizations) into the attitudes (for individuals) and policies (for organizations) to direct them, so that in the final observed outcome, people will act and apply at the practical level of behaviour or operation, and organizations will utilize managerial practices. By its nature (and as implied from its title), this is an active system, always in perpetual motion, since it needs to respond to both external requirements (the environment) and internal requirements (both the organization and the people). These requirements alter on a continuous base (think about yourself – have your future plans stayed similar to those you had while in school? When you started university? Now?).

The CAST perspective encompasses three levels of analysis for the understanding of careers management. It covers both individual and organizational perspectives, and associates them together. Following Chapters 2 and 3, which focused on individual careers, the CAST concept helps to facilitate a further step of integrating the needs and provisions of the two principal participants in the system:

Table 4.1 The Career Active System Triad: presentation of levels

Level	Individual	Organization
Values	Aspirations	Philosophy (strategy)
Approaches	Attitudes	Policies
Behaviours	Actions	Practices

the individual and the organization. The third major participant, which lies more in the background, is general society – the local community, area, state, region and humanity in general.

EXHIBIT 4.1

Metaphors exercise

Using the concept of metaphors (*see* below, and for a further perspective, Morgan, 1980, 1993, 1997), try to envisage how a theatre metaphor may be applied to explain the CAST. As in casting a play, the management need to decide which person will take each role, to plan ahead to find the right people, to train them for their specific roles, and make sure that a replacement can step in, if a member of the cast leaves (voluntarily or involuntarily).

Note: The interested reader may find a fascinating and useful application of this metaphor in the real-life entertainment industry in a *California Management Review* article by DeFillippi and Arthur (1998).[8]

Metaphor

The application of a name or a descriptive term or phrase to an object or action to which it is imaginatively but not literally applicable (e.g. a glaring error).
The Concise Oxford Dictionary (1990)
   Other examples are the city as a jungle; an organization as a beehive.
   Metaphors may provide an enhanced understanding of a phenomenon, in our case, a richer portrayal of the meaning of career systems within organizational life. For more on the use of metaphor in career studies *see* Chapter 5.

Let us explore how the CAST corresponds with the individual As and organizational Ps:

The individual three As

Individuals have career **aspirations** about what they want to achieve in their wider life and in their working career. Their career aspirations are reflected in their goals and aims. Of course, it is not enough to have an aspiration, since competence is required to reach career goals. If a person has no ability, skills or talent to fulfil his or her aims, the aspiration will become irrelevant or, worse, misleading and frustrating. A realistic approach will help the individual in setting career targets that relate well to their aspirations (hence their interests) as well as to the ability to gain them. These career aspirations will influence people's attitudes towards work, career and life in general. With their aspirations in their minds, and with cultural, educational and family influence, and the surrounding community, people develop **attitudes** – towards their work, their organization and, subsequently, their career. At the practical level, the individuals will move on to **actions** and behaviour. They will apply career activities to plan and manage their careers. Taking part in specific training, workshops, finding the right mentor, focusing on specific roles, and many other activities, will enable a person to improve their chances of success in their career. The three levels are associated with each other – actions are subject to attitudes, and both are derived from aspirations.

The organizational three Ps

Organizations have a certain **philosophy** and strategy that guides them in their development, growth and maintenance. This philosophy provides a direction to the organization. To manage well organizations should aim to apply best practice at the operational level and target it to fulfil their strategic goals. Such strategic decisions will focus on career issues too (e.g. *see* Chapter 7 for strategic choice in managing expatriation or Chapter 8 on diversity strategies). To translate the strategic goals into operational activities, the organization develops a wide variety of **policies**, many of which are concerned with people issues. These serve to direct actions, i.e. at the operational level the HRM unit will apply a wide range of career **practices** (*see* elaboration in Chapter 6) that maintain the continuity of the human resource part of the organization.

Put together, the CAST helps to comprehend and interpret the relationship between individual and organizational career planning and management.

EXHIBIT 4.2	**Your CAST**

- What are your career aspirations?
- How do they evolve from your approach to life? To work?
- What actions do you take to fulfil your aspirations?

EXHIBIT 4.3	**Your organization CAST**

You may be working now, you may be a full-time student. Still you probably have in mind certain dreams about the organization which you most wish to work for.
SO ... the questions are:

- In a perfect world, what type of philosophy would you like your organization to hold?
- How should the organization translate this philosophy into a set of clear, directive policies?
- What type of practices will enable your 'dream employer' to facilitate your career to fulfil your own aspirations?

Organizational career systems

Contemporary organizational career systems need to be based around several remits. First, the organization is no longer the only, or maybe not even the main focal point for career management. Sociological, economic and technological trends summarized in Chapter 1 contribute to an increased involvement and responsibility on the individual side. These are mirrored, for example by the protean career concept (Hall, 1976, 1986,[9] presented in Chapter 3) that means more emphasis is placed on individuals' responsibility for taking their destiny into their own hands. The world of work and employment experience presents a significant transition in psychological relationships between employers and employees, and in the growing number of new work arrangements. Sparrow (2000)[10] mentioned teleworking/telecommuting, virtual teams, international assignments, small and medium enterprises, and small project-based forms of organizations (*see also* DeFillipi and Arthur, 1994 and further in this chapter).[11] To these we can add new forms of work arrangements such as contingent work, multiple part-time employment and cyberspace employment. Several trends require the upgrading of the traditional methods of career planning and managing, as conducted by the organization. Among these trends are the competitive markets and business environments that, with other forces, initiated the globalization of business, redundancy and delayering and the boundaryless career. In addition there are conflicting trends, which produce a set of different contingencies for career systems.

One of the most dramatic processes that emphasize such a chaotic environment is the contradictory trends in organization size. On the one hand we find the rise of large organizations such as huge conglomerates (many due to mergers and acquisitions), and on the other hand, the flourishing of small businesses and start-up enterprises. The growth in mergers and acquisitions is partially responsible for the creation of mega-corporations (Cartwright and Cooper, 1996).[12] A few well-documented examples from the end of the twentieth century and the beginning of the twenty-first are the Exxon-Mobil amalgamation in 1999, the Swiss Bank takeover of Warburg and later merger with UBS in 1998 and the PriceWaterhouseCoopers creation (*see* below). The latter has shrunk the Big Six accountancy giants to the Big Five (formerly known as the Big Eight, and with the possible collapse of Arthur Andersen perhaps to become the Big Four). The merger of pharmaceutical giants Glaxo-Wellcome and Smithkline-Beecham, to form the world's largest drugs developer and producer, is another prominent example from a different business sector. Legal issues have arisen in relation to the HP merger with Compaq in 2002. Such mergers create major challenges to the companies' career systems, and hinder their ability to retain all the talented people from both firms.

EXHIBIT 4.4	**Mergers**

UBS acquiring PaineWebber

The acquisition of PaineWebber by UBS in 2000 is just one example of the continuity of this trend and the consequences for individual careers. The primary impetus

Exhibit 4.4 continued

for the merger came from UBS, which wished to widen their retail network by acquiring PaineWebber, renowned for their strong position in the US market. However, in other countries PaineWebber's operations were minor.

This acquisition caused many employees, who lost the status they had held in the small operation, to re-think their positions. Although they now had career opportunities in the larger UBS open to them, for example in the City of London headquarters, many did not wish to become just a cog in the machine. Some of them would rather have the broader responsibility they enjoyed in the small operation.

Exxon-Mobil

The merger of Mobil and Exxon created a giant company, ranked second in the Fortune 500 at the time of writing. It was presented as a merger, but many former Mobil employees saw it as a takeover. Most senior positions are held by former Exxon personnel. The headquarters of the new conglomerate is located in Texas, and many Mobil executives who refused to leave Virginia have left the amalgamated company.

A different area, involving acquisitions rather than mergers, has developed with the globalization of businesses. This trend has also meant the penetration of foreign manufacturing operators through the purchasing of local plants in different countries to exploit gaps in labour markets. Such an approach has wide implications for career opportunities and the developmental options for companies opting for this method. The operators of the Japanese companies Toyota and Honda in the USA and Nissan in the UK, and the German company Volkswagen in Brazil come to mind in the car sector.

While mergers and acquisitions can create giant successful corporations, many do fail. According to Cartwright and Cooper (1993),[13] failures are usually due more to cultural mismatch than to the strength of or the lack of financial attractiveness of the deal. Human factors can make or break a newly formed company. Different career paths, contrasting approaches to the management of people, lack of sensitivity, all contribute to the failure of some mergers and acquisitions.

Alongside the Big Five many small consulting companies strive, while the large ones maintain different career paths. For example, before the Enron affair, Andersen Consulting employed more than 65 000 people in 48 countries. Andersen Consulting emphasized their dominant global status and their commitment to transforming the e-commerce marketplace. Such global consultancy firms work with highly dynamic, new and agile e-commerce businesses through consulting, developing new dot-com and business ventures. Many of the consultants in the Big Five or the Big Four are working with start-ups and spin-offs. The case of Andersen Consulting sadly shows that even the best and most highly regarded career is subject to luck, in that case, the bad luck of working for a company which apparently bowed to greed rather than professionalism.

Many people choose to be consultants but not necessarily for large accounting firms. Some may be redundant engineers, marketing, operations and other executives, who decide to create their own business. Often, their starting point and first customer is their former employer.

Another Big Five global consultancy firm is PricewaterhouseCoopers, which has some 160 000 people on board, about 9000 of whom are partners. They have a presence in 150 countries and territories. The history of today's PricewaterhouseCoopers is paved with a sequence of mergers and acquisitions. The major one was the merger of two firms – Price Waterhouse and Coopers & Lybrand – each with historical roots going back some 150 years. Set out in Exhibit 4.5 are some of the key milestones in the history of both firms (taken from the company's website).

EXHIBIT 4.5	
1849	Samuel Lowell Price sets up a business in London
1854	William Cooper establishes his own practice in London, which seven years later becomes Cooper Brothers
1865	Price, Holyland and Waterhouse join forces in partnership
1874	Name changes to Price, Waterhouse & Co.
1898	Robert H. Montgomery, William M. Lybrand, Adam A. Ross Jr. and his brother T. Edward Ross form Lybrand, Ross Brothers and Montgomery
1957	Cooper Brothers & Co. (UK), McDonald, Currie and Co. (Canada) and Lybrand, Ross Bros & Montgomery (US) merge to form Coopers & Lybrand
1982	Price Waterhouse World Firm formed
1990	Coopers & Lybrand merges with Deloitte Haskins & Sells in a number of countries around the world
1998	Worldwide merger of Price Waterhouse and Coopers & Lybrand to create PricewaterhouseCoopers

Being a partner in a Big Five firm is the ultimate career success dream of many accountants and MBA graduates. This position brings power and influence as well as immensely high earnings. The career path in a consultancy firm offers a clear goal to each apprentice: to become a partner, and in larger firms there is an even higher level – that of senior partner.

A contrasting trend is the increasing growth of start-up firms and small businesses, a trend largely supported by governments. The cliché that each large corporation started as a small business is true, and serves as a source of inspiration to many entrepreneurs. The small-business sector produces increasing numbers of new job openings, and many are taken by people who have left their former large employers (voluntarily or otherwise). The individualistic aspirations of many of the X generation combined with new opportunities, many of which are provided on the Web or via its use, all contribute to the emergence of a multitude of small enterprises. The X generation may feel much safer in virtual organizations, another fast-developing sector with innovative career options.

Merging organizations, merging career systems

One great challenge that faces organizations, following a merger, is the creation of a single coherent and sustainable career system, from two different, usually distinct, career systems. The differences are due to different structures, hierarchies, compensation systems, performance appraisal systems, and different systems succession planning, where these exist.

In a large merger in the late 1990s, two merging companies had compensation systems that were similar in terms of cost to the organizations, but different from the employees' viewpoint: salaries were higher in one organization than in the other, but training was minimal, and people were expected to invest in their own development. In the other partner, which paid lower salaries, there was widespread investment in training and development. The difference in salaries in the range of $120 000 (typical in these companies), was about $20 000 per annum. The HR challenge was to merge the two different compensation systems in a cost-effective manner.

Management buy-out: business innovation, career novelty

The purchase of a substantial shareholding in a company by its managers – 'the management buy-out' (MBO) – was pioneered in the USA in the early 1970s. Since then MBOs have become an everyday global feature of corporate life and an established stage in the corporate cycle.[14] In any private enterprise society, where the ownership of productive businesses may change hands, there will be opportunities for suitably motivated managers to run such organizations more efficiently than their current owners. The impetus for many buy-outs may come from the managers themselves. They are capable of realizing that the parent company is not able or willing to invest sufficiently in their subsidiary or that the constraints imposed by head office are preventing the growth of their business. Buy-outs, like greatness, are nevertheless often thrust upon people. Taking over one's own workplace is very different from being employed by it.

MBO: new career frontiers

The MBO offers the leading managers the status of ownership. It has also created a niche labour market. This comprises venture capital companies, investing banks, solicitors and deal-makers, all of whom are engaged in providing financial and managerial support for the managing team. The strength of the managers both as individuals and as a team is widely accepted as the most important success factor of MBOs (Baruch and Gebbie, 1998).[15] The buy-out process is a time of great opportunity and high risk, but the end results can be tremendous in terms of financial and personal career gains.

Organizational frames and career dynamism

While the previous discussion depicts a wide range of novel organizational frames and career dynamism, there are still many traditional and conventional organizations, in both production and services, with traditional career systems characterized by a relatively clear hierarchy, career paths and central control systems. Among them there are organizations with bureaucracy-based structures and conventional career ladders. Sometimes these are associated with particular occupations. In teaching, the civil service, and certainly in the armed forces, the police and the health sector, career systems still offer a relatively clear hierarchy and alternative paths. In certain systems, the vocation dictates a flat career structure (such as teaching), whereas in others there are clear routes for managerial development up multiple ladders.

Organizations, whether they are a small, medium or a large conglomerate, a traditional bureaucracy or a novel organizational framework, play a significant role in the management of careers. Line managers and HR units share the role of running the operational part of career systems. In small enterprises this role is carried out by general managers, in addition to their broad operational roles. The larger the organization, the more can (and should) be done in the specific area of career systems. At the micro level, HR should aim to help individuals to gain a balance between work and other facets of life, in particular the family. This involves a shift from the 'telling' role of the paternalistic approach, to consultation and mutually shared planning. In the emerging career systems, organizations are taking on a supportive, consulting role. At the macro level, the HR manager, director or vice president will deal with strategic issues of HRM and with the strategic alignment between HRM and the operation of the organization, including career-related aspects.

Strategic HRM, strategic career systems

The strategic HRM approach was introduced in the early 1980s by Devanna, Fombrun and Tichy (1981), Fombrun, Tichy and Devanna (1984), and Beer *et al.* (1984), and continued to be a major topic of research (Salaman, 1992; Hendry, 1995; Tyson, 1995; Lundy and Cowling, 1996; Wright and Snell, 1998).[16] According to strategic HRM, the HR strategy should be developed alongside the general strategy of the organization, to acquire a cultural fit within the organization and with the outside environment. Such strategic alignment should lead to high organizational effectiveness and performance (Holbeche, 1999).[17] Strategic alignment or business integration focuses on aligning the people, processes, and technology with the organization's evolving strategy. It enables organizations to make the most of their capabilities by implementing their strategic vision through a systematic approach.

For individuals, strategic alignment offers increasingly significant learning opportunities, especially in today's environment where the parameters of business are rapidly changing. It provides versatile options for developing various different career paths in which employees can enrich their competencies and skills, develop new ones and generate future career options.

Taking a strategic view of the management of people, and seeing human resources as the most essential ingredient for organizational success, the resource-based view (RBV) can serve as a useful framework. Wernerfelt (1984) and Prahalad and Hamel (1990) built the resource-based theory around the internal competencies of the firm (Russo and Foults, 1997).[18] Grant (1991)[19] classified organizational resources as tangible, intangible and personal based. The RBV puts the emphasis on the internal resources of the organization (Hoskisson *et al.*, 1999).[20] For the organization, a resource could be tangible and intangible assets which bring a high return on investment over extended periods of time (Wernerfelt, 1984).

The predominant property of the human asset is that it is an intangible asset. People are one of the organizational assets, perhaps the most crucial, that enhance firm performance, and HRM is the system designed to obtain output, measurable in terms of company performance compared with investment in HRM (Delaney and Huselid, 1996; Harel and Tzafrir, 1999).[21] Competitive advantage is based on the internal resources of the firm, and in particular the human capital. While optimizing the human asset is cited as the most important for increasing competitiveness, managing it becomes a crucial element in gaining competitive advantage (cf. Pfeffer, 1994, 1998).[22] Part of the work is acquiring these resources (recruitment and selection), which takes a very short time. The other part is maintaining the people, developing, growing, and improving this resource, or in other words, managing their career. That part is spread over a much wider time frame – the duration of employment of the people, which can last for their entire working life (a common phenomenon in the past, now quite rare).

A crucial consideration when developing HR strategy (hence career management and system strategy) is the need to match HR strategy and organizational strategy. Such a need for congruency was most notably depicted by Meshoulam and Baird (1987) in their discussion of the association between the organizational and HR stages of development.[23] They argue that while it is important to develop an HR strategy, it would be disadvantageous for the organization to have its HR strategy lagging behind its overall organizational strategy, and similarly there would be problems in having a highly developed HR strategy while the organizational strategy is in its infancy. In their framework they provide five-scale level of strategy development: initiation, functional growth, controlled growth, functional integration and, finally, strategic integration. Efficiency will be best achieved when the levels of HR strategy and organizational strategy match, they claim.

Hand in hand with the emergence of the strategic HRM conceptual framework, came theoretical works relating to careers as a system within the organization,[24] and relating them to strategy and HR practice. However, Lengnick-Hall and Lengnick-Hall (1988)[25] have identified a wide gap between corporate policies and their applications in practice, in line with both the Meshoulam and Baird's framework and the CAST concept. In addition, there has been little examination of the actual process of career management within organizations. Hall (1986)[26] emphasized the importance of career practices and activities and the increasing efforts exerted by top management in many organizations. These career practices will be elaborated upon in Chapter 6. Organizations have assumed more responsibility within this area, even if not always by means of traditional, long-term approaches, and the career management practices that they employ need to be better understood.

However, the practices utilized derive from the strategy. In fact, this is what principles of good management dictate, but of course, many organizations apply 'off-the-shelf' practices without strategic consideration. How strategy guide practice – the framework of Sonnenfeld and Peiperl (*see* Exhibit 4.6) – provides a general answer.[27]

<table>
<tr><td>**EXHIBIT 4.6**</td><td>## Strategic career systems – the Sonnenfeld and Peiperl model</td></tr>
</table>

Sonnenfeld and Peiperl have integrated several streams of research to create a contingent framework for understanding organizational career systems as a strategic approach. They posited that, rather than there being one best model for organizational careers, the particular type of career system used should be appropriate to the strategy of the firm, linking the typology with the four strategic types: *prospectors, defenders, analysers and reactors* proposed by Miles and Snow (1978).[28]

The typology (*see* Figure 4.1 for an adaptation of Sonnenfeld and Peiperl's 'four archetypes' of career systems) contains two dimensions: Supply Flow, which ranges from completely internal supply to largely external supply of managerial labour; and Assignment Flow, which indicates the degree to which assignment and promotion decisions are based on individual performance on the one hand as against overall contribution to the group or organization on the other. According to the model, organizations vary in terms of these dimensions, which generate four career system 'types' (one for each quadrant): *Academy, Club, Baseball Team* and *Fortress*.

Academy

The *Academy* is represented in the quadrant having internal supply flow and individual-based assignment flow. Firms of this type are characterized as being committed to early-career hiring and long-term professional growth. Firm-specific skills, lateral or dual career paths and the tracking and retention of talent typify this group.

Entry characteristics include a strictly early career and the ability to grow.

Career development includes primary human resources practice, extensive training for specific jobs, tracking and sponsorship of high potential employees, and elaborate career paths/job ladders.

Exit characteristics are a low turnover, retirement and dismissal for poor performance.

Typical organizational examples are large established blue-chips such as IBM and GM.

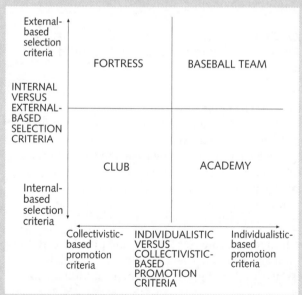

Figure 4.1 The Sonnenfeld model of career systems

Source: Based on J.A. Sonnenfeld and M.A. Peiperl (1988) 'Staffing policies as a strategic response: A typology of career systems', *Academy of Management Review*, 13(4), 568–600. Reproduced with permission.

Exhibit 4.6 continued

Club

The *Club* is the name applied to organizations in the internal supply flow/group-based assignment flow quadrant. Here 'security and membership are the essence of commitment', and there is strong concern for status in a fixed hierarchy. Clubs typically have some kind of monopoly protection from markets, often combined with a public interest kind of mission (such as might be found in a utility, military or religious organization).

Entry characteristics are an early career and an emphasis on reliability.

Career development is general, with slow paths, required steps and an emphasis on commitment.

Exit characteristics show a low turnover and include retirement.

Typical organizational examples are utilities and banks.

Baseball team

The *Baseball Team* designates the external supply flow/individual assignment flow quadrant. Such organizations would not offer employment security and are most concerned with innovation and star performance. Commitment to the organization is low, but energy and ambition are high, as everyone perceives a chance to become a star. When such expectations are dashed or when the firm is perceived to be in trouble, people quickly move to new organizations, often in similar businesses.

Entry characteristics include primary human resources practice, an emphasis on credentials and expertise, and recruitment at all career stages.

Career development means on-the-job training, with little formal training and little succession planning.

Exit characteristics show a high turnover and cross-employer career paths.

Typical organizational examples are entertainment, advertising and law firms.

Fortress

Lastly, the *Fortress* has both external supply flow and group-based assignment flow. These are firms fighting for survival, because of either economic conditions in their industry or crises specific to their business.

Entry characteristics include passive recruitment, being drawn to the industry by one's own interests and background, and selective turnaround recruitment.

Career development is made by an effort to retain the core talent.

Exit characteristics show that layoffs are frequent and seniority is respected.

Typical organizational examples are airlines, hotels and retailers.

This model focuses on the need to associate HRM theory and practice with the general organizational operation and strategy. The model was supported by case material and was used successfully to illustrate the movement of individuals in the managerial labour market.

Source: Based on J.A. Sonnenfeld, M.A. Peiperl and J.P. Kotter (1988) 'Strategic determinants of managerial labor markets: a career systems view', *Human Resource Management*, 27(4), 369–88.

Question

> If you had a choice, which type of career system would best fit your own career aspirations and attitudes?
>
> This is a relatively easy question. The more difficult is:
>
> How can you learn in advance about the type of career strategy adopted by an organization that has advertised a job you may wish to apply for?

Flexibility and competitive advantage

Flexibility means the ability to meet a variety of needs in a dynamic environment.[29] This environment is both internal and external to the organization. Sanchez distinguished between resource flexibility (the extent to which a resource can be applied to a wide range of alternative uses), and coordination flexibility (the extent to which the organization can rethink and redeploy resources). In terms of the human factor, the resources reside with the people, their competencies and skills, knowledge and abilities, and in their commitment and loyalty. Such flexibility needs to be manifested via the utilization of a variety of career management practices (*see further* in Chapter 6).

Wright and Snell (1998) applied the Sanchez framework to encompass the HRM perspective, as presented in Table 4.2.[30]

Table 4.2 Strategic HRM indicators of resources and coordination flexibility

	Flexibility in	
Factor	*Assets/Resources*	*Operation/Coordination*
Application	(1) Applicability (2) Rigidity versus flexibility of application	• Malleability of practices • Speed of feedback on impact of practices
Competence	(1) Skill spectrum (2) Ability to acquire new skills	• Variety of skills in the workforce • Ability to acquire diverse skills (e.g. via contingent workers)
Action	(1) Rigidity versus flexibility of script application	• Complementarity/conflict between scripts of different groups

Source: Adapted from R. Sanchez (1995) 'Strategic flexibility in product competition', *Strategic Management Journal*, 16, 135–9 and P.M. Wright and S.A. Snell (1998) 'Toward a unifying framework for exploring fit and flexibility in strategic human resource management', *Academy of Management Review*, 23(4), 756–72.

Flexibility as a strategic response

Organizations embrace flexibility as a strategic option to gain competitiveness.[31] In terms of HRM, flexibility has several meanings. There is functional flexibility, numerical flexibility, time and space flexibility and, above all, mind flexibility. Functional flexibility means the ability of the organization to utilize people's competencies in more than one role. This should not be restricted to job enhancement/enrichment, but also to a multiple choice of needed competencies, developing the missing or needed qualities. Numerical flexibility is manifested via different level of anticipated commitment and formal legal contractual ties. The company may define a 'core' group of employees, those responsible for the company's competitive advantage, and distinguish them from peripheral employees. The latter would have different contracts, sometimes short term, sometimes on an hourly or a daily basis. Time and space flexibility are all about where and when jobs are done. Working from 9 to 5 at the office/plant no longer needs to be the standard convention, not even the rule for the majority of the employees. Later in this chapter these aspects will be elaborated.

Question	Are you flexible (i.e. can your organization rely on your flexibility in order to maintain the flexible management of people)? Can you offer functional flexibility (i.e. how many roles can you fulfil within the realm of your organization's operations)? What competencies would you need to develop that will enable you to fill possible further roles? Do you see yourself as a 'core' employee, or are you able and ready to work in different organizations if needs change? Are you flexible in terms of time and space – would you consider working from home? During non-conventional working hours? What other qualities of flexibility can you offer your employer?

These types of flexibility help both individual and organizations, and are now quite established. However, what enabled these practices to emerge and succeed is what I call the mind flexibility of the managers who accepted such non-traditional principles at the time. Mind flexibility, thus, is the most important for the management of people and for career management, as mind flexibility will enable and develop future types of flexibility in management. It is up to executives on both the HR and operations side to realize that there is no one best way to deliver; and that although enabling a variety of options might look (and indeed is) complex, such an approach will enable better output via creativity and innovation. In this sense creativity refers to the generation of novel ideas, whereas innovation to their successful implementation.[32]

The first strategic decision organizations need to make is which type of career system will be applied. The two basic options are the traditional system or a system embodying a certain kind of flexibility in the employment relationship. Of course an organization may decide to apply a hybrid employment relationship arrangement. It will become apparent, through reading this book, that most organizations will have to adopt a flexible system that will take into account both the nature of the individual inclinations of the new generation, and the turbulent nature of the economic market. For most it will be impossible or illogical to try and adhere to old-style bureaucracy when hierarchical ladders lose their meaning and relevance in most systems. Still some organizations (e.g. the Army, the Church) will not be able to move fast, and for them it might be better to stick to the traditional ways.

The concept of flexibility is not free from academic criticism: Pollert (1991) went so far to claim that there is no real meaning to the concept of the flexible workforce.[33] In her view there is conflicting evidence for the reality beyond the rhetoric of flexibility (*see also* Legge, 1995, on rhetoric v. reality in the HRM area).[34] Pollert also indicated national variations: in France and the UK 'flexibility' means 'fixed short-term contracts' whereas in Sweden and Germany it means multi-skilling, qualifications and training. As Walsh (1991) has pointed out, the impetus for flexibility derives frequently from the need for cost control rather than a genuine interest in developing employees.[35]

Competitive advantage and redundancy programmes

Why is the concept of 'competitive advantage' associated so closely with redundancies, layoffs and job cuts? Being competitive is concerned with the ratio between organizational inputs and outputs. Outputs mean products or services. Inputs are organizational assets – capital, which may be land, buildings, machinery, money, knowledge and, above all, people. The inputs form the major difference for each of the outputs. A competitive organization produces more or better products or provides better services with the same level of assets, or uses less assets to achieve the same outcome. Labour and labour costs play a central role most of the time. Realizing that numerical flexibility is an 'easy choice', many executives opt for job cuts as a first resort.

Even when labour costs are not relatively high they are more open to manipulation than other fixed organizational costs.[36] Doganis (1994) provides the example of airline operations, where labour costs represent only 25–35 per cent of total operational costs.[37] Nevertheless, the costs of aircraft and fuel price are highly rigid, whereas labour costs are subject to (a) numerical and (b) pay level flexibility, thus people on the payroll are one of the few available variable elements of costs, at least in the short term. Regarding the human component of the organization as a cost centre rather than an investment base is the foundation of this approach. In addition, using the metaphor of 'cutting fat', there may be some justification for certain cases of reducing workforce size.

However, when this becomes the first resort in operational restructuring, redundancies might be reduced to a vicious cycle, ending with poor organizational outcomes. There is intriguing evidence that might surprise some chief executive officers. In contrast to the widely held belief that 'cutting fat' is an effective strategic response, De Meuse, Vanderheiden and Bergmann (1994) analysed all 52 relevant cases of Fortune 100 companies to come up with surprising findings.[38] Contrary to expectations, financial analysis indicated worsening financial performance over a long time frame (five years), which followed substantial cuts in the labour force. When this is added to the traumatic impact of the 'survivor syndrome',[39] it requires organizations to have second thoughts before imposing redundancies.

Incidentally, new evidence indicates how the survivor syndrome following massive redundancies can be avoided or minimized.[40] Such evidence re-emphasizes the crucial role of 'best practice' in career management, in particular if the organization has no alternative but to make people redundant.

EXHIBIT 4.7	How would you like to be treated?

If you were working for a large company facing financial difficulties, how would you wish to be treated in terms of decision making, communication, fairness and justice?

The blurring of boundaries

In their book *The Boundaryless Organization*, Ashkenas *et al.* (1995)[41] wrote about the diminishing traditional boundaries within organizations, and mentioned the following four aspects to demonstrate the breaking of the chains of organizational structure:

- vertical
- horizontal
- external
- geographic

By vertical they were referring to the breaking down of rigid hierarchies, which this book discusses widely. Diminishing horizontal boundaries means merging the different departments and units within an organization. The traditional structure divided the organization into various departments according to their specific function (e.g. marketing; logistics; production; HR; etc.). Today's organization needs to react to environmental changes and be proactive at the same time, thus such separation is not healthy for the functioning of the organization. Of course this implies that career paths for future managers will include non-traditional options. By external, Ashkenas *et al.* meant that the distinction between the organization as such and the environment, is now not as clear-cut as it was. In HR, for example, performance appraisal can build on customers, suppliers, and others that deal with the organization's members. People may be seconded to other organizations (*see* Chapter 6 for further details), external personnel can act as consultants, and employees can be working for temporary agencies. The last aspect is geography: many organizations now do not have a specific location. The virtual organization is an extreme case, but many other types of operation are not restricted to a specific place. The physical building is no longer the essence and representation of the organization.

In addition to these boundaries we can identify others that represent further disintegration of the traditional separation between the organization and its environment. Clear boundaries once existed between the domain of work and other facets of life, but these are fading away now. There are several dimensions where such distinction between work and non-work boundaries are diminishing. Time, space, and commitment are mingled in the current fluid organizational systems. The first two are quantifiable and measurable, whereas the latter is involved with inner thinking and feelings. As was pointed out earlier, 'mind interaction' means that individuals think and have emotions about work-related issues during their time away from work, and about home/family issues while working. This phenomenon occurs in conventional settings to a certain extent, but where boundaries are blurred the distinction between work and non-work is harder to maintain.

One framework where mind interaction can be managed effectively is that of teleworking or telecommuting (discussed later in this chapter). For this mode of work to be effective, people need to be judged by results rather than by their physical presence at a place of work. However, teleworkers might find it quite difficult to manage mind interactions. Baruch and Nicholson (1997)[42] found that telecommuting reduced work-related stress but increased home- and family-related stress (although the overall impact was stress reduction). More important for the organization, they supported early contentions that teleworking enables better performance. Such indications encourage both individuals and organizations to see telecommuting as offering new career opportunities. In some cases, though, social isolation and detachment from face-to-face networking is thought to have detrimental effects on career future prospects.

Outsourcing

Another totally different way to gain flexibility is concerned with outsourcing HR activities, including career management practices. The advantages are clear – outsourced activities can be conducted by professional external vendors as needed. Costing will be clearer (though not necessarily cheaper), and such activities will be performed within the available budget.

Much has been written on outsourcing HR (cf. Greer, Youngblood and Gray, 1999)[43] but very few have tried to clarify what they mean by the term HR outsourcing. The convention relates to outsourcing HR activities rather than the determination of HR strategy. In the career area there are certainly many practices that can be easily outsourced, while outsourcing others would give rise to grave doubts about the organizational commitment of decision makers.

Activities such as developing a performance appraisal system, and even analysis of the outcome of the process can be done by external agencies. Of course, eventually line managers have to make their own evaluations, and the HR department has to make the relevant decision based on that analysis. Similarly job analysis can be conducted by professional agencies, and pre-retirement and other career workshops can be outsourced. Cultural training (preparing expatriates for the new culture to which they are to be exposed) is better done by external people who are better acquainted with those cultures. Recruitment and selection, in particular for top jobs, has, of course, for a long time been carried out by HR agencies and head-hunters.

However, some decisions can only be taken by the organization itself. An external agency may prepare the salary accounts, but the organization needs to decide who receives what level of income (and external tools such as the Hay system can be useful in that task). Other tasks cannot be outsourced – mentoring (a positive facet), discipline (a negative one), industrial relations, career planning – these activities should stay under organizational control and management.

In addition to the nature of the activities feasible for outsourcing one needs to be able to assess the benefits of having top-quality services from vendors, compared to what can be provided from within the organization. Moreover, once an activity is outsourced and the internal capability of performing it is dismantled, it would be very difficult and costly to gain it back.

To sum up, outsourcing career practices is a way to gain flexibility, which can be cost-effective, and is low risk in the short term, but in the long run makes the organization dependent on external agencies.

Question

> Whom would you like to provide you with career advice – your line manager, HR department or external agency? Who would be your preferred mentor – a manager from within or a private consultant?

Work stress and control over time

Stress at work has become of great concern for organizational managers as well as for political leaders. Stress is having an enormous negative impact. At the practical level it is a major cause of work-related illness and absenteeism. At the wider context of concern for this book is the major long-term outcome of people totally abandoning employment, or moving to lower-level work, producing less added-value output in their jobs, as a result of high stress levels. The cumulative effects of stress have a highly detrimental impact upon individual well-being and health, as well as on organizational processes.[44] Ever-increasing stress causes many to focus on work and neglect other domains of life. The 'TINS' syndrome (two incomes, no sex) is an extreme manifestation of the way work might take over our life. Much of people's feelings depends on their perception of time sovereignty, i.e. who is in charge.

As regards working hours, there are two contrasting trends in the industrial world. First, due to social legislation, and the influence of trade unions (which still have a certain level of power in Europe and other countries), the permitted number of weekly hours worked is being reduced overall, mostly in the manufacturing and some service industries. This reduction helps to preserve jobs that might otherwise be made redundant. The second factor is derived from two major issues that have an opposite effect – the market demand for a 24-hour, 365-days-a-year response, and global competitiveness, which implies a demand for long working hours, and in particular for managers to work overtime (which is coupled with the compensation practice that pays no overtime to employees in managerial positions). Geography has an impact too. In many economies organizations need to operate across several time zones, even within the same country (e.g. USA, the EU, or Russia).

Another distinction exists between different 'classes' of employees, in particular between managerial staff and professionals as opposed to rank and file employees. In Spain, for example, the number of hours worked by employees is similar to that in many other European countries, but the daily pattern is different. Most workers go home in the middle of the day for *la Comida*, the lunch break, and later return to their place of work. In contrast, their managers take no break, and work more than 50 hours a week on average. Similarly the relatively long working week of British employees (averaging 42 hours a week) includes many less skilled workers, working shorter hours, and managers and professionals working 60 or even 70 hours a week.

These conflicting trends in the pattern of working hours create a distinction between the haves and the have-nots – in terms of time (and subsequently in terms of quality of life). Those covered by the legislative protection of the EU's Working Time Regulations have a reasonable workload while those not so covered, mostly managers and professionals, work overtime without direct compensation. In France and the USA most managers are in the exempt category. In other parts of the world working hours are longer. Both managers and workers in manufacturing in South Korea work long hours. In Samsung, for example, a day shift of eleven hours, for twenty-seven days a month is the routine.[45] With so much time devoted to work, both life and careers will focus around the workplace, and work-related stress might become an influential factor in people's lives.

Murphy (1988) offers a three-level analysis of stress prevention: primary, of stress reduction, secondary, of stress management, and tertiary, of organizational support mechanisms.[46] All levels should be treated by the organization, and the career system can take a leading role, in particular at the last level, in providing organizational support, beginning with alternative work arrangements, and ending with employee assistance programmes (Cooper, Liukkonen and Cartwright, 1996).[47] Cartwright and Cooper (1997)[48] include job security and job performance (or its evaluation) as two career development issues in stress management, that need to be dealt with by the organization. While job security is difficult to achieve, self-efficacy (*see* Chapter 3), the development of competencies and improved employability can serve as relevant factors in reducing career stress.

Stress and time management

Control over one's career gives one greater control over one's time and life. A wide range of options are now recognized as pertinent by organizations and individuals. These include teleworking, multiple part-time jobs, job sharing and a myriad of other time management options. However, in many cases competitiveness and retaining a managerial job means endless working hours, as when Dilbert's boss tells him he must work 18 hours a day to compete in the industry. Dilbert suggests in reply that they just *say* they work such long hours, and that then perhaps their competitors will die trying to match them. The sarcastic boss asks, 'Would it work?', to which the equally sarcastic Dilbert answers, 'It almost worked on us'.

Question

How much time, ideally, would you like to devote to work? Would you be ready to work long hours? What may cause you to agree to work 45 hours a week? 50? 60? 70?

If an important project deadline is approaching, would you be willing to work during the weekend? If yes, what if such project deadlines arrive as frequently as once a month? Once a week? What will your spouse say about it? What would you do if you have young children and wish to see them also in daylight?

Moreover:

As an executive, what moral right do you have to ask a manager reporting to you to stay till late at night? (And do you know if her husband/his wife is able to be at home to care for their children?)

However:

Doesn't organizational commitment require a readiness to exert effort and sacrifice something for the success of the organization? It should be reasonable for the organization to expect people who accept responsibility to do whatever is necessary to make sure their job is done properly. And for 'impression management' purposes, working long hours will mark you as someone who is ready to invest in his/her job and career.

Assignment (can be a group assignment)
Prepare a draft of an organizational policy on overtime work for managerial and professional workers. Remember that this draft policy should be derived from your organizational culture and values, and it must be capable of being translated into operational practices.

Alternative work arrangements

Gottlieb, Kelloway and Barham (1998)[49] list an array of flexible work arrangements that characterize practices, all of which have implications for career management. At the core of these practices is the need of organizations to recognize and be proactive in dealing with the interface between home, family and work. Various flexible ways of managing people and people's careers have been developed to enable the most effective utilization of human resources.

To benefit from using a diversity of human resources, organizations need to find ways to maximize their use of, first, their own people who otherwise would be left on the outside (e.g. via teleworking), and then the external labour market, to ensure the best fit between resources and expected outputs. A curious aspect of the employment situation in recent years is that there was high unemployment at a time of otherwise full employment (in the 1970s and early 1980s), and yet unemployment reached new low levels in the West (in particular in the USA) following the large-scale redundancies of the 1990s and early 2000s. Part of the explanation may be the growth of part-time employment, and another part perhaps the disillusionment of many unemployed people, especially the older generation, that have given up altogether any hope of future employment.

One of the most effective and successful methods of alternative work arrangements is telecommuting (also called home working or teleworking). Telecommuting is enabled by technological improvements and an increase in the use of information technology (IT) on the one hand, and on the other hand, by an unconventional managerial approach, which takes it that work is what you do, not a place where you go to. The initial idea was originated by Jones (1957, 1958).[50] Toffler (1980)[51] suggested that the information age 'could shift literally millions of jobs out of the factories and offices into which the Industrial Revolution swept them right back to where they came from originally: the home'. Telecommuting was expected to be the 'next workplace revolution' in the 1980s (Kelly, 1985), but more balanced views (e.g. Davenport and Pearlson, 1998) indicate that the growth of telecommuting is not matching expectations.[52] While limited success is apparent in Western societies, both in the Far East and Eastern Europe (not to speak of the developing world), the phenomenon is in its infancy.

Baruch and Nicholson (1997) studied the requirements for effective telecommuting.[53] While indicating the many positive impacts of telecommuting, they identified four aspects, each of which must be right for telecommuting to be effective. Figure 4.2 depicts the four aspects, and indicates perhaps why telecommuting has not yet grown as much as many futurists forecasted (due to the overlap needed between the aspects). Similarly, Figure 4.3 presents two ways by which telecommuting can become a blessing or a curse for organizational outcomes.

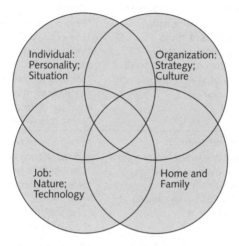

Figure 4.2 Telecommuting: the four aspects and their overlap

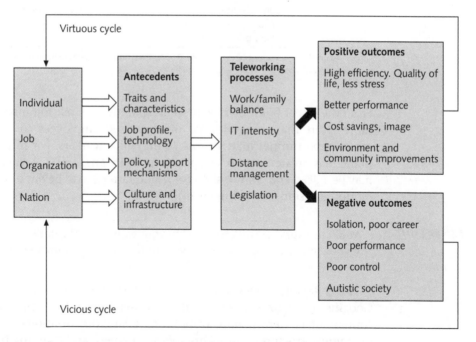

Figure 4.3 The virtuous versus the vicious cycle of teleworking

Note: Only one example from each of the four levels is given in each box, for illustrative purposes.

Source: Reprinted from Y. Baruch, (2001) 'The status of research on teleworking and an agenda for future research', *International Journal of Management Review*, 3(2), 113–29, with permission from Blackwell Publishing.

Table 4.3 Possible benefits and shortcomings of teleworking

Level	Possible benefits	Possible shortcomings and challenges
Individual	*Improved performance/higher productivity *Less time spent on commuting *Satisfying need for autonomy *Improved quality of working life (e.g. working environment) *Less work-related stress *More time with the family *Could be the only way to work at all (mothers of infants, people with disabilities, etc.)	*Fewer opportunities for affiliation, detachment from social interactions *Less influence over people and events at workplace *Questionable job security and status *Fewer career development options *Lower 'visibility'/promotability *Work-related use of private space and resources *More home-related stress *Management of work-home interface without time/space buffers *More time with the family
Organizational	*Higher productivity *Wider labour market to draw upon *Space and overheads savings *Less absenteeism *Image of a flexible workplace *Legal requirements	*Control over teleworkers' activities and monitoring performance *Control over health and safety *Need for alternative motivation mechanisms *Less committed employees *Loss of team-working benefits
National	*Less commuting, less pollution, congestion, fewer accidents *Support for local, in particular rural, communities *More people can work *Less discrimination	*Creation of an autistic society (i.e. individuals atomized and isolated from social institutions) *Need to adapt legal system

Source: Adapted and developed from Y. Baruch (2000) 'Teleworking: benefits and pitfalls as perceived by professional managers', *New Technology, Work & Employment*, 15(1), 34–49.

From the career point of view it seems that, overall, telecommuters need to exert more effort than conventional office-located employees to ensure that their career opportunities match those of the office workers. For some, working from home may create new career opportunities (Evans, 1993),[54] whereas for others it may be a dead end: Out of sight (of headquarters) may be out of mind (when promotion decisions are being taken).

Question	Would teleworking work for you? In your early career? Later on? What proportion of your time will you, ideally, devote to teleworking, compared to time on-site?

Novel flexible modes of work do not start or end with telecommuting. Lobel, Googins and Bankert (1999)[55] offer a wide framework which takes into account contemporary trends: globalization, increasing organizational flexibility, changing family structures and technological changes, and examine both operational and strategic implications for managers, as well as research implications.

At another level of work flexibility and the employment relationship we find the new phenomenon of the Multiple Part-Time (MPT) work pattern. MPT is a new alternative work arrangement, forming part of the emerging 'New Deal' in employment. MPT represents a shift away from paternalistic and benevolent secure employment, to an emphasis on continuous responsibility for self-development and employability on the part of the employee.

Part-time work (indeed, single part-time work) grew very quickly in the last quarter of the twentieth century, especially in Europe (Cette, 1999) and received much attention in academic research (*see* Feldman, 1990 and Barling and Gallagher, 1996 on the nature and consequences of part-time work).[56] This evolution has been linked mainly to four factors. The first is the high rate of unemployment in many developed countries. The second is the increased participation of women in the labour force (Cette, 1999): women's rate of part-time work is higher than that of men. The third is the need of business firms to cut costs, to enhance operational flexibility, or to increase access to scarce human capital and to enlarge the pool of talent upon which the organization can build (Belous, 1989; Hipple, 1998).[57] Finally, state incentives, in particular in Europe (Bloch and Galtier, 1999; Cette, 1999), aiming to increase employment rate have increased the use of part-time jobs.[58]

While MPT work has not been widely studied, a USA population survey (Stinson, 1997)[59] demonstrates that 7.8 million American employees were multiple jobholders, and 22 per cent of them were multiple part-timers. Furthermore, as Kimmel and Powell (1999)[60] found, US multiple jobholders typically combine a full-time job with a part-time job (sometimes termed 'moonlighting'). The same is true of Canadians. Thus, despite its apparent absence from the literature, MPT is utilized by a significant minority of the workforce, and its popularity is growing steadily.

Organizations that opt to hire part-time employees may realize that their part-time workers have another part-time job, which means a divided commitment, but also is a possible valuable source of knowledge and experience to be shared.

Another flexible work arrangement, which is less concerned with career options, but arises more as a means to enable people to balance work and career effectively is flexi-time. By this term it is meant the flexibility to change the time of work from the conventional 9 a.m.–5 p.m. schedule. Arrangements vary from starting and ending work earlier or later than the 'standard' to working according to pressure when work is subject to different demands. Such demands can be on a weekly, monthly, or annual basis. For example, in the accounting profession there is greater pressure of work at the end of the month, and on a yearly base, in April and December. It would make sense to enable employees to work fewer hours during the year, and work for longer hours when financial reports have to be completed. The extent to which management accept such an option is a clear sign of the amount of mind flexibility, mentioned earlier, possessed.

Job sharing is yet another alternative work arrangement, which enables more than one person to share a certain role. It came mostly as a response to the needs of working females and mothers, but might mean a loss of opportunities for advancement for those working under such arrangements, as reported by Gottlieb *et al.* (1998) in relation to Canadian bank employees.[61]

A form of labour market flexibility is the use of contingent work. In relation to such an arrangement, it must be asked whether employers are still looking for a highly committed workforce. They may seek commitment from their 'core' people. However, recent evidence suggests that temporary workers may have similar psychological contract and even higher job satisfaction and commitment to the organization (McDonald and Makin, 1999).[62] Similarly, Krausz, Sagie and Bidermann (2000)[63] found no difference between part-time and full-time workers in their work attitudes. In fact they identify the advantage for contingent workers of being able to control the scheduling of their work. Contingent work can be an invaluable source of knowledge and learning for the organization (Matusik and Hill, 1998).[64] Nevertheless, finding an appropriate career system to fit the needs of a contingent workforce is a challenging task for organizations.

The CAST and alternative work arrangements

Applying the CAST framework to alternative work arrangements means that individuals will act according to their aspirations. For example, people who put an emphasis on work-life balance or have the ideal of 'family first' may be more likely to be attracted to alternative work arrangements. Many aspects of attitudes to work, for example, commitment, are associated with people's career aspirations. Their behaviour or their action of opting, for example, for telecommuting is subject to their attitudes to work. Among the attitudes to work are the needs identified by McLelland.[65] Thus, people may have a high need for autonomy (which would pull people to telecommute), a high need for affiliation (which would push people away from telecommuting) and a high need for control (which will prevent managers from allowing telecommuting to flourish). People who wish to explore a multitude of experiences may prefer working on a temporary basis, moving from one workplace to another continually. For organizations, the CAST framework implies that if their philosophy puts a high value on a culture of flexibility in management, this will need to be translated into having policies reflecting all types of flexible work arrangements – numerical, functional, etc. (Atkinson, 1984).[66]

Gottlieb *et al.* (1998)[67] define five major alternative work arrangements:

- Flexitime: allows employees to start and/or end the working day earlier (or later) than usual.
- Compressed hours: where employees work fewer (or no) hours some days, and longer hours on other days (e.g. work 37.5 hours in 4 days, with 1 day off).
- Telecommuting: staff work from home for all or part of the working week.
- Part-time: staff work less than 30 hours a week.
- Job-sharing: two employees share the responsibility and benefits of one full-time position.

Exhibit 4.8 presents the expected positive impact and challenges on HR presented by each of these alternative work arrangements.

EXHIBIT 4.8	**The pros and cons of alternative work arrangements**

Alternative work arrangement	Expected positive impact	Challenges
Flexitime	Enabling the employee to schedule their working hours in a way that they will not clash with their personal activities and commitments	(a) The flexibility of certain policies is limited (b) Eventually work is expected to take place on employer's premises
Compressed hours	Enabling employees to benefit from chunks of time off work when they need it	(a) It might be difficult to find time for 'paying back' those chunks (b) Such arrangements imply that on certain days people will work extremely long hours, which could lead to fatigue and stress
Telecommuting	(a) Self management of time and operation (b) Reducing travel – saving time (discussed later in this chapter)	(a) Reduced teamwork (b) Reduced visibility (c) Social isolation (discussed later in this chapter)
Part-time	(a) Enables people who would otherwise have to quit work to participate in the workforce (b) Can provide variety if combined with another part-time job	(a) Part-timers might be regarded as 'second-class' citizens; they may have lower levels of compensation and other benefits (b) Part-timers tend to have low job security
Job-sharing	High-potential employees that otherwise would drop from the labour market can perform tasks that usually require a full-time employee	There might be an issue of equity and comparability of inputs from different people

Source: Reprinted from B.H. Gottlieb, E.K. Kelloway and E. Barham (1998) *Flexible Work Arrangements*, Chichester, Wiley, p. 12, © John Wiley & Sons Limited, reproduced with permission.

Organizational developments and career systems

The development of career theory follows naturally from the development of organizational theory. Changes in organizations and society alter the structure and the culture in which careers develop, as well as the basic assumptions of the nature of career progress. In 1978 Schein introduced the Career Cone model.[68] This represented a mould-breaking approach to career modelling, from functional, hierarchical progress within a single sector to a multidisciplinary approach that enables sideways development. The Cone model allows for spiral

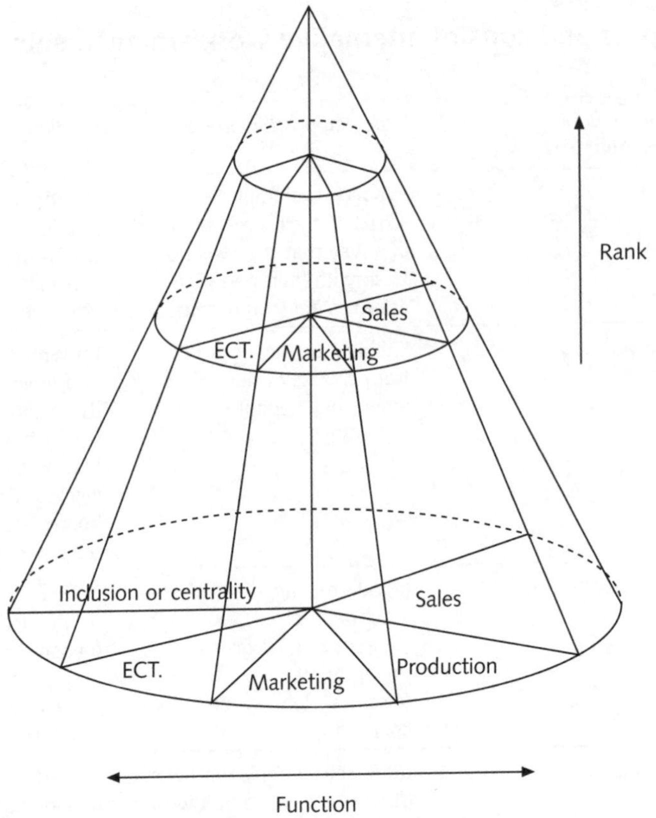

Rank

Sales

ECT. Marketing

Inclusion or centrality

Sales

ECT.

Marketing

Production

Function

Figure 4.4 Schein's organizational cone

Source: Taken from http://152.30.22.232/kirk/CDTheories/schein_organ_cone.html.

progress that integrates knowledge and practice from a variety of functional sections in the organization.

The Sonnenfeld and Peiperl model (1988),[69] presented in Figure 4.1, is one of the more analytical models of organizational career systems. Their typology posited that, rather than there being one best model for organizational careers, the particular type of career system used should be appropriate to and derived from the strategy of the firm.

In the 1990s several models broke organizational boundaries yet again. The Peiperl and Baruch post-corporate career[70] is one example of the next leap forward in career horizons, which are now legitimately spread outside the organization. They claim that, faced with fewer prospects for advancement, many people have become disillusioned with careers in large organizations. Thus work and careers are moving out of these organizations altogether, into smaller, more entrepreneurial firms and into individual, consultant-type roles. To a certain extent this represent a cycle where models of careers and career systems have evolved, as presented in Figure 4.5 (see further in Chapter 5).

As presented in Chapter 1, Herriot and Pemberton (1996)[71] outlined four properties they feel an established career model should possess. These are:

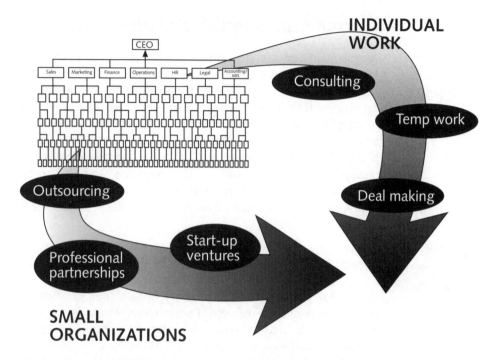

Figure 4.5 Contemporary careers: leaving the organization behind

Source: Reprinted from M.A. Peiperl and Y. Baruch (1997) 'Back to square zero: the post-corporate career', *Organizational Dynamics*, 25(4), 7–22, copyright 1997, with permission from Elsevier Science.

(a) Contextualization (i.e. taking into account not merely the organization, but also the business, political and economic environment).

(b) The cyclical and processual nature of the model.

(c) Subjectivity (rather than normativity) for the meaning of career success.

and

(d) The interactive nature of the relationship between the organization and the individual.

The core of this model is the requirement to match individual and organizational needs/wants and provisions. Added to this are the concepts of procedural and distributive justice, as well as the development of relationships (or 'psychological contract', to use another term) as an end output. Procedural justice may be defined as the degree to which the rules and procedures specified by policies are properly followed whenever they are applied. In the organizational career context procedural justice concerns the means (rather than the ends) of social justice decisions (Furnham, 1997; Folger and Cropanzano, 1998; Greenberg and Cropanzano, 2001), i.e. the basis on which career decisions are made.[72] Employees will be willing to accept organizational policies and practices if these are based on fair procedures. They value not just being treated with dignity and respect, but also being provided with adequate information about these procedures (Cropanzano and Greenberg, 1997).[73]

Recruitment, selection and career systems

Recruitment and selection are usually not perceived as integral parts of the organizational career system. Their role is to make sure there is a match between the individual and the nature and demands of the role within the specific organizational context. Two issues, however, make the distinction between the recruitment process and the career system artificial. First – it is still desirable to recruit a person for a career, rather than for a job. Second, to make sure the right match is found, the organization needs to have as clear an idea as possible about the requirements for each position. If these issues are borne in mind, the process of selection will be part of the strategic management of the human resources (e.g. applying the competencies framework – see Iles, 1999).[74] Let us look at these two issues.

EXHIBIT 4.9	Selection and recruitment

Iles (1999) suggested a framework for understanding selection and recruitment based on four distinct theoretical perspectives. These are: (a) the strategic management approach; (b) the psychometric approach; (c) the social process approach; and (d) the critical discourse perspective on assessment.

Each is concerned with selection and recruitment as part of the overall career.

Recruitment for a job or for a career? Once career was a job for life (or rather an employer for life). For a few this is true even today. Teachers, for example, can start and end their career in the same position. For most professions and vocations the nature of the job includes systematic development, sometimes associated with a higher status level and further progress within the hierarchy. Again, in the past it was common to find people developing along certain vocational career paths in a single organization. However, for most changes in the world of careers have altered that situation. The average time people spend in one organization had been reduced to a few years by the end of the twentieth century (the average tenure on the job in the USA being about four years,[75] thus career horizons within a single organization are limited. In fact Hall (1996: 5)[76] cited the CEO of General Electric describing contemporary psychological contracts as 'one-day contracts'. Nevertheless it is the core people, those who would stay for longer and develop within the organization, that are the real target of the organizational career system. Moreover, many people would still like to experience a long-term relationship with their employing organization, if not as a promise, at least as a possible option.

There is a difference in the perspectives on matching for different hierarchy levels, in particular for managerial levels (cf. Forbes and Piercy, 1991).[77] At the lower managerial level the focus is on performance, efficiency, qualifications and needed competencies (know-how), whereas at the executive level the focus is on a match with the business strategy and culture, and fit with the other members of top management. Moreover, for top roles and CEO posts, evidence of strong networking is of particular relevance – what the individual can bring to the organization in terms of external resources and contacts (know-whom). As for rank-and-file positions, qualifications and work experience play a significant role.

Chapter 2 highlighted people's need for advancement, and promotions within the organizational ranks are the most visible way of achieving this aim. From the organizational viewpoint promotion is a process comprising decision making, political interventions and setting future directions for organizational performance and effectiveness. It aims to maintain the continuity and survival of the system in relation to jobholders.

'New deals'

The current radical restructuring of many organizations has changed the traditional concept of the career and subsequently the way they manage their career systems. A prominent change was the developing and maintaining of a psychological contract between employers and employees. Table 4.4 presents the main features of the changing nature of psychological contracts. The table is based on several complementary works and reviews, most notably Herriot and Pemberton (1995), Sullivan (1999) and Cascio (2000).[78]

The idea of the 'Psychological contract' was presented in Chapter 1, and here we can see how it is reflected in a wide variety of innovative approaches to careers, which organizations must recognize. As elaborated on in Chapter 1, the roots of such contracts are probably deeper than those of formal legal contracts, and we can examine the Social Contract of Jean-Jacques Rousseau (1762, 1997)[79]

Table 4.4 The changing nature of psychological contracts

	Old Deal	New Deal
Employee offers	Loyalty, conformity, commitment	Long hours, added responsibility, broader skills, and tolerance of change and ambiguity, and willingness to work in a dynamic situation (as long as it fulfils their needs)
Employer offers	Security of employment, career prospects, training and development and care in trouble	High pay, reward for performance, and above all, having a job (employment for as long as business need exists)
Employee expects in return	Lifelong employment, pay related to tenure, vertical promotion	Development, investment in employability, learning environment, updated technology, flexibility
Employer expects in return	Organization needs take over individual needs	Self-reliant, resilient employees, ready for flexibility
General	Standard, rigid structure and work pattern, predictability	Unconventional flexible structure and work pattern, uncertainty
Values	Loyalty, stability, paternalism	Self-reliance, versatility

as a framework of social order where people have agreed upon certain 'rules of the game' with society. Similarly, the psychological contract focuses on the tacit dialogue between the individual and the organization. This is in the 'unspoken promise, not present in the small print of the employment contract, of what the employer gives, and what employees give in return' (Baruch and Hind, 1999).[80]

Psychological contracts differ from formal, legal employment contracts in their context and expected impact (Spindler, 1994).[81] They have been described by Hall and Moss (1998)[82] as a learning and development contract with the self rather than with the paternalistic and protective organization. Most of the new psychological contracts deal with situations where there are no long-term contracts but a commitment on the part of the organization to provide the employees with training and development, in order to develop a 'portable portfolio' of skills. With this they will be able to find alternative employment if the company no longer needs their services (Handy, 1989).[83]

The beginning of the 1990s saw this significant change in the nature and notion of the psychological contract (e.g. Hiltrop, 1995).[84] The new contracts are based on an interactive (relational) process and an exchange (transactional) model (Shore and Terick, 1994).[85] Robinson and Morrison (1995)[86] studied the impact of such changes to discover the role played by trust in mediating the adverse impact of breaking the old style of psychological contract.

Employees do not always welcome the transformation. The new contracts do not offer lifelong employment (or a promise of such), nor the necessity of mutual commitment and loyalty. The typical old, traditional deal was that employees offered loyalty, conformity and commitment whilst the employers offered security of employment, career prospects, training and development within the company and care in time of trouble. Both sides based the relationship on 'trust'.

Under the new deal, employees offer long hours, assume added responsibility, provide broader skills and tolerate change and ambiguity, whereas employers offer high pay, reward for performance, flexibility and, ideally, the opportunity for lifelong learning and development (Herriot and Pemberton, 1995).[87] Under such conditions, when there is readiness for change and adjusted expectations, there will not be a process of disillusionment and a feeling of betrayal on the part of employees, as suggested by Brockner, Tyler and Cooper-Schieder (1992).[88]

New terminology has sprung up around the contemporary psychological contract, which was presented in Chapter 3: DeFillippi and Arthur (1994) and Arthur (1994) were perhaps the first to use the term 'boundaryless career', while Ashkenas *et al.* (1995) wrote about the boundaryless organization.[89] Later, Arthur, Claman and DeFillippi (1995) suggested the phrase 'intelligent careers'.[90] Waterman *et al.* (1994) with 'career resilient workforce' and Peiperl and Baruch (1997) with the 'post-corporate career' used different terms, but all reflect a change from what we had known in the past.[91] Managers need to re-create commitment and maintain confidence and performance using different expectations and incentives based on the new contract.

Instead of a sequence of promotions and pay rises within an organization, individuals have suffered a loss of security of employment and prospects of promotion. The consequences for employees' morale and organizational innovation are beginning to be felt, and organizations are at a loss as to how to manage careers in the future. Individuals, likewise, are trying to maintain their employability in the labour market by developing marketable skills (Herriot and Stickland, 1999).[92]

> What is your preferred psychological contract? Can you identify dimensions of your expectations that differ from those of your employer? Can you identify what would be fair for your employer to expect from you? Appendix 4.1 at the end of this chapter is provided to help you identify your ideal psychological contract.

Empowerment

Empowerment is not a new buzzword introduced merely to inspire current trends in management science. It comprises an innovative approach to working with people and a shift from the top-down management styles which have dominated control mechanisms and managerial concepts in both theory and practice since the Industrial Revolution (Baruch, 1998).[93] According to the New Deal and the new psychological contract, organizations now empower people not only in operational terms, but also in managing their career, their development, their progress. Weick (2001, p. 207)[94] argues that traditional career management by the organization is replaced by more self-reliance. This implies empowerment in terms of a self-managed rather than an organization-led career.

Empowerment means 'finding new ways to concentrate power in the hands of the people who need it most to get the job done – putting authority, responsibility, resources and rights at the most appropriate level for the task. It also means the controlled transfer of power from management to employees in the long-term interest of the business as a whole'.

Empowerment is part of a set of motivational techniques designed to improve employee performance through increased levels of employee participation and self-determination (Vecchio, 1995).[95] Traditional paradigms were based predominantly on strong managerial control, a concept originating from the Greek philosopher Plato some 2400 years ago.[96] The modern concept of empowerment relates primarily to the delegation of decision-making power to people at lower organizational levels, but empowerment means more than merely delegation (Malone, 1997).[97] It is concerned with trust, motivation, decision making and basically, breaking the inner boundaries between management and employees as 'them' versus 'us'. However, there is a difference between the meaning of empowerment and the rhetoric of its implementation, and the latter is not always in line with the good intentions of its originators (Hales, 2000).[98]

Conger and Kanungo (1988)[99] viewed empowerment in the organizational context as a set of conditions necessary for intrinsic task motivation. Thomas and Velthouse (1990)[100] define four components of empowerment:

- choice – not only providing employees with genuine job enrichment and opportunities to have their voice heard, but also giving them real power to control and influence work processes;
- competence – enabling people to be confident of their capacity to make these

choices; enhancing their self-efficacy as a pre-condition to making decisions and standing by them;

- meaningfulness – valuing the work done by the empowered people; and
- impact – letting people have influence over what is going on in the organiz-ation, ensuring that their decisions make a difference.

All of these components apply to the transformed organizational career system. Many of the roles traditionally held by the organization have been passed to indi-vidual employees. This transfer is not always, however, the best course, as some transferred responsibilities should remain with the organization.

Baruch's (1998)[101] model of empowerment offers four ways of classifying organ-izational approaches to empowerment. The model proposes that the perceptions, attitudes, beliefs, and values of senior management can be described by constraints that can be grouped into two domains, labelled *belief* and *fairness*. Subsequently a 2×2 model emerges for analysis of empowerment in organizations, which may be relevant to career systems as well as in general empowerment.

The two dimensions of the model are:

- *Belief*: the extent to which top management genuinely believe in the underly-ing ideas of empowerment and its potential benefits. This will depend on the values the people at the top hold. The *bona fide* notion of empowerment implies the transfer of actual and rectified delegation of power and decision making to the lower echelons of the organization. In terms of career manage-ment it means passing responsibility to both line managers and the employees themselves.
- *Fairness*: the extent to which the approach of senior management to employees is fair and just/honest. Here we have a clear problem – for justice and fairness are loaded terms, not easily measured. In terms of a career fairness may relate to the support the organization is prepared to give to help people in their career.

Combined, these dimensions project four prototypes of the organizational approach to and the interpretation of empowerment. The first dimension, belief, determines whether career empowerment will be applied in the organization; the second, fairness, implies the support and investment of the organization for the empowered people. These are portrayed below.

If the organization and its representatives do not believe in the concept, and apply a 'fair' approach, they will take 'career empowerment' off the agenda. If they do believe in the concept, and apply a 'fair' approach, they will delegate decision making to individuals and will support them accordingly.

If the organization and its representatives do not believe in the concept, but for reasons to do with political correctness, compliance with fashionable theories and image building prefer to be seen as applying best practice, they may try to apply simulated career empowerment. Lastly, if they believe in the concept, but do not wish to play a 'fair' game, they may just off-load the burden of career management on to employees.

These four dimensions have been labelled respectively as the **Dissociated**, the **Enlightened**, the **Fraudulent** and the **Miser** (or **mean-spirited**) (*see* Figure 4.6).

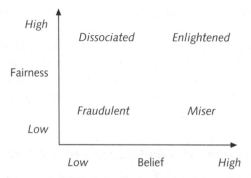

Figure 4.6 The four dimensions of the empowerment model

Career management and the litigious society

The surge in employment-related litigation is apparent in Western society. In the UK, with a labour market of 26 million, the central agency for advisory, conciliation and arbitration services (ACAS) witnessed about three-quarters of a million legal inquiries, culminating in 167 354 individual action against employers in 1999 (*The Times*, 29 August 2000). Many other private individual cases reach court via different channels. The sharp rise can be attributed to several elements: a decrease in the level of unionism, improved employment rights, an increase in the sophistication of people with multiple competencies and wider knowledge, a proactive approach by individuals and fewer bonds between employers and their workforces because of the increasing flexibility and individualization of work.

The implications of such actions on the management of employment relationships with a large workforce are destructive. Taking a matter to court means ending a trust-based relationship, and long-term career development is based on such relationships. A large proportion of employment-related cases concern career issues, in particular the issue of promotion and equal employment opportunities. One issue which may possibly lead to litigation is the management of diversity and equal employment opportunities. More on this will be presented in Chapter 8.

A major emphasis in this book is on how to determine best practice in various HR-related decisions, if there is any 'best practice' (*see* the argument of Cappelli and Crocker-Hefter 1996[102] who claimed no such 'solution' is feasible). Baruch (1998b)[103] advised HR managers how to walk the tightrope of people management by trying to find the golden route, a balanced way between extremes, in both strategy and practice. Acute problems concern the ambiguity and complexity of the issue of managing people. And people are the most difficult asset to manage – they are unpredictable (at least to some extent), they have their own will and plans (which do not necessarily fit with those of the organization), and they are affected by the external and internal organizational environments. These issues affect how career management can be dealt with, and limit what executives can expect from organizational career management systems.

To put it at its most basic level, the role of HR is 'To obtain and retain employees' (Cuming, 1986).[104] 'Retaining' is basically career management. To find the right people, HR managers have to engage in an explicit search to identify the implicit qualities needed for effective management in the organization. Maintaining motivation requires the investment of even greater effort. It requires a continuous role of developing people, responding to individual and organizational needs and being proactive in inspiring as well as in directing people (Baruch, 1998b).[105] Applying best practice and fairness is the best answer to the prospect of litigation on the part of both individuals and external agencies (such as government, unions, etc.).

Organizational learning mechanisms concerning career practices

One important question about practices is how far they are applied. Chapter 6 reviews a wide portfolio of career practices. It is feasible to evaluate, for each practice, how far employees (as well as senior managers) are aware of its existence, to what level they utilize these practices and how they feel about the outcomes of these practices.

Perhaps the most important question to be asked is, 'Does this make a difference?' What are the consequences for the individual and for the organization? As shown by Baruch and Rosenstein (1992),[106] there is a strong connection between the implementation of CPM techniques and career planning and management by individuals (r = .54). Other positive correlations were found with satisfaction measures (e.g. organizational satisfaction, career satisfaction) and the implementation of CPM.

Baruch's (1996)[107] survey indicates a clear gap between top managers in HR and those outside HR in their perceptions of what organizations offer their employees in terms of career practices. The results presented in Table 4.5 indicate that employees have little knowledge of the techniques, considerably below the expectations of HRM theorists and practitioners. Probably the most interesting question to be examined is why some practices are used more than others. The answer could be connected to fear on the part of organizations of creating career expectations in their employees. These concerns increase both in times of recession, and in response to changes and instability in business life. Long-term planning becomes more difficult, sometimes irrelevant, and organizations tend to plan career developments mainly in the short term. Even if planning long-term developments, organizations will present and discuss them in vague terms rather than as a commitment.

A second, crucial, aspect of the results is the disagreement, both among senior managers and among employees, about whether the techniques were in use. This disagreement may be due to two main reasons: a) the ambiguity of the nature as well as the definition of the different techniques; b) a genuine lack of knowledge that can be caused by distortions in organizational communication.

Storey's (1995: 5)[108] definition of HRM includes the wording: 'HRM is a distinctive approach to employment management which seeks to obtain competitive advantage through the strategic deployment of a highly committed and skilled workforce, using an array of cultural, structural and personnel practices.' How can HR and career managers in organizations gain a true picture of employees' perceptions of career systems? A simple way is to use internal employees surveys.

Table 4.5 The existence of OCPM techniques – management viewpoint

No.	Technique	%	%	%
1.	Use of PA as a basis for career planning	56.7	26.7	16.7
2.	Career counselling by direct supervisor	35	28.3	36.7
3.	Career counselling by HRM unit	16.7	26.7	56.7
4.	Books and/or pamphlets on career issues	8.3	15	76.7
5.	Common career paths	28.3	36.7	35
6.	Assessment centre	41.7	26.7	31.7
7.	Other ways of identifying management potential	11.7	10	78.2
8.	Dual ladder	43.3	26.7	30
9.	Postings regarding internal job openings	43.3	16.7	40
10.	Appraisal committees	18.3	15	66.7
11.	Formal education as part of career development	98.3	1.7	–
12.	Career workshops	10	8.3	81.7
13.	Written personal career planning for employees	6.7	10	83.3
14.	Retirement preparation programmes	33.3	55*	10
15.	Mentoring	43.3	–	55
16.	PA as a basis for salary review	63.3	18.3	18.3
17.	Management inventory (Succession planning)	28.3	30	41.7
18.	QC (for identification of management potential)	30	23.3	46.7
19.	Training programmes for managers	70	–	23.3

PA: performance appraisal
QC: quality circles
* This high percentage includes organizations that stated that such a technique is unnecessary at the present stage of their organizational life (young organizations).
No. of organizations: 60 (51 in Israel, 9 in the UK).

Source: Reprinted from Y. Baruch (1996) 'Career planning and managing techniques in use', *Career Development International*, 1(1), 43–52, with permission from MCB UP Ltd.

These may be use for comparative analysis, but their validity is questionable. Additional sources include sessions with mentors, managers, sample employees, and some recommend using exit interviews.

Evaluating career systems

In a similar way to performance appraisal at the individual employee level, organizations should evaluate their business unit performance and effectiveness. Management should be able to evaluate the operational and performance quality of its units, departments and subdivisions for two major reasons: first, the need to be well acquainted with what is happening in the organization; second, in order to identify and isolate possible problems and difficulties which might be due to poor performance (Baruch, 1997).[109] However, it is never simple to evaluate the 'soft' management issues covered by HRM. Moreover, different clients or constituencies have various expectations of HRM, as defined by Tsui (1987, 1990).[110]

One way to conduct such an evaluation is to look at 'customer satisfaction' – and one major customer is the employees as a whole. Attitude surveys have several advantages and are widely used (cf. Florkowski and Schuler, 1994).[111] However, they are limited to employees' perceptions, and their shortcomings include accuracy problems, questionable reliability and validity, and the fact that it is not only employees who are the clients of HRM. Furthermore, employees may not be familiar with some of HRM practices, such as succession planning.

Another means of evaluation is to measure the extent to which the unit has achieved its goals, which in career system management may be manifested by employees' career satisfaction, and by a proper flow of appointments at the organizational level (e.g. there is no need for crisis head-hunting when people leave the organization). Nevertheless, 'goal attainment' requires criteria to be defined in terms of clear, measurable objectives, and in people-related issues it is difficult to reach agreement about the meaning and importance of such objectives (Harrison, 1987).[112] Also the time scale that is needed to assess goal attainment in the area of HRM is fairly long.

A different evaluation method will focus on analysing the career practices applied by the organization. This builds on Townley (1994)[113] who referred to HRM as a set of practices and techniques. Baruch argued that such evaluation should relate to both *what* is being done and *how* it is being done.

Each of these three methods can be utilized to evaluate organizational career systems. Goal attainment can be assessed by comparisons with either specific organizational goals, or wider goals (e.g. set by national professional bodies). Employee surveys can include employees' perceptions of career management. Chapter 6 provides a comprehensive set of career practices that can serve as a basis for conducting an evaluation.

There are several methods of obtaining feedback on organizational career systems (and other HR systems). Certain unique knowledge may derive from **exit interviews**, which may take the form of a survey, or phone or face-to-face sessions. Most argue for conducting exit interviews at the time of leaving, or on the last day/in the last week. This is not always the best option (*see* Exhibit 4.10).

EXHIBIT 4.10	**Exit interviews**

John Sullivan of San Francisco State University argues that 'exit interviews' should be conducted 3–6 months after the departure date since there is a significant difference between the answers given then and those given on leaving. There are several reasons for this. First, leaving may be traumatic and such an interview can provide an opportunity for people to air their frustrations. Second, it is only after some time that people can compare the new employer to the former one. Another aspect is that in an interview at the time of leaving the employee must be polite, bearing in mind that the former employer will be providing a reference (recommendation letter) for future employers.

Thus it is not surprising to find problems with exit interviews and surveys. AT&T's experience with post-exit questionnaires, posted to the home of former employees, was poor also. There being no real incentive to return the survey, most responses were from very disgruntled employees who frequently ranted about how

Exhibit 4.10 continued

bad the company was while offering little in the way of substantive, useful information.

In view of such disappointing outcomes (http://ourworld)[114] HR can opt for pre-exit interviews, sometimes called 'Why do you stay?' interviews, as opposed to 'Why are you leaving?' interviews. An organization being strategic and proactive will ask its key people why they stay and what the barriers to their productivity are. By identifying symptoms before they get out of hand an organization may be able to prevent the cause.

The practicality of evaluating career systems

Baruch and Peiperl (2000)[115] suggested a descriptive model for understanding contemporary career systems and practice along two dimensions: 'Sophistication of the career management practices', and 'Involvement necessary on the part of the organization' to apply them appropriately. Baruch (2003)[116] advanced this framework by adding four dimensions to enable deeper and better understanding of career systems, and their evaluation. These are: 'Strategic orientation'; 'Developmental focus'; 'Organizational decision-making relevance'; and 'Innovative approach'.

'Strategic orientation' is based on strategic the HRM approach (Fombrun, Tichy and Devanna, 1984)[117] that implies that HRM should not be seen as a set of distinct practices but as part of organizational strategic management as a whole.

'Developmental focus' questions the relevance of career management practice to the personal development of employees, as compared to the simple acquisition of specific organizational needs. With human resources being seen as the core asset and as the source of competitive advantage for the firm, it is in the interest of companies to develop this resource (Cappelli and Crocker-Hefter, 1996).[118] This means, of course, investment in developing people's competencies, but will be reflected in the bottom-line outcomes of the firm (Pfeffer, 1998).[119]

The third additional dimension is the degree to which the practice is relevant to 'Organizational decision-making issues', such as the selection of top executives (cf. Mitchell and Beach, 1977; Nutt, 1999).[120]

Lastly, 'Innovative approach' (in contrast to conventional and orthodox approaches) concerns the extent to which specific practice reflects novel ideas and concepts. Among the academic contributions of the last decade of the twentieth century are several innovative concepts that require a non-traditional career approach.

All in all, the updated six-dimension model offered by Baruch aims to further develop career theory by offering and critically examining a normative model for integrating the available portfolio of organizational career practices. Such a model also assists an understanding of management practice in the area of careers. It can help to facilitate guidelines for evaluating organizational career systems, i.e. along these six dimensions:

- **Involvement**: from a very low to a very high level of organizational involvement needed when dealing with the specific career practice.
- **Sophistication and complexity**: from very simple to highly sophisticated and complex.
- **Strategic orientation**: from very practical or 'tactical', to very strategic.
- **Developmental focus**: from low to high relevance for developing individuals.
- **Organizational decision-making focus**: from low to high relevance for organizational decision-making processes.
- **Innovative**: from very traditional or conventional, to innovative and unorthodox.

Summary

In this chapter we moved from the individual to an organizational perspective, from a focus on psychology to a focus on management theory. The Career Active System Triad (CAST) framework was introduced and discussed in detail, representing the basis of organizational career systems.

Further, we dealt with career dynamism and how contemporary careers are significantly different from traditional style careers, in terms of both the practice and the strategy. A dominant theme was the need for flexibility, both as a strategic response and as a tool for gaining competitive advantage.

Dealing with new trends in managing organizations and people we discovered the blurring of boundaries, the advantages and possible perils (such as increased stress). Alternative work arrangements, 'New deals' and empowerment were presented as part of the new career system construct. Lastly, we looked at a method for evaluating career systems.

Key terms

- The CAST
- Organizational career systems
- Mergers
- Management buy-outs
- Strategic career management
- Flexibility
- Working hours
- Alternative work arrangements
- Telecommuting
- Multiple part-time work
- Moonlighting
- New deals
- Empowerment
- Litigious society
- Opinion surveys
- Exit interviews

DISCUSSION QUESTIONS

Class CAST exercise

Write down one of your career aspirations, try to analyse how it is reflected in your career attitudes, and point out an action you conducted as a result. Now compare your 'set' of three with the student who sits next to you.

Lessons and food for thought

1 *For HR managers*: Using the CAST concept, how would you distinguish between practices, policies (e.g. do you have a set of established policies?) and strategies (if they exist). Do you have an organizational strategy? Is there a match between this strategy and the HR strategy? Were they developed simultaneously?

2 *For the HR consultant*: What would be your advice to HR managers in developing a comprehensive approach to an organizational career system?

3 *For the HR teacher*: How would you integrate new forms of organizations (mergers and acquisitions, MBOs, new ventures, the virtual organization) in the traditional teaching of career systems?

4 *For the student*: What is the timespan of your career plan, and how far would you genuinely involve your organization in your career plan? How would you obtain involvement and commitment from your organization towards the development of your competencies and skills to ensure further advances in your career?

Review questions

1 Show how the psychological contract concept translates into actions in terms of your career-related behaviours.

2 In what ways would your university learn about how to improve its operations if it were to listen carefully to an *exit interview* which might be conducted with you after your studies? When will you be in the best position to provide fair and useful feedback – as soon as you finish? A couple of months later? Or further on in your career?

Critical thinking and ideas probing

1 If you are a student now looking for your first job, what are you looking for: a job; a career; an experience?

2 Which type of alternative work arrangements would you be ready and willing to adopt?

3 What would be a realistic career expectation, from your viewpoint, from: (a) your organization; (b) your direct manager?

4 What would empowerment mean for you in your job? What type of empowerment will you delegate to your subordinates?

Notes

[1]   Christensen, L.T. (1995) 'Buffering organizational identity in the marketing culture', *Organization Studies*, 16(4), 651–72; Hostager, T.J., Al-Khatib, J. and Dwyer, M.D. (1995) 'National, social and organizational identity: The effective managerial exploration of diversity', *International Journal of Management*, 12(3), 297–304; Elsbach, K.D. and Kramer, R.M. (1996) 'Members' responses to organizational identity threats: Encountering and countering the Business Week rankings', *Administrative Science Quarterly*, 41(3), 442–76.

[2]   Stapley, L. (1995) *The Personality of the Organization: A Psychodynamic Explanation of Culture and Change*, London: Free Association Books.

[3]   Dutton, J.E. and Dukerich, J.M. (1991) 'Keeping an Eye on the Mirror: Image and Identity in Organizational Adaptation', *Academy of Management Journal*, 34(3), 517–54.

[4]   Levinson, D.J. (1978) *The Seasons of Man's Life*, NY: Knopf.

[5]   Lipman-Blumen, J. and Leavitt, H.J. (1999) 'Hot groups "with attitude": A new organizational state of mind', *Organizational Dynamics*, 27(4), 63–73.

[6]   Roth, G. and Kleiner, A. (1998) 'Developing organizational memory through learning history', *Organizational Dynamics*, 27(2), 43–59.

[7]   Sutton, R.I. (1983) 'Managing organizational death', *Human Resource Management*, 22, 391–412.

[8]   DeFillippi, R.J. and Arthur, M.B. (1998) 'Paradox in project-based enterprise: The case of film making', *California Management Review*, 40(2), 125–39.

[9]   Hall, D.T. (1976) *Careers in Organizations*, Glenview, IL: Scott, Foresman; Hall, D.T. (1986) *Career Development in Organizations*, San Francisco: Jossey-Bass.

[10] Sparrow, P.R. (2000) 'New employee behaviors, work designs and forms of work organization: what is in store for the future of work?', *Journal of Managerial Psychology*, 15(3), 202–18.

[11] DeFillippi, R.J. and Arthur, M.B. (1994) 'The boundaryless career: a competency-based career perspective', *Journal of Organizational Behavior*, 15(4), 307–24.

[12] Cartwright, S. and Cooper, C. L. (1996) *Managing Mergers Acquisitions & Strategic Alliances*, 2nd edn, Oxford: Butterworth-Heinemann.

[13] Cartwright, S. and Cooper, C.L. (1993) 'The role of culture compatibility in successful organizational marriages', *Academy of Management Executive*, 7(2), 57–70.

[14] Wright, P.M., Thompson, S., Chiplin, B. and Robbie, K. (1991) *Buy-ins and Buy-Outs*, London: Graham & Trotman.

[15] Baruch, Y. and Gebbie, D. (1998) 'Cultures of success: the leading UK MBOs', *Journal of Business Venturing*, 13(5), 423–39.

[16] Devanna, M.A., Fombrun, C.J. and Tichy, N.M. (1981) 'Human Resource Management: Strategic Perspective', *Organizational Dynamics*, 9(3), 51–67; Fombrun, C.J., Tichy, N.M. and Devanna, M.A. (1984) *Strategic Human Resource Management*, NY: John Wiley & Sons, pp. 19–31; Beer, M., Spector, B., Lawrence, P.R., Mill, Q.D. and Walton, R. E. (1984) *Managing Human Assets*, NY: The Free Press; Salaman, G. (1992) *Human Resource Strategies*, London: Sage; Hendry, C. (1995) *Human Resource Management, A strategic approach to employment*, Oxford: Butterworth-Heinemann; Tyson, S. (1995) *Human Resource Strategy*, London: Pitman; Lundy, O. and Cowling, A. (1996) *Strategic Human Resource Management*, London: Routledge; Wright, P.M. and Snell, S.A. (1998) 'Toward a unifying framework for exploring fit and flexibility in

strategic human resource management', *Academy of Management Review*, 23(4), 756–72.

[17] Holbeche, L. (1999) *Aligning Human Resource and Business Strategy*, Oxford: Butterworth-Heinemann.

[18] Wernerfelt, B. (1984) 'A resource-based view of the firm', *Strategic Management Journal*, 5, 171–80; Prahalad, C.K. and Hamel, G. (1990) 'The core competence of the corporation', *Harvard Business Review*, 68(3), 79–91; Russo, M.V. and Foults, P.A. (1997) 'A resource-based perspective on corporate environmental performance and profitability', *Academy of Management Journal*, 40(3), 534–59.

[19] Grant, R.M. (1991) 'The resource-based theory of competitive advantage', *California Management Review*, 33(3), 114–35.

[20] Hoskisson, R., Hitt, M., Wan, W. and Yiu, D. (1999) 'Theory and research in strategic management: Swings of a pendulum', *Journal of Management*, 25(3), 417–56.

[21] Delaney, T.J. and Huselid, A.M. (1996) 'The impact of human resource management practices on perceptions of organizational performance', *Academy of Management Journal*, 39, 949–69; Harel, H.G. and Tzafrir, S.S. (1999) 'The effect of human resource management practices on the perceptions of organizational and market performance of the firm', *Human Resource Management*, 38(3), 185–99.

[22] Pfeffer, J. (1994) *Competitive advantage through people: Unleashing the power of the work force*, Boston: Harvard Business School Press; Pfeffer, J. (1998) *The Human Equation*, Boston: Harvard Business School Press.

[23] Meshoulam, I. and Baird, L. (1987) 'Proactive human resource management', *Human Resource Management*, 26(4), 483–502.

[24] Sonnenfeld, J.A. and Peiperl, M.A. (1988) 'Staffing Policy as a Strategic Response: A Typology of Career Systems', *Academy of Management Review*, 13(4), 568–600; Von Glinow, M.A., Driver, M.J., Brousseau, K. and Prince, J.B. (1983) 'The Design of a Career Oriented Human Resource System', *Academy of Management Review*, 8(1), 23–32.

[25] Lengnick-Hall, C.A. and Lengnick-Hall, M.L. (1988) 'Strategic HRM – a review of the literature and a proposed typology', *Academy of Management Review*, 13(3), 454–70.

[26] *See* note 9 above.

[27] *See* note 24 above.

[28] Miles, R.E. and Snow, C.C. (1978) *Organizational Strategy, Structure, and Process*, NY: McGraw-Hill.

[29] Sanchez, R. (1995) 'Strategic flexibility in product competition', *Strategic Management Journal*, 16, 135–9.

[30] *See* note 16 above.

[31] Birkinshaw, J. (2000) 'Network relationships inside and outside the firm, and the development of capabilities', in J. Birkinshaw and P. Hagstrom (eds) *The Flexible Firm*, Oxford: Oxford University Press, pp. 3–17.

[32] Srica, V. (1996) 'Innovation Management', *International Encyclopedia of Business and Management*, London: Thompson Int.

[33] Pollert, A. (1991) 'The Orthodoxy of Flexibility', in A. Pollert (ed.) *Farewell to Flexibility*, Oxford: Blackwell, pp. 3–31.

[34] Legge, K. (1995) *Human Resource Management – Rhetoric and Realities*, Basingstoke: Macmillan.

[35] Walsh, T. (1991) '"Flexible" employment in the retail and hotel trades', in A. Pollert (ed.) *Farewell to Flexibility*, Oxford: Blackwell, pp. 104–15.

[36] Noon, M. and Blyton, P. (1997) *The Realities of Work*, Basingstoke: Macmillan.

[37] Doganis, R. (1994) 'The impact of liberalization on European airline strategies and operations', *Journal of Air Transport Management*, 1(1), 15–25.

[38] De Meuse, K.P., Vanderheiden, P.A. and Bergmann, T.J. (1994) 'Announced layoffs: their effect on corporate financial performance', *Human Resource Management*, 33(4), 509–30.

[39] Brockner, J. (1992) 'Managing the Effects of Layoffs on Survivors', *California Management Review*, 34(2), 9–28; Brockner, J., Grover, S., Reed, T.F. and DeWitt, R.L. (1992) 'Layoffs, job insecurity, and survivors' work effort: Evidence of an inverted-U relationship', *Academy of Management Journal*, 35, 413–25; Brockner, J., Tyler, T.R. and Cooper-Schieder, R. (1992) 'The influence of prior commitment to institution on reactions to perceived unfairness: The higher they are, the harder they fall', *Administrative Science Quarterly*, 37, 241–61.

[40] Baruch, Y. and Hind, P. (1999) 'Perpetual Motion in Organizations: Effective Management and the impact of the new psychological contracts on "Survivor Syndrome"', *European Journal of Work and Organizational Psychology*, 8(2), 295–306; Baruch, Y. and Hind, P. (2000) 'The Survivor Syndrome: A management myth?', *Journal of Managerial Psychology*, 15(1), 29–41.

[41] Ashkenas, R., Ulrich, D., Jick T. and Kerr, S (1995) *The Boundaryless Organization*, San Francisco: Jossey-Bass.

[42] Baruch, Y. and Nicholson, N. (1997) 'Home, Sweet Work: requirements for effective home-working', *Journal of General Management*, 23(2), 15–30.

[43] Greer, C.R., Youngblood, S.A. and Gray, D.A. (1999) 'HR Outsourcing', *Academy of Management Executive*, 13(3), 85–96.

[44] Cartwright, S. and Cooper, C.L. (1997) *Managing Workplace Stress*, London: Sage.

[45] Hillriegel, D., Slocum, J.W. and Woodman, R.W. (1992) *Organizational Behavior*, 6th edn, St. Paul: West, p. 212.

[46] Murphy, L.R. (1988) 'Workplace interventions for stress reduction and prevention', in C.L. Cooper and R. Payne (eds) *Causes, Coping and Consequences of Stress at Work*, Chichester: Wiley.

[47] Cooper, C.L., Liukkonen, P. and Cartwright, S. (1996) *Stress Prevention in the Workplace*, Dublin: European Foundation.

[48] *See* note 44 above.

[49] Gottlieb, B.H., Kelloway, E.K. and Barham, E. (1998) *Flexible Work Arrangements*, Chichester: Wiley.

[50] Jones, J.C. (1957, 1958) 'Automation and Design', parts 1–5, *Design*, 103, 104, 106, 108 and 110.

[51] Toffler, A. (1980) *The Third Wave*, London: Collins.

[52] Kelly, M.M. (1985) 'The Next Workplace Revolution: Telecommuting', *Supervisory Management*, 30(10), 2–7; Davenport, T.H. and Pearlson, K. (1998) 'Two cheers for the virtual office', *Sloan Management Review*, 39(4), 51–65.

[53] *See* note 42 above.

[54] Evans, A. (1993) 'Working at Home: A New Career Dimension', *International Journal of Career Management*, 5(2), 16–23.

[55] Lobel, S.A., Googins, B.K. and Bankert, E. (1999) 'The future of work and family: critical trends for policy, practice, and research', *Human Resource Management*, 38(3), 243–54.

[56] Cette, G. (1999) *Le temps partiel en France*, Conceil d'Analyse Economique, La Documentation Francaise; Feldman, D.C. (1990) 'Reconceptualizing the nature and

consequences of part-time work', *Academy of Management Review*, 15, 103–12; Barling, J. and Gallagher, D. (1996) 'Part-time employment', in C.L. Cooper and I.T. Robertson (eds) *International Review of Industrial and Organizational Psychology*, London: Wiley and Sons, vol. II, pp. 243–77.

[57] Belous, R.S. (1989) *The contingent economy: The growth of the temporary, part-time and subcontracted workforce.* Washington, DC: National Planning Associates; Hipple, S. (1998) 'Contingent work: results from the second survey', *Monthly Labor Review*, November, 22–35.

[58] Bloch, L. and Galtier, B. (1999) 'Emplois et salaries a temps partiel en France', in G. Cette *Le temps partiel en France* Conceil d'Analyse Economique, La Documentation Francaise; Cette (1999), *see* note 56 above.

[59] Stinson, J.F. Jr. (March 1997) 'New data on multiple jobholding available from the CPS', *Monthly Labor Review* (USA Bureau of Labor Statistics), 3–8.

[60] Kimmel, J. and Powell, L.M. (1999) 'Moonlighting trends and related policy issues in Canada and the United States', *Canadian Public Policy*, 25(2), 207–31.

[61] *See* note 49 above.

[62] McDonald, D.J. and Makin, P.J. (1999) 'The psychological contract, organizational commitment and job satisfaction of temporary staff', *Leadership & Organization Development Journal*, 21(2), 84–91.

[63] Krausz, M., Sagie, A. and Bidermann, Y. (2000) 'Actual and preferred work schedules and scheduling control as determinants of job-related attitudes', *Journal of Vocational Behavior*, 56(1), 1–11.

[64] Matusik, S.F. and Hill, C.W. (1998) 'The utilization of contingent work, knowledge creation, and competitive advantage', *Academy of Management Review*, 23(4), 680–97.

[65] McClelland, D.C. (1985) *Human Motivation*, Glenview, IL: Scott Foresman.

[66] Atkinson, J. (1984) 'Manpower strategies for flexible organisations', *Personnel Management*, 16(8), 28–31.

[67] *See* note 49 above.

[68] Schein, E.H. (1978) *Career Dynamics: Matching Individual and Organizational Needs*, Reading, MA: Addison-Wesley.

[69] *See* note 24 above.

[70] Peiperl, M.A. and Baruch, Y. (1997) 'Back to square zero: the post-corporate career', *Organizational Dynamics*, 25(4), 7–22.

[71] Herriot, P. and Pemberton, C. (1996) 'Contracting careers', *Human Relations*, 49(6), 757–90.

[72] Furnham, A. (1997) *The Psychology of Behavior at Work*, Hove, UK: The Psychology Press; Folger, R. and Cropanzano, R. (1998) *Organizational Justice and Human Resource Management*, Thousand Oaks, CA: Sage; Greenberg, J. and Cropanzano, R. (eds) (2001) *Advances in Organizational Justice*, Stanford, CA: Stanford University Press.

[73] Cropanzano, R. and Greenberg, J. (1997) 'Progress in organizational justice', in C. Cooper and I. Robertson (eds) *International Review of Industrial and Organizational Psychology*, NY: Wiley.

[74] Iles, P. (1999) *Managing Staff Selection and Assessment*, Buckingham: Open University Press.

[75] BW (1997) 'Job mobility, American-style', *Business Week*, 27 January 1997, p. 20; WSJ (1997) 'Staying on the job', *Wall Street Journal*, 11 February 1997, p. A1.

[76] Hall, D.T. (1996) *The Career is Dead – Long Live the Career*, San Francisco: Jossey-Bass.

[77] Forbes, J.B. and Piercy, J.E. (1991) *Corporate Mobility and Paths to the Top*, NY: Quorum Books.

[78] Herriot, P. and Pemberton, C. (1995) *New Deals*, Chichester: John Wiley; Sullivan, S.E. (1999) 'The changing nature of careers: A review and research agenda', *Journal of Management*, 25(3), 457–84; Cascio, W.F. (2000) 'New Workplaces', in Jean M. Kummerow (ed.) *New Directions in Career Planning and the Workplace*, 2nd edn, Palo Alto, CA: Davies-Black Publishing.

[79] Rousseau, J.J. (1762, 1997) *The Social Contract*, Cambridge: Cambridge University Press. (Translation by V. Gourevitch.)

[80] *See* note 40 above.

[81] Spindler, G.S. (1994) 'Psychological contracts in the workplace – a lawyer's view', *Human Resource Management*, 33(3), 325–33.

[82] Hall, D.T. and Moss, J.E. (1998) 'The new Protean career contract: helping organizations and employees adapt', *Organizational Dynamics*, 26(3), 22–37.

[83] Handy, C. (1989) *The Age of Unreason*, London: Hutchinson.

[84] Hiltrop, J.-M. (1995) 'The changing psychological contract: The human resource challenge of the 1990s', *European Management Journal*, 13(3), 286–94.

[85] Shore, L.M. and Tetrick, L.E. (1994) 'The psychological contract as an explanatory framework in the employment relationship', *Journal of Organizational Behavior*, 1, Trends in OB supplement, 91–109.

[86] Robinson, S.L. and Morrison, E.W. (1995) 'Psychological contracts and OCB: The effect of unfulfilled obligation on civic virtue behavior', *Journal of Organizational Behavior*, 16(3), 289–98.

[87] *See* note 78 above.

[88] *See* note 39 above.

[89] DeFillippi and Arthur (1994), *see* note 11 above; Arthur, M.B. (1994) 'The boundaryless career: A new perspective for organizational inquiry', *Journal of Organizational Behavior*, 15(4), 295–306; Ashkenas *et al.* (1995), *see* note 41 above.

[90] Arthur, M.B., Claman, P.H. and DeFillippi, R.J. (1995) 'Intelligent enterprise, intelligent careers', *Academy of Management Executive*, 9(4), 7–22.

[91] Waterman, R.H. Jr., Waterman, J.A. and Collard, B.A. (1994) 'Toward a career-resilient workforce', *Harvard Business* Review, 72(4), 87–95; Peiperl and Baruch (1997), *see* note 70 above.

[92] Herriot, P. and Stickland, R. (1999) 'The Management of Careers: Introduction', Special issue of *European Journal of Organization and Work Psychology*.

[93] Baruch, Y. (1998) 'Walking the Tightrope: Strategic Issues for Human Resources', *Long Range Planning*, 31(3), 467–75.

[94] Weick, K.E. (2001) *Making Sense of the Organization*, Oxford: Blackwell.

[95] Vecchio, R.P. (1995) *Organizational Behavior*, 3rd edn, Fort Worth: The Dryden Press.

[96] *See* Clemense, J.K. and Mayer, D.F. (1987) *The Classic Touch*, Homewood, IL: Dow Jones-Irwin.

[97] Malone, T.W. (1997) 'Is empowerment just a fad? Control, decision making and IT', *Sloan Management Review*, Winter, 23–35.

[98] Hales, C. (2000) 'Management and Empowerment Programmes', *Work, Employment & Society*, 14(3), 501–19.

[99] Conger, J.A. and Kanungo, R.N. (1988) 'The empowerment process: Integrating theory and practice', *Academy of Management Review*, 13(3), 471–82.

[100] Thomas, K.W. and Velthouse, B.A. (1990) 'Cognitive elements of empowerment: An "interpretative" model of intrinsic task motivation', *Academy of Management Review*, 15, 666–81.

[101] *See* note 93 above.

[102] Cappelli, P. and Crocker-Hefter, A. (1996) 'Distinctive human resource are firms' core competencies', *Organizational Dynamics*, 23(4), 7–22.

[103] Baruch, Y. (1998b) 'Empowerment Models in Organizations', *Career Development International*, 3(2), 82–7.

[104] Cuming, M.W. (1986) *Personnel Management*, London: Heinemann.

[105] *See* note 103 above.

[106] Baruch, Y. and Rosenstein, E. (1992) 'Career planning and managing in high tech organizations', *International Journal of Human Resource Management*, 3(3), 477–96.

[107] Baruch, Y. (1996) 'Career Planning and Managing Techniques in Use', *Career Development International*, 1(1), 43–52.

[108] Storey, J. (1995) 'Human resource management: still marching on, or marching out?', in J. Storey (ed.) *Human Resource Management: A Critical Text*, London: Routledge, pp. 3–32.

[109] Baruch, Y. (1997) 'Evaluating quality and reputation of Human Resource Management', *Personnel Review*, 27(5), 377–94.

[110] Tsui, A.S. (1987) 'Defining the practices and Effectiveness of the Human Resource Department: A Multiple Constituency Approach', *Human Resource Management*, 26(1), 35–69; Tsui, A.S. (1990) 'A Multiple-Constituency Model of Effectiveness: An Empirical Examination at the Human Resource Subunit Level', *Administrative Science Quarterly*, 35, 458–83.

[111] Florkowski, G.W. and Schuler, R.S. (1994) 'Auditing Human Resource Management in the Global Environment', *International Journal of Human Resource Management*, 5, 827–51.

[112] Harrison, M.I. (1987) *Diagnosing Organizations*, Newbury Park, CA: Sage.

[113] Townley, B. (1994) *Reframing Human Resource Management*, London: Sage.

[114] http://ourworld.compuserve.com/homepages/gately/pp15js00.htm

[115] Baruch, Y. and Peiperl, M.A. (2000) 'The Impact of an MBA on Graduates' Career', *Human Resource Management Journal*, 10(2), 69–90.

[116] Baruch, Y. (2003) 'Career systems in transition: A normative model for organizational career practices', *Personnel Review*, in press.

[117] *See* note 16 above.

[118] *See* note 102 above.

[119] *See* note 22 above.

[120] Mitchell, T.R. and Beach, L.R. (1977) 'Expectancy theory, decision theory, and occupational preference and choice', in M.F. Kaplan and S. Schwartz (eds) *Human Judgment and Decision Process in Applied Settings*, NY: Academic Press; Nutt, P.C. (1999) 'Surprising but true: Half the decisions in organizations fail', *Academy of Management Executive*, 13, 75–90.

Appendix 4.1
Psychological contract exercise*

The short questionnaire below is intended to help you in formulating your 'most preferred New Deal' in employment. It is hoped that filling it in will lead you to a better understanding of the ways in which individuals and their employing organizations can develop mutually rewarding relationships in the future.

Should you expect your future organization to fulfil **all** your needs? Certainly not! Yet, we hope that our organization will meet some of our most important needs. The table below asks you to compare a list of possible expectations that you wish your future organization to fulfil with what you actually expect in practice. Perhaps only a few of the options are important to you, and you will try to build your relationship with the organization around them. Do not expect your employer to meet all your expectations, just as you would not expect a partner to meet all your needs within one relationship.

Please circle the number that best represents your answer (1 being the lowest, 7 the highest).

What I want	Expectation	What I am reasonably expecting
1 2 3 4 5 6 7	professional challenge	1 2 3 4 5 6 7
1 2 3 4 5 6 7	filling in my time	1 2 3 4 5 6 7
1 2 3 4 5 6 7	shelter from family/spouse demands	1 2 3 4 5 6 7
1 2 3 4 5 6 7	learning environment	1 2 3 4 5 6 7
1 2 3 4 5 6 7	emotional support	1 2 3 4 5 6 7
1 2 3 4 5 6 7	social companionship	1 2 3 4 5 6 7
1 2 3 4 5 6 7	skill development	1 2 3 4 5 6 7
1 2 3 4 5 6 7	opportunity to manage others	1 2 3 4 5 6 7
1 2 3 4 5 6 7	opportunity to be managed	1 2 3 4 5 6 7
1 2 3 4 5 6 7	financial provider	1 2 3 4 5 6 7
1 2 3 4 5 6 7	source of inspiration	1 2 3 4 5 6 7
1 2 3 4 5 6 7	social status	1 2 3 4 5 6 7
1 2 3 4 5 6 7	career aspiration	1 2 3 4 5 6 7
1 2 3 4 5 6 7	job security	1 2 3 4 5 6 7
1 2 3 4 5 6 7	open communication	1 2 3 4 5 6 7
1 2 3 4 5 6 7	professional development	1 2 3 4 5 6 7
1 2 3 4 5 6 7	personal guidance	1 2 3 4 5 6 7
1 2 3 4 5 6 7	good working conditions	1 2 3 4 5 6 7
1 2 3 4 5 6 7	source of motivation	1 2 3 4 5 6 7
1 2 3 4 5 6 7	life structure	1 2 3 4 5 6 7
1 2 3 4 5 6 7	safe working environment	1 2 3 4 5 6 7
1 2 3 4 5 6 7	feeling needed and valued	1 2 3 4 5 6 7
1 2 3 4 5 6 7	fair treatment	1 2 3 4 5 6 7
1 2 3 4 5 6 7	increased employability	1 2 3 4 5 6 7
1 2 3 4 5 6 7	honesty in dealing with me	1 2 3 4 5 6 7

You may add here any other expectations you have, not mentioned above:

....

Similarly, should you expect yourself to fulfil **all** your organization's requirements? Again, certainly not. This table asks you to compare what the organization may expect from you and what you are actually planning to give in return. As before, do not expect yourself to meet all the expectations in the relationship.

What may be expected from me	Organizational expectation	What I will actually give
1 2 3 4 5 6 7	high-quality performance	1 2 3 4 5 6 7
1 2 3 4 5 6 7	long hours	1 2 3 4 5 6 7
1 2 3 4 5 6 7	commitment	1 2 3 4 5 6 7
1 2 3 4 5 6 7	desire and ability to learn	1 2 3 4 5 6 7
1 2 3 4 5 6 7	emotional support to others	1 2 3 4 5 6 7
1 2 3 4 5 6 7	punctuality	1 2 3 4 5 6 7
1 2 3 4 5 6 7	be a source of motivation to others	1 2 3 4 5 6 7
1 2 3 4 5 6 7	maintain a safe working environment	1 2 3 4 5 6 7
1 2 3 4 5 6 7	being managed	1 2 3 4 5 6 7
1 2 3 4 5 6 7	managing others	1 2 3 4 5 6 7
1 2 3 4 5 6 7	represent the organization positively	1 2 3 4 5 6 7
1 2 3 4 5 6 7	be flexible	1 2 3 4 5 6 7
1 2 3 4 5 6 7	develop the organization	1 2 3 4 5 6 7
1 2 3 4 5 6 7	open communication	1 2 3 4 5 6 7
1 2 3 4 5 6 7	be a good 'organizational citizen'	1 2 3 4 5 6 7
1 2 3 4 5 6 7	loyalty	1 2 3 4 5 6 7
1 2 3 4 5 6 7	honesty in dealing with them	1 2 3 4 5 6 7

You may add here any other expectations you have, not mentioned above:

....

* The questionnaire was developed by Yehuda Baruch from the University of East Anglia and Patricia Hind from Ashridge Management College.

5 The dynamic nature of career management

LEARNING OBJECTIVES

After reading this chapter you should be able to:

- Understand the nature of career dynamics.
- Be acquainted with the career as metaphor.
- Critically analyse labour markets.

CHAPTER CONTENTS

Question

The DilbertZone is a website renowned for its sharp cynicism, in all areas of management, in particular in the management of people, including, of course, the career area. Below are two comments (adapted from the DilbertZone), that manifest a high level of career cynicism:

- Have you ever noticed how the words 'loyal' and 'layoff' sound similar but mean the opposite?
- PHBs (Pointed Hair Bosses) at our consulting firm think that announcing pay

cuts, layoffs, imaginary reward systems and fewer promotions will help retain the 'good' people. Yeah, as in 'good' bye!

How will you feel about your employer if you experience a high level of exploitation and readiness to shed jobs without further thought for the well-being of employees? How will this affect your commitment and loyalty?

Transitions

This chapter deals with the implications of environmental and organizational changes on career systems. Peiperl and Baruch (1997)[1] considered past and current career models and set out a vision of future careers that differs from past careers. They highlighted one primary attribute of this change – the existence of horizontal links that transcend organizational and systems boundaries, including geographical ones. As these links continue to develop, they will provide more opportunity and flexibility than was ever available under previous systems. The new rules of the game would best fit those who have the competencies – mostly knowledge and skills – to take advantage of them, and those who will be proactive.

Organizations have always been subject to change and cutbacks, and individuals within them were subject to competition and, occasionally, layoffs. The difference now relates to the scope and pace of the phenomenon – the number of organizations whose career systems have been thrown into disarray, and the number of people affected, seem to have reached a critical mass. It is now the norm, rather than the exception, for organizations to have no fixed career paths and for individuals in them to see no further than a few years ahead, if that, in their own careers. We can no longer depend upon career tracks (themselves subject to stable organizational structures) to ensure that we progress merely because we are competent and work hard. And many people who came into their organizations with an expectation of such career progress are learning this lesson the hard way.

Organizations just cannot offer any longer a commitment and loyalty-based relationship, thus moving to a transactional relationship or trying to generate relational relationships based on transformational leadership. One of the novel ideas of developing transactional relationship is the concept of employability which, Baruch (2001)[2] argues, will benefit individuals, but can hardly serve as a substitute for loyalty on the organizational side of the equation.

The idea of employability has emerged as employers deserted the old deals. To keep a balance in the relationship, employability has come to offer people a different kind of psychological contract so that they will feel a fair deal exists, so that they will not feel betrayed. The organization can no longer afford to offer (or to promise) people a stable workplace and a long-term commitment to employment. In the information age this should be understandable. To replace this traditional notion, an alternative promise is to be made – people will receive 'employability'. As part of the new deal, the organization makes a fresh promise: We will invest in you, make you attractive for other employers so that if you have to leave (i.e. when we fire you), you will be able to find a new job easily. To put it bluntly, this is the essence of employability, according to many who have written of the concept (e.g. Byron, 1995; Fagiano, 1993; Ghoshal, Bartlett and Moran, 1999; MacLachlan, 1996; Martin, 1995; Skoch, 1994; Waterman, Waterman and Collard, 1994).[3] These scholars and others have rightly suggested that once organizational changes, in particular those due to the global competitive market, took place, it was not feasible to stick to the former relationship. There is an imbalance in the relationship. The solution, they argue, is for the organization to offer employability in the psychological contract. However, the present workforce consists of sophisticated, highly educated people. For them, employability can also be read as: in the future we will prepare you for the next round of restructuring, when you will be made redundant. This fits well with the cynicism presented at the start of this chapter (Baruch, 2001).[4]

Figures 5.1 to 5.4 show the dynamic nature of HRM and career systems.

Question

How will you check whether or not you gained employability, working for your present employer?

The practical answer should alarm HR managers who believe in employability as an incentive the organization has to provide: the ultimate way to check one's own employability is to apply for a different job! This way the person will know whether they can indeed be easily employed. The peril of this exercise, for the present organization, is that the 'test' can be so successful that the employee will decide to accept a job offer.

In a workshop done in a leading business school for bank executives, about half of them (all mid–senior-level managers) admitted that during the last year they had applied for different jobs elsewhere, not intending to accept the offer, but just to see if they would be offered the job. Of course, the executives participating in the training, were still employed by the bank. We cannot know how many others had tried and succeeded in the test, and had already left.

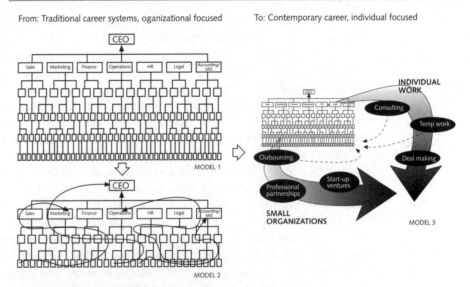

Figure 5.1 The transformation of career planning

Source: Reprinted from M.A. Peiperl and Y. Baruch (1997) 'Back to square zero: the post-corporate career', *Organizational Dynamics*, 25(4), 7–22, copyright 1997, with permission from Elsevier Science.

Figure 5.1 implies that a sea change is needed in organizational career systems, in particular in the planning element. Many unpredictable elements enter the equation. The diversity of options requires the HR manager to have excellent networks not merely within the organization but also in the relevant labour market environment, to anticipate both possible departures and either likely or imaginable options for replacement and alternative resourcing. On the other hand, even with the end of conventional thinking about career ladders, a hierarchy still exists in medium and large organizations. Exploring new options does not mean fully abandoning the traditional system that is still applicable for a vast number of people.

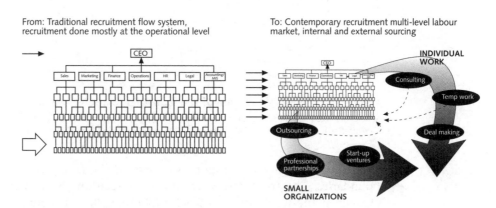

From: Traditional recruitment flow system, recruitment done mostly at the operational level

To: Contemporary recruitment multi-level labour market, internal and external sourcing

Figure 5.2 The transformation of recruitment

Source: Reprinted from M.A. Peiperl and Y. Baruch (1997) 'Back to square zero: the post-corporate career', *Organizational Dynamics*, 25(4), 7–22, copyright 1997, with permission from Elsevier Science.

Figure 5.2 emerges as a direct consequence of the implications of Figure 5.1. The traditional recruitment flow for most organizations was into the entry level, for both rank-and-file and managerial posts. Occasionally a few managerial openings would occur at higher levels, a few in particular at the top executive level. The Sonnenfeld and Peiperl (1988)[5] model depicts it as a 'supply flow', that is, a source of new employees. The flow can be internal (only or mostly from the lower grades), or external – at all hierarchy levels. The transformational model depicted in Figure 5.2 indicates that the trend is towards an external supply flow, due not necessarily to choice but to necessity, as the dynamics of careers enforce a need to re-fill positions at all levels when necessary. Individuals taking control of their own careers do not have the traditional barriers that force them to stay within the organization, thus may leave at any time.

While Ghoshal, Bartlett and Moran (1999) and Hammer and Champy (1993) argue for the need to cut the number of managerial levels, in practice organizational control mechanisms still rely heavily on hierarchy and lines of authority.[6] In addition people depend on these levels to re-establish their own identities and achievement levels. In any case, career entry points are now spread fairly evenly throughout existing managerial levels. As a result there is a growing need to acquire managers at all levels of management in organizations.

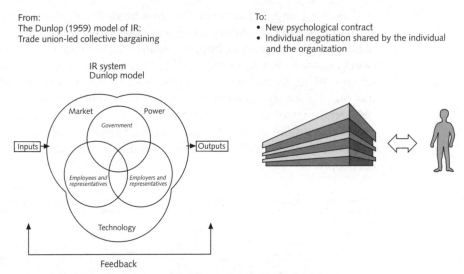

Figure 5.3 The transformation of the industrial relations system

Source: Reprinted from M.A. Peiperl and Y. Baruch (1997) 'Back to square zero: the post-corporate career', *Organizational Dynamics*, 25(4), 7–22, copyright 1997, with permission from Elsevier Science.

Figure 5.3 posits a stimulating perspective for US, European and other national boundaries. The transition of employment relations is apparent although the change in the legal and industrial relations system is conventionally slow to respond to fast environmental, sociological and organizational developments. From the traditional Dunlop model (1959)[7] of simplicity and a structured relationship of identifiable players at the three representative levels (employees' representation, organizations and governments) there is a transition to the ambiguous and multivariate level of analysis depicted in Figure 5.3 as the 'fluid' model. The new model clearly distinguishes negotiation between the organization and the individual and the distance between core and peripheral employees. The New Deal model is obviously distinct from the traditional one. Negotiation now takes place between several constituencies of the organization: management (and HR representing the organization) and individuals on both 'hard' issues of payment and conditions as well as 'soft' elements of employability, commitment and investment in people (e.g. competencies). There is a difference between core and peripheral employees, and some negotiations are conducted with external agencies and sub-contractors responsible for outsourced work. In most cases unions have lost their wide and strong powers. However, there is an interesting aspect of the change in labour markets. Traditionally trade unions had a strong hold in manufacturing and public service industries (e.g. government bodies). As the share of public services rises, paradoxically union membership grows also. Nevertheless, the bargaining power that derives from the ability to strike has become less of a threat to employers. In 2000 Ford warned workers in its European plants that strikes would lead to the closure of plants. In October 2002, Fiat, the Italian car manufacturer, announced that it would lay off one-fifth of its 40 000-strong workforce due to overcapacity (the demand for Fiat cars is about two million a year, while the firm can produce well over three million cars a year). The car workers' union could not object to such realities of the market, and only try to negotiate a better deal for those leaving. Cheap labour on a global scale elsewhere has posed a dilemma for trade unions – if they play too hard they might lose the whole employment deal. The trend towards individualism also means that the legal aspects of industrial relations are dealt with more often via individual contracting than via collective bargaining.

Psychological theory would suggest that individuals affected might feel bitter towards organizations for changing the comfortable and uncomplicated structure of the conventional hierarchy. They might lament the loss of the recognition and appreciation of loyalty and commitment which this hierarchy provided.

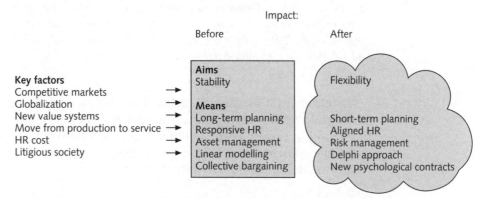

Figure 5.4 The transformation of strategic HR planning: an emergent model

Source: Reprinted from M.A. Peiperl and Y. Baruch (1997) 'Back to square zero: the post-corporate career', *Organizational Dynamics*, 25(4), 7–22, copyright 1997, with permission from Elsevier Science.

Figure 5.4 depicts the influence of several factors on strategic HRM planning and consequently on a long-term career system development. The outcome is a move from familiar and approachable systems characterized by stability and enabling long-term planning, to vagueness and ambiguity, resulting in short-term planning.

Career dynamism

> Beginning to reason is like stepping onto an escalator that leads upwards and out of sight. Once we take the first step, the distance to be travelled is independent of our will and we cannot know in advance where we shall end.
>
> Peter Singer (1982)[50]

We live in exciting times. The realities of the workplace can be harsh, but can bring thrills and enthusiasm to people and organizations. Change makes life interesting, as the old Chinese proverb says.

Cascio (2000, citing Bulkeley, 1998 and Ulrich, 1998)[8] listed six key business trends that inflict changes in the world of work. These are globalization, technology, change, intellectual capital, speed of market change, and cost control. To these we can add continuing socioeconomic developments and individual consciousness, discussed earlier.

EXHIBIT 5.1	360 degrees – an indication of the dynamism in career system practices

360-degree feedback will be discussed in Chapter 6, but it serves as a good example of the dynamism of developments in both the theory and practice of HR, with implications for career systems.

Performance appraisal (PA) grew out of organizations' need for a more objective measure than informal managerial networking for managing people (e.g. for promotion, training needs, etc.). PA provided feedback on employees' input and contributions, as well as their needs. But PA was based on a single source of information, and suffered from poor reliability and invalid measurement. In the early 1990s researchers were advocating 360-degree feedback (e.g. *see* Tornow, London *et al.*, 1998).[9] By the end of the 1990s some misgivings have been raised, and HR faces new challenges (*see* Chapter 6).

A philosophical perspective on the basis for change may focus on the shift from a collectivist to an individualistic society (reflected, in the career context, in Hall's protean career). Post-modern values reflect this shift. People develop high individual consciousness, with a pre-eminent focus on individualism and concern with self (Singer, 1997; Wolfe, 1998).[10]

Question	What can and should organizations do to help and promote positive development, and at the same time identify and prevent negative deterioration? What, then, would you advise line managers and HR executives about how to approach the new realities of organizational career systems? In what way did the understanding of the individual perspective (presented in Chapters 2 and 3) help you in reaching your conclusions?

Implications for organizations

In managing careers organizations should start looking for different models. They need to realize that one should no longer act as if the old notion of organizational commitment and loyalty is valid and applicable. Greater awareness of the multiple commitments employees have is necessary and especially the decreasing importance of organizational commitment within these multiple commitments. Organizations can no longer ask for too much (and expecting full commitment to the organization is probably too much). Moreover, long-term stable relationships are not longer valid. Major and rapid changes characterize both individuals and organization.

Lewin's field theory (1951)[11] was useful for describing and analysing changes in a relatively stable period. He suggested that there are three basic stages for any change. Change should be perceived as occurring in a field of forces, in which 'push' and 'pull' forces operate in different directions. For a change to occur there needs to be a 'de-freezing' stage, then change develops, and this is followed by a final stage of 're-freezing', leading back to stability, till a further need arises, which will occasion the next change. The model works well (i.e. has strong explanatory power) within a time frame that allows the three stages, ending with re-freezing, to occur. However, today it seems that organizations are subject to constant changes that do not permit any re-freezing. Fluidity rules. Some thirty years ago, in his book *Future Shock*, Toffler (1970)[12] warned that there was a feeling that the rate of change was accelerating, and that 'change was out of control'.

Peiperl and Baruch (1997)[13] describe how career systems develop. In man's earliest days, all had similar roles, that of the hunter-gatherer. Nicholson (1998, 2000)[14] claims that the ways of thinking and feelings developed in those days are still deeply rooted in our cognitive map. Later, even when civilization started to flourish, there was no career system for most of the population: the vast majority of people worked on the land, in workshops or primitive industries, and generally did so near their homes. Careers and their management is a relatively modern phenomenon. Peiperl and Baruch show how models of careers have evolved, with an interesting return to 'square zero', but not literally – perhaps it has been more of a spiral than a circular development.

EXHIBIT 5.2	### Hidden work

Hidden work is work that takes place outside the legal system. It is usually undertaken by individuals (but is sometimes arranged in syndicates). Hidden work is prominent in some Eastern Europe countries, following the collapse of communism. In Western societies much money moves through illegal drug trading, a relatively new sector among the many 'traditional' sectors of hidden employment. Hidden work is understudied for obvious reasons, in particular accessibility, but deserves more attention (Noon and Blyton, 1997).[15]

The majority of people, however, are engaged in conventional employment, where paradigms are changing.

Perpetual motion

The survivor syndrome

In a time of recurrent changes, what can replace the old paradigms and how do organizations manage the processes concerned with motivating people and keeping their commitment when job security is no longer a valid concept? With the old paradigms and concepts no longer relevant, the challenge is to get the best out of people in a new framework. The term 'Survivor Syndrome' has been coined to refer to and describe the reaction of people who remain in employment after an organization has undergone a redundancy or downsizing programme. It has been argued that those who stay in an organization often experience the adverse effects of change as profoundly as those who have left (Brockner, 1992; Astrachan, 1995).[16] Scholars have suggested a multitude of negative consequences of survivor syndrome: for example, O'Neil and Lenn (1995)[17] argued that inappropriate redundancy will end in anger, anxiety, cynicism, resentment, resignation and retribution. Job insecurity and fear of further restructuring are factors acknowledged as adding to stress in the workplace (cf. Hartley *et al.*, 1991).[18] To these negative effects Downs (1995)[19] added low morale, overworking and the possibility of sabotage. The impact on survivors can be destructive: Church (1995) in the USA, cited in Jackson (1997), and Doherty and Horsted (1995) in the UK found a dysfunctional impact on commitment, loyalty and performance (*see also* Brockner *et al.*, 1992; Baruch, 1998; Baruch and Hind, 2000; Mowday, 1999).[20] Another prominent writer on downsizing, Cameron (1994, 1996)[21] has cited overload, burnout, inefficiency, conflict and low morale as possible negative consequences of survivor syndrome. Businesses that understand these attitudinal and motivational issues will be able to manage the process in order to enhance the performance of these survivors and thus of the organization (Doherty and Horsted, 1995).[22]

As Baruch and Hind (1999)[23] state, organizations must overcome the psychological transition from 'It won't happen here' to 'When is it going to happen?'

How to manage the survivor syndrome

When an organization is considering specific factors to focus on in order to preserve employee morale during downsizing, Mishra, Spreitzer and Mishra (1998)[24] suggest the following:

1 Deciding: use downsizing as a last resort; construct a credible vision, based on the business case; and ensure downsizing is not seen as a short-term fix.
2 Planning: form a cross-functional team, who are agreed on the reasons for downsizing, identify all constituents and address their concerns, use experts such as outplacement counsellors to smooth the transition, provide training to managers and supply adequate information on the state of the business.
3 Making the announcement: explain the business rationale, announce the decision, notify employees in advance where possible, be specific, time the announcement appropriately, offer employees the day off.
4 Implementing the decisions: tell the truth and even over-communicate, provide job search assistance for leavers, announce subsequent separations as planned, be fair in implementing separations, be generous to leavers, allow for voluntary separation, involve employees in implementation, provide career counselling and train the survivors where necessary.

Baruch and Hind (1999)[25] argue that, although detailed, the above list is lacking in two respects. First, it consists of a set of separate, dissociated issues, and does not provide a coherent, comprehensive framework (which they produce – *see below*, Figure 5.5). Second, several key elements are missing. Mishra *et al.* ignore the trade union issue – perhaps because they refer mostly to the US private sector. For this reason their advice may be of little help in organizations with unionized and protected labour. This may be a critical factor, as many employees may view the new psychological contract as a threat. Another factor omitted, again perhaps of crucial importance, is the provision of counselling to survivors as well as leavers. Often, counselling is offered only to those exiting the organization. One of the most important elements in a downsizing programme is the perception of the process used to select those to be made redundant (Jackson, 1997).[26] The selection needs to be based on clear, performance- and operational-related criteria, with obvious links to the business case and rationale. 'Best Practice' should be implemented in managing downsizing. It is also important to implement decisions swiftly.

Figure 5.5 presents a flow-chart diagram of downsizing/redundancy, representing the options and their determinants. The figure suggests a sequence that organizations should anticipate in managing the survivor syndrome effect. What is to be expected, then, and what should be done?

The first stage is characterized by relative stability and traditional psychological contracts. Such conditions represent utopia in the industrial world, but may still exist in certain sectors or some developing countries. If an organization has managed to maintain a feeling of stability and the 'Old deal', any deviation will cause survivor syndrome, argue Baruch and Hind. However, in most business environments, 'perpetual change' is already the new way of life. For example, most large organizations, and the vast majority of *Fortune 500* companies, have already gone through redundancy cycles (e.g. in the five years 1987–91, 85 per cent of *Fortune 500* companies suffered massive redundancies, according to Cameron, 1994).[27]

If a state of perpetual change is not recognized, organizations must first create awareness of the concept of a 'fast-changing environment'. Generating an atmosphere of urgency enables people to go through a transformation process, which will permit them to operate and perform while realizing that they are doing so in a 'perpetual change' mode.

In the following stage (characterized by perpetual change, which is recognized by both employees and management), the organization should develop a new psychological contract. This in itself is necessary, but not sufficient. The next stage

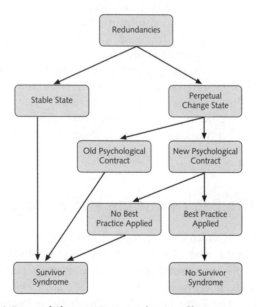

Figure 5.5 Downsizing and the surviver syndrome effect

Source: Y. Baruch and P. Hind (1999) 'Perpetual motion in organizations: Effective management and the impact of the new psychological contracts on "Survivor Syndrome"', *European Journal of Work and Organizational Psychology*, 8(2), p. 297.

is using 'best practice'. Only when all three pre-conditions are met, may the organization hope to avoid the survivor syndrome, according to Baruch and Hind.

Best practice indeed? Are there do's and don'ts for downsizing?

What is best practice? Is there one general 'best practice' or are there many possibilities? Several scholars, practitioners as well as academics, have suggested various concepts to use in developing 'best practice'. Given the existence of so many sets of conditions, environments and other antecedents, more than one contingency should be considered to achieve a smooth process and to minimize the survivor syndrome effect. Chapter 6 provides a general framework for 'best practice' in terms of general career planning and management practices. Regarding downsizing, the advice for organizations is to use redundancy only as a last resort. It is advisable to prove to or show employees that it was indeed the last resort, after all feasible options have been tried. Such options or alternative practices include:

- early retirement;
- reducing or halting recruitment for a limited period (but not for too long, otherwise organizations will have a 'missing a generation' in the future);
- selling part of the company (e.g. via a buy-out);
- job-sharing.

Of course, when it eventually implements the process the organization should be supportive towards leavers, help in their job search, provide training and career counselling (*see* Chapter 6), etc.

Question

An example of worst practice.

It is clear that communication has a lot to do with the way a message about redundancy is delivered. The short history of mass redundancies tells us how employees heard about the demise of their job via the media – be it television, radio or newspaper article! Perhaps the worst way to deliver the message was demonstrated in May 2003 when thousands of Accident Group employees in the UK received a text message(!) telling them about cancellation of pay day, and asking them to call a number where most where told about losing their job.

Can you think of a more humane and dignified manner to deliver such a message?

The Peter Principle and organizational career systems

The art of ensuring people are effective is the principal role of career systems. In the past, one of the most problematic obstacles to the effective management of people and consequently to organizational effectiveness was the Peter Principle. It was seen as a valid concept in the traditional hierarchy-based organizational structure. The Peter Principle is simple: in a bureaucracy, employees progress up the hierarchy until they reach their level of incompetence, i.e. where their performance is unsatisfactory, and at that level they will stay. This paradoxical idea is found in many organizations where people progress 'up the ladder', where tenure is the most significant factor in decisions on promotion and where redundancies are rare.

Where the Peter Principle applies, organizational effectiveness deteriorates. This was particularly true in many rigid organizations, and was an unfortunate phenomenon while job security was the rule. The change in industrial relations systems and the loss of job security have meant that the Peter Principle has become less of a threat to organizations. People who cannot function according to their level of responsibility and authority have to leave, as the ICL case (*see* Figure 5.6 below) depicts.

Like Parkinson's Law (i.e. that bureaucracy grows irrespective to the need of their services), and stripped of its humorous elements, the concept is disturbing due to its valid reflection of real-life situations. The lack of an option to get rid of 'dead-wood' made the Peter Principle a fact of life in the 1950s to 1970s. However, the changing nature of HRM and career management created a different climate. Those incapable of performing, unfit to perform well in a position, can no longer maintain that position. Lateral and even downward movement became feasible, and redundancies became the norm.

Rothwell (1995)[28] associates HR planning with careful career planning, and even more important, with corporate policy towards career-matched policies and approach. She cites Beattie and Tampoe's (1990)[29] description of the revised operational and HR strategy of ICL, a large UK-based corporation which developed a manpower/career planning framework that aimed to implement a 80 : 20 insider : outsider ratio of managers. (In fact the company has a preference for employing internal labour.) The programme was based on segregating internal labour into the following segments: a fast stream, a slower stream, the 'right level' group (for lateral movement) and the Peter Principle group, the latter destined to look for employment elsewhere.

Figure 5.6 depicts the meaning of organizations becoming lean and mean: no more room for 'fat' or reserves; no options left for people who are not performing to their best. The luxury of maintaining slack means less competitiveness, and organizations cannot afford this.

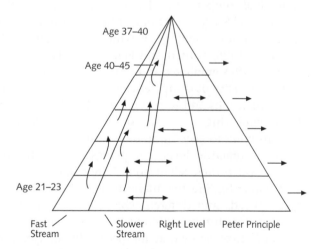

Figure 5.6 Providing different career patterns

Source: Reprinted from D.F. Beattie and F.M.K. Tampoe (1990) 'Human resource planning for ICI', *Long Range Planning*, 23(1), p. 21, copyright 1990, with permission from Elsevier Science.

| EXHIBIT 5.3 | **Abandoning the system – the case of Oticon** |

Oticon, a Danish high-tech firm in the hearing-aid industry (the third largest in the world), went through a radical change in the early 1990s. This came via a new leadership vision, which followed budget and operational crises (Larsen, 1996)[30] for the company, which employs 4000 people (1300 of whom are in Denmark). They abandoned the traditional hierarchy, cut out the entire managerial structure, and established a project-based firm, a fluid organizational structure (DeFillippi and Arthur, 1998).[31] The implications for the career management system were overwhelming (Larsen, 2002).[32] In the new career development system there was no rigid, and hardly any structure at all. Each staff member could become a project leader, and at the same time retain a position as project member in other projects. There was only one layer of top management, with no intermediate level. A few former experienced managers have become 'centres of professional expertise'. This led at first to certain feelings of a lack of HRM input, therefore a new type of role was introduced – that of 'coaches', to serve as mentors and holding HR responsibility. This framework requires people to match their career expectations to a totally different system, and many in **Oticon** felt they could not go through such a change and left. The rest, however, continue to make **Oticon** a success story.

Qualities dynamism

In the past what mattered was having formal qualifications. Competencies, and even more, the ability to learn, have taken the place of qualifications. Self-efficacy, self-esteem and resilience are the basis of the successful career path for the new careerist.

One of the most crucial core competencies of organizations is the knowledge of their employees. People strive and build their success on knowledge and other individual competencies. These can be professional/vocational related, or managerial. Table 5.1 lists a set of competencies that individuals may gain from managerial education, and all of which are sought by MBA graduates (Baruch and Leeming, 1996; Baruch and Peiperl, 2000b).[33] The table also shows differences between MBA graduates and non-MBA managers on these competencies.

The diversity of competencies possessed by individuals enables them to flourish in their jobs and to survive in a tough labour market. At the organizational level, employing a diversity of employees will be of benefit. It is a managerial responsibility to keep up to date with labour market trends.

At the practical level, companies wishing to ensure a diversity of qualities should widen their talent pool. Here demographic diversity can help (for which *see* Chapter 8). Effective management of diversity requires the harnessing of the special needs and different characteristics of different people, which may be associated with their different life and career stages. Chapter 6 presents, among other practices, some that are specifically directed towards particular groups, e.g., dual-career couples, the pre-retirement population or high-flyers. Career plans need to incorporate the singular qualities of all individual members of the organization. Succession planning (*see* Chapter 6) provides an example: in a well-

Table 5.1 Competencies and managerial education

| | Perceived Competence | | |
	MBAs	Others	Sig
1. Effective reading	5.32	4.93	**
2. Oral presentations	5.21	4.83	**
3. Written presentations	5.54	5.04	***
4. Time management	5.05	4.4	***
5. Interviewing	4.75	4.56	ns
6. Financial skills	4.89	4.35	***
7. Managing change	5.25	4.89	**
8. Stress management	4.54	4.36	ns
9. Career management	4.52	4.03	**
10. Research skills	5.07	4.49	***
11. Accountancy skills	4.02	3.27	***
12. Working in teams	5.40	5.14	ns
13. Negotiating skills	4.75	4.55	ns
14. Self-confidence	5.33	5.01	*
15. Decision making	5.51	5.28	**
16. Interpersonal skills	5.18	5.09	ns
17. Abstract thinking	4.91	4.58	ns
18. Managing others	5.12	5.02	ns
Mean all (CMPT)	5.03	4.66	***

ns: non-significant difference, $*\alpha<.1$, $** \alpha<.05$, $*** \alpha<.001$.
Source: Based on Y. Baruch and M.A. Peiperl (2000) 'The Impact of an MBA on Graduates' Career, *Human Resource Management Journal*, 10(2), 69–90; and Y. Baruch and A. Leeming (1996) 'Programming MBA programme – the Quest for Curriculum', *Journal of Management Development*, 15(7), 28–37.

planned scheme each person would have several options for career moves, whereas for each position there would be several candidates to fill it.

Career communities

Parker and Arthur (2000)[34] associated the intelligent career's 'three ways of knowing' (Know why, Know how and Know whom) with a diversity of career communities. The idea of people having multiple sets of commitment is not new: each individual can have commitments in more than one realm of their life. Multiple commitments refer to several levels of meaning: identification, association and relationship (as discussed in Chapter 3). These relationships can also depend on the career stage that a person has reached (Cohen, 1991).[35] In the careers context, Parker and Arthur offered a basic list, which is elaborated below: Industry (sector); Occupation and professional association; Region (from local to national); Ideology; Religion; Alumni (of school, university, military or reserve forces service where applicable); Support groups; Family; Virtual; and Organization. Within the organization, commitment need not be general to the organization, but is usually shared among different constituencies: the organization, leader and/or mentor; the team; the department/unit; the project (or product); peers/colleagues. Commitment to a union can be classified as work-related, but its boundaries lie across organizational borders. For the organization this means that individuals manage a very complex network of commitments within multi-level communities, and the organization cannot and should not see itself as the core base for employees' self-identity and the focal point of their life.

Question | What are the major communities from which you gather your strength and hope for the future? What role would the ideal organization play for you as one of these communities?

Career networking

As indicated in Chapter 4, much of the success of individuals and the organizational system depends on the ability to develop and utilize effective networks for communication and learning. These help to identify and initiate the best next career move.

What is the position of a person who has no network, if they have worked for years for a company that encouraged internal networking and practically barred external career networking? When such a person is made redundant they face a severe problem of re-entering the labour market. If that is the case, the company may show a degree of responsibility and support by offering outplacement services, either internally, or via the use of external agencies (*see* Exhibit 5.4).

EXHIBIT 5.4 | Outplacement services: Doubting Thomas

Tom Money arrived at our offices depressed and angry. He had been informed on the previous Friday afternoon that his style did not fit the new organisation culture. He was 'Too aggressive, too uncomfortable to have around and his job no longer existed'. He was offered outplacement counselling as part of his severance package.

Tom was convinced that outplacement was conscience money from his employers.

That first meeting had Tom primarily living in the past – going over meetings and conversations to try to understand how things had come to this.

We dealt with his feelings and his focus, which was entirely internal. It took some time to even get him to consider the future and how we could help. We convinced him that he was our client and that we were here to help him irrespective of who paid for our service.

He reluctantly agreed to do some homework before our next meeting. This work consisted of Tom identifying the things which he had found of value in both his career and his personal life, and also to write a description of himself and his life to date.

At our second meeting a few days later Tom had started to realise that his life to date had been pretty successful. He had married and raised two lovely children. He was a home-owner and well regarded within the community. His career had been

Exhibit 5.4 continued

successful up until this point. Tom hadn't changed – the environment had. The skills and attributes which had made him successful would be valued in many companies.

This self analysis provided a powerful reinforcement of Tom's self-esteem.

It provided the basis for examining and identifying his life and career goals. At 42, Tom wanted to use the skills he had developed in his previous two companies to continue his career trajectory. We discussed other options such as consultancy or running his own business. Tom was concerned about the risks these options may place on his family.

Having completed a comprehensive analysis we were ready to prepare a marketing plan. This included CV development, targeting sectors, companies and relevant consultancies. Approach letters and advert analysis also featured.

Tom's depression receded and returned on a number of occasions usually associated with rejection letters. We kept him doing positive things and maintained a high level of momentum. His interview skills were developed using video feedback to help him modify his behaviour and present himself in a positive manner. Our extensive access to job and company databases helped keep his activity level high. He also accessed our web facilities regularly.

He then started to get first interviews followed by rejections which lowered his morale. We analysed each interview in detail and discovered that some residual bitterness was coming through.

We convinced him to put the past behind and look at his current situation as an opportunity. Eventually after three months Tom found a vacancy on our database. It was in his discipline but outside his previous sectors. His first and second interviews went well and the company made him an offer. He was unsure if he should accept so we did a positive/negative analysis which showed that the positives far outweighed the negatives. We helped with his negotiation tactics and secured the best offer possible.

Tom started his job with our jointly developed integration plan to help make an impact and maximise his early effectiveness. He is doing well and has taken to his new sector, bringing added value by his cross-sector expertise. We talk regularly and he knows we are here for him if it does not work out. His Christmas card read 'Thanks for listening, thanks for the guidance, the outplacement experience has affected me in a way I would not have thought possible'.

This case was kindly provided by The Quo Group Ltd.

Careers as metaphors

In Chapter 4 we noted how the use of metaphors 'the application of a name or a descriptive term or phrase to an object or action to which it is imaginatively but not literally applicable, e.g. a glaring error' *The Concise Oxford Dictionary*, 1990 can be helpful for understanding career concepts. There are many ways to describe careers in a metaphorical way.

Metaphors

The use of metaphors for understanding organizations has been advocated by, among others, Morgan (1980, 1986, 1997) and Hatch (1997), and it is a well-established practice in depicting organizational features (e.g. Smircich, 1983; Rich, 1992; Jeffcutt, 1994).[36] Dunford and Palmer (1996)[37] cited a number of theoretical contributions which employed metaphors for management studies.

Applying metaphors in the study of organizations has contributed to the development of organizational, as well as many other types of theory. The advantage of using metaphors for understanding organizations has been well demonstrated by Morgan in his conceptual framework, and is widely applied in organizational studies (cf. Czarniawska, 1997).[38] Metaphors transposed from more established sciences, for use within the science of management, can be advantageous, in the sense that the analogy can enhance the understanding of relevant phenomena. 'Metaphor facilitates change by making the strange familiar, but in that very process it deepens the meaning or values of the organization by giving them expression in novel situations' (Pondy 1983: 164).[39] In addition, Avelsson (1995: 45), building on earlier work of Brown (1976),[40] claims that certain phenomena are always regarded from a certain point of view. This means that all knowledge is metaphoric, since knowledge is perspective dependent.

An example of a metaphorical use to capture the meaning of the interim manager's career was presented by Inkson, Heising and Rousseau (2001).[41] They suggested a series of complementary metaphors, including: displaced person, spare part, dating agency/marriage bureau client, hired gun, and bee. Together these series of vivid images encapsulate the transience, alienation, mobility, ambiguity and temporary fragile nature of the interim manager's career.

The use of linguistic metaphors can become more complex: Paleonymics means retaining old names while grafting new meaning upon them (Culler, 1982: 140).[42] Boje, Rosile, Dennehy and Summers (1997)[43] use the term re-engineering to demonstrate Paleonymics: the 're' in re-engineering is an example of paleonymic grafting. It marks a difference or a gap in the word 'engineering' that is being supplemented. The 're' in re-engineering is a supplement, a little something extra added to complete engineering. The 're' also signifies adding a little something extra to bureaucracy. In the context of redundancy Downs (1995)[44] went so far as to use the context of capital punishment in his book title. In similar vein is the Desert Generation metaphor, and we can also identify the new meaning of resilience in Waterman et al.'s (1994)[45] Career Resilience, both mentioned earlier in this book.

A more positive orientation is to look at career management via the gardening metaphor. It can be used as strong analogy for career practice management in organizations. Bearing in mind the constant need for nourishment and support, developing people and nurturing plants share much in common. In his book *Being There*, Jerzy Kosinski (1970)[46] depicted a gardener who is assumed to be able to care for people, and even more.

EXHIBIT
5.6
The garden metaphor

Jerzy Kosinski writes, 'It's not easy sir,' he said 'to obtain a suitable place, a garden in which one can work without interference and row with the seasons...'

'Very well put Mr Gardiner, isn't that the perfect way to describe what a real business man is.'

The garden metaphor (as well as the will of people to hear what they want to hear) is quite convincing: Rand invites the president to meet Chance; the president was already told that Chance is a very intelligent business man. When Chance repeats the statement about the garden the president doesn't doubt for one second that Chance is being metaphorical. 'I must admit, Mr. Gardiner,' the president said, 'That what you have just said is the most refreshing and optimistic statement I have heard in a very, very long time.'

Source: Jerzy Kosinski (1970) *Being There*, New York: Bantam Books, p. 45.

Let us look at caring for people via the metaphorical analogy of gardening (Table 5.2).

The garden metaphor is not the only one to be used. The role of the organization in career management can be understood via other metaphors, revealing several layers. Some of the more popular metaphors are outlined below.

Career as a journey, travelling the roads. This metaphor is perhaps the one most commonly used to tell stories of life and career. A career is a

Table 5.2 Nourishing careers: a gardening metaphor

Garden, for plants	Career, for people
No two plants are alike – different soil, sun and watering conditions will get the best out of different plants	No two people are alike – different conditions will get the best out of different people. The person-environment fit concept is applied here.
Don't let them all ripen at the same time	We don't want all managers to be ready for further progress at the same time.
Start with seeds and small plants	Use the internal labour market: in developing people it is important to get them early – so that they will acquire values, attitudes and culture.
Don't let the tall ones block the light and take the space of the growing one	Allow development for a new generation of managerial layers, don't let existing managers hinder the development of new talent.
Use only best quality seeds	Make sure your recruitment and selection get you the best people for your needs.
Give the better plants enough space and good conditions. Thin out the poor one and the weeds.	Don't hesitate to make non-performers redundant.

journey, which you may plan, but you never know where or even when it will end. The organization paves the roads, develops new paths and holds the map. However, people can take different roads, even outside the plan set by the organization. Career decisions, according to this metaphor, occur whenever people reach a road junction. Robert Frost, in his poem 'The Road Not Taken' said:

'Two roads diverged in a wood, and I –
I took the one less travelled by
And that has made all the difference.'

Several variations of this metaphor are:

- **Career as rowing down a river**. Starting from the spring, merging with flows from new directions; no way back; and the pattern of the river may change in the future, so will be different for those that come later.
- **Career as climbing up a mountain**. Almost the opposite to the former, but a strong metaphorical image is the climbing – and in today's career landscape it need not be a single mountain, but a group of hills, a chain of summits, each calling for climbers, posing a challenge. Starting from the plains, focusing on reaching the top, but with many alternative routes, people look on it as an adventure.
- **Career as navigating at sea**. No path, the way is navigated via tacit knowledge, one does not always know the destination, how long it will take to get there, or what obstacles there may be on the way (under water?).
- **Career as wandering in space**. No road map, random progress and development, lost in space (actually cyberspace).

The metaphor most frequently used, the career as a journey, implies that we use maps to navigate. In most of these metaphorical models, career structures are constructed around maps, and the organization holds the key, while the level of transparency varies. The options for mobility, the boundaries, and the landscape are becoming more transparent so that individuals can take a more active role in navigating their career in this uncertain world.

In contrast to the innovative, contemporary metaphors, the old-fashioned one sees the organization as a ladder or steps to climb.

Career as moving up in a building or up a ladder. The organization constructed the building or set up the ladder and gives you the best ways to move about. The walls are rigid, the steps are fixed and determined. Some places you will never see (i.e. if your career is in marketing you will never experience operations or finance).

More than the others, the following career metaphor can help us in understanding and confronting the role of the individual *vis-à-vis* that of the organization. It is the metaphor of the **Career as a play in the theatre of the world**. The management of careers is divided between the two players:

- Individual career management – which mask do we put on in each episode?
- The organization – stage management, setting the scene, ensuring continuity.

This is a metaphor that sees employment as a theatre. Career development is a part of a play, and in the play we perform different roles according to the mask we are wearing at the time. People can put on a 'Manager' mask, a 'Big Boss' mask, but also a 'Caring' mask, as well as many others. In different circumstances people play several parts and roles in the theatre of organizational life. A manager may need to wear the mask of Mentor for supporting a protégé, five minutes later wear the 'Tough guy' mask for dealing with the union representative, and then swap to the 'Visionary' mask when seeking to inspire shareholders. This mask/theatre metaphor reflects the general behaviour of people at work, not just career management, but has strong implications for career systems. The organization can teach, educate and train managers to use different 'masks' for their different career-related roles. Different qualities are needed in mentoring and in disciplining.

Organizational career systems resemble, for this metaphor, setting the stage, while the HR manager takes the role of director or producer of the play. However, life is never as structured and rigid as this implies, and theatrical improvisation may represent a more suitable metaphor in this case. What is clear and fits well with this metaphor is the way we are all expected to put on a 'mask' to fit the specific role or circumstances we face. What make the theatre of life more complicated for many people is the discrepancy between their own inner qualities and the requirements of the role, especially when they have to perform a variety of roles. This happens, for example, in differences between work and home, e.g. when the tough policeman returns home and becomes the loving father, but also in the work situation when at one time you are appraising the performance of a subordinate, and the next you are facing your boss for your own appraisal.

Lastly, the metaphor that may best depict the relationship between employee and employer is that of **marriage** (with job separation resembling divorce, there being so much similarity in the feelings of people going through the process). Both relationships (marriage and employment) have suffered a severe blow in recent times. In both there has been a shift from an unconditional loyalty-based relationship to conditional attachment.

Companies may now see themselves as 'teams' rather than 'families', partly because you cannot fire a member of a family; but you can fire a member of a team.

From marriage to conditional attachment

One may see a strong association, correlational rather than just metaphorical, between the nature of marriage and employment relationships. In the past both marriage and employment were considered to be lifelong relationships, at least at the intentional level. In the latter part of the twentieth century both establishments were cracking. Marriage has ceased to be the only form of cohabitation. Many people live together on a trial basis, and only if this works do they get married. Similarly there are many temporary workers or people on short-term contracts, which can be converted to full employment if all goes well. Many marriage terminations occur because divorce is possible. Similarly many employees, perhaps the majority, enter employment relationships with no intention of maintaining them for life. And the typical termination of an employment relationship does not occur at the time of retirement from a single employer. Employment relationships most frequently end as a result of redundancy or voluntary exit.

Despite all the changes to career systems, one metaphor that is still valid is that of the **Tournament**. With fewer managerial layers, and people's strong need for visible progress, the Tournament element of careers can become fierce. This perspective of career progress was initially offered by Rosenbaum (1979)[47] to describe career mobility in large corporations. It has strong explanatory power, especially in a male-dominated workplace.

Changes in specific occupations and the emergence of new vocations and business sectors

While some occupations are relatively stable, new occupational systems have emerged and evolved. Among these are some that existed in the past as a hobby-related activity, and others which are totally new.

One area that has expanded is sport as a career. If you were a football player in the 1960s–1970s, this was a spare-time activity. You had to have a job to earn your living. Hanging up your shoes at the end of a sporting career at the age of 30–35 usually meant going back to low-level jobs. If you were particularly successful, e.g. a leading player in the premier league, you might open a pub or sports shop and hope that your former fans will form a base of loyal customers. Times have changed, and the sums people earn in the top leagues in Europe have made a career in football a lucrative one. A retired footballer may move directly to the stock exchange to play with the money he has amassed or invest in a whole retail network. The same implies to other branches of sport too, most notably tennis and golf.

Another area of growth is that of emotional work. This includes not just psychology and psychiatry, both of which started as professions in the twentieth century, but a wide range of consultancy and conciliatory work. Noon and Blyton (1997)[48] argue that the need for this work is on the increase.

Changes in the labour force and operational sectors

There have been gradual changes over the centuries in the labour market – first from the hunter-gatherers of prehistory to the introduction of agriculture, the development of trading and the growth of a service sector and small-scale industry. The Industrial Revolution led to the development of large-scale manufacturing, the growth of cities and a reduction in the numbers employed in agriculture. In the twentieth century improvements in technology led to further changes in the balance of employment in Western economies, with service-sector employment exceeding that in manufacturing. Unemployment in both old and new sectors has continued to rise, as the pace of production and efficiency have improved.

A question for the future is what will happen to the people who are no longer needed in agriculture, production or services. Most want to work but we do not know where, in what or how they will keep their jobs. The last chapter of this book offers some insights into this issue.

The pace of the changes described above was by no means uniform. The first took millions of years, the second, a couple of thousand years, the following one, a few hundred, and the last, only a few dozen years. At present time there are many career options for those left out of the labour market, ejected from conventional jobs. One of the most amazing qualities of human beings is the ability to adapt, to develop, to transform. This ability, however, is limited, and depends on the pace and depth of change. When the environment changes slowly, or when time is not a scarce resource, most people can adapt to change or cope with it effectively. However, if what is needed is an all-encompassing change, leading in a totally new direction, and with severe time restrictions, it is unlikely to be achieved without severe adjustment problems.

Another associated change in the pace of change is the spread of practices and labour market divisions from Western societies to the rest of the world. The great advances in transportation and telecommunications have made geographical boundaries less significant (although cultural and legal boundaries remain intact). They have accelerated the spread of changes from the leading economies to the rest of the world.

A significant general trend reiterated in this book is that of transferring responsibility for the management of careers from organizations to individuals. One aspect that individuals need to consider is how to promote themselves in a world in which the patronage of the organization is lacking or entirely missing, how to stand out from the crowd. One way of 'self-promotion' is impression management and career signalling (*see* Chapter 2).

Change versus stability: implications for career systems

Table 5.3 compares change and continuity and looks at the implications for careers (building on Noon and Blyton, 1997: 204).[49]

Summary

In this chapter we explored career dynamism by seeking to understand the phenomenon of employability and its implications for individuals and organizations. We looked at redundancies and the prospect of the survivor syndrome, trying to identify best practice. We explored new career perspectives via career communities and networking, and by examination of a set of career metaphors. The chapter concluded by placing the discussion in historical perspective and analysing past and future changes.

Table 5.3 Change and continuity: implications for careers

Change	Continuity	Career implications
New patterns of production and consumption	Persistence of work ethic	New ways of work, but strong need for work persists
Rise of service sector	Continual existence of routine, boring jobs	Innovative career patterns alongside traditional roles based on division of work
Technological change with some growth of high-skilled jobs	New types of low-skill low-discretion jobs	Career frustration for highly educated new generation
Increase of emotional labour	Underevaluating of social abilities as skills	A gap between professional inner satisfaction and remuneration levels
More women in the labour market	Gendered division of labour; unfair discrimination	Need for management of diversity in light of continuous perceived or actual discrimination
New forms of work and working time patterns	Traditional working methods and forms of control	Stratified labour markets; variety of career systems approaches
New management initiatives for work intensification	Traditional methods of control and reliance on employee consent	Applying empowerment and trust-based relationships
Emergence of Post-Fordism organizations	Taylorism/Fordism organizations remain	Dualism in career management, based on organizational operation and ethos

Source: Based on M. Noon and P. Blyton (1997) *The Realities of Work*, Basingstoke: Macmillan.

Key terms

- Employability
- Career cynicism
- Survivor syndrome
- Best practice
- The Peter Principle
- Career communities
- Career networking
- Career metaphors

DISCUSSION QUESTIONS

Lessons and food for thought

1 *For the HR manager:* What kind of changes can you detect in your immediate business environment that will have a profound effect on the way you manage careers in your organization?

Discussion questions continued

2 *For the HR consultant*: What kind of changes can you detect in your immediate business environment that will have different effects for different organizations? What will the different effects be and how would you recommend organizations to adapt their career systems to such a change?

3 *For the HR teacher*: To what extent should you incorporate into your HRM teaching elements from history, sociology, geography and technology to clarify trends and dimensions in career systems, but not to distract your students from the main subject?

4 *For the student*: Here is an interesting exercise you can do yourself to analyse the changes the world of careers is experiencing. The list below, of attributes people may look for in their career, is part of the Psychological contract exercise – *see* Appendix 4.1. First complete this for yourself (placing the attributes in order of importance for you from 1 to 12). Then ask members of your parents' generation (one of the parents, uncle, aunt, etc.) to fill in the same form; and if at all possible, do the same for members of your grand-parents' generation. Can you see a trend? Does it fit with what you have learned by now from the book?

What do (did) you expect from your employer?	*Order of importance*
professional challenge	
financial provider	
source of inspiration	
social status	
job security	
professional development	
good working conditions	
source of motivation	
life structure	
safe working environment	
feeling needed and valued	
increased employability	

Class exercise

The suggested exercise for the student (above) can be developed into an interesting class comparative session, using the 12-level ranking and comparing responses for the different attributes.

Notes

1   Peiperl, M.A. and Baruch, Y. (1997) 'Back to square zero: the post-corporate career', *Organization Dynamics*, 25(4), 7–22.

2   Baruch, Y. (2001) 'Employability: A substitute for loyalty?', *Human Resource Development International*, 4(4), 543–66.

3   Byron, W.J. (1995) 'Coming to terms with the new corporate contract', *Business Horizons*, 38(1), 8–15; Fagiano, D. (1993) 'Training is the new job security', *Management Review*, 82(8), 4; Ghoshal, S., Bartlett, C.A. and Moran, P. (1999) 'A new manifesto for management', *Sloan Management Review*, 40(3), 9–22; MacLachlan, R. (1996) 'Liberté, egalité and now employabilité', *People Management*, 24(2), 16; Martin, P. (1995) 'Performance appraisal', *Management Accounting – London*, 73(3), 67; Skoch, D.A. (1994) 'Ask for commitment, not loyalty', *Industry Week*, 243(21), 21 November, p. 38; Waterman, R.H. Jr., Waterman, J.A. and Collard, B.A. (1994) 'Toward a career-resilient workforce', *Harvard Business Review*, 72(4), Jul/Aug, 87–95.

4   *See* note 2 above.

5   Sonnerfeld, J.A. and Peiperl, M.A. (1988) 'Staffing Policy as a Strategic Response: A Typology of Career Systems', *Acdemy of Management Review*, 13(4), 568–600.

6   Ghoshal, Bartlett and Moran (1999) – *see* note 3 above; Hammer, M. and Champy, J. (1993) *Reengineering the Corporation*, NY: Harper Business.

7   Dunlop, J.E.T. (1959) *Industrial Relations Systems*, New York: Holt.

8   Cascio, W.F. (2000) 'New Workplaces', in Jean M. Kummerow (ed.) *New Directions in Career Planning and the Workplace*, 2nd edn, Palo Alto, CA: Davies-Black; Bulkeley, W. (1998) 'Corporate seers', *Wall Street Journal*, 16 November, pp. R37, R39; Ulrich, D. (1998) 'A new mandate for human resources', *Harvard Business Review*, 76(1), 124–34.

9   Tornow, W.W., London, M. *et al.* (1998) *Maximizing the Value of 360-Degree Feedback*, San Francisco: Jossey-Bass.

10   Singer, P. (1997) *How are We to Live? : Ethics in an Age of Self-interest*, Oxford: Oxford University Press; Wolfe, A. (1998) *One Nation, After All: What Middle-Class Americans Really Think about God, Country, Family, Poverty, Racism, Welfare, Homosexuality, Immigration, the Left, the Right, and Each Other*, New York: Viking.

11   Lewin, K. (1951) *Field Theory in Social Science*, NY: Harper & Row.

12   Toffler, A. (1970) *Future Shock*, London: Pan Books.

13   *See* note 1 above.

14   Nicholson, N. (1998) 'How hardwired is human behavior?', *Harvard Business Review*, 76(4), 134–47; Nicholson, N. (2000) 'Motivation-selection-connection: An evolutionary model of career development', in M. Peiperl, M. Arthur, R. Goffee and T. Morris (eds) *Career Frontiers*, Oxford: Oxford University Press.

15   Noon, M. and Blyton, P. (1997) *The Realities of Work*, Basingstoke: Macmillan.

16   Brockner, J. (1992) 'Managing the Effects of Layoffs on Survivors', *California Management Review*, 34(2), 9–28; Astrachan, J.H. (1995) 'Organizational departures: The impact of separation anxiety as studied in a mergers and acquisitions simulation', *Journal of Applied Behavioural Science*, 31(1), 31–50.

17   O'Neil, H.M. and Lenn, D.J. (1995) 'Voices of survivors: words that downsizing CEOs should hear', *Academy of Management Executive*, 9(4), 23–34.

18   Hartley, J., Jacobso, D., Klandermans, B., van Vuuren, T., Greenhalgh, L. and Sutton, R. (1991) (eds) *Job Insecurity: Coping with Job Insecurity*, London: Sage.

19   Downs, A. (1995) *Corporate Executions*, NY: AMACOM.

20 Church, A.H. (1995) 'From both sides now organizational downsizing: What is the role of the practitioner?', *The Industrial/Organizational Psychologist*, July; Jackson, P.R. (1997) 'Downsizing and deselection', in N. Anderson and P. Herriot (eds) *International Handbook of Selection and Assessment*, Chichester: Wiley, pp. 619–36; Doherty, N. and Horsted, J. (1995) 'Helping survivors to stay on board', *People Management*, 12, 26–31; Brockner, J., Grover, S., Reed, T.F. and DeWitt, R.L. (1992) 'Layoffs, job insecurity, and survivors' work effort: Evidence of an inverted-U relationship', *Academy of Management Journal*, 35, 413–25; Baruch, Y. (1998) 'The Rise and Fall of Organizational Commitment', *Human System Management*, 17(2), 135–43; Baruch, Y. and Hind, P. (2000) 'The Survivor Syndrome: A management myth?', *Journal of Managerial Psychology*, 15(1), 29–41; Mowday, R.T. (1999) 'Reflections on the study and relevance of organizational commitment', *Human Resource Management Review*, 8(4), 387–401.

21 Cameron, K.S. (1994) 'Strategies for successful organizational downsizing', *Human Resource Management*, 33, 189–211; Cameron, K.S. (1996) 'Downsizing', in M. Warner (ed.) *International Encyclopaedia of Business and Management*, London: Thompson International, vol. 2, pp. 1050–6.

22 *See* note 20 above.

23 Baruch, Y. and Hind, P. (1999) 'Perpetual Motion in Organizations: Effective Management and the impact of the new psychological contracts on "Survivor Syndrome"', *European Journal of Work and Organizational Psychology*, 8(2), 295–306.

24 Mishra, K.E. Spreitzer, G.M. and Mishra, A.K. (1998) 'Preserving employee morale during downsizing', *Sloan Management Review*, Winter, 83–95.

25 *See* note 23 above.

26 *See* note 20 above.

27 *See* note 21 above.

28 Rothwell, S. (1995) 'Human Resource Planning', in J. Storey (ed.) *Human Resource Management: A Critical Text*, London: Routledge, pp. 167–202.

29 Beattie, D.F. and Tampoe, F.M.K. (1990) 'Human Resource Planning for ICL', *Long Range Planning*, 23(1), 17–28.

30 Larsen, H.H. (1996) 'Oticon: Think the unthinkable: radical (and successful) organizational change', in J. Storey (ed.) *Cases in Human Resource Management*, Oxford: Blackwell.

31 DeFillippi, R.J. and Arthur, M.B. (1998) 'Paradox in project-based enterprise: The case of film-making', *California Management Review*, 40(2), 125–39.

32 Larsen, H.H. (2002) 'Oticon: career development in a project based organization – Think the unthinkable', *Human Resource Planning*, in press.

33 Baruch, Y. and Leeming, A. (1996) 'Programming MBA programme – the Quest for Curriculum', *Journal of Management Development*, 15(7), 28–37; Baruch, Y. and Peiperl, M.A. (2000b) 'The Impact of an MBA on Graduates' Career', *Human Resource Management Journal*, 10(2), 69–90.

34 Parker, P. and Arthur, M.B. (2000) 'Careers, organizing and community', in M.A. Peiperl, M.B. Arthur, R. Goffee and T. Morris (eds) *Career Frontiers: New Conceptions of Working Lives*, Oxford: Oxford University Press, pp. 99–121.

35 Cohen, A. (1991) 'Career stage as a moderator of the relationships between organizational commitment and its outcomes: A meta-analysis', *Journal of Occupational Psychology*, 64, 253–68.

36 Morgan, G. (1980) 'Paradigms, metaphor and puzzle solving in organizational theory', *Administrative Science Quarterly*, 25, 605–22; Morgan, G. (1997) *Images of Organizations*, Thousand Oaks, CA: Sage; Hatch, M.J. (1997) *Organization Theory*, NY:

Oxford University Press; Smircich, L. (1983) 'Concepts of Culture and Organizational Analysis', *Administrative Science Quarterly*, 28, 339–58; Rich, P. (1992) 'The organizational taxonomy: definition and design', *Academy of Management Review*, 17(4), 758–81; Jeffcutt, P. (1994) 'From interpretation to representation in organizational analysis: Postmodernism, ethnography and organizational symbolism', *Organization Studies*, 15(2), 241–74.

[37] Dunford, R. and Palmer, I. (1996) 'Metaphors in popular management discourse: the case of corporate restructuring', in D. Grant and C. Oswick (eds) *Metaphor and organizations*, London: Sage, pp. 95–109.

[38] Czarniawska, B. (1997) 'A four times told tale: combining narrative and scientific knowledge in organization studies', *Organization*, 4, 7–30.

[39] Pondy, L.R. (1983) 'The role of metaphors and myths in organization and in the facilitation of change', in L.R. Pondy, J. Frost, G. Morgan and T.C. Dandridge (eds) *Organizational Symbolism*, Greenwich: JAI Press, pp. 157–66.

[40] Avelsson, M. (1995) *Management of Knowledge-Intensive Companies*, Berlin: Walter de Gruyter; Brown, R.H. (1976) 'Social Theory as Metaphor', *Theory and Society*, 3, 169–97.

[41] Inkson, K., Heising, A. and Rousseau, D.M. (2001) 'The interim manager: prototypes of the 21st century worker?', *Human Relations*, 54, 259–84.

[42] Culler, J. (1982) *On Deconstruction: Theory and Criticism After Structuralism*, Ithaca, NY: Cornell University Press.

[43] Boje , D.M., Rosile, G.A., Dennehy, R. and Summers, D. (1997) 'Restorying reengineering: some deconstructions and postmodern alternatives', *Communication Research*, 24(6), 631–68.

[44] *See* note 19 above.

[45] *See* note 3 above.

[46] Kosinski, N. Jerzy (1970) *Being There*, New York: Bantam Books.

[47] Rosenbaum, J.L. (1979) 'Tournament mobility: career patterns in a corporation', *Administrative Science Quarterly*, 24, 221–41.

[48] *See* note 15 above.

[49] *See* note 15 above.

[50] Singer, P. (1982) *The Expanding Circle: Ethics and Sociobiology*, New York: Farrar, Straus & Giroux.

Career management practices

LEARNING OBJECTIVES

After reading this chapter you should be able to:

- Define career practices.
- Identify the existing portfolio of career practices.
- Understand how they are associated with each other.
- Explain how organizations can develop a career practices system to match their needs.

CHAPTER CONTENTS

Question

> Think what your organization can do for you, not (just) what you can do for your organization.
>
> How well would you like to be treated by your organization? What kind of career planning and management activities would you expect? What may your organization plan for you without your knowing about it?
>
> In this chapter we dwell on the third 'P', the practical level: the activities, actions and operations that form the practice of career planning and management.

Creating the function

Here is a question I used to give my HRM students in their final exam:
You have just been recruited by a company which employs some 1000 employees, a company that previously did not have an HRM/Personnel department, for historic reasons and because the former CEO believed that HR issues should be dealt with directly by line managers. However, a new CEO is now in charge, and she believes that there should be a specific professional unit within the organization to deal with HRM/personnel issues. You have been recruited to create the new department and head it. The HR manager will be one of the board level team (you would not have accepted the offer had this not been the case).

On your first day you set yourself the task of building a comprehensive system to include all the necessary HR practices. In particular, you need to decide which practices to apply and how these will be integrated.

Questions

If the situation in the company was satisfactory under the old system, and since we believe in delegation, why not continue letting the line managers be the HR managers?

What impact will the type of organization and its characteristics have on your answer? The above scenario may vary, depending on such factors as: whether it is a production or service based firm; whether it is an established or new enterprise; which sector it is in – high or low technology; what form of control – centralized or decentralized, and others.

Question

As a consultant, the scenario depicted above may face you with a challenge: If you are asked to advise an HR director about how to rebuild their HR department from scratch, what would you be doing in terms of the constituencies of the department?

Introduction

This chapter takes on the more pragmatic task of focusing on career practices, a subsection of overall HR practices. The chapter outlines a comprehensive portfolio of HRM practices, which can be conducted by organizations to plan and manage employees' careers. It develops and expands upon earlier work of the author.[1] The chapter provides a systematic presentation and critical examination, rooted in both theory and practice, of a range of career management practices, techniques, activities and programmes. For each career practice referred to, an explanation is given of how it may be utilized by organizations in the 2000s. The chapter also integrates these practices into a comprehensive organizational framework.

The importance and prominence of organizational Career Planning and Management (CPM) as part of HRM has been widely recognized.[2] From the early writing on modern career systems to recent inputs, academic scholars have emphasized that organizational career systems should ensure the fit between individual needs and aspirations and organizational requirements.[3] However, as pointed out in Chapter 2, much of the literature on careers has focused on the individual whereas there is an acute lack of conceptual and theoretical formulation of organizational practices. An exception is the Baruch and Peiperl model presented in this chapter, a model developed as a result of empirical investigation, and integrating a variety of organizational career practices.

A good starting point for establishing a comprehensive updated organizational career system is to examine what was available in the 1980s and 1990s. The chapter goes on to project which career practices will remain valid and relevant, which will need significant change and adaptation, which might become obsolete, and which new ones may emerge. The first part of the chapter critically examines a traditional portfolio for career practices.

There have been several attempts to establish what comprises a conventional set of organizational career practices. Several sources in the literature suggest specific lists of career practices.[4] Walker and Gutteridge (1979)[5] identified 10 career activities, although some of these were closer to other constituencies of HRM than to career management. A different problem occurs with the work of Gutteridge and Otte (1983),[6] which focused on some aspects of career practices, limiting the discussion to 10 practices and evaluating only three of them. Perhaps the most comprehensive list was that provided by Gutteridge, Leibowitz and Shore in their study of careers in the United States.[7] However, their study concentrated on large business organizations only (the top 1000 US corporations), and might thus have been non-representative of broader practice.

EXHIBIT 6.2	Analysis

In the USA, the 1000th largest company (PC Connection, in the *Fortune 1000* list) employs some 1500 people. Number 200 in the *Fortune 500*, Entergy Corporation, with annual revenues of nearly $10 billion, has more than 15 000 employees. The size in terms of employee numbers varies, with some companies employing more than 100 000 people. However, the US labour market consists of about 126 million people. Thus, the majority of people work in small or medium-sized companies. While all have career, whether they all need a formal career system is another matter.

Question

At what stage in terms of size of the organization should an HR function be introduced into an organization? At what stage in terms of size should a career management function be introduced into the HR unit? What organizational and environmental characteristics will influence your answer?

The use of career practices: empirical evidence

The list of practices presented and discussed in this chapter evolved from several earlier works on CPM practices. Most practices were covered in many sources, but some new ones were added to the list, including induction, special programmes

Table 6.1 Use of career practices in 1990s studies

Career practices	Scale of 1–7		Per cent use by the organizations		
	A		B1	B2	C
	mean	sd	%	%	%
Job postings	5.62	1.65	55	89	68
Formal education/tuition reimbursement	5.08	1.48	100	100	78
PA for career planning	4.80	1.63	82	89	
Counselling by manager	4.52	1.62	59	89	97
Lateral moves (job rotations in USA)	4.33	1.6			60
Counselling by HR	4.16	1.78	41	56	67
Pre-retirement programmes	4.15	2.15	90	78	5
Succession planning	3.6	1.75	63	33	69
Formal mentoring	2.95	1.79	43	44	44
Common career paths	2.73	1.8	67	56	
Dual ladder	2.42	1.77	75	44	34
Career booklets/pamphlets	2.41	1.6	22	33	19
Written individual career plans	2.38	1.82	14	33	
Assessment centre	2.34	1.79	69	67	23
Peer appraisal	2.26	1.73			
Career workshops	2.15	1.6	14	44	24
Upward appraisal	2.04	1.7			
Appraisal committees			37	11	30
Training programmes for managers			75	44	30
Orientation programme					78
Special needs (dual-career couples)					13

A – Baruch and Peiperl 1997: use in 194 UK organizations. Scale of 1–7: 1 = not applied at all; 7 = applied extensively.
B1 – Baruch 1996b: use in 51 high-tech firms in Israel.
B2 – Baruch 1996b: use in 9 high-tech firms in the UK.
C – Gutteridge, Leibowitz and Shore (1993): use in 256 large firms in the USA.

Sources: Derived from Y. Baruch and M.A. Peiperl (1997) 'High flyers: glorious past, gloomy present, any future?', *Career Development International*, 2(7), 354–8; Y. Baruch (1996) 'Organizational career planning and management techniques and activities in use in high-tech organizations', *Career Development International*, 1(1), 40–9; T.G. Gutteridge, Z.B. Leibowitz and J.E. Shore (1993) *Organizational Career Development*, San Francisco: Jossey-Bass.

for unique populations, and secondments (temporary assignments to another area/organization). Table 6.1 summarizes findings from studies in the 1990s, all of which tested the use of career management and planning practices in organizations. The sources for the data in these studies are responses from HR managers, as they are considered most likely to be best acquainted with career practices, both as professionals and as representatives of the organization.

The rest of the chapter is devoted, first to an elaboration of each practice, and then brings them together in an integrated framework. The presentation of the practices is in line with the classification offered by Baruch and Peiperl's (2000a) model,[8] which comprises five clusters of career practices (*see* Figure 6.1). It is a descriptive model (*see* Exhibit 6.3), i.e. based on field-research data, gathered from almost 200 organizations, and was constructed using the statistical procedure of factor analysis, a procedure utilized to measure interrelationships among variables. The classification is configured along two dimensions: degree of practice sophistication and level of organizational involvement.

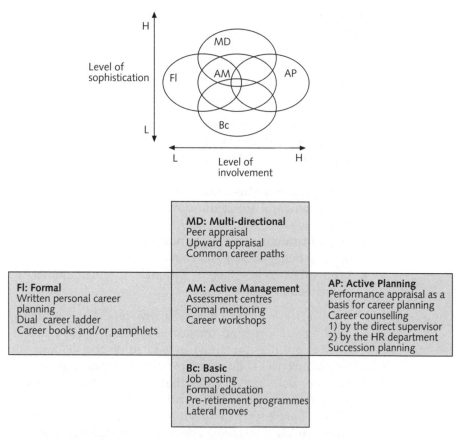

Figure 6.1 Two-dimensional model of career management practices

Source: Y. Baruch and M.A. Peiperl (2000) 'Career management practices: An empirical survey and implications', *Human Resource Management*, 39(4), 347–66 © John Wiley & Sons, Inc., reproduced with permission.

EXHIBIT 6.3

Normative versus descriptive models

A normative model is one that tries to establish what *should be* the right way to do something – to conduct a process, to develop a product, to form a relationship, etc. In this case, it is to develop a comprehensive set of organizational career practices and to find out how they may be associated with each other.

A descriptive model is one based on factual reality, i.e. how things *are* in real life. It is based on data collected and assembled, and is subjected to analysis that checks the relationships among constructs or variables.

While the majority of clusters in the model appear to be logical, and clearly based on factual evidence (i.e. a descriptive model, based on actual organizational cases), it is not necessarily the best model for developing a career system. Another way to look at clusters of career practices would be to develop a normative model – a model which tries to establish what career practices *should* be applied, and when establishing connections, to point to the right way to classify the clusters. In this sense, a normative model may add to our understanding and to the development of organizational career systems. The following set of dimensions may provide insights into the nature of each career practice (the first two were used in the Baruch and Peiperl (2000) model, the rest were introduced by Baruch, 2003).[9] These dimensions were presented in Chapter 4 and are listed again for the convenience of the reader.

- **Involvement**: from very low to very high level of organizational involvement needed while dealing with the specific career practice.
- **Sophistication and complexity**: from very simple to highly sophisticated and complex.
- **Strategic orientation**: from very practical, 'tactical', to very strategic.
- **Developmental focused**: from low to high relevance for developing individuals.
- **Organizational decision making focused**: from low to high relevance for organizational decision-making processes.
- **Innovative**: from very traditional or conventional, to innovative and unorthodox.

Using a Delphi approach, a normative model was generated from the views of 16 leading scholars from the Career division of the Academy of Management. The career practices presented were rated on the six dimensions. In view of the variety of practices and the complexity of working life, the advantage of this analytical approach appears to be that it utilizes the wide base of knowledge and depth of understanding of the participants.

Table 6.2 presents the evaluation of the practices along the six dimensions.

The relatively low standard deviations in Table 6.2 indicate considerable agreement amongst the respondents about the rating of the practices across the dimensions. The developmental-oriented dimension ratings were the highest, indicating that present career practices are highly directed towards individual development, as suggested by much of the writing on contemporary career systems. However, the application of career practices is still associated with a high level of organiz-

Table 6.2 Descriptive statistics and inter-correlation between the six dimensions

	Mean	SD	1	2	3	4	5
1. Developmental oriented	3.64	0.52					
2. Decision making oriented	2.82	0.59	0.48 (0.02)				
3. Innovative oriented	2.81	0.53	0.62 (0.00)	0.53 (0.01)			
4. Organizational involvement level	3.57	0.51	0.33 (0.12)	0.82 (0.00)	0.61 (0.00)		
5. Sophistication and complexity of practices	2.94	0.67	0.67 (0.00)	0.75 (0.00)	0.90 (0.00)	0.76 (0.00)	
6. Strategic oriented	3.05	0.63	0.56 (0.00)	0.85 (0.00)	0.65 (0.00)	0.75 (0.00)	0.82 (0.00)

Note: Coefficient/(cases)/two-tailed significance

Source: Reprinted from Y. Baruch (2003) 'Career systems in transition: A normative model for organizational career practices', *Personnel Review*, 32(2), 231–51, with permission from MCB UP Ltd.

ational involvement. At the lower end of the scale we find the decision-making element and innovation, indicating the need for HR professionals to develop further the practices used to manage people's career in organizations.

CPM practices: clusters

Basic

The practices below were grouped under the title Basic (low on sophistication, medium on involvement) by the Baruch and Peiperl model:

- Postings regarding internal job openings
- Formal education as part of career development
- Lateral moves to create cross-functional experience
- Retirement preparation programmes

Formal

The practices below were grouped under the title Formal (medium on sophistication, low on involvement) by the Baruch and Peiperl model:

- Booklets and/or pamphlets on career issues
- Dual ladder (parallel hierarchy for professional staff)
- Written personal career planning

Active management

The practices below were grouped under the title Active Management (medium on sophistication, medium on involvement) by the Baruch and Peiperl model:

- Induction
- Assessment centres
- Mentoring
- Career workshops

Active planning

The practices below were grouped under the title Active Planning (medium on sophistication, high on involvement) by the Baruch and Peiperl model:

- Performance appraisal as a basis for career planning
- Career counselling by direct supervisor
- Career counselling by HR Department
- Succession planning

Multi-directional

The practices below were grouped under the title Multi-directional (high on sophistication, medium on involvement) by the Baruch and Peiperl model:

- 360-degree performance appraisal systems
- Common career paths
- Special programmes for ethnic minorities, women, disabled, dual career couples, etc., expatriates and repatriates, high-flyers

New CPM practices

The following additional practices listed by managers are not classified under any cluster in the Baruch and Peiperl model:

- Building psychological contracts
- Secondments
- Intrapreneurship

Another general career practice is:

- Training programmes for managers to enable them to handle careers issues

This practice is needed to provide managers with the skills required for handling their employees' careers. It is not one specific practice but combines several of the above-mentioned practices and activities, and is part of a training programme for managers.

Career practices for whom?

Each person, be they the porter or the CEO, has a career. Many develop their career outside the boundaries of large organizations. Among these are the self-employed, people who run small businesses, free-lancers, the unemployed. However, most working people are in organizations, usually as employees. Career practices are carried out by organizations to meet employees' needs. They exist to support employees at all organizational levels, but in particular those in the higher echelons. Managerial and professional careers are more complex than those of some of the rank and file personnel. Consequently certain career practices are conducted only for managers. Throughout this chapter a distinction is made between practices directed mainly or exclusively at the managerial population and those aimed at employees at various hierarchy levels.

In considering career practices it may be advisable to review the above-mentioned practices to ascertain which are still valid and necessary, and which might be deemed unnecessary in the context of the twenty-first century. Even those expected to be essential in the future may need to be revised and adapted, e.g. in the light of contemporary organizational and environment turbulence.

The reader should bear in mind that the practices vary in their applicability and relevance to different kinds of organizations: small companies usually need fewer official bureaucratic and regulated systems, since informal procedures can be applied successfully. Organizations operating in different industrial sectors and countries may apply different sets of practices, or apply the same practice differently. Centralization versus de-centralization will also influence the application and structure of the CPM system. A special case is large multinational companies operating in diverse cultures. For such companies a variety of approaches in their different subsidiaries may be appropriate.

The final consideration is the impact that future innovations in information technology (IT) systems are expected to have on how careers are managed. The implications of the ever-increasing use of the Internet is just one example. However, the pace of technological breakthroughs in IT means that any attempt at forecasting long-term future practices may prove risky.

Career practices: detailed discussion

Advertising internal job openings

Whenever a vacancy occurs, the organization can look to fill it with either internal or external people. The choice depends on the level and type of position and the norms of the organization's career management practices (*see* Chapter 4 for the Sonnenfeld and Peiperl model[10] which identifies the dimension of external versus internal recruitment, and *see also* the Derr and Laurent model).[11]

For vacant rank and file positions, people may be hired from outside, even though there may be internal personnel who wish to apply for the new post, so creating another vacancy. When the search focus is internal, the vacancy can be advertised within the organization. Many organizations have a policy that jobs are advertised internally before any external search is conducted. The growing importance of internal job advertising as part of a comprehensive organizational career system was demonstrated by Douglas Tim Hall and others. Extensive use of internal job advertising indicates to employees that the organization prefers internal promotion to recruiting managers from outside (i.e. a focus on the internal labour market).

Traditionally, jobs were advertised internally either on notice-boards or in the company newsletter. During the 1990s we witnessed a shift to advertising via internal e-mail and e-notice-boards, advertisements which may subsequently be distributed outside on external networks via the Internet.

Our people make the difference

We need good people for great jobs.

- Departments
- College Recruiting
- Search Careers
- Submit Resume
- Hourly Employment

- Application for Employment
- Benefits
- Diversity
- Life in Northwest Arkansas
- Success Stories

Note that for such a complex organization, there are several streams of applications (plus a separate one for Walmart.com, a subsidiary of some 250 employees which deals with their e-business only).

Figure 6.2 Web job openings for Wal-Mart stores

Source: www.walmart.com

Formal education as part of career development

Organizations may select people of managerial or technical potential and send them on a formal training or study programme as part of their career development path. The formal education may be a first degree in engineering, an MBA, or other graduate or postgraduate studies for managerial personnel, or professional and vocational qualification courses for non-managerial employees. Once an organization has identified an immediate future appointment need, such education can provide a solution. Even if there is no acute need, the organization may identify people who are worth the investment and justify the trust associated with such investment. Alternatively individuals can propose themselves for such a programme. As the timespan for HR planning gets shorter, and with widespread redundancies, many organizations have been less prepared to offer such long-term investment in people. This is due not just to the short-term nature of modern job contracts, but also to the lower level of mutual commitment organizations might expect. This tendency is expected to continue, and organizations will prefer to acquire people who already possess the necessary qualifications rather than those who need to be sent on study programmes. As a consequence, short-term specific training may replace academic studies sponsored by organizations.

The qualification most frequently utilized to develop managerial competence is the Master in Business Administration (MBA) degree. Several studies have indicated the importance of the MBA, and the reputation of certain business schools.[12] An MBA degree from a leading business school can make a difference for its holder in terms of managerial competence, career progress and remuneration[13] but the problem organizations face is the insecurity and instability of investment in people. Employees are not the property of the employer; they can move on to different jobs and organizations, with the new employer (who may be a competitor) benefiting from the former employer's investment.

All in all, organizations need to be very careful in their long-term investment in training and development. If employees are promised that they will gain 'employability', investment in terms of training is the most visible manifestation of the commitment on the part of the organization to fulfil its role in this respect.

EXHIBIT 6.4	**Is it good for your company to have managers with an MBA qualification?**

Here are two stories of leading global companies which place a high value on an MBA.

Verizon

Some 10–15 per cent of **Verizon**'s managerial workforce has an MBA. For **Verizon**, an MBA is a valuable asset, and it expects the holder of an MBA to have a better strategic perspective and orientation, more sophisticated knowledge and awareness of its application and a more balanced set of skills than a person without an MBA or

Exhibit 6.4 continued

one who is a specialist in a particular business discipline. However, in terms of who gains the most from an MBA, the perception is that the individual gets more upfront benefits. The benefits to the organization are harder to quantify and observe. When organizations are filling management positions, an MBA can be a tie-breaker and evidence of achievement, focus, skills and commitment.

Still, when on looks at what has happened in the past to **Verizon** employees who earn an MBA, one sees that they have not done especially well. For a number of reasons **Verizon** generally does not attract MBA graduates (perhaps because it is a mature business or because it has a 'sales culture').

EDS

At **EDS**, with more than 1500 MBA graduates, the contribution of MBA studies stems from the knowledge and skills associated with an MBA curriculum which, according to **EDS**, benefits the company in all aspects of their business, but primarily in finance and accounting, strategic planning and management development. However, since **EDS** does not impose a requirement to obtain an MBA for any particular job, there is no company policy on MBAs. Still, in terms of who gains the most from an MBA, the MBA graduate or **EDS** as their employing organization, the answer is clearly both. Thus, in hiring for management positions, an MBA tends to generally be more of an advantage. In practice, the MBA tends to give an advantage to the MBA graduate, which propels the individual forward in his or her career. All in all, while a benefit to start with, it is the knowledge and the performance that matters. MBAs from the 'Top' schools do tend to produce very distinguished graduates. However, even among the graduates from a nearby state university evening programme, **EDS** finds good talent.

Lateral moves to create cross-functional experience

Lateral moves to create cross-functional experience are increasing, and it seems this trend will continue. These may be seen as elementary career planning and management practices which most organizations with HRM systems need to apply. The flattening of organization was one of the flagships of the 1990s. When there are fewer hierarchy levels and horizontal communication is the key to success, people will no longer move up the ladder so fast. A slow climb to the top, perhaps in the Japanese style, became quite typical in Western organizations.[14] Organizations need to indicate clearly that such a route reflects career success rather than failure; this is a shift from the past practice, which perceived only 'climbing up' as evidence of career success. People should be advised that career advancement is not necessarily along the traditional upward path.

Some of these lateral movements may take the form of developing new ventures, secondments and cross-functional moves. In 1978, Edgar Schein presented the spiral cross-functional move, but that too was part of upward progress (*see* Figure 6.3).[15] Lateral moves (*see* Figure 6.4) will characterize the career path of the future manager, while job rotations and role changes will be frequent for the

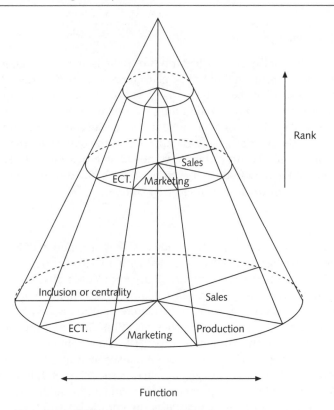

Figure 6.3 Schein's organizational cone

Source: Schein (1978). Taken from http://152.30.22.232/kirk/CDTheories/schein_organ_cone.html

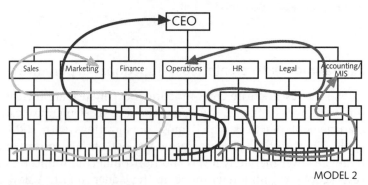

MODEL 2

Figure 6.4 Lateral moves

Source: Reprinted from M.A. Peiperl and Y. Baruch (1997) 'Models of careers: back to square zero', *Organizational Dynamics*, 25(4), 7–22, copyright 1997, with permission from Elsevier Science.

rank-and-file workforce. Relevant examples of this trend include the moving of insurance agents and bank clerks to direct marketing jobs.[16]

Retirement preparation programmes

This practice is directed at the target population of employees – those approaching retirement and about to leave the organization. These programmes can be short, e.g. a three-day workshop, taking place a couple of months before retirement. In addition to the 'standard' programme, large corporations may have a diversity programme, such as pre-retirement planning for women or minorities. They can also be longer, in terms of both programme time and its spread over a wider timespan. An investment in this practice is evidence of high commitment on the part of the organization to its employees, an essential part of developing mutual trust and commitment.[17] In these programmes the employee is prepared for retirement in several ways. Much time is devoted to financial considerations and ensuring that participants understand pension conditions and learn tax regulations. However, the better programmes take into account also the psychological need to adjust to life without work, a transformation that, if not managed, might end in deterioration of the health and well-being of people used to full-time hard work. Information on leisure activities and other fulfilling tasks forms a significant part of the better programmes, and in some of them the spouse is invited to take part too.

| EXHIBIT 6.5 | Pre-retirement programmes |

Companies may run their own programmes or acquire one from an external consultancy.

Career Management Consultants is one of many consultancies who offer companies to manage their retirement programmes to assist employees to plan for the transition to retirement. The preparation includes emotional adjustments and lifestyle preparation. Their specific programme takes into consideration:

- Financial realities
- Geographic preferences
- Physical and emotional services
- Planning for positive change
- Decision making
- Career change
- Volunteering
- Dealing with family reactions and adjustments
- Aiming towards happiness

An internal programme is offered by the Wisconsin Department of Employee Trust Funds. Their motto is 'Retirement – A New Beginning'. The pre-retirement planning programme takes the form of a 12-hour course held in the evening for two hours a week for six weeks. The content of the course will typically include:

- Financial planning
  - Social security
  - Retirement benefits
- Insurance
  - Life insurance
  - Health insurance/Medicare
- Legal tips (e.g. taxes, wills and lawyers)
- Consumerism, housing, employment and retirement, wellness in retirement, and leisure.

The heavy redundancies of recent years mean that fewer people are remaining at the workplace until the legal retirement age (70 in the USA and 65 in most EU countries). Thus traditional pre-retirement programmes might become quite rare in the future. The need for this practice obviously depends also on the age of the organization and the maturity of its employees. For organizations that have been in existence for about 20–30 years, with most founders being aged about 30 at the time of the start-up, there is no real need for formal institutionalized pre-retirement programmes. If there are only a very few due to retire, the issue may best be dealt with by a private consultancy that will conduct an internal organizational programme of preparation for retirement, in line with the present-day approach of outsourcing HR functions.

If large-scale redundancy programmes are likely to prevail in the near future, pre-retirement programmes may be transformed into pre-redundancy programmes. In this kind of programme, the organization will first prepare the employees for the possibility that 'it could happen to you, too'. Subsequently the focus will move to what can be done, how an employee whose career has reached a plateau stage can be trained to look successfully for a new job in declining industrial sectors. In addition to such a pre-redundancy programme, the same organization will need an after-redundancy programme, to deal with the 'survivor syndrome' which might affect those who have stayed. Professional use of best practice may combat survivor syndrome successfully.[18]

Booklets and/or pamphlets on career issues

Booklets, pamphlets or leaflets are part of an organization's formal stock of career-related information. They introduce what career opportunities the organization offers and provide an introduction to all available CPM practices. Information that may be covered includes career paths, the competencies required for each position on the path, time scales (e.g. the minimum time to be spent in a certain position before promotion), conditions for certain developments. The aim of such booklets is to provide everyone in the organization with relevant information, releasing the direct manager from the job of presenting that information to subordinates.

Such information is directed at all employees, but is important especially for newcomers, either those recently recruited to the organization, or those recently promoted to the managerial ranks. In the 2000s we expect fewer of these booklets to exist. Complex company re-structurings, mergers and acquisitions will make most written forms obsolete very quickly. Booklets may be made available in electronic form as part of the company website, with access either limited to the employees of the company who have the password, or open to all.

With companies facing an increasing number of lawsuits due to a failure to satisfy employees' expectations, employers do not like to present what might later be seen as unfulfilled promises. This factor, coupled with the lower potential for long-term planning, means that the importance of such booklets is declining, and they are being replaced by different forms, such as electronic boards and directories which can incorporate structural change fed into the system, resulting in an updated version of an electronic booklet.

Dual ladder

The dual ladder is a parallel hierarchy, created for non-managerial staff, such as professional or technical employees. The major role of such a 'ladder' is to provide 'upward mobility' and recognition for those who cannot or do not wish to hold a managerial role. The dual ladder emerged in response to the need to provide professionals in non-managerial roles a different promotion path. A typical case is that of the excellent, promising engineer who is promoted to a managerial role (because there is no alternative means of recognizing or remunerating them within the professional roles). Such promotions often end with an accomplished professional transformed into a poor manager.

The dual ladder is very important, but is suitable only for the particular group (professionals without managerial skills or with no aspiration to become managers). Many large firms use this technique (Feuer, 1986), and its use is continually growing (Badway, 1988).[19] The reason for creating the dual ladder will still be valid in the 2000s, and perhaps even more so, as a new sector of professionals will be involved – professional experts, counsellors, etc. – not managers, but people working in crucial roles, with a responsibility and remuneration level similar to that of managers. The CPM system will need to identify the population eligible for this status, and ensure that only a small proportion enter the stream. Otherwise it will lose its power as an alternative system of recognition for those few who deserve it.

Induction

The process of introducing people to their new organization is the first CPM practice a new employee experiences (it will be entitled induction or socialization). This is a process whereby all newcomers learn the behaviours and attitudes necessary for assuming roles in an organization (Van Mannen, 1976).[20] Part of it is formal, led by organizational officials, whereas other aspects are learned in an informal manner, not necessarily in line with organizational formal norms and policies (*see*, for example, Ashford, 1986).[21] Newcomers are not always passive in their search for information (Morrison, 1993).[22] The set of mutual expectations in the boundaryless organization will be different from the one most people have experienced in the past (for further elaboration *see* the discussion of psychological contracts later in this chapter). Nevertheless, it remains essential that employers should introduce newcomers to the varied aspects of their organizational life and their role within it. These can be related to ideology or philosophy, culture, policies, rules and regulations, norms, expected behaviours and performance, and any other information, including social, which will help them to master their jobs and become integrated into the new workplace. One of the main changes witnessed in the 1990s is the much wider age span of newcomers. Whereas in the old type of careers people joined organizations at an early age, and in many cases stayed for their whole working life in the same workplace, people now tend to have a multiple career path, and frequent changes of employers are common. An induction process for the experienced professional or manager is very different from that directed at young school leavers or new graduates.

The long-lasting impact of this early experience for newcomers on their later life in the organization should not be underestimated (Bauer and Green, 1994).[23]

Assessment and development centres

Assessment centres have attracted much interest in academia and from organizational practitioners. They have been found as a reliable and valid tool for career development (c.f. Tziner, Ronen and Hacohen, 1993; Thornton, Tziner, Dahan, Clevenger and Meir, 1997; Iles, 1999) and are expected to continue to play an important role in the twenty-first century (Howard, 1997).[24] In the recent past, assessment centres were used for two main purposes: as a selection tool for managerial recruitment, and as an indicator of managerial potential; now they are also being used for developmental purposes (Spychalski, Quinones, Gaugler and Pohley, 1997).[25] Development centres evolved from assessment centres, and share many features with them, but are directed not necessarily towards selection but rather to general development and enhancement of the manager, preparing him/her for future roles. There is widespread discussion of assessment centres in the literature and most studies provide strong support for their effectiveness (e.g. Bray, 1985; Portwood and Granrose, 1986; Laser, 1990).[26] Large organizations may have their own assessment centres whereas small firms generally use external institutions. The use of assessment centres for selection is expected to decline, as fewer positions will be available following the trend towards downsizing (Cameron, 1996).[27] Thus we may witness more use of assessment centres for developmental purposes and identification of managerial potential (Iles, 1999).[28]

Mentoring

The principal aim of mentoring is to bring together a person with managerial potential and an experienced manager, who is not necessarily that person's direct manager. The senior manager can provide advice and tutoring, serving as a kind of 'uncle' or 'godfather' in the workplace. Thus mentoring is directed mostly at managerial personnel, and is used frequently in graduate recruitment programmes. The potential of this practice has been suggested in many studies (e.g. Baird and Kram, 1983; Clawson, 1980; Kram, 1985; Scandura, 1992; Baugh, Lankau and Scandura, 1996, and others).[29] In particular Kram (1986)[30] argues that both mentors and protégés benefit from this practice, and that the organization can shape the kind of mentoring relationships it wants. Such a win-win situation, when achievable, will be needed in the future too. Moreover, the organization is a clear beneficiary from having mentoring practice (Scandura and Viator, 1994),[31] in terms of protégés' attitudes and performance.

Mentoring, though acclaimed as a novel and esteemed approach for managerial development, also has pitfalls. Scandura (1998)[32] analysed the main dysfunctions of mentoring, which she saw as negative relations, sabotage, difficulty and spoiling. Another significant problem associated with mentoring is the possible collision of interests between the direct manager and the mentor. Cross-gender mentoring can also give rise to questions of possible sexual harassment on the one side and creating or encouraging unintended types of relationships on the other. Problems of this sort can be prevented by same-gender mentoring, which will be more feasible when more females enter managerial positions. The availability of mentors may also be a problem: with fewer hierarchical layers in the 2000s organization it will be more difficult to find enough people to serve as mentors – a factor which might reduce the present considerable use of this practice. To overcome these problems novel ideas are offered, for example the introduction of peer mentoring. A different approach to encourage senior managers to take on protégés would be to emphasize that being a mentor is a sign of seniority and recognition. Thus mentoring may replace position in the formal hierarchy as a status symbol for mature and loyal managers, those who wish to contribute to the success of the organization and at the same time to be recognized as a senior member of the organization.

Career workshops

Career workshops are short-term workshops focusing on specific aspect(s) of career management, and aiming to provide managers with relevant knowledge, skills and experience (*see* Figure 6.5). Participating in career workshops can contribute to the effectiveness of the employee (Sweeney, Haller and Sale, 1989).[33] Career workshops usually focus on specific aspects such as identifying future

Career workshops		
Career resilience workshop		
Altman and Baruch (2002)[35] developed a workshop to help individuals identify their resilience and coherence with their employing organization. An extract from the workshop is presented below (participants are asked, among other activities, to evaluate several statements about themselves and their workplace).		

Evaluation scales:

1	2	3	4	5	6	7
low	moderately low	neither low nor high	moderately high	high	very high	extremely high

	Actual presence	Valence – how important this is for you
1. Individuals are encouraged to take responsibility for their own development	1 2 3 4 5 6 7	1 2 3 4 5 6 7
2. Employees are encouraged to take initiatives to enhance their own employability	1 2 3 4 5 6 7	1 2 3 4 5 6 7
Etc.		

Intelligent career workshop

Parker and Arthur (2002)[36] developed a workshop based on sort cards to identify and analyse individual 'components' of career intelligence. Further information can be found in Parker and Arthur (2002).

Figure 6.5 Career workshops

opportunities, rather than just general development (e.g. interviewing skills). With frequent structural changes in organizations people certainly need adaptation mechanisms, and workshops of this kind will help in this. Career workshops can improve the employability of the participants, enhancing their career resilience (Waterman, Waterman and Collard, 1994).[34] The impetus for sending people to workshops can come from their manager or mentor or the HR counselling system as well as self nomination. With an increasing number of organizations making redundancies or undergoing restructuring, future career workshops may concentrate on inter- and intra-organizational opportunities. Among the many ideas on which workshops can focus are how to increase employability, how to create new satellite companies or joint ventures, the concept and practice of the management buy-out. These and other ideas can help participants to develop new insights into the future of their career – within the organization or elsewhere.

Performance appraisal as a basis for career planning

Numerous works emphasize the need for a close connection between the performance appraisal (PA) system and career development (e.g. Jacobson and Kaye, 1986; Weitzel, 1987; Murphy and Cleveland, 1995).[37] Hall, Posner and Harder (1989)[38] demonstrated the gap between the theory behind PA systems and their implementation, suggesting the need to combine CPM with the PA system. PA systems were found to operate in most of the organizations studied.

Of all the CPM practices, PA is perhaps the most fundamental. It can be utilized in HRM in a very similar way to that by which accountancy reports (such as the profit and loss account or the balance sheet) cater for the finance and accountancy systems. Valid and reliable PA would identify who should be promoted, who should be made redundant at a time of downsizing, and identify training and development needs. In terms of choosing people for future development, e.g. the selection of high potential employees for assessment centres, can be done on the basis of their PA results. A variety of CPM practices, such as appointing mentors or building succession planning, depend on the PA system. If the system is valid and reliable it may serve as the foundation stone for an integrated CPM system.

Career counselling

Career counselling is a two-way communication with the employee and two main sources are available for conducting this. The first is the direct manager (or another higher manager) who has a good knowledge of the employee's attitudes, behaviours, skills, etc.; the second is an HRM manager. Depending on the complexity of an organization, and its financial resources, external counselling can also be provided. This practice can be closely associated with the core of the Herriot and Pemberton (1996) model,[39] which shows the need to match organizational requirements and possibilities with individual career aspirations and abilities. Many agencies now provide career counselling services to both individuals and organizations (some examples are presented in Chapter 2 – *see* Exhibit 2.2).

Career counselling by direct manager and by the HRM unit

In many organizations the direct manager is in the best position to conduct career counselling, because he or she has perhaps the most accurate and up-to-date knowledge of the person. On the other hand, for such counselling to be fruitful, the person conducting it needs to have good standing in the organiz-ation, and to know the career options available and the direction of future organ-izational developments. In addition serving as a counsellor can conflict with other roles of the manager, such as loyalty (i.e. whether his/her loyalty resides with the organization or with the subordinate). Career counselling can be con-ducted also by the HRM unit staff. The advantages of their doing the counselling include knowledge of organizational goals and development; familiarity with HRM planning for the whole enterprise and knowledge, skills and experience of counselling in general. The obstacle that frequently prevents HRM from carrying out this task is its detachment from the professional life of the organization.

One of the long-standing problems relating to this practice is the fact that direct managers frequently see it as a bureaucratic burden, as Walker and Gutteridge (1979) found.[40] They also found that most of the supervisors in their survey (87 per cent) were not trained for counselling. A new problem is that there may be major changes of which the direct manager may have no prior knowl-edge. For example, in mergers and acquisitions, many layers of management become aware of a significant organizational structural change only after its announcement. In the 2000s we expect HRM to be more closely aligned with the general business strategy, so that the HR manager will be more aware of future plans, and consequently will be better equipped to deal with individual career counselling.

One solution could be to make two or three counsellors available – the direct manager and an HRM manager, with the option also of external counselling. Sometimes counselling can touch on sensitive issues, and individual employees may prefer the latter option. For personal matters which may require confiden-tiality, integration is not recommended (e.g. certain issues should not be reported to the formal PA system), but on the other hand, individual interest in second-ments (*see* the discussion later in this chapter) could be expressed and identified through counselling.

EXHIBIT 6.6	External counselling

A worldwide downturn in the sales of machine tools caused an engineering company located in Birmingham to review its capacity, resulting in the loss of more than 100 jobs. The job losses included labourers, warehousing, operators, clerical, supervision, management, engineers and apprentices.

They selected an outside consultancy (the Quo Group) due to their extensive knowledge and experience of the Midlands job market. They were able to provide counsellors with relevant sector expertise along with the empathy to work with the varying levels of skills and attributes in the company.

The programme consisted of a series of two-day workshops for all non-managerial staff* to attend. These workshops concentrated on: identifying life and career goals, developing the appropriate action plan (including CV and interview preparation), mapping routes to the job market (including advertisement analysis, job and government agencies and networking), and dealing with offer negotiations.

Clients were seen in the consulting firm's premises and/or in individual sessions depending on their needs.

Major elements in the success of the programme were a mailshot to more than 500 companies within a 5-mile radius of the site, coupled with contacting local job agencies. These resulted in hundreds of enquiries. The Quo Group provided a job researcher who matched enquiries to skills and arranged interviews for all concerned. In addition a helpline was in place for those individuals who required support after the programme was completed.

Six weeks after the end of the programme only 4 per cent of those wanting jobs were still unemployed.

*Managers were provided with the Quo Group's one-to-one Executive Programme.

Source: This case was kindly provided by the Quo Group Ltd.

Succession planning

Miner and Miner (1985)[41] suggested a framework of organizational planning in which the organization decides on the possible replacement of every manager within the organization, and evaluates the potential for promotion of each manager. By its nature, this programme is primarily directed towards the managerial workforce. Succession planning (also termed a management inventory) can be valuable in the context of long-term planning. It will be different, but not less important, in a flattened organization where lateral movements occur. In the latter, succession planning will be more complicated but will still show who should first be considered when a new vacancy arises or job rotation is planned.

It should be noted that succession planning builds on the internal labour market, and looks mostly within the organizational boundary (Rothwell, 1994; Sessa and Campbell, 1997).[42] With less loyalty and a higher turnover of employees, and managers in particular (Baruch, 1998), succession planning may possess less predictive power in the 2000s.[43]

A different approach was advised by Leibman, Bruer and Maki (1996),[44] who suggested a new concept, entitled 'succession management', should replace succession planning. They emphasized the gap between the traditional and the contemporary approaches, the former prone to be rigid in form, based on skills and experience, whereas the latter is dynamic and flexible. The gap could be bridged if HR focuses on the competencies and leadership qualities of managers. Inputs for the creation and updating of succession planning will come from several sources – primarily the PA system, and then mentors' perceptions, assessment centre results and career counselling. Special attention is needed in responding to equal employment opportunities (EEO) and particular groups that may have specific requirements. Careful analysis of any succession planning programme will look at its implications for other CPM practices such as formal education training programmes, or appropriate and relevant secondments.

Figure 6.6 presents an example of a succession planning form.

Comp MD (or CEO if in US):
Ms Power
A/T/P: 55/12/3
Opt 1: Mr Yuth
Opt 2: Ms Monetar

Comp Secretary
Mr Borden
A/T/P: 60/35/5
Prom: C
Perf: **
Opt 1: Mr Perfor
Opt 2: Ms Mark

Comp Marketing MD
Mr Youth
A/T/P: 42/5/3
Prom: B
Perf: ****
Opt 1: Mr Perfor
Opt 2: Ms Future

Comp Finance MD
Ms Monetar
A/T/P: 52/15/10
Prom: B
Perf: ***
Opt 1:
Opt 2:

Comp Operation MD
Mr Perfor
A/T/P: 50/25/4
Prom: C
Perf: ***
Opt 1:
Opt 2:

Comp Finance MD
Ms Monetar
A/T/P: 52/15/2
Prom: A
Perf: *****
Opt 1:
Opt 2:

Marketing North
Mr Rough
A/T/P: 50/30/7
Prom: C
Perf: ***
Opt 1:
Opt 2:

Marketing Central
Mr Stable
A/T/P: 37/15/3
Prom: D
Perf: **
Opt 1:
Opt 2:

Marketing SE
Mr Mark
A/T/P: 42/12/5
Prom: A
Perf: ****
Opt 1:
Opt 2:

Marketing SW
Ms Const
A/T/P: 60/40/7
Prom: B
Perf: ***
Opt 1:
Opt 2:

Marketing Planning
Ms Future
A/T/P: 40/15/3
Prom: A
Perf: *****
Opt 1: ...
Opt 2: ...

Key:

A/T/P: Age in years (clear indication of time before retirement) / Tenure (and within the company it can be decided whether it is tenure in the company, in the sector, or in a managerial position in general / Time in present position (indication of readiness for a new move).
Prom: Promotability, with different letters indicating whether the person is:
   A: top performer, ready for next career upward move;
   B: good performer; maybe move to a similar level job;
   C: reasonable, all round performer;
   D: unsatisfactory performance level;
   F: a failure, must be replaced ASAP;
   &: not enough time in job to be evaluated.
A different sign may be added to indicate readiness for promotability in the short or long term (or that the person has reached the highest possible level).

For example, Ms Monetar may be excellent in her job, but having been there only 2 years means she should not yet be moved.

Perf: Performance level, from 1 to 5 stars (*) according to whatever PA system is used at Comp.

Opt 1, 2...: Who is a prospective successor – can be from the same hierarchy level or from one level below – either in the same department or from another department; lack of options means a need to recruit from outside (as no viable option exists within). The company may decide to add a line of 'crisis replacement': who can step in if the manager leaves with short notice or suffers health problems or death.

Figure 6.6 Succession planning form

360-degree performance appraisal systems

The late 1990s saw a growth in unorthodox methods of PA, mainly 360-degree feedback (*see* the special issue of the journal *HRM* in 1993) with a variety of PA methods applied (Tziner, Kopelman and Joanis, 1997).[45] 360-degree feedback can take the form of peer appraisal, upward appraisal, committee appraisal, or a combination of several sources in addition to appraisal by the direct manager (Baruch and Harel, 1993; Bernardin, Kane, Ross, Spina and Johnson, 1995).[46] Self- and upward appraisal (Baruch, 1996a and Bernardin, 1986, respectively)[47] are also valuable sources of PA, increasing the reliability and validity of the process. All signs indicate that this trend will continue, with PA being used more as a feedback tool and for development purposes rather than being used in gathering information for organizational decision making. The latter use will persist where individual performance-related PA is practised (cf. Kessler and Purcell, 1992; Kessler, 1994).[48] While the literature supports the use of 360-degree feedback (cf. Tornow, London, *et al.*, 1998),[49] it should be noted that this practice is very demanding in terms of time invested and analysis required, so it may not be easy to apply it routinely in organizations.

Special programmes for ethnic minorities, women, people with disabilities, dual-career couples, etc.

Chapter 8 will deal specifically with diversity management. Here it is sufficient to note that organizations should develop special programmes to tackle all possible kinds of discrimination, such as the 'glass ceiling' effect for women, i.e. not being promoted above certain managerial level (Morrison, White and Van Velsor, 1987).[50] Many programmes are intended to support the population discriminated against, sometimes even to apply 'positive discrimination'. It is important, though, that such 'positive discrimination' does not imply the abandonment of a policy of selection according to skills, competencies and suitability for the job. Problems of discrimination exist for many groups, not just women. Discrimination on the basis of ethnic background, disability, age and religion can prevent appropriate people from making a full contribution. For example, mass early retirements accepted by or imposed on people in their 50s might deprive organizations of a pool of talented and experienced people. Disabled people can be highly committed and productive when that disability is irrelevant to the requirements of the role under consideration. Organizations which recognize these issues will benefit from pursuing different career management practices with respect to particular populations with specific needs.

Special programmes are not necessarily concerned with discrimination. The case of dual-career couples raises another matter, i.e. how to enable two people to develop side by side when both have a career. With the continuing growth in education and equality in employment we will see even more dual-career couples in the 2000s. The HR system must recognize this, especially where international relocations become necessary as part of career progress (Baruch, 1995; Harvey, 1997).[51] The trend of globalization is expected to continue and managing expatriates will be a crucial issue in the twenty-first century (*see* Punnett, Crocker and Stevens, 1992, and also the next section of this chapter).[52]

Special programmes for expatriates and repatriates

Global career management will be dealt with in Chapter 7. Here I will note only that international HRM is a fast-developing issue in the management of people (Kopp, 1994).[53] For multinational/global enterprises, the management of expatriates is a crucial part of their CPM agenda (Black, Gregersen and Mendenhall, 1992; Borg and Harzing, 1995).[54] In addition, there are growing concerns about the special attention needed for the management of repatriation: Rodrigues (1996)[55] referred especially to the 'reverse culture shock' effect. Evidence indicates a high rate of failure in the management of expatriates (Marquardt and Engel, 1993; Zetlin, 1994).[56] The most important aspect of this management is rigorous preparation for the assignment, with emphasis on cultural induction, maintaining communication with expatriates and paying attention to the repatriation period. As argued previously, the expatriate population is likely to expand in the future, as globalization spreads. Career paths in multinational corporations will include overseas posts as a crucial part of the developmental process for the managerial workforce.

Special programmes for high-flyers

All employees, as the prime asset of the organization, deserve investment in their career by their organization. However, the so-called high-flyers are perceived as a special asset, with the potential to make a unique contribution to the future of the organization, and thus worthy of having greater attention and resources dedicated specifically to them. Derr, Jones and Toomey (1988) look at high-flyers as a scarce resource, and because of the reduction in workforce numbers, including managerial layers, suggest that organizations will look for more ways of developing future leaders.[57] In contrast with the variety of separate practices discussed in this chapter, 'Special programmes for high-flyers' could form a group of practices and activities from those mentioned in the list, applied extensively to the high-flyers.

London and Stumpf (1982) suggested a two-part model for organizational CPM, especially designed for high-flyers.[58] The first part relates to the identification of the high-flyers at the beginning of their careers while the second refers to the accelerated path set for them. Such a development programme provides the high-flyer with a unique opportunity and wider options for fast development, but might also create pressure and stress for the individual. Recent developments, however, question the necessity for specifically designated high-flyer programmes, due to the unpredictable nature of the present-day workplace, and constant structural changes (Baruch and Peiperl, 2000a).[59] Trends already under way in the 1990s indicate that what will be required from the twenty-first century high-flyer is entrepreneurship competencies rather than the ability to exercise control and power in a bureaucratic system. In a boundaryless organization, a boundaryless career is called for (Ashkenas, Ulrich, Jick and Kerr, 1995; Arthur, 1994).[60]

New CPM practices for the 2000s

Building psychological contracts

The concept that a psychological contract exists between the employee and the workplace was discussed earlier in this book, and is acknowledged as a crucial aspect of the relationship between both sides. Recent works examine the results of breaking these contracts (cf. Rousseau, 1996; Morrison and Robinson, 1997).[61] The beginning of the 1990s saw a significant change in the nature and notion of the psychological contract. In future employers will have to clarify this concept – as a set of mutual expectations which need to be agreed upon, explicitly or implicitly – to their employees (*see also* Herriot and Pemberton, 1995).[62] These expectations are, first, what the organization perceives as a fair contribution from the employee, and second, what the organization will provide in return. Employees will be persuaded and required then to 'sign' this unwritten contract. This is in line with Wanous' (1992) ideas of the realistic job preview, taking it in the broader sense of the realistic career preview (*see also* Semmer and Schallberger, 1996).[63] The cycle of career planning and development for each person joining the workforce will start with the establishment of a mutual agreement, a psychological contract, which sets the type and style of future relationships. Two different populations will be involved here: existing employees, for some of whom the old psychological contract will be altered (for many this process occurred in the 1990s), and the newly hired, for whom the essential part will be delivered during the induction period, with reinforcement to follow later.

Secondments

Secondment is the temporary assignment of a person to another area within the organization, or sometimes to another associated organization (such as a customer or supplier). In a recent study, Baruch and Peiperl (2000a)[64] asked HR managers to refer to a list of career practices and also to indicate whether they used additional practices. Several of the 194 respondents suggested 'secondments' as an additional practice. Secondment is a period in which the manager acquires a different perspective within the company boundaries or from the outside; and a period of time spent in marketing, HRM or finance can improve a production manager's knowledge of organizational processes, help build interrelations with colleagues and increase communication thereafter. At a more advanced level, secondments can be taken outside the organization. Exchange programmes under which managers and executives serve a period of time in another company, sharing knowledge and gaining some insight in return, can provide a win-win situation for both companies involved.

As in the other practices described, the impetus to offer people secondments can come from their manager or mentor, or from HR counselling and PA systems. A possible problem with secondment programmes is the need for long-term HR planning and for mutuality, thus making it feasible mostly for large or well-established corporations. There is a risk of losing successful managers to the company they are seconded to, and there is also the usual risk of benchmarking, where it might be that only one side benefits from the deal. If the practice of creating satellite firms develops in the West, as in Japan for example, the use of secondments will expand and it is possible that the 2000s may see more of this practice in a wider range of organizations.

Intrapreneurship

As seen in Chapter 3 (in the discussion of the Desert Generation phenomenon), different people have different approaches to their life and career. Employers should identify those who possess the qualities needed to generate new business within the organization. Organizations should encourage organizational learning, and provide employees with options for inner sources of growth, via intrapreneurship. Instead of outsourcing activities and operations, organizations can use people from within who desire to develop something new, but still remain within the organization.

EXHIBIT 6.7	**Company case: Intrapreneurship at The Times of India Group**

The Times of India Group is the largest media and entertainment company in India with an annual turnover exceeding US$320 billion or £210 million. It employs some 7000 people in the company directly, and about 1000 on contractual appointment, a ratio typical in this business sector, and publishes 4 Newspapers, 2 Magazines, 1 Tabloid, has 12 Radio stations, 10 Retail stores and divisions in Music (Times Music, the largest music company in India), the Internet, Multimedia and News Syndication. A fast-growing group, with a heritage of 164 years, it is perceived as a highly vibrant and creative media company.

The Times of India Group has long recognized that the company can grow only when entrepreneurship thrives within the organization. Thus, the Board of Directors have always encouraged employees to start new brands, sub-brands and new ventures which augment the organization's mission to grow as the largest information and entertainment company in Asia. The company's 26 main brands and 116 sub-brands are largely accounted for by such encouragement of intrapreneurship.

In addition, the company has ventured into the Internet (www.indiatimes.com), with some eight hundred million page views per month. For most professionals one of the most exciting reasons to work with the group has been the constant pace of growth of the company and the freedom offered to do one's job and to play with ideas and give birth to new ventures and for those who have latent entrepreneurship talent ... this has been a constant source of encouragement.

Many health surveys conducted in different companies show that most people at some stage in life want to do something new, fresh, relevant in a field that they are passionate about. Organizations like the Times Group offer this opportunity to harness the creative potential of each individual to benefit the company. In such a scenario, both the organization and the individual win.

Thanks to Ashoke K. Maitra, HR Director of The Times of India Group for providing this case.

CPM practices which require reassessment for the 2000s

Common career paths

A career path is the most preferred and recommended route for the career advancement of a manager in an organization. Such career paths can lead people through various departments and units within the organization and, in multinational companies, in overseas subsidiaries. The use of career paths spread rapidly in the 1970s and 1980s in many organizations (Portwood and Granrose, 1986)[66] and its significance was demonstrated by Carulli, Noroian and Levine (1989) and Boyle and Leibovitz (1990).[67] The use of career paths is more widespread in larger organizations, whereas one may find more informal paths or a complete lack of paths in smaller organizations. The base for career path planning is stability and a wide range of layers and positions. With traditional hierarchical structures flattening and diminishing (*see* Cameron, 1996)[68] and with the creation of boundaryless and virtual organizations, it is likely that career paths will not develop much in future. The consequences for career paths are that there are fewer fast tracks in organizations, including large ones. As Peiperl and Baruch (1997)[69] argued, it is now the norm, rather than the exception, for organizations to have no fixed career paths and for individuals in them to see no further than one or two years ahead.

Written personal career planning for employees

Written documents generate commitment, at least on the organization's part. Long-term commitment (e.g. life-time employment) became virtually extinct as a feature of organizational life in the 1990s and this trend seems sure to continue in the 2000s. Written personal career plans are problematic also because they create expectations. Past experience of such plans provides examples of frustration as where a plan suggests the same job for several people, which only one can attain. Few organizations use this technique (Baruch, 1996b),[65] and it could be that this practice will die out in the 2000s, for reasons similar to those suggested for the common career path.

EXHIBIT 6.8	Company case: High-flyers and career paths at The Times of India Group

The Times of India Group has a long history of capacity building and talent development. Let us look at their Management Trainee scheme. Over the last 30 years, the company has inducted bright young professionals at entry levels in Marketing, Manufacturing, Finance and HRD. In 2002, their Directors in Marketing, Production, Modernization, Sales, and all the heads of publishing centres have come from the several Management Trainee schemes in the company.

In marketing, the recruitment team goes every year to the best management schools and selects management trainees in marketing. The new entrants are put in the sales job for about 2 years. After that they are put in charge of a group, where they have 6–8 people reporting to them. Once they effectively supervise the group, they are then appointed as category head to be in charge of a total category. Categories in the newspaper industry are sections like appointments or displays, etc. The category head of appointments is in charge of generating revenues through recruitment advertisements. Similarly, displays are large advertisements for products. Once a person has successfully been a category head for 2–3 years, the person is then given charge of an entire branch, where s/he not only has to head the advertising function, but also look after all the other areas like corporate communication, human resources, industrial relations, material management and finance. After the person has been a successful branch head for 2–3 years, s/he is then put either in charge of a region, say the southern part of India or given a Brand to develop. If a person performs effectively and demonstrates greater potential, the person could perhaps become Director of the company or could be given an opportunity to start new brands.

Exhibit 6.8 continued

In the production function, the company selects two kinds of trainees. The first are those with a diploma in printing, who start on the shop floor and later are put in charge of specific areas as unit heads. The selected people later advance to the level of Works Manager. The company also recruits Graduate Engineer Trainees from professional engineering colleges with Bachelors in Engineering in the area of production, manufacturing, mechanical and electronics. These students initially work on the shop floor for about 2 years, later they are put in charge of a section for about 4–5 years and then offered complete responsibility for one of the smaller production factories. Once they have successfully run a factory, they are put in a large printing establishment in charge either of the printing operation or processing or of colour. Later, they are promoted to head the total factory.

Thus we see that common career paths are still valid in large organizations that benefit from relative stability and growth.

Thanks to Ashoke K. Maitra, HR Director of The Times of India Group for providing this case.

From a collection to a collective: integrating practices into a system

Throughout this chapter, career practices have been discussed mostly in isolation, almost as if they are unrelated, albeit grouped in several clusters. However, careers in organizations are meant to be planned and managed in a joint manner. A system should be designed to answer the needs and requirements of both the individual and the organization. Professional, effective HR management will make sure that the career system operates in a well-integrated, comprehensive way.

Applying a two-fold level of integration is necessary to achieve a fit and to make the optimal use of career practices. These levels are the 'internal', amongst the variety of practices, and the 'external' – integration between the career system and the organizational culture and strategy. Both internal and external integration should be strategy led: an HRM strategy that is part of and aligned with the whole organizational strategy, including the career area.[70] Day-to-day management of career practices is derived from the strategy. Strategy, for example, will determine whether an organization should go international or stay within its national borders. The derived implementation of career practices following this strategy will deal with expatriation and repatriation policies and practices. HRM strategy will determine which is the preferred labour market (i.e. internal or external) and career practices will determine which type of job advertising will be implemented. Similarly, organizations will develop career practices according to the organization's wider HRM strategy.

Internal integration

Internal integration relates to the level of harmony between the various career practices; a fit for which there is a dire need. This has been demonstrated throughout the chapter in discussions of the relationships between specific practices: how the PA system is associated with other practices, how inputs from one practice (mentoring, for example) influence the use of others (e.g. workshops, secondments).

As indicated and presented above, career practices may appear in clusters, where groups of practices are interrelated. The wide range of career management practices may naturally be clustered in groups according to their common use and interrelations among them. Further, these clusters are associated with certain organizational characteristics such as size, age or culture and the clusters vary according to the sophistication and extent of involvement of the organization in the career management process.[71] The future seems to promise more managerial complexity, resulting in a need for more sophisticated career systems. The involvement of the organization will vary too, according to the target population (e.g. characteristics such as employees' level of education, lifestyle, etc.), the culture of the organization and the business sector.

The integration may follow the 'cafeteria method'. Cafeteria-style career management programmes are among the newer approaches to career pluralism in organizations.[72] Fundamentally, cafeteria plans provide an array of career-track options, training opportunities, performance evaluation schemes and reward systems to enable employees to have career experiences that are most in line with their own career concepts and motives and with the strategy of the organization.

One of the most important ingredients of internal integration is the use of advanced IT systems. Internal e-mail systems can be used for the distribution of information not only on job vacancies but also on career workshops, booklets, training and the development opportunities and other features. As suggested previously, having a website has become the norm for organizations. Part of the information available on organizations' websites relates to career options in the organization, the type of people who work there and their roles (such data are available now for most universities or at least those of the industrial world). One may also find information on how to apply for jobs, and more and more data will be accessible as organizational information continues to grow and expand. This is subject to the stability of the Internet, which is not guaranteed: the Internet might collapse as a result of misuse, abuse, or even terrorist action (including the spread of computer viruses).

Support systems, increasingly the IT-based ones, have an important role to play in the management of career systems. The results of PA are likely to be processed by IT, particularly in view of the complexity of 360-degree PA systems. These systems require much integration and comparative analysis for the understanding and utilization of the data. Similarly, creating reliable and valid succession planning depends on the use of IT systems to gather and analyse information from many sources. We are seeing an increase in the number of organizations utilizing performance related payment (PRP), with remuneration depending partially on individual and/or group performance. This seems to be the direction for the near future, in particular for knowledge workers. For complex PRP systems, IT may combine the career and payment systems to generate an integrated output, which will consider the variety of inputs into an accepted two-fold output. Internal integration will not be limited to the tangible element of payment. It will also enable flexibility and reflect the new type of psychological contracts between the employer (or employers, when individuals work in more than one workplace) and the employee.

External integration

As far as external integration is concerned, we observed that the career system that best fits the organization depends on the operational strategy of the whole enterprise. The Sonnenfeld and Peiperl (1988) career system model,[73] presented earlier in Chapter 4, was based on the Miles and Snow organizational strategic model.[74] This is in line with the theoretical works of the early 1980s, introducing the concept of strategic HRM.[75] The career system should be developed in line with business objectives and needs.[76] The types of practices carried out will depend on the culture of the organization. In a bureaucratic system, which is relatively stable (e.g. the civil service, traditional manufacturing), common career paths can still be applied for long-term career progress. In a dynamic, turbulent sector (e.g. IT companies), career paths will have to be revised every year or two. In this latter type of work environment career practices such as mentoring become even more important, although it becomes increasingly difficult to identify enough senior managers suitable and ready to serve as mentors. In terms of the continuum from individualism to collectivism, another recognized dimension in organizational culture studies, succession planning or secondment will appeal to individualistic cultures whereas group-oriented cultures will probably focus on developing induction programmes, workshops and special practices for supposedly disadvantaged groups. The organizational culture will help in shaping the career practices and their use, but in a complementary way, career management can help in the reshaping of organizational culture.

Impact factors

Several factors are expected to influence the way career practices will be integrated. The most prominent are size, age, globalization, workforce diversity and the chosen labour market. These factors will determine whether certain practices are applied and the importance of their implementation.

Size is crucial, as small organizations neither have nor need the resources required to implement practices such as succession planning or a dual ladder. In terms of age, new organizations will not need retirement-preparation programmes and will be less inclined to encourage secondments. The level of globalization of the company will determine the need for special expatriation programmes and the type of mentoring imperative for overseas appointments. Workforce diversity will influence not only special career programmes but also the tone of career counselling, booklets, workshops and other practices, and focus on either the internal or the external labour market will have to be taken into consideration in any induction programme, mentoring, succession planning and psychological contracts.

Implications for organizations

Organizations will find it increasingly difficult to rely upon textbook prescriptions. Solutions developed to fit the latter part of the twentieth century are not expected to match the needs of the twenty-first century organization. As a general rule, more responsibility will lie with the individual. It will be very much up to the individual to look for information and to learn of opportunities inside and outside their present workplace. The role of the employer is changing similarly. As Peiperl and Baruch argued: 'The successful organizations of the next century will be those whose people have control of their own work and who make decisions to align that work with the goals of the organization'.[77]

As suggested here and elsewhere, a new type of psychological contract emerged in the 1990s and it may be the sort that we will have to live with in the coming decades. Employers will need to offer employees a psychological contract that they will appreciate and believe in and employers must ensure that they are able to fulfil their side of the new contracts. Sometimes the content of these contracts is demonstrated by the use of buzz-words such as Empowerment or Employability. Career management needs to create the right balance between empowering people to seek their own destiny and creating essential organizational support mechanisms to maintain and direct people's careers.

Outsourcing is another option – for non-core roles and activities. It should be used wisely, and not as a first resort. It seems better for an organization to use its own people when feasible, but outsourcing increases flexibility. Sometimes outsourcing works best with external providers of a temporary workforce. Whereas once such agencies mostly dealt with low-skilled workers, more professional roles and even managerial-level roles (i.e. the interim manager) can be filled by external agencies. To increase flexibility it may be useful for organizations not only to provide information on job opportunities within company boundaries, but to create a network of suppliers, customers, even competitors, which will generate a labour market of benefit not only to the organization's own staff but to all participants.

The general advice for organizations is – support your staff. Employees do not wish to be managed in an old-style paternalistic manner, but they need support mechanisms to enable them to fulfil their aims and ambitions. In a turbulent era people need more assistance. Organizations should ensure that their managers and HR people have both the capacities, not only to make tough decisions and confront the consequences, but also to provide emotional support. Some will be incapable of managing these seemingly two contradictory requirements – but the options should be made available anyway. Even those who appear tough may need support systems, not necessarily the same systems as for those who are made redundant – and for these, and especially for the survivors, individual counselling will be needed more then ever.

Summary

This chapter has outlined a comprehensive portfolio of HRM career-related practices, i.e. practices which can be used by organizations to plan and manage employees' careers. The practices have been discussed in no specific order of importance, but an attempt has been made to group them according to their role in a comprehensive organizational career system. Most of the career practices in use are expected to be developed and cultivated in the future, although some may disappear, as there is no apparent managerial need for them. This will be mainly due to structural developments within organizations, coupled with the new type of psychological contract. This characterizes a relationship between employees and employers which will be continued and developed in the organization of the future.

The portfolio has included a separate discussion of each practice, and an analysis of its fit for the future. The whole set of career practices have been combined into a broad integrated package which organizations may apply when implementing career systems. While I hope that the list is comprehensive and covers the whole area of organizational career planning and management, I make no pretensions to having provided a full or precise prescription, either for the present or for the future. First, with so many changes affecting individuals, organizations and nations, it is very difficult to make forecasts. Second, there is huge variety within organizations, even within the boundaries of one nation or one sector of industry. Based on the outlines presented in this chapter, it is left to HR managers in each organization to determine and decide what practices are needed to answer their specific situation, using sense, sensibility and professionalism.

Key terms

- Career Planning and Management (CPM)
- CPM portfolio
- Career practices
- Integrated career system
- Internal and external integration

DISCUSSION QUESTIONS

1 How can one determine one's own organization's needs in terms of the matched career practices portfolio?
2 What can individuals manage?
3 If you are employed or can refer to an organization you know:
   - How will you develop such a system effectively?
   - The customers of the system – who are they and what are their needs?
4 In what way would the following factors influence the relative importance and relevance of the various career practices described above?
   - Sector of activity
   - Country of origin
   - In case of a MNC – working in the home country or in a subsidiary

Discussion questions continued

- Size of organization in terms of number of employees
- Geographic distribution of company location
- Level of education of most employees
- Demography of workforce in terms of
  - Gender
  - Age
  - Ethnicity

Class exercise

HR outsourcing   In the continuous debate about organizational core versus periph-eral operations, it was argued that certain operations, activities and practices can be outsourced to gain better effectiveness and flexibility. Such operations include clean-ing services, special marketing campaigns, IT maintenance, etc.

There are arguments both for and against outsourcing the HR operation.

Critically examine each of the career practices presented in this chapter, and classify them according to the following three categories:

- Practices that certainly can (or should) be outsourced.
- Practices that should not be outsourced under most circumstances.
- Practices for which you find conflicting arguments about the possible benefits and pitfalls of outsourcing them.

Compare and contrast your list with others in small group discussion.

Lessons and food for thought

Let us now reconsider the question given at the beginning of this chapter (*see* Exhibit 6.1):

Imagine that you are the HR director of a company, and your CEO/Board are asking you to recreate the organizational career system (note – this is a reactive HR approach) or that you have decided that the organization needs an updated career system (a proactive HR approach). What would your plan look like? Which career practices would you apply, and in what order would they be introduced to the organizational setting? Bear in mind:

- Organizational characteristics: size, sector of operation, level of prosperity.*
- The individual level: be aware of the different needs that may stem from the age distribution of employees, diversity within the workforce, professions.
- The society/national level: labour markets, economic conditions, the environment.

Comment – if you are not working in an organization, assume you work for a con-sultancy, and were asked to advise an HR manager of an organization of your choice.

* What difference would it make if the organization has 10 000 employees rather than 1000? What if there are only some 200? What difference would it make if the organization operates in the hotel or the software development industry? Give the logical and theoretical base to support your answer.

Notes

1   Baruch, Y. (1996b) 'Organizational career planning and management techniques and activities in use in high-tech organizations', *Career Development International*, 1(1), 40–9; Baruch, Y. (1999) 'Integrated Career systems for the 2000s', *International Journal of Manpower*, 20(7), 432-57; Baruch, Y. and Peiperl, M.A. (2000a) 'Career Management Practices: An Empirical Survey and Implications', *Human Resource Management*, 39(4), 347–66.

2   Van Mannen, J. and Schein, E.H. (1977) 'Career Development', in J.R. Hackman and J.L. Suttle (eds) *Improving Life at Work: Behavioral Science Approaches to Organizational Change*, Santa Monica, CA: Goodyear, pp. 30–95; Schein, E.H. (1978) *Career Dynamics: Matching Individual and Organizational Needs*, Reading, MA: Addison-Wesley; Gutteridge, T.G. (1986) 'Organizational Career Development Systems: The State of the Practice', in D.T. Hall, *Career Development in Organizations*, San Francisco: Jossey-Bass, pp. 50–94; Hall, D.T. (1986) *Career Development in Organizations*, San Francisco: Jossey-Bass, pp. 50–94; Gutteridge, T.G., Leibowitz, Z.B. and Shore, J.E. (1993) *Organizational Career Development*, San Francisco: Jossey-Bass; Herriot, P., Gibbons, P., Pemberton, C. and Jackson, R. (1994) 'An empirical model of managerial careers in organizations', *British Journal of Management*, 5(2), 113–21; Leach, J. (1977) 'The notion and nature of careers', *The Personnel Administrator*, 22(7), 53–63.

3   Schein, E.H. (1978) *Career Dynamics: Matching Individual and Organizational Needs*, Reading, MA: Addison-Wesley; Herriot, P. and Pemberton, C. (1996) 'Contracting Careers', *Human Relations*, 49(6), 757–90.

4   A comprehensive list of such sources is: Baruch, Y. (1996b) 'Organizational career planning and management techniques and activities in use in high-tech organizations', *Career Development International*, 1(1), 40–9; Baruch, Y. and Peiperl, M.A. (2000a) 'Career Management Practices: An Empirical Survey and Implications', *Human Resource Management*, 39(4), 347–66; Bowen, D. and Hall, D.T. (1977) 'Career planning for employee development: a primer for managers', *California Management Review*, 20(2), 33–5; Herriot, P., Gibbons, P., Pemberton, C. and Jackson, R. (1994) 'An empirical model of managerial careers in organizations', *British Journal of Management*, 5(2), 113–21; London, M. and Stumpf, S.A. (1982) *Managing Careers*, Reading, MA: Addison-Wesley; Louchheim, F. and Lord, V. (1988) 'Who is taking care of your career?' *Personnel Administrator*, 33(4), 46–51; Walker, J.W. and Gutteridge, J.G. (1979) *Career Planning Practices: An AMA Survey Report*, NY: AMACOM.

5   *See* note 4 above.

6   Gutteridge, T.G. and Otte, F.L. (1983) 'Organizational career development: what's going on out there?' *Training and Development Journal*, 37(2), 22–6.

7   *See* note 2 above.

8   *See* note 1 above.

9   Baruch, Y. and Peiperl, M.A. (2000a) 'Career Management Practices: An Empirical Survey and Implications', *Human Resource Management*, 39(4), 347–66; Baruch, Y. (2003) 'Career systems in transition: A normative model for organizational career practices', *Personnel Review*, 32(2), 231–51.

10 Sonnenfeld, J.A. and Peiperl, M.A. (1988) 'Staffing policy as a strategic response: a typology of career systems', *Academy of Management Review*, 13(4), 568–600.

11 Derr, C.B. and Laurent, A. (1989) 'The Internal and External Career', in M.B.

Arthur, D.T. Hall and B.S. Lawrence (eds) *Handbook of Career Theory*, Cambridge: Cambridge University Press, pp. 454–71.

[12] Lorinc, J. (1989) 'Class action', *Canadian Business*, 62(9), 68–76.

[13] Baruch, Y. and Peiperl, M.A. (2000b) 'The Impact of an MBA on Graduates' Career', *Human Resource Management Journal*, 10(2), 69–90; Baruch, Y. and Leeming, A. (2001) 'The Added Value of MBA Studies – Graduates' Perceptions', *Personnel Review*, 30(5), 589–601.

[14] Bailyn, L. (1980) 'The slow burn to the top: Some thoughts on the early years of organization careers', in C.B. Derr (ed.) *Work, Family and Careers: New Frontiers in Theory and Research*, NY: Praeger, pp. 94–106.

[15] Schein (1978), *see* note 2 above.

[16] Peiperl, M.A. and Baruch, Y. (1997) 'Models of careers: back to square zero', *Organizational Dynamics*, 25(4), 7–22.

[17] Eisenberger, R., Fasolo, P. and Davis-LaMastro, V. (1990) 'Perceived organizational support and employee diligence, commitment, and innovation', *Journal of Applied Psychology*, 75(1), 51–9.

[18] Brockner, J., Tyler, T.R. and Cooper-Schieder, R. (1992) 'The influence of prior commitment to institution on reactions to perceived unfairness: The higher they are, the harder they fall', *Administrative Science Quarterly*, 37, 241–61; Baruch, Y. and Hind, P. (1999) 'Perpetual Motion in Organizations: Effective Management and the impact of the new psychological contracts on "Survivor Syndrome"', *European Journal of Work and Organizational Psychology*, 8(2), 295–306.

[19] Feuer, D. (1986) 'Two ways to the top?', *Training*, 23(2), 26–34; Badway, M.K. (1988) 'What we've learned managing Human Resources', *Research-Technology Management*, 31(5), 19–35.

[20] Van Mannen, J. (1976) 'Breaking in: Socialization to work', in R. Dubin (ed.) *Handbook of Work, Organization and Society*, Chicago: Rand McNally, pp. 7–130.

[21] Ashford, S.J. (1986) 'The role of feedback seeking in individual adaptation: A perspective', *Academy of Management Journal*, 29, 465–87.

[22] Morrison, E. W. (1993) 'Newcomer information seeking: Exploring types, modes, sources, and outcomes', *Academy of Management Journal*, 36(3), 557–89.

[23] Bauer, T. and Green, S. (1994) 'Effects of newcomers' involvement in work-related activities: A longitudinal study of socialization', *Journal of Applied Psychology*, 79, 211–23.

[24] Tziner, A., Ronen, S. and Hacohen, D. (1993) 'A four-year validation study of an assessment center in a financial corporation', *Journal of Organizational Behavior*, 14(3), 225–37; Thornton III, G.C., Tziner, A., Dahan, M., Clevenger, J.P. and Meir, E. (1997) 'Construct validity of assessment center judgements: analysis of behavioral reporting method', *Journal of Social Behavior and Personality*, 12(5), 109–28; Iles, P. (1999) *Managing Staff Selection and Assessment*, Buckingham: Open University; Howard, A. (1997) 'A reassessment of assessment centers: challenges for the 21st century', *Journal of Social Behavior and Personality*, 12(5), 13–52.

[25] Spychalski, A.C., Quinones, M.A., Gaugler, B.B. and Pohley, K. (1997) 'A survey of assessment center practices in organizations in the United States', *Personnel Review*, 50(1), 71–90.

[26] Bray, D.W. (1985) 'Fifty years of Assessment Centres: A retrospective and perspective view', *Journal of Management Development*, 4(4), 4–12; Portwood, J.D. and Granrose, C.S. (1986) 'Organizational career management programmes: what's available? What's effective?', *Human Resource Planning*, 19(3), 107–19; Laser, S.A. (1990) 'Management Development in a Changing Environment', in R.J. Niehaus and K.F. Price, *Human Resource Strategies for Organizations in Transition*, NY: Plenum Press, pp. 255–63.

[27] Cameron, K.S. (1996) Downsizing, an entry in M. Warner (ed.) *International Encyclopaedia of Business and Management* (Thompson Int.), V2, 1050–6.

[28] *See* note 24 above.

[29] Baird, L. and Kram, K.E. (1983) 'Career dynamics: Managing the supervisor-subordinate relationship', *Organizational Dynamics*, Summer, 46–64; Clawson, J.G. (1980) 'Mentoring in Managerial Careers', in C.B. Derr (ed.) *Work, Family, and the Career*, NY: Praeger; Kram, K.E. (1985) *Mentoring in the Work*, Glenview, IL: Scott, Foresman; Scandura, T.A. (1992) 'Mentorship and career mobility: An empirical investigation', *Journal of Organizational Behavior*, 13, 169–74; Baugh, S.G., Lankau, M.J. and Scandura, T.A. (1996) 'An investigation of the effects of protégé gender on responses to mentoring', *Journal of Vocational Behavior*, 49, 309–23.

[30] Kram, K.E. (1986) 'Mentoring in the Workplace', in D.T. Hall, *Career Development in Organizations*, San Francisco: Jossey-Bass, pp. 50–94.

[31] Scandura, T.A. and Viator, R.E. (1994) 'Mentoring in public accounting firms: An analysis of mentor-protégé relationships', *Accounting Organizations & Society*, 19(8), 717–34.

[32] Scandura, T.A. (1998) 'Dysfunctional mentoring relationships and outcomes', *Journal of Management*, 24(3), 449–67.

[33] Sweeney, D.S., Haller, D. and Sale, F. (1989) 'Individually controlled career counselling', *Training and Development Journal*, Aug., 58–61.

[34] Waterman, R.H. Jr, Waterman, J.A. and Collard, B.A. (1994) 'Toward a career-resilient workforce', *Harvard Business Review*, 72(4), 87–95.

[35] Altman, Y. and Baruch, Y. (2002) *Career Resilience Workshop*, Working Paper, School of Management, University of East Anglia.

[36] Parker, P. and Arthur, M.B. (2000) 'Careers, organizing and community', in M.A. Peiperl, M.B. Arthur, R. Goffee and T. Morris (eds) *Career Frontiers: New Conceptions of Working Lives*, Oxford: Oxford University Press, pp. 99–121.

[37] Jacobson, B. and Kaye, B.L. (1986) 'Career development and the performance appraisal: it takes two to tango', *Personnel*, 63(1), 26–32; Weitzel, W. (1987) 'How to improve performance through successful appraisals', *Personnel*, 64(10), 18–23; Murphy, K.R. and Cleveland, J.N. (1995) *Understanding Performance Appraisal*, Thousand Oaks, CA: Sage.

[38] Hall, J.L., Posner, B.Z. and Harder, J.W. (1989) 'Performance appraisal systems', *Group & Organizational Studies*, 14(1), 51–9.

[39] Herriot, P. and Pemberton, C. (1996) 'Contracting Careers', *Human Relations*, 49(6), 757–90.

[40] Walker and Gutteridge (1979), *see* note 4 above.

[41] Miner, J.B. and Miner, M.G. (1979) *Personnel and Industrial Relations: A Managerial Approach*, NY: MacMillan, pp. 208–31.

[42] Rothwell, W.J. (1994) *Effective Succession Planning: Ensuring Leadership Continuity and Building Talent from Within*, Saranac Lake, NY: AMACOM; Sessa, V.I. and Campbell, R.J. (1997) *Selection at the Top: An Annotated Bibliography*, Greensboro, NC: Center for Creative Leadership.

[43] Baruch, Y. (1998) 'The Rise and Fall of Organizational Commitment', *Human System Management*, 17(2), 135–43.

[44] Leibman, M., Bruer, B.A. and Maki, B.R. (1996) 'Succession management: the next generation of succession planning', *Human Resource Planning*, 19(3), 16–29.

[45] Tziner, A., Kopelman, R. and Joanis, C. (1997) 'Investigation of raters' and ratees' reactions to three methods of performance appraisal: BOS, BARS, and GRS', *Canadian Journal of Administrative Sciences*, 14(4), 396–404.

[46] Baruch, Y. and Harel, G. (1993) 'Combining multi-source performance appraisal: An empirical and methodological note', *Pubic Administration Quarterly*, 17(1), 96–111; Bernardin, H.J., Kane, J.S., Ross, S., Spina, J.D. and Johnson, D.L. (1995) 'Performance appraisal design, development and implementation', in G.R. Ferris, S.D. Rosen and D.T. Barnum (eds) *Handbook of Human Resource Management*, Cambridge, MA: Blackwell, pp. 462–93.

[47] Baruch, Y. (1996a) 'Self performance appraisal vs. direct manager appraisal: A case of congruence', *Journal of Managerial Psychology*, 11(6), 50–65; Bernardin, H.J. (1986) 'Subordinate appraisal: A valuable source of information about managers', *Human Resource Management*, 25, 421–39.

[48] Kessler, I. And Purcell, J. (1992) 'Performance related pay: objectives and application', *Human Resource Management*, 2(3), 16–33; Kessler, I. (1994) 'Performance related pay: contrasting approaches', *Industrial Relations Journal*, 25(2), 122–35.

[49] Tornow, W.W., London, M. *et al.* (1998) *Maximizing the Value of 360-Degree Feedback*, San Francisco: Jossey-Bass.

[50] Morrison, A.M., White, R.P. and Van Velsor, E. (1987) 'Executive women: Substance plus style', *Psychology Today*, 21, 18–26.

[51] Baruch, Y. (1995) 'Business globalization – the Human Resource Management aspect', *Human Systems Management*, 14(4), 313–33; Harvey, M. (1997) 'Dual-career expatriates: expectations, adjustment and satisfaction with international relocation', *Journal of International Business Studies*, 28(3), 627–58.

[52] Punnett, B.J., Crocker, O. and Stevens, M.A. (1992) 'The challenge for women expatriates and spouses: some empirical evidence', *International Journal of Human Resource Management*, 3(3), 585–92.

[53] Kopp, R. (1994) 'International human resource policies and practices in Japanese, European, and United States multinationals', *Human Resource Management*, 33(4), 581–99.

[54] Black, J.S., Gregersen, H.B. and Mendenhall, M.E. (1992) *Global Assignments*, San Francisco: Jossey-Bass; Borg, M. and Harzing, A.W. (1995) 'Composing an International Staff', in A.W. Harzing and J.V. Ruysseveldt (eds) *International Human Resource Management*, London: Sage, pp. 179–204.

[55] Rodrigues, C. (1996) *International Management*, Minneapolis/St. Paul: West Publication.

[56] Marquardt, M.J. and Engel, D.W. (1993) 'HRD competencies for a shrinking world', *Training & Development*, 47(5), 59–65; Zetlin, M. (1994) 'Making tracks', *Journal of European Business*, 5(5), 40–7.

[57] Derr, C.B., Jones, C. and Toomey, E.L. (1988) 'Managing high-potential employees: current practices in 33 US corporations', *Human Resource Management*, 27(3), 273–90.

[58] *See* note 4 above.

[59] *See* note 1 above.

[60] Ashkenas, R., Ulrich, D., Jick, T. and Kerr, S. (1995) *The Boundaryless Organization*, San Francisco: Jossey-Bass; Arthur, M.B. (1994) 'The boundaryless career: A new perspective for organizational inquiry', *Journal of Organizational Behavior*, 15(4), 295–306.

[61] Rousseau, D.M. (1996) 'Changing the deal while keeping the people', *Academy of Management Executive*, 10(1), 50–9; Morrison, E.W. and Robinson, S.L. (1997) 'When employees feel betrayed: A model of how psychological contract violation develops', *Academy of Management Review*, 22(1), 226–56.

[62] Herriot, P. and Pemberton, C. (1995) *New Deals*, Chichester: John Wiley.

[63] Wanous, J.P. (1992) *Organizational Entry: Recruitment, Selection, Orientation, and*

Socialization of Newcomers, 2nd edn, Reading, MA: Addison-Wesley; Semmer, N. and Schallberger, U. (1996) 'Selection, socialisation, and mutual adaptation: Resolving discrepancies between people and work', *Applied Psychology: An International Review*, 45(3), 263–88.

64 *See* note 1 above.

65 *See* note 1 above.

66 *See* note 26 above.

67 Carulli, L.M., Noroian, C.L. and Levine, C. (1989) 'Employee-driven career development', *Personnel Administrator*, 34(3), 66–70; Boyle, T.J. and Leibovitz, S.J. (1990) 'Hiring thoroughbreds: Pitfalls to avoid and the rules to follow', *Business Horizons*, Nov–Dec, 28–33.

68 *See* note 27 above.

69 *See* not 16 above.

70 Gunz, H.P. and Jalland, R.M. (1996) 'Managerial careers and business strategies', *Academy of Management Review*, 21(3), 718–56.

71 Baruch and Peiperl (2000a), *see* note 1 above.

72 Brousseau, K.R., Driver, M.J., Eneroth, K. and Larsson, R. (1996) 'Career pandemonium: Realigning organizations and individuals', *Academy of Management Executive*, 10(4), 52–66.

73 *See* note 10 above.

74 Miles, R.E. and Snow, C.C. (1978) *Organizational Strategy, Structure, and Process*, NY: McGraw-Hill.

75 Devanna, M.A., Fombrun, C.J. and Tichy, N.M. (1981) 'Human Resource Management: Strategic Perspective', *Organizational Dynamics*, 9(3), 51–67; Fombrun, C.J., Tichy, N.M. and Devanna, M.A. (1984) *Strategic Human Resource Management*, NY: John Wiley & Sons, pp. 19–31.

76 Holbeche, L. (1999) *Aligning Human Resource and Business Strategy*, Oxford: Butterworth-Heinemann; Purcell, J. (1995) 'Corporate Strategy and human resource management', in J. Storey (ed.) *Human Resource Management – A Critical Text*, London: Routledge, pp. 63–86; Tyson, S. (1997) 'Human Resource Management comes of age: Strategic integration', in S. Tyson (ed.) *Human Resource Strategy*, London: Pitman, pp. 1–15.

77 Peiperl and Baruch (1997), *see* note 16 above.

7 Global career management

LEARNING OBJECTIVES

After reading this chapter you should be able to:

- Distinguish between individual and organizational management of global careers.

- Analyse organizational global positioning within several theoretical frameworks.

- Identify the variety of strategic options for applying global career systems.

- Understand the impact of individual background and organizational policies on global careers.

- Understand how organizations can avoid losing their global workforce.

CHAPTER CONTENTS

Introduction

In the 1960s, Hofstede conducted what is probably the largest comparative international study of work-related values (Hofstede, 1980).[1] The results were published, using a false name (*Hermes*) for the company. However, it was very clear at the time, given that the company under discussion was a high-tech company, with operations in more than 40 countries, that it must be IBM. Today it would not be so easy to identify a company by the size of its multinational operations: most of the high-tech corporations (and others) in the *Fortune 500* list have global operations in a considerable number of countries. Even today IBM is still typically used to demonstrate the archetype global corporation. Nevertheless most companies over a certain size operate globally, and need to manage their human resources internationally. Moreover, the IBM model is not necessarily the best strategy for them to follow.

In this chapter we will look at how, when an organization moves from a country-based to a global-based operation, this process is reflected in career systems for individuals and their employing organization.

The internationalization of careers: individual perspective

It is some time since the 1960s, when the world was first depicted as a 'global village' (MacLuhan, 1960).[2] For many companies, indeed, the globe rather than their home country is the arena for their business, their market and their labour market. Regularly operating across geographical borders has become the rule rather than the exception, in particular for large, blue-chip companies. From the career management perspective this means that people need to manage and to be managed beyond both geographical and cultural horizons. Few would challenge what has by now become the 'bread and butter' of executive careers in multinational corporations (MNCs). Global managers are needed to provide answers for the challenges of global management (Cornelius, 1999; Sparrow and Hiltrop, 1997).[3] Truly 'global' managers are sought for, be they 'home-', 'host-' or 'third-' country nationals (*see* Exhibit 7.1) as companies aim for global competitiveness (Arthur and Bennett, 1995; Drucker, 1999).[4] Companies invest in the development of future global leaders (Conner, 2000)[5] to ensure competitiveness in the international market. Of course, not every manager is expected to be international, but 'a small core of international employees will be a key to successful globalization' (Shackleton and Newell, 1997).[6]

| EXHIBIT 7.1 | **Home country**: the country where the main operation was established, where the headquarters is situated, and most importantly, which defines strategy, retains control and manages the operation of the organization. Most multinationals have a distinct culture determined by the home company (and national) culture. Employees from the home country will be sent as expatriates to the host countries. |

Exhibit 7.1 continued

Host countries are countries where the home company ('mother company') oper-ates. They will have mostly local, 'host-country' national employees, but also some expatriates, usually in managerial or professional technical positions. There may also be some employees who are '**Third-country** nationals' – people who have moved from a different country altogether to work for the company. Some of them may have moved from an operation in one host country to one in another host country.

However, a clear definition of a global manager does not exist, since there may be several meanings to the title 'global manager'. It can be (a) an expatriate man-ager (cf. Black and Gregersen, 1999);[7] (b) a manager who works across borders (cf. Bartlett and Ghoshal, 1992);[8] or simply (c) a manager in a company which oper-ate across borders. While the last option is too all-encompassing, the first two are valid, and indicate the distinction between expatriates and globetrotters, 'travel-ling managers'. The expatriate is an employee who works in an overseas sub-sidiary of a company, for a considerable period of time, and is usually accompanied by their immediate family (if they have one); the 'travelling man-ager' is a manager who routinely operates across borders, but has a base in one country, usually, the country where the core operation is located. In their roles within MNCs, 'travelling managers' need to make frequent visits to different locations around the globe. There are others who operate similarly, e.g. agents, merchants, solicitors, etc. who perceive the whole world as their operational field.

EXHIBIT 7.2   A globetrotting career

MC is known to his friends as the 'Flying Dutchman'. He worked in the past for IBM, Unisys and Logica in The Netherlands, and as part of his career was expatri-ated to the UK and later to the USA. Now he works both as an interim manager for an MNC, and at developing his own business, Quandar. His career motto is: 'They don't wait for you ... so you have to take the initiative, create your own space.'

His present career has emerged from the earlier stages, but subject to his own inclinations. After more than twenty years in corporate life he has decided to embark on an entrepreneurial venture. Quandar Marketing, which he established, is a company specialising in marketing-on-demand services for businesses that want to outsource their marketing activities. In addition, since in the first stages of devel-opment such a company would not be needed on a full-time basis, he acts as an interim manager for an international communication consultancy firm. In this role, which require some three working days a week, MC divides his working time among San Francisco, Amsterdam, and London. He has a six months' contract, where he has to spend most of his time at the Amsterdam operation, regularly visit the headquarters, which is in San Francisco and deal with many customers located in London, where he lives.

MC is not concerned about the amount of travelling, especially as the flight time from London to Amsterdam is less than an hour. He is fluent in Dutch and English (and also in German and French), and knows the local cultures at first hand. Living in London was his choice, and MC really sees himself as a citizen of the world.

Individual characteristics of global managers

Defining a Global Manager would never be simple but some have tried. Borg and Harzing (1995) tried to 'profile' the international manager using both Tung's (1982) and Mendenhall and Oddou's (1985) criteria.[9] Tung identified four groups of variables that determine the success of the global manager: technical knowledge and job skills; interpersonal relationships; ability to cope with environmental constraints; and lastly, family situation. Mendenhall and Oddou referred to a different set of dimensions: self-orientation (self-esteem, self-confidence, etc.); features that enhance capability to interact effectively with host nationals; the ability to perceive what the locals have in mind; and ability to deal with cultures that are very different from one's own. Baruch (2002)[10] claims that these and other sets of criteria are all prerequisites for success in any managerial job, thus 'there is no such thing' as a global manager, although, to succeed in such a position one needs, perhaps, a 'global mind-set', a readiness and willingness to work within a global environment, to accept differences and to benefit from such diversity. Baruch argues that while the concept of globalization reflects true business reality, the idea that there is a certain profile, which one should fit in order to be a successful global manager seems flawed. Similarly, in terms of personality (e.g. the 'Big Five' – *see* Goldberg, 1990)[11] it is difficult to identify specific attributes that will distinguish a person more likely than others to succeed in an international career. It seems that what makes an individual a 'global manager' is more a state of mind, an openness and willingness to cross borders – geographical and cultural – as part of the career. It is no surprise, then, to find that global assignments pose great challenges for managers.

EXHIBIT 7.3	Could you be a global manager?

What do you believe are the qualities and specific circumstances that would make you a successful global manager? What do you believe are the qualities and specific circumstances that might prevent you from becoming a successful global manager?

Do these concern your inner qualities? Your job-related competence? Your family situation?

Global psychological contracts?

Guzzo, Nooman and Elron (1994)[12] placed the issue of global HRM, in particular that of expatriation, within the current debate on the psychological contract. Viewed from this theoretical perspective, expatriation is a specific case of the employment relationship. Guzzo *et al.* (1994) argue that these relationships will be relational rather than transactional. One indeed may have to make sacrifices when agreeing to expatriation, but on the other hand, one may gain in the long term. Nevertheless, many HR managers will challenge the contention of Guzzo *et al.*, recognizing that in order to persuade employees to accept expatriation to a 'difficult' country, a higher salary has to be offered.

The relationship can be influenced also by individual characteristics. However, the effect of such characteristics is not straightforward. For example, age may have different implications: young people, especially those without children, may agree to expatriation quite willingly, as may older people whose children have left home and who have no responsibility for elderly relatives, while middle-aged people might find an international move problematic. Because age is quite closely associated with hierarchical level, and most expatriate positions are for middle-level personnel, rather than very junior employees or senior executives, there are considerable challenges for HR managers in filling these positions.

Other individual issues include gender and marital status. Empirical evidence suggests that in most cases expatriates tend to be males. Markham (1987) has pointed out that women may be less willing than men to accept relocation.[13] This tendency may become stronger in overseas relocation. Organizations need to be realistic in assigning female managers to overseas posts. In certain cultures female managers may face barriers, in the shape of reluctance to collaborate, or even legal obstacles to employment. However, as experience in Japan shows (Taylor and Napier, 1996), this is not necessarily so.[14] Their suggested explanation was that in Japan US female managers were accepted primarily as professionals, as American and as managers, and less as females.

Career systems must accommodate the marital status of employees. This is even more true in the case of expatriation. Dual-career couples, single parents and people with caring responsibilities for elderly relatives or with teenage children pose challenges for the system. This means that when HR managers take career management decisions, they have to be very aware of the specific personal circumstances of their employees. Seeking such information might, of course, be perceived as intruding.

Harvey (1997)[15] focused on the issue of selecting dual-career couple employees for international assignments. Their dual careers pose a major obstacle in terms of their readiness and willingness to accept expatriation. Dual-career couples find it hard for one of them to leave their job or to serve as a housewife/husband while the spouse is on an overseas assignment. It is difficult for spouses in professional and managerial positions to find suitable roles elsewhere. An innovative solution on the part of the company may be to offer either work or support in finding work for the spouse.

EXHIBIT 7.4	**Wider perspective?**

The framework of global management may be extended to include the issue of immigration and the way multicultural communities interact in a different cultural realm. Leong and Hartung (2000)[16] discuss how career interventions such as counselling may be influenced by the target population (they focused on people of Chinese origin who grew up in Western cultures). They argue for the need to move from multiculturalism based on demographics to one that is based on mindsets.

The Push/Pull model

A combination of individual values and needs, organizational approaches (*see* further discussion later in this chapter), and national culture is manifested in Baruch's Push/Pull model (Baruch, 1995).[17] This model is based on Lewin's field theory (1951),[18] and takes into account the economic, rights and cultural realms (*see* Figure 7.1). Whenever a proposal to move across borders is put to any employee, there will be two forces operating in conflicting directions. One pulls the employee to move to the new place, the other pushes him or her back, i.e. to reject the move. Each person will decide according to the strength of these forces, and these forces operate in all three realms. For example, the organization may increase the pull factor by offering high economic incentives. A push factor might be a strong dislike of the culture of the host country, or even of its physical climate. There are many legal constraints relating to the movement of people across borders, such as the need for a work permit, or which other-country nationals can work in specific countries. Cultural forces can pull people too – for those looking for adventure, some exotic places would have an appeal, whereas other people might resent being sent to those places. A difficult situation for the human resource department in any MNC is dealing with a refusal to accept expatriation (Punnett, 1997).[19] Not only does a refusal leave a hole in the system to be filled, but it might have a snowball effect, in that people may refuse to step in once the post has been rejected by others. Thus, organizations need to assess in advance how likely people are to accept or refuse global assignments.

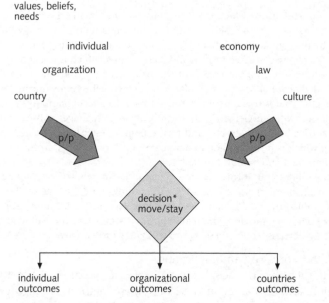

* can be taken in each level – usually the person

Figure 7.1 The Push/Pull model

Source: Reprinted from Y. Baruch (1995) 'Business Globalization – the Human Resource Management Aspect', *Human Systems Management*, 14(4), p. 316, with permission from IOS Press.

Different national managerial cultures

Companies that operate across borders realize that even in Western cultures, there are different national cultures. A vivid example relevant to career management is the answer to the question, 'Which are the most important criteria for managerial success?' Scheneider and Barsoux (1997)[20] compared and contrasted different answers.

In the USA culture the right answer is drive and ability. In France the criterion is whether or not the manager studied at one of the *Grands Ecoles*. The German model emphasizes technical and functional competence, whereas in the UK what matters is classical education and a generalist approach. The Japanese value a qualification from a top university, compliance and loyalty.

Thus, when MNCs operate in a country different from the headquarters country, the development of a career system will have to take into account such differences, and even so, the managers will face misunderstandings that stem from different managerial cultures.

EXHIBIT 7.5	**Hamburger discipline**

I heard the following story from Dan W., an American executive who worked for Mobil Oil (now Exxon-Mobil) as an expatriate in several countries, including Japan, Germany, UK and, of course, the USA. This story manifest the different metaphorical hamburger you will encounter when you are disciplined in different cultures:

> When you work in the USA and make a mistake, your manager will call you up to his/her office. At first you will be told something along the lines of, 'We know how good you are, valued by the company, and that usually your work is fine' (lower bun). Then will come the 'meat': 'Yesterday you acted in such and such manner, which is not according to our policy' and so on. So a warning or comment will be entered on your file. Then the manager will say, 'We do know that it was a one-off event, and we value your work, and wish to leave this behind, etc.' That is the upper bun. You got your 'balanced' hamburger.
>
> But if you work in Germany, most probably your manager will call you up to his/her office, and will tell you exactly and to the point: 'Yesterday you acted in such and such manner, which is not according to our policy' and so on. So a warning or comment will be entered on the file. That's it. Just 'meat'.
>
> On the other hand, if this were to happen in Japan, your manager would call you up to his (probably not her) office, and tell you something along the lines of, 'We know how good you are, valued by the company, and that usually your work is fine'. Then he will go on, praising your work, providing more nice positive comments, and will send you out (just the buns). Nevertheless, you will know, you will know indeed why you were called up.

This was the story. Now for implications.

First, in each country, people are easily able to recognize the method of disciplinary action, and how severe it is. Second, these methods are highly dependent on national culture. A problem will emerge, though, when people from different cultures mingle work together. For example, imagine that an employee with the German cultural orientation is placed in Japan, and is called in for a disciplinary procedure. He or she will probably never get the message. Or imagine a worse

Exhibit 7.5 continued

scenario, where a Japanese employee stationed in Germany is disciplined in 'the German way' by the local manager – it might lead to immediate departure or some other disastrous outcome.

No doubt people from each of the cultures feel that their way is the right one. But the question is not who is right. What matters is that the message needs to be delivered and understood, wherever the company operates. So now you get a feeling for the challenge.

Moving on from the metaphorical illustration of cultural differences, the typical progression into and out of organizations varies significantly across countries. As indicated in earlier chapters, in the UK and the USA, people may enter the organization at the rank and file level, and then develop within the organization, or may enter a managerial position (e.g. via graduate recruitment) and develop within that role, or they may be head-hunted to fill an executive position. Similarly they may leave the organization from any position. In Germany and Japan entry is almost exclusively to the lower echelons, and people will tend not to leave the organization. In Japan congruence, compliance and obedience are crucial for promotion. In many Western cultures, being confrontational, playing the Devil's advocate, is a better way to introduce oneself to top management.

Informal career networking

In studying management it is sometimes implied that organizational managerial processes are planned and managed in a systematic way, and that both individuals and organizations have a well-structured and formalized system for managing. This may be true for mechanistic aspects, operations and regulations. However, in people management, informal relationships are no less crucial for the future career than formal relationships. Networking, discussed in Chapter 4, will usually have a stronger impact on the future career. When people cross borders, they need to find how to become a part of local networks. The way to enter the system, of course, is different in each country, and sometimes entry is almost impossible, but the first step is to identify the network. In the UK networking is usually simple – it occurs in the pub, just after work is finished. In France the best way to connect may be during long lunch sessions. In small countries it might prove difficult, as many networks develop from one's schooldays, and in countries where a period of armed service is compulsory many of the networks are formed during this service. From networks one gains informal advice, knowledge that cannot be delivered in formal meetings, the support of a key person for the next career move. The expatriate manager should figure out how the local informal system works, and do their best to get involved, if they wish to become part of the system.

Question | Can one become president of the USA without the support of the Freemasonry network? (Rumour has it that Bill Clinton was a rare exception.)

A final point to consider in the context of the global management of careers relates to the fact that the same company operates in a variety of cultures and career systems. The MNC still needs to obtain and retain the right people, and to apply 'best practice'. And clearly what may be perceived as 'best practice' in one place will not be so perceived in another. Thus, one major challenge for global career management is to find the right balance across the different operations, setting a policy that will take into account the strategy of the organization as well as local requirements.

A further major challenge concerned with career management is the management of expatriates and their expatriation and repatriation process. Both challenges are dealt with in the next section.

Global career systems: the organizational perspective

Organizational models of global management of people

The earlier part of this chapter dealt with the individual point of view. However, it was the combination of economic and social factors that caused the increase in global competition and global operations, and subsequently an acceleration of traffic in expatriation and repatriation (cf. Laurent, 1986; Porter, 1989; Porter and Tansky, 1999).[21] Organizational-level analysis generates a different perspective on the management of international careers, or on the introduction of an international assignment to the organizational post portfolio. Organizational models of the global management of people are those of Perlmutter (1969); Bartlett and Ghoshal (1992); and Baruch and Altman (2002).[22]

There are two major aspects of global career management. One is the management of HRM across borders in a company that operates in more than one country. The other concerns moving people across borders – expatriation and repatriation.

HRM operating across borders: 'glocalized' careers

How does an organization become 'glocal'? Operating in different countries poses a challenge to the management of career systems. First, there needs to be congruence and matching across the operation (i.e. being global), but then the operation is carried out in different countries, each with a different economy, legal system and culture (i.e. being local). Even what may be perceived as simple for one person is not necessarily so. Very often, the secret of success lies in finding the right combination or level of compromise in reaching 'glocalization'. Let us look at the following issues: remuneration, performance appraisal, training and development, industrial relations and health and safety.

Remuneration

The system of remuneration or compensation is problematic since one cannot use the same measure across borders. The principal question is what should be the basis for payment, and the major two options are similarity of amount of money and similarity of buying power. Other questions will derive from this basic issue. For example, what should a company do with regard to variation in taxation levels?

Dowling et al.[23] present five objectives a firm's remuneration system needs to satisfy. The policy should:

- be consistent and fair;
- enable the firm to attract and retain the necessary employees;
- facilitate the transfer of employees in a cost-effective manner;
- be consistent with the firm's strategy, structure and business needs;
- ensure that employees are motivated.

What is not simple, for example, is the definition of fair. What would you consider 'fair' payment? Also the concept of consistency loses its meaning when the system has to accommodate the requirements of different populations requiring separate systems (e.g. local managers and expatriates). The system can relate to both extrinsic and intrinsic components of payment (Logger, Vinke and Kluytmans, 1995).[24]

Generally, a firm must decide whether the base for payment will be the country of the headquarters, the home country of the person involved, or the host country. If a company has a similar operation and hierarchy structure in two countries, the salaries of the local employees should relate to salaries in that country. For example, if a Swedish or American company has branches in Britain and Madagascar, the salary of the British branch manager should match the salary of a branch manager of a similar-sized operation in Britain, not that of the manager of Madagascar. Similarly, in determining the Madagascan branch manager's salary, the benchmark should be the remuneration of other branch managers in Madagascar, not the salary of USA, British or Yemeni managers in their own countries. Of course, the situation become more complex when expatriation is involved: for example, if an American IT firm sends two IT support technical managers, one to Japan and one to Brazil, or one to Switzerland and one to Portugal (both within Europe, it should be noted), should they have the same salary in dollar terms? The buying power of the dollar in the various economies is certainly different. The required quality of life may be a better measure. But then the company should realize that a portion of the family income is devoted to savings, or to paying a mortgage. This share can be kept at the level of the home country. In addition, the company should envisage the reaction of locals to marked disparity. Recent evidence from a Chinese study suggests that local workers might still feel that there is unfair disparity if expatriates earn much more than they do, but this feeling can be reduced if the expatriates receive salaries that are not too far above those of their local counterparts (Chen, Choi and Chi, 2002).[25] In 2003, oil workers in Nigeria held many expatriates hostage as part of an attempt to improve their pay.

If the company has a policy of similar payments for similar positions, what needs to be done about tax differences? Even within the EU, the top rate of tax varies from some 40 per cent to more than 70 per cent. Again, a 'fair' but costly solution for the company is to pay the difference to compensate the employee.

In calculating pensions, an issue of considerable importance is where people will live when they are retired? Of course, this cannot be determined early in the career of an expatriate. The importance and relevance of this issue may be reduced or even eliminated in the future, as there is a clear tendency in many companies to offer their employees private pension schemes. These pass the burden and the decision to the expatriates themselves (but then they may need to have financial advice about pensions at the time of their expatriation).

One thing companies are certainly expected to pay is relocation costs. These may also include yearly visits for the expatriate to the home operational base, to keep in touch with the home business, to meet with his or her mentor and career adviser, with colleagues and others. Policies will vary across companies, and according to the status of the expatriate and financial constraints and budgets. Among the issues to be decided are who will fly economy, business or first class, and whether all family members are covered, what constitutes a reason for visiting the home country. What if, to deal with a family problem, the expatriate (or their spouse) must return home, and who defines what is a 'must' (a funeral for a deceased parent certainly is, but how about the birth of a niece, the marriage of a brother, etc.)? Companies should have a general policy and guidelines on these issues too.

An assignment of two or three years will be paid according to a certain scale of remuneration. This should be treated as a temporary appointment. However, if the expatriation becomes very long term or permanent (either in the same country or via a sequence of expatriate postings), the compensation should be reviewed and revised to keep pace with local levels of payments as compared with costs of living.

To sum up, while the general guidelines should lead to a 'fair' and constructive system, situational factors will force companies to be inventive and flexible in setting and managing the remuneration system across borders. In addition, companies can rely on external systems that are designed to evaluate needed adjustments for spending power parity (such as the Hay system of Hay Management Consultants).

Question	What do you feel would be the right combination that would be fair compensation for you if you were asked to move to a country in Europe? In South America?

Performance appraisal

When implementing a PA system the firm should decide which kind of system and what format (or forms) should be utilized. There is a variety of options for choosing relevant criteria, and in the global context these differ across countries. The system needs to be based on an appropriate measurement instrument or scale, e.g. ranking, behavioural appraisals (Graphic rating scales, Anchored rating scales, Observation scales, to name a few), the management by objective approach, and others. Some of these measurement scales would be suitable for individualist societies whereas others would suit the needs of collectivist societies. The MNC has three options: (a) to apply the same system across the board; (b) to apply different systems for different operations (either per country or per region); or (c) to find a compromise.

To achieve coherence across functions the system should be identical in different countries of operation. However, for many reasons, starting with legal, but also cultural, a company may find that forms that are accepted and effective in one country cannot be utilized similarly in another country. This can be particularly relevant if the PA system is also used as a basis for performance related pay (PRP). If this is the case issues of remuneration discussed above are affected too (cf. Kessler and Purcell, 1992; Kessler, 1994).[26]

A clear example is the use of 360-degree feedback. In some countries this would be the best option for providing employees with rich feedback. Earlier studies show the benefits of such a system in different cultures (Bernardin *et al.*, 1995; Baruch and Harel, 1993).[27] Self and upward PA (Baruch, 1996 and Bernardin, 1986, respectively)[28] can also be included as valuable PA sources, increasing the reliability and validity of the process. In other cultures people might resent the use of this form of evaluation (the Hofstede concept of Power Distance can serve to explain and forecast anticipated problems).[29]

Bernardin *et al.* (1995)[30] argue that any PA system should apply: (a) legally defensible appraisal procedures; (b) legally defensible appraisal content; (c) legally defensible documentation of appraisal results and (d) legally defensible raters. Thus, legal advice is important in adapting the global system to local considerations, and local legal systems vary considerably.

Another practical issue is that of mergers and acquisitions in international organizations. This means that when a MNC acquires a local company, the HR system is part of the purchase, and the mother company needs to decide if or how to apply the PA system to the new company. Doing this can be quite difficult if this is an overseas operation.

Question	How would you feel about a 360-degree feedback PA system if you were appointed to work in a country in Europe? In South East Asia?

Training and development

The wider the spread of a MNC, the more training is needed. The reasons for this include: reaching common ground within the company, encouraging an exchange of knowledge within the company, and preparing internal people for different operations across borders (mostly, but not only, for expatriates). The standard training programme of a one-nation company becomes complex when it needs to accommodate the different educational systems in various countries. What may be perceived as global knowledge in one country may be an exception in another. In addition, unless the training and development is restricted to executive positions, it will have to be translated into many languages.

In addition to the general challenges of providing comprehensive training and development around the globe, there is the need for specific training programmes for expatriate managers. Such programmes should prepare them for the local culture, operation and management practices. The training should include the legal system, the financial system, and most important – the local culture. In addition, language training is essential – it is important that the expatriate achieves at least conversational level of competence in the local language. Many programmes try to involve the family also in such training – both cultural and language.

Cultural training should include various aspects of local ways of behaviour, and in particular the approach to negotiation. Baumgarten[31] provides an overview of available options for cross-cultural training, and offers the following:

- simulations (such as role playing, case studies, instructional games);
- programmed instruction (cultural assimilation);
- expositive instruction (e.g. lectures, tutorials, reading and audio-visual presentations);
- sensitivity training (as in T-groups);
- behaviour modification methods (such as modelling);
- field experience (i.e. visits, assignments to micro-cultures, and meeting with experienced former expatriates or locals); and
- on-the-job training.

Industrial relations

Local industrial relations vary considerably between nations. In some countries unions, although not necessarily concerned with career systems, may have a say in decisions on promotion. This may go against the culture, ethics and ethos of many American executives (where the level of unionization is less than 15 per cent of the workforce), but is practical and relevant where most employees are trade union members, including managers. The union can object to certain appointments, and it may be wise to consult the union in advance rather than have a dispute later on. Legal advice on local employment laws should be obtained and considered.

Health and safety

Question

> Should your company provide condoms, free of charge (and encourage their use) to all employees? Including managers? Only to drivers?
>
> The answer would be strongly negative for many countries, but not for an operation in Africa, South East Asia, or parts of Eastern Europe, where the Aids epidemic forces companies to apply quite non-traditional methods. Studying large Tanzanian companies, Baruch and Clancy (1999)[32] (*see* Exhibit 7.6) found a high level of Aids, in particular when transportation employees were involved. And the level of infection was spread evenly across the hierarchy.

As with the issue of PA, legal considerations in relation to health and safety matters will vary across nations. In addition environmental effects may be relevant, and in some countries bodies such as Greenpeace can cause companies publicity problems, which might affect a company's reputation and people management issues (as happened to Shell in relation to the demolition of the Brent-Spar oil rig). The basic issue concerns which standard the company should adopt – that of the home base, or the local one. Adopting the home base standard may ensure better health and safety conditions, but may prove more costly than the local standard, and thus might make the operation less competitive than other local operations. The decision will inevitably include ethical questions relating to the value the company places on the health of its local workers. A different situation arises when, perhaps to its surprise, the MNC discovers that the local regulations and customs impose a higher level of safety than is standard in its home country. This may be for security reasons (e.g. areas subject to terrorist activities), a hazardous environment (e.g. a tough climate), or an epidemic (*see* Exhibit 7.6).

| EXHIBIT 7.6 | Managing careers in AIDS-infected areas |

Africa tends not to be a focus for global HRM studies, but nevertheless many MNCs operate in Africa. The general finding of Baruch and Clancy is that discrimination against HIV/AIDS will not be tolerated in the long term by governments and public opinion, and is expected to become illegal in most places. Thus they suggest that flexible career planning should be implemented, with regularly updated succession plans, as well as the following support mechanisms:

- Support groups
- Education and promotion of anti-AIDS policies and practices
- Supply of medical advice
- Setting fair and reasonable policies for financial assistance in case of emerging cases and in cases of death
- Establishing organizational policies to cover:
  - recruitment and selection of new employees (no discrimination)
  - insurance
  - career management – succession planning
  - educational programmes, brochures and other information available
  - sexual behaviour at work
  - supply of reactive prevention (condoms) and active treatment
  - financial cover for infected people

Certain issues will be specifically relevant to MNCs operating in Africa. These mostly concern expatriation and repatriation to and from Africa.

In selecting people for overseas assignments, should the MNC use African nationals as third-country nationals (TCNs)? In practical terms, since there is an acute shortage of skilled personnel in most African countries infected by Aids, it seems unlikely that the MNC would choose this route anyway. The anticipated direction of flow of personnel for MNCs would be to send expatriates and/or TCN personnel to countries with high levels of HIV/AIDS. This poses the question – how can possible resistance to this on the part of employees be tackled? According to Baruch's Push/Pull model (*see* Figure 7.1), to encourage acceptance of the assignment the company needs to balance the negative push that HIV/AIDS has for assignees, and this can be done by a variety of measures (compensation, planned career path, fit with personal attributes, etc.).

Fair treatment and a proactive approach can improve a company's image and reputation. In particular the proper treatment of company employees suffering from HIV/AIDS will enhance the image of the company for the larger population.

Source: Based on Y. Baruch and P. Clancy (2000) 'Managing AIDS in Africa: HRM challenges in Tanzania', *International Journal of Human Resource Management*, 11(4), 789–806.

Expatriation and repatriation career strategies

Expatriation is the clearest manifestation of globalization from an HR perspective (Brewster and Scullion, 1997; Porter and Tansky, 1999; Selmer 1996).[33] Theuerkauf (1991)[34] suggested that for the global organization, career planning right from the recruitment stage, through to the top, should involve international assignments.

One indication of the problem career systems face when dealing with international assignments relates to failure. The literature indicates that failure rates are high. Failure may be defined as early return, poor performance on assignment and lack of learning from the international experience. However another disturbing finding is that between 30 per cent and 40 per cent of expatriates leave their companies within two years of repatriation (cf. Dowling *et al.*, 1994; Stroh, 1995).[35] A wider definition of failure should therefore include leaving the company after repatriation, as Black and Gregersen (1999)[36] argue. An employee who leaves an organization soon after repatriation causes heavy expense to the company, and may even pose a business risk (Selmer, 1998).[37]

Four elements concerned with career management and expatriation are: choice of candidate, pre-posting preparation for executive and family (both prior to the expatriation), support and maintenance of relations with the home organization while on the assignment, and facilitation of a smooth return to the home base upon completion (Mendenhall *et al.*, 1987; Zetlin, 1994).[38] The following theoretical frameworks may help in understanding companies' approaches to the management of expatriation and repatriation.

One seminal classification of strategic approaches to global management strategy was offered by Perlmutter (1969).[39] His classification differentiates among global organizational configurations: ethnocentric (home-country oriented), polycentric (host-country oriented) and geocentric (worldwide oriented). Later, Heenan and Perlmutter (1979)[40] added the regiocentric (region oriented).

This classification (ethnocentric, polycentric, geocentric and regiocentric) fitted well with the American international outlook in the second half of the twentieth century, and it is still appropriate for many MNCs.

In the ethnocentric model, most or all of the decision makers in the host operation will be people from the home country, sent as expatriates from headquarters. The reasons for opting for such a strategy include: a lack of trust in local people, a need for strong control by the mother company, being in the initial stage of operations (before moving on to other strategies), or simply a lack of technological or of a specific type of knowledge in the host country. While these may be valid reasons, applying this model frequently suffers from a misunderstanding of local culture and local ways of working, which might hinder the success of the home country managers. Another undesirable outcome is that host-country managerial personnel are prevented from progressing beyond a certain level in the organization and as a result they might lose their motivation and move elsewhere.

The polycentric model favours the appointment of local personnel to managerial positions. This leaves locals with ample development options, helps in reducing the costs of expatriation and the length of time it takes an expatriate manager to adapt to local conditions. In particular circumstances this model helps to overcome local political hurdles and sensitivities. The major problem with using this model concerns contact between the home and host companies, which might suffer possible detachment as compared with the position under the ethnocentric model. The latter, in many cases, aims to transfer the home culture to the host country operation. Also, the whole idea of multinational/international/global integration is inapplicable under this model, as a segregation remains in place.

The geocentric model shows a way to overcome the problems of the first two models. The basic premise of the geocentric model suggests that there should be no issue of nationality when making appointment decisions in a MNC. The person most suitable for the job will get it, no matter what his/her nationality is. While in principle this sounds like a 'best practice' approach, this model is quite utopian or idealistic, in the sense that it may take many years for such a model to be fully developed across the globe. In fact this model works quite well within the USA (across the states), and can work in many European nations. This model, though, will not help in transferring home country and company core values and culture in the way the ethnocentric model does. In practice, moving people around on a continual basis is quite costly in terms of training and remuneration.

The regiocentric model is an attempt to compromise and divide an operation into several regions, with the effect being that people move within, but not across, regions. This model allows host-country nationals to develop their careers further than in the polycentric model, but the barrier is not eliminated, just moved to the regional level. It can be a good intermediate strategy until the MNC can move on to geocentric.

Another influential framework was that suggested by Bartlett and Ghoshal (1989).[41] Their categorization of MNC strategic models classifies organizations according to a two-dimensional matrix comprising level of integration, and level of responsiveness. This matrix forms a four-quadrant model with the following categories: international (low on integration and responsiveness), global (low on responsiveness, high on integration), multinational (high on responsiveness, low on integration) and transnational (high on both).

The classification offers an alternative and complementary approach to that often featured in the literature. For example, Bartlett and Ghoshal's concept suggests a stages-based model, where firms can develop up to the final *transnational* stage. This strategic model implies that the HRM strategy, in particular in managing expatriates, is aligned according to the four 'levels'. The 'transnational' model, which is similar to Perlmutter's geocentric model, is the ultimate goal. Both present a utopian model rather than actual working cases. One exception, perhaps, is Nestlé – the Swiss company with less than 5 per cent of its workforce and operations located in Switzerland.

In contrast, a model suggested by Baruch and Altman (2002)[42] argues for five distinct options, each with their relative advantages and disadvantages, and not necessarily on a graduated scale whereby each model is expected to be better than the former. The options are grounded in practice, and can match organizational strategies in globalization for both the business and the HR function. This concept supports the strategic alignment of HRM with business strategy (Gratton et al., 1999; Holbeche, 1999),[43] and provides benchmarking for the strategic choices companies have to make in developing their policies and practices. All in all, the set of options reflects the variety of cultural perspectives of a global economy at the start of the twenty-first century.

This theoretical framework focuses on the HR management of expatriation and repatriation as part of organizational career systems. A five-option classification expresses a variety of approaches organizations may take in managing expatriate careers. The main contribution of this approach is to break the mould of the model to which many well-known blue-chip MNCs aspire. Many MNCs desire to become 'transnational', i.e. borderless company, but Hu (1992)[44] claims that in fact there exist only national companies, which operate across borders. The fact remains that in most cases most of the employees and operations or the management and headquarters are located in the mother company's country (Nestlé, mentioned above, and Shell, located in both the UK and The Netherlands, are well-known, but rare exceptions).

Baruch and Altman's (2002)[45] five options are different models or approaches for organizations to adopt in managing expatriation and repatriation. These are based on several dimensions – values, time, global as opposed to local focus, individual as opposed to company criteria, and nature of the psychological contract. Each option implies a different organizational approach to the management of careers and the meaning of international assignment as a part of people's career within the organization.

The five options are discussed in the following paragraphs.

1 *The Global (or Empire)*: This is the 'archetype' large global MNC, with an established reputation in expatriation management. The Empire corporate philosophy views expatriation as integral to organizational life. Both individual and organizational expectations accept it when planning careers, and period(s) of expatriation are an inevitable part of the career path for any executive. Some may not wish to be expatriated, but in this they will deviate from the norm, and thus they will be excluded from the mainstream career path. For the Empire organization, globalization is not a goal as such. It is an inherent property and part of the organizational ethos. The company will have a comprehensive set of procedures and practices in place. Moreover, people in the company as well as those joining would expect expatriation to be at the core of their professional and managerial career.

2 *The Emissary (or Colonial)*: The Colonial company has established overseas markets and a long-term view as to its international aspirations; however it is firmly rooted in a particular culture and this serves as the basis of its ideology, its power base and its source of expatriates. It is characterized by an organizational culture indoctrinated with an ingrained obligation – a sense of duty backed with high commitment and loyalty. Under the Colonial option some people may be asked to accept an expatriate role, and in line with the ethos 'for God, King and Country' are not expected to refuse.

3 *Peripheral*: This model fits companies operating in peripheral locations, where the experience of expatriation is highly desirable. Here expatriation is a means

of benefiting employees. Globalization for the Peripheral company is an expansion strategy, as local markets are insufficient to offer growth. Or indeed the company may have chosen to target itself as export oriented. What is different in the Peripheral option is that people will be queuing up to get the chance of expatriation. It will be perceived as a perk by both the individuals and the employer.

4 *Professional*: The Professional strategic option is based on buying in knowledge and expertise. Its goal is to concentrate on home-country strengths and keep its people within specified geographical borders. Hence the ideology drives the organization towards outsourcing cross-border activities, and delivery through people external to the company. These may be local people, or TCN specialists. The company prefers to use external people, in effect outsourcing the expatriation process.

5 *Expedient*: This is the emergent approach for newcomers to the global scene, which characterizes most firms in the process of developing policies and practices. An ad hoc and pragmatic approach, the expedient option is quite a 'mixed bag'. It encompasses a wide range of companies that are entering globalized markets or wishing to become global players.

The principles that form the basis for distinguishing among the options are discussed in the following paragraphs.

1 *Values as the strategic drivers*, be they at the individual, organizational or national level, underpin attitudes and behaviours. Values are the bedrock of a company's philosophy and, consequently, strategy, on numerous issues. So, for example, the core philosophy of the Global company may be portrayed by the idea of Organization Man; the manifest ideology of the Emissary organization is 'spreading the gospel'; hedonism encapsulates the Peripheral ideas of expatriation as a perk; while the Professional option is based on confined transactional relationships. Lastly, the Expedient strategy, driven by pragmatism and immediacy, thrives on entrepreneurial values.

2 *The time dimension* (or assignment length): for the Global employee, though the career may be construed as a string of relocations, each one is short term (usually no more than three years' duration); an Emissary expatriate may have a somewhat longer-term posting; the Professional expatriate opts for an extended period of expatriation voluntarily; the Peripheral as well as the Expedient expatriate experiences more erratic expatriation assignments, but for different reasons. For the Peripheral expatriate, it is a perk to be shared with the many; for the Expedient expatriate expatriation is ad hoc and therefore less predictable.

3 *Where to look for expatriates*: orientation. For the Global expatriate, as with the geocentric or transnational model, geography is of little consequence; while for the Professional organization, an international focus means sourcing from outside the home country. The Peripheral organization builds on the eagerness of its employees to experience the big world; the Emissary organization expects its people to give up the security and convenience of the home organization. The Expedient organization, with its ad hoc emphasis, is likely to be inconsistent in its sourcing.

4 *Individual as opposed to company criterion*: the core of the Peripheral and Professional organizations is the individuals – whether the professional expatriates in the Professional option or employees' expectations in the Peripheral company – and it is the individuals who drive expatriation. The reverse is true for both the Emissary and the Global company, since it is the company's requirements that drive the process. For the Expedient company, resolutions will be ad hoc and variable.

5 *What psychological contract?* In the Global case, the psychological contract is open-ended, with employees and organization anticipating a long-term career. For the Emissary option, it is relational, underscoring the mutual commitment of employee and organization. The Professional option is transactional (market based) as is that for the Peripheral option (based on the lure of a lucrative position). As for the Expedient option, the psychological contract has to be developed for each case.

The five options are posited as 'ideal type' models, while in reality organizations have to respond pragmatically in managing expatriation processes. Therefore one often encounters variations, i.e. a hybrid of two or more options. The variations among the options are expected to be mirrored in the career systems and opportunities expected in each option of the model. In the Global option, the career prospects for managers are truly borderless. For the Emissary option, executives may be expected to contribute a few years' service for the sake of the company, while in the Peripheral option the motive to embark on an international career derives from individual eagerness to explore the world. The Professional option is a market-led career, and some people are lifelong expatriates, moving among companies that need their services. In the Expedient option a career overseas is an exception and involves negotiations with the company about future prospects, especially following repatriation.

Globalization will continue, and while much depends on political trends and legal requirements, international careers will prevail in the future.

EXHIBIT 7.7	All in all, evidence suggests that individuals as well as organizations should evaluate the prospective benefits of expatriation as against the possible pitfalls and the investment needed.

Will repatriation be needed?

Where will your people end up? Borg (1988)[46] offered four categories for identifying where people sent on an international assignment ended up. He found that only 38 per cent of the 200 managers in his study had a single global assignment and simply returned home. The rest either stayed in the country to which they were sent (25 per cent), or moved on to a global career with several consecutive global assignments, some remaining abroad (22 per cent), whereas 15 per cent returned home after a series of assignments.

What Borg does not tell us is what happened to people who did not stay with the company. Departure is an indication of the indirect failure of either the expatriation or the repatriation.

Table 7.1 Expatriation and repatriation dimensions of HR

Strategy

Option	Philosophy/ideology	Goals/aims	TNCs	Time–org. dimension	Time–ind. dimension	Level of analyses *	Examples **
Global	Lifestyle: the expected career pattern	Globalization as a key org. Characteristic	Non-issue	Long term	Short term	The firm	Nestlé Exxon Lafarge
Emissary	Cultural agent: organizational long arm	Expansion: branching out	Frowned upon	Long term	Mid term	The firm & national/cultural	Sony Vivendi Matsushita
Peripheral	Expatriation as a perk	A growth strategy	Undesirable	Variable	Ad hoc, usually short term	The firm & national	Ericsson Corus Jypex
Professional	Foreign legion: annexed for expat. Missions	Segregate between 'internal' and 'external'	Common	Mid-long term	Mid-long term	The firm & the individual	Gillette KPMG Teva
Expedient	Opportunistic: reactive	Responsive to emergent opportunities	Possible	Ad hoc	Ad hoc	The firm & the individual	NU Brintons Barclays

HR practice

Option	Recruitment & selection	T&D	Policies	Career development: retention	Level of analyses *
Global	Internal–(enforced)	Regular, ongoing	Established	Integral career path	The firm
Emissary	Internal–(normative)	Regular, specific	Developed	Loyalty and long term; relational	The firm & national/cultural
Peripheral	Internal–(desired)	Ad hoc	Evolving	Distributive justice as an issue	The firm & national
Professional	External	Buy-in	Outsourcing	Contract-based relationships	The firm & the individual
Expedient	Internal or external	None (time & budget constraints)	(Lack)	Exceptional case; dealt as per need	The firm & the individual

(continued on next page)

Table 7.1 Expatriation and repatriation dimensions of HR (continued)

| Option | Advantages | HR consequences | | Level of analyses * |
		Challenges		
Global	Steady flow of candidates, ongoing learning	Managing the flow		The firm
Emissary	Long-term commitment	Maintaining attachment, low turnover		The firm & national/cultural
Peripheral	Easy to recruit	Difficult to re-patriate, 'politicized'		The firm & national
Professional	Cost effective, flexible	Lack of commitment, high turnover		The firm & the individual
Expedient	Unstable, flexible	Managing the chaos		The firm & the individual

* Level–while the stress in our framework is on the organizational (firm) level, we acknowledge that other levels of analysis apply; for example, the Professional is individual oriented in its practices whereas national location (geography and mentally) would play a significant role in the Peripheral option and national culture in the Emissary option.

** Although many of the prototypes chosen need no explanation, in particular the Globals, others may be less known to the US readership. Even within the Globals, one example is Lafarge, a French construction company with more than 65,000 employees, most of them outside France; at Lafarge being expatriate is a condition for getting into the upper echelons of the firm. Vivendi (formerly Suez Lyonnaise des Eaux) is a French utility company, which has more than 220,000 employees worldwide, some 150,000 of them in 120 countries outside France. The company maintains the Emissary option for their operation in the UK water industry. Matsushita is a Japanese conglomerate that applies the Emissary option in its policy and practice. Sony had to use the Emissary for many Japanese employees (and also reinforce the message with considerably high salaries for expatriates)–although even in Japan many employees would be happily expatriated for the option to observe and perhaps absorb other cultures.

Ericsson is a Swedish MNC in the mobile-phone market, for which the issue of expatriation is never a problem when looking for local Swedes to spend some time in southern countries. Corus Group was formed following a merger between Dutch company Hoogovens and British Steel. With 60,000 employees (headquartered in the UK), they have just over 200 expatriates, but the number is growing. For the former part based in The Netherlands the company applies the Peripheral option successfully: however, with wide experience in the global market and a well-developed policy they do not usually face repatriation problems. The company is certainly aiming to move to the Global approach. Jypex, a medium sized electric infrastructure company, is based in the French Caribbean islands of Guadeloupe and Martinique. While the French fly to Martinique for regular meetings, it is the Guadeloupians who are expatriate to Paris.

While Gillette and KPMG need no introduction (KPMG also applies the Global approach alongside the Professional), Teva is an Israeli pharmaceutical company with 3,500 employees, which used to utilize the Peripheral option, but now has transformed its expatriation approach to the Professional mode, and has very few expatriates. Brintons is a top international (UK-based) carpet manufacturer, with a workforce of 4,000, of which almost 1,500 are located overseas, but similarly to NU only a couple of dozen are expatriates. One may utilize the Expedient approach also as a large organization, such as Barclays Bank does, with hundreds of expatriates.

Source: Reprinted from Y. Baruch and Y. Altman (2002) 'Expatriation and repatriation in MNC: A taxonomy', *Human Resource Management*, 11(4), 789–806 © John Wiley & Sons, Inc., reproduced with permission.

Table 7.2 Expatriation and orientation

	Single global assignment	*Multiple global assignments*
Ending up abroad	Naturalized	Cosmopolitan orientation
Ending up at home	Local orientation	Unsettled

Source: Based on M. Borg (1988) *Intentional Transfer of Managers in Multinational Corporations*, Stockholm: Almqvist & Wiksell Int.

What is failure, how many fail?

Several studies have tried to analyse the failure rate of expatriation. One problem with these studies is the lack of clear acceptance of the meaning of failure. One indication is an early return, a pre-planned departure from the role. However, a more comprehensive approach should take into account the level of performance (or lack of it) while on assignment. Lastly, a wider perspective would take into account also repatriation failure, e.g. leaving the company after repatriation.

Of course, it is not merely the company, but also the host country of the MNC that will influence the prevalence, the nature and the success or failure of expatriation. A possible reason for the discrepancy in the literature on failure rates may be due to differences among cultures. There is empirical evidence that failure rates in Europe and Japan are lower than in the USA (Tung, 1988; Scullion, 1991; Harzing and Ruysseveldt, 1996).[47]

One thing is quite clear – the costs of failure of expatriation are considerably higher than those for failing in a conventional job. The real cost must take into account the loss of training, relocation costs and the indirect costs of loss of reputation and further difficulties in finding a replacement. Thus the actual cost of failure depends very much on the specific assignment – the destination, the training undertaken, the salary and the two-way relocation costs wasted. What cannot be calculated is the loss of reputation and the damage caused to the future of expatriation in the relevant organization. An estimate of the average costs (Mendenhall and Oddou, 1985)[48] is in the range of $US55 000–80 000 per expatriation for US companies. Other costs, claim Dowling *et al.* (1994)[49] include loss of political contacts, morale and productivity. Finally, as is elaborated below, the one who may pay the highest cost is the individual involved. And this will also mean a loss for the company, if the individual's decision is to leave the firm as a consequence.

What are the reasons for failure? The answer depends not only on company practice, but also on the cultural origin of the expatriate. Tung (1982)[50] found that for Europeans and Americans, the major constraint was the inability of their spouse to adjust. The Americans added other factors, the fifth on the list being the inability of the manager to cope with larger overseas responsibility. In contrast, this was the first and major reason for failure for the Japanese expatriates studied. The spouse's inability to adjust came only fifth in the list of factors for the Japanese expatriates. (It is quite likely that cultural values relating to the role of women were of significance in this ranking. At the time the study was undertaken, most of the Japanese expatriate population were males, and this is largely true today. Another factor is that many of the spouses opted to stay in Japan rather than accompany their husbands overseas.)

Other factors include the level of hospitability of the people of the host country. Paris is notoriously unsympathetic to foreigners, as vividly presented by Dowling *et al*. The climate also has an impact. People from Spain may find north Canada or Sweden too cold whereas people from northern countries will metaphorically melt in the heat of the Middle East. Other countries pose even more challenges for strangers, ranging from religious differences to terrorist activities and danger from frequent kidnapping. Business visitors to Georgia are advised to hire a bodyguard to accompany them. Assignments in Afghanistan and Pakistan have cost the lives of many expatriates. Even the simple fact that alcohol is banned in many of the Gulf states would deter expatriates from some Western countries from spending a significant amount of time there on assignment.

Repatriation and reverse culture shock

One of the most neglected aspects of expatriation is the repatriation process. In many cases HR managers, line managers and colleagues assume that people will just happily return home, in the belief that there is no place like home. However, this has been proven only too often to be a totally wrong assumption. Some of the problems stem from managerial and direct career issues. Others concern reverse culture shock (RCS), the effect whereby people are surprised and shocked to encounter a new culture when they return home to what is apparently known territory.

Reverse culture shock occurs as a result of several sets of changes. First, people change. In terms of their managerial role, the expatriate assignment gives people an invaluable experience. Many are given greater responsibility than they have held before, perhaps as head of an operation, having to make strategic decisions. Upon returning home, they find that even if they are at a similar level in the organizational hierarchy, they become a 'cog in the machine', and the vast experience they have gained is not appreciated – as found by Baruch *et al*. (2003)[51] in a company that lost some 50 per cent of its returning expatriates within a couple of years of repatriation.

Even more disturbing may be the changes that occur in the company while the expatriate is away. At one extreme there is the full collapse or disappearance of the company, with the result that the returning expatriate comes back to an entirely different company from that which they left. (Enron, Exxon and Mobil are just a few recent examples of such changes.) Even more subtle changes can also have a strong impact – restructuring, widespread downsizing, changing of market niche – all these would change the career system to which an expatriate might have been hoping or preparing to return.

In terms of cultural differences, people learn how things can be done differently, sometimes better. They gain an understanding of others in another culture. If they believe they have seen better working practices overseas, they will have an extremely difficult time trying to persuade their colleagues to adopt such practices (and will almost certainly make themselves unpopular in the process).

| EXHIBIT 7.8 | **Alcohol** |

In the USA, one cannot legally drink alcohol before the age 21. In the UK the age is 18. Conversely, in the UK the pubs stop selling drinks at 10.30 or 11.00 pm, whereas no such limit exists in the USA.

A returning expatriate may be critical of some practices in their home country, comparing them unfavourably with those in the country where they have just spent some time. (The same may be true of their children also.)

Another issue is that while an expatriate is overseas, unexpected changes may occur in their home country. For example, an expatriate who spent three to five years overseas during the 1990s might have been very surprised at the huge growth in the use of mobile (cellular) phones, and could have found the disturbance they caused to quiet commuting time most unwelcome. Moreover, being away means being away from local networking, missing out on important, and less important, events. It creates 'Black Holes' of knowledge about what has happened during the absence. People might become out of touch and feel disconnected from their former culture, yet not really part of the overseas culture that they have now left behind.

| EXHIBIT 7.9 | **Detachment** |

MC and his wife (*see* Exhibit 7.2) suffered severely from RCS when they returned to The Netherlands after six years in the UK and the USA. They found that both the country and the company to which MC returned, remained the same, whereas they had moved forward. Personally, they were expected by everyone, family and old friends, to return and revert to what they had been in the past. In the company, the same people who managed it six years before were still in the same positions. MC was not able to express and utilize the rich experience and knowledge he gained. The 'Black Holes' in their knowledge of day-to-day life at home left the family detached. After a couple of years of trying to settle down in The Netherlands, they decided to return to the UK. This was their way to overcome the RCS, and they saw the UK as a reasonable compromise between the European culture they loved, and the American Anglo-Saxon approach in which they preferred to work.

What relevance does the cultural gap or distance between the home country and the host country have on the level of RCS? I wish to offer here two contradicting hypotheses, which refer to the cultural difference between the home country and the host country.

The first hypothesis suggests that the 'closer' the cultural differences between the home country and the host country, the LESS RCS impact will be found. This simplistic hypothesis relies on the theory of Person-Environment Fit, and suggests that it would be easier to return to a culture after serving time within a relatively similar culture.

An alternative hypothesis suggests, on the contrary, that the 'closer' the cultural differences between the home country and the host country, the more RCS impact will be found. The case for this hypothesis reflects the idea that when there are huge, significant differences between the cultures, in particular when the host country is seen as a 'less desired destination', people do not 'get used to it', will not blend in or try to adapt to local patterns of work and non-work life. They will always be waiting to return home, not making any attempt to change themselves. On the other hand, if a person (and their family) spends a considerable time in a culture that is relatively close (e.g. Americans spending time in the UK or Australia), they can easily adapt to the host country culture, which is nevertheless different from their own, and on their return will experience different behaviour patterns, lifestyle, etc.

Which hypothesis is valid is not known yet, but even the presentation of the hypotheses serves to challenge HR managers in planning and preparing expatriates for their return.

How can a company anticipate RCS, and what can be done? Can cultural gap be measured at all? Measurement of 'culture' is a sensitive matter, and the main measure, that developed by Hofstede, is subject to debate. There are, however, other concepts for evaluating cultural differences (*see* the works of Ronen and Shenkar (1985) and Trompenaars and Hampden-Turner (1997)[52] that can indicate the strength of the cultural gap. The model depicted in Figure 7.2 lists the factors that may influence the existence and level of RCS.

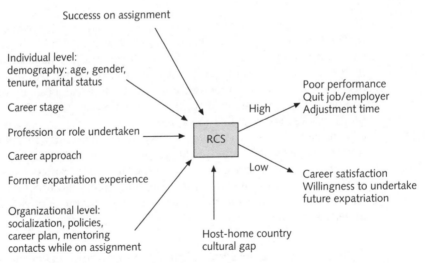

Figure 7.2 Factors affecting reverse culture shock

The implications for MNCs are very relevant. Identifying the problem is the first step in rectifying the outcomes. Recognition that repatriation requires attention will cause organizations to introduce repatriation programmes. Such programmes will be designed to prevent RCS, and will be tailored to each situation, and will depend on the cultures of both home and host country and the gap between them.

EXHIBIT 7.10	**Prepare yourself for the repatriation surprise**

What will you do if, upon repatriation, you find that...

You have been forgotten by most of your former peers and superiors?

Most of your former peers and superiors have left while you were away?

Your place in the career development system has been taken by others?

The role formerly designated for you on your return has disappeared due to restructuring?

You (and your family) cannot easily re-adapt to cultural changes that have happened at home?

Your job is no longer involved with strategy making – you returned to become a cog in the operational machine?

During your expatriation, your mentor has quit, been transferred, lost status, etc.?

Now, what will you do, *while on expatriation*, to *prevent* the above or their consequences from occurring?

Virtual expatriation

Do we really need to expatriate people for them to operate for a company in a different country? Not always. Many call centres of UK companies are located far from the main premises of the organization. The first call centres were in Scotland, where unemployment was higher, and labour cheaper than in southeast England, and companies turned later to India to gain even better cost effectiveness, using highly skilled employees in a low-paid area. Crabb (1995)[53] tells us of how UK organizations employ people in India, benefiting from the wage gap, without moving people across borders: software engineers in India earn some £1000 a year – a small fraction of the salary of their counterparts in the UK. The employment of such people is very tempting for employers, and it does not require expatriation and repatriation, with all their difficulties and challenges. The application of new technology can save companies on the costs of their people management. Not all is bright, though: in practical terms there is a five-hour gap in time zones between the UK and India, and this may cause operational problems (or cause Indian employees to work late at night). Politically, moving work overseas means fewer jobs at home, and this might cause political and image problems for companies, as happened in late 2002 to Prudential when they decided to close a UK operation and move the work to India.

Summary

The chapter focuses on the internationalization or globalization of careers and career systems. It starts with the individual perspective, trying to identify, if possible, the characteristics of global managers and whether a global psychological contract has developed. It proceeds to offer the general framework of the Push/Pull model to understand career movements, in light of different national and managerial cultures. Moving on from the individual to the organizational perspective, the chapter addresses two aspects of global career systems. The first is the implication for HRM and career management when HRM has to operate across borders (and the chapter discusses in depth the issues of remuneration, performance appraisal, training and development, industrial relations and health and safety). The second area is expatriation and repatriation, and the chapter presents three prominent models or frameworks for understanding expatriation and repatriation career strategies from the organizational perspective (at the three Ps levels: practice, policy and philosophy). The chapter ends with a discussion of the reverse culture shock phenomenon.

Key terms

- Global career
- Global manager
- Expatriation
- Repatriation
- Glocalization
- The Push/Pull model
- Perlmutter's classification (ethnocentric, polycentric, geocentric and regiocentric)
- Bartlett and Ghoshal's classification (international, global, multinational and transnational)
- Baruch and Altman's classification (global, emissary, professional, peripheral and expedient)
- Reversed cultural shock

DISCUSSION QUESTIONS

Lessons and food for thought

1 *For the working student*: What will make you agree, or be willing, to accept (or dissuade you from accepting) an international assignment as your next job? In five years? Are you proactive or reactive in reaching your career goals? What kind of company model best matches your own organization?

2 *If you aim to become an HR consultant*: (a) How prepared are you to provide advice to people seeking a global career route? Which questions will you ask a manager before advising on a change to an international career? In what ways might your approach be different for female managers?

(b) Which organizational policies and practices will you suggest to an organization that wishes to embark on an international operation in the following countries: Germany, Sweden, Peru, Saudi Arabia? Can you analyse an organizational approach and place it within one of the models described in this chapter?

Notes

[1] Hofstede, G. (1980) *Culture's consequences: international differences in work-related values*, NJ: Sage.

[2] MacLuhan, M. (1960) *Explorations in Communication*, Boston, MA: Beacon Press.

[3] Cornelius, N. (1999) *Human Resource Management: A Managerial Perspective*, London: International Thomson Business Press, p. 215; Sparrow, P.R. and Hiltrop, J.M. (1997) 'Redefining the field of European HRM: A battle between national mindsets and forces of business transitions?', *Human Resource Management*, 36(2), 201–19.

[4] Arthur, W. Jr. and Bennett, W. Jr. (1995) 'The international assignee: the relative importance of factors perceived to contribute to success', *Personnel Psychology*, 48(1), 99–114; Drucker, P.F. (1999) *Management Challenges for the 21st Century*, Oxford: Butterworth-Heinemann, p. 61.

[5] Conner, J. (2000) 'Developing the global leaders of tomorrow', *Human Resource Management*, 39(2 and 3), 147–57.

[6] Shackleton, V. and Newell, S. (1997) 'International assessment and selection', in N. Anderson and P. Herriot (eds) *International Handbook of Selection and Assessment*, Chichester: Wiley, p. 82.

[7] Black, J.S. and Gregersen, H.B. (1999) 'The Right Way to Manage Expats', *Harvard Business Review*, 77(2), 52–62.

[8] Bartlett, C.A. and Ghoshal, S. (1989) *Managing Across Borders. The Transnational Solution*, Boston, MA: Harvard Business Press.

[9] Borg, M. and Harzing, A.W. (1995) 'Composing an international staff', in A.W. Harzing and J.V. Ruysseveldt (eds) *International Human Resource Management*, London: Sage, pp. 179–204; Tung, R.L. (1982) 'Selection and training procedures of US, European and Japanese multinationals', *California Management Review*, 25(1), 57–71; Mendenhall, M. and Oddou, G.R. (1985) 'The dimensions of expatriate acculturation: a review', *Academy of Management Review*, 10(1), 39–47.

[10] Baruch, Y. (2002) 'No such thing as a global manager', *Business Horizons*, 45(1), 36–42.

[11] Goldberg, L.R. (1990) 'An alternative "description of personality": The Big Five factor structure', *Journal of Personality and Social Psychology*, 59, 1216–29.

[12] Guzzo, R.A., Nooman, K.A. and Elron, E. (1994) 'Expatriate managers and the psychological contract', *Journal of Applied Psychology*, 79(4), 617–26.

[13] Markham, W.T. (1987) 'Sex, relocation and occupational advancement – the "real cruncher" for women', in A.H. Stromberg, L. Larwood and B.A. Gutek (eds) *Women and Work, an annual Review*, Vol. 2, pp. 207–32, NJ: Sage.

[14] Taylor, S. and Napier, N. (1996) 'Working in Japan: lessons from women expatriates', *Sloan Management Review*, Spring, 76–84.

[15] Harvey, M. (1997) 'Dual-career expatriates: expectations, adjustment and satisfaction with international relocation', *Journal of International Business Studies*, 28(3), 627–58.

[16] Leong, F.T.L. and Hartung, P.J. (2000) 'Adapting to the changing multicultural context of career', in A.W. Harzing and J. V. Ruysseveldt (eds) *International Human Resource Management*, London: Sage, pp. 212–27.

[17] Baruch, Y. (1995) 'Business Globalization – the Human Resource Management Aspect', *Human Systems Management*, 14(4), 313–26.

[18] Lewin, K. (1951) *Field Theory in Social Science*, NY: Harper & Row.

[19] Punnett, B.J. (1997) 'Towards effective management of expatriate spouses', *Journal of World Business*, 32(3), 243–57.

[20] Scheneider, S.C. and Barsoux, J.-L. (1997) *Managing Across Cultures*, Harlow, England: Prentice Hall, p. 144.

[21] Laurent, A. (1986) 'The cross cultural puzzle of IHRM', *Human Resource Management*, 25(1), 91–102; Porter, M.E. (1989) *The Competitive Advantage of Nations*, London: Macmillan; Porter, G. and Tansky, J.W. (1999) 'Expatriate success may depend on a "Learning Orientation": considerations for selection and training', *Human Resource Management*, 38(1), 47–60.

[22] Perlmutter, H.V. (1969) 'The tortuous evolution of the multinational corporation', *Columbia Journal of World Business*, Jan.–Feb., 9–18; Bartlett, C.A. and Ghoshal, S. (1992) 'What is a global manager', *Harvard Business Review*, 70(5), 124–32; Baruch, Y. and Altman, Y. (2002) 'Expatriation and repatriation in MNC: A Taxonomy', *Human Resource Management*, 41(2), 239–59.

[23] Dowling, P.J., Schuler, R.S. and Welch, D.E. (1994) *International Dimensions of Human Resource Management*, Belmont, CA: Wadworth, p. 149.

[24] Logger, E., Vinke, R. and Kluytmans, F. (1995) 'Compensation and appraisal in an international perspective', in A.W. Harzing and J.V. Ruysseveldt (eds) *International Human Resource Management*, London: Sage, pp. 144–55.

[25] Chen, C.C., Choi, J. and Chi, S.-C. (2002) 'Making sense of local-expatriate compensation disparity: mitigation by local referents, ideological explanations, and interpersonal sensitivity in China-foreign joint ventures', *The Academy of Management Journal*, 45(4), 807–17.

[26] Kessler, I. and Purcell, J. (1992) 'Performance related pay: objectives and application', *Human Resource Management*, 2(3), 16–33; Kessler, I. (1994) 'Performance related pay: contrasting approaches', *Industrial Relations Journal*, 25(2), 122–35.

[27] Bernardin, H.J., Kane, J.S., Ross, S., Spina, J.D. and Johnson, D.L. (1995) 'Performance appraisal design, development, and implementation', in G.R. Ferris, S.D. Rosen and D.T. Barnum (eds) *Handbook of Human Resource Management*, Cambridge, MA: Blackwell, pp. 462–93; Baruch, Y. and Harel, H.G. (1993) 'Combining multi-source performance appraisal: An empirical and methodological note', *Public Administration Quarterly*, 17(1), 96–111.

[28] Baruch, Y. (1996) 'Self performance appraisal vs. direct manager appraisal: A case of congruence', *Journal of Managerial Psychology*, 11(6), 50–65; Bernardin, H.J. (1986) 'Subordinate appraisal: A valuable source of information about managers', *Human Resource Management*, 25, 421–39.

[29] *See* note 1 above.

[30] *See* note 27 above.

[31] Baumgarten, K. (1995) 'Training and development of international staff', in A.W. Harzing and J.V. Ruysseveldt (eds) *International Human Resource Management*, London: Sage, p. 214.

[32] Baruch, Y. and Clancy, P. (2000) 'Managing AIDS in Africa: HRM challenges in Tanzania', *International Journal of Human Resource Management*, 11(4), 789–806.

[33] Brewster, C. and Scullion, H. (1997) 'A review and agenda for expatriate HRM', *Human Resource Management Journal*, 7(3), 32–41; Porter and Tansky (1999) – *see* note 21 above; Selmer, J. (1996) 'Expatriate or local boss? HCN subordinates' preferences in leadership behaviour', *International Journal of Human Resource Management*, 7(1), 165–78.

[34] Theuerkauf, I. (1991) 'Reshaping the Global Organization', *McKinsey Quarterly*, 3, 1023–119.

[35] Dowling, Schuler and Welch (1994) – *see* note 23 above; Stroh, L.K. (1995) 'Predicting turnover among repatriates: can organizations affect retention rates?', *International Journal of Human Resource Management*, 6(2), 443–56.

[36] *See* note 7 above.

[37] Selmer, J. (1998) 'Expatriates: corporate policy, personal intentions and international adjustment', *International Journal of Human Resource Management*, 9(6), 996–1007.

[38] Mendenhall, M., Dunbar, E. and Oddou, G.R. (1987) 'Expatriate selection, training, and career pathing', *Human Resource Management*, 26(3), 331–45; Zetlin, M. (1994) 'Making tracks', *Journal of European Business*, 5(5), 40–7.

[39] *See* note 22 above.

[40] Heenan, D.A. and Perlmutter, H.V. (1979) *Multinational Organizational Development*, Reading, MA: Addison-Wesley.

[41] *See* note 8 above.

[42] *See* note 22 above.

[43] Gratton, L., Hope Hailey, V., Stiles, P. and Truss, C. (1999) *Strategic Human Resource Management*, New York: Oxford University Press; Holbeche, L. (1999) *Aligning Human Resource and Business Strategy*, Oxford: Butterworth-Heinemann.

[44] Hu, Y.S. (1992) 'Global or Stateless Corporations Are National Firms with International Operations', *California Management Review*, 34(2), 107–26.

[45] *See* note 22 above.

[46] Borg, M. (1988) *International Transfer of Managers in Multinational Corporations*, Stockholm: Almqvist & Wiksell Int.

[47] Tung, R.L. (1988) *The New Expatriates: Managing Human Resources Abroad*, NY: Harper & Row; Scullion, H. (1991) 'Why companies prefer to use expatriates', *Management*, November, 20–1; Harzing, A.W.K. and Ruysseveldt, J.V. (1996) *International Human Resource Management*, London: Sage.

[48] *See* note 9 above.

[49] *See* note 23 above.

[50] *See* note 9 above.

[51] Baruch, Y., Steele, D.J. and Quantrill, G.A. (2002) 'Management of expatriation and repatriation for novice global player', *International Journal of Manpower*, 23(7), 659–71.

[52] Ronen, S. and Shenkar, O. (1995) 'Clustering countries on attitudinal dimensions: a review and synthesis', *Academy of Management Review*, 10, 435–54; Trompenaars, F. and Hampden-Turner, C. (1997) *Riding the Waves of Culture*, Irwin Professional Publishers.

[53] Crabb, S. (1995) 'Jobs for all in the global market?', *People Management*, January, 22–7.

8 Managing career diversities

LEARNING OBJECTIVES

After reading this chapter you should be able to:

- Define diversity.

- Distinguish between a variety of diversities.

- Identify the advantages and possible pitfalls in managing diversity.

- Understand the impact of diverse individual backgrounds on careers.

- Distinguish between the legal and managerial arguments in managing diversity.

- Understand the role of diversity in career systems management.

CHAPTER CONTENTS

Introduction

What is the largest minority in the workforce in most Western labour markets (e.g. Europe, USA)?

Answer
White males.

True. There is no longer a majority of any single group of people, and even what was once the dominant part and certainly the majority of the workforce is now still the largest of all the groups, but it is not the majority. With the representation of women in the workforce close to 50 per cent, and a significant number of other minorities, white males comprise less than 50 per cent of the workforce. White males have become a minority in the labour market, due to the rapid increase in female employment, coupled with an increasing level of ethnic minority representation in the workforces of Western countries. For example, in the USA the Hispanic population is growing, there are a considerable number of black people and there is a continuous stream of Asian immigrants entering the country. Within a few years it is anticipated that white males' share of the US labour market will be reduced to about one-third.

However, white males hold the majority of managerial positions, and this disproportionate representation increases the higher up the organizational echelons one travels. White males' salaries are higher than those of women and other disadvantaged groups. The substantial earnings gap between males and females varies in level, according to the country, the profession and the sector. It is not unusual to find a 20 per cent, 30 per cent or higher pay gap. On a positive note, it should be noted that the gap has been shrinking dramatically in the recent past.

What is diversity?

No two people are the same. We all have unique qualities, each person possesses a distinctive combination of internal and external characteristics that makes him or her different from any other person. Yet we share many characteristics with certain other people, forming collectives of groups with specific common characteristics (e.g. sex, skin colour, etc.).

Within the work, organization and career context, diversity relates to the existence of a variety of sub-groups in the workforce. The first is women (being the largest group that suffers discrimination). The others are related to: race, ethnic minority, disability, minority religion, age (both young and old, though discrimination against old people is more prevalent in labour markets), sexual orientation and nationality. And the list is not conclusive. Most of these sources of diversity are observable (e.g. skin colour) or easily detectable (accent that reflects a national origin), whereas some are not clearly identifiable (e.g. sexual orientation, religion, some disabilities). Harrison, Price and Bell (1998)[1] refer to 'surface-' versus 'deep-' level diversity. 'Surface' diversity refers to demographic, mostly visible background characteristics of people, whereas 'deep-' level diversity refers to attitude or approach of people. They claim that the effect of time will mostly neutralize the effect of 'surface' diversity, and will enhance the effects of 'deep-level' diversity.

What is discrimination?

Discrimination means treating certain people unfavourably because they belong to a certain sub-group. This discrimination will usually be illegal if it is not anticipated that their belonging to the sub-group will influence performance in the job. For example, if a white male wishes to work as a midwife in a hospital that serves mostly black people, and a black woman with lower qualifications is appointed to the job, he will rightfully feel discriminated against. In practice, though, it is usually people of the minority groups that suffer from discrimination.

Most discrimination on the basis of diversity is illegal, but not all of it. Discrimination on the grounds of nationality means that one cannot gain employment because of one's nationality – nationals of some countries may need to have a work permit, and gaining it requires substantial efforts. Within the EU, though, EU nationals can work in any country without the need for a work permit. For some employers, sexual orientation is a cause for discrimination (e.g. the navy).

Discrimination does not need to be direct. Indirect discrimination occurs when one condition or requirement for a job or a position implies that the person belongs to a certain group which is then discriminated against. For example – if one is required to be at least taller than the average or a specific measure, this may lead to indirect discrimination: people of Asian origin are often shorter than those of Anglo-Saxon origin, thus a requirement for a policeman to be above a certain height causes most applicants of Chinese origin to be turned down. This was found to constitute indirect discrimination. A different case in the UK found that relying solely on referrals or recommendations for hiring in a plant where most of employees were white males constituted indirect discrimination against black people.

What is management of diversity?

Management of diversity means working systematically towards a workplace where the composition of the employees' diversity will reflect that of the general society. This involves taking proactive steps to promote a culture and atmosphere of equality and to ensure that there is no unjustified discrimination in the selection of people – both into the organization, and in promotion decisions.

Why manage diversity?

There are two principal reasons why organizations should manage diversity, in particular, career diversity: first, the legal aspect, and, second, organizational performance, effectiveness and outcomes. To be more explicit, Cox and Blake

$(1991)^2$ presented six managerial arguments to support the management of diversity in organizations.

(a) **Cost**: the organization needs to be able to manage the full spectrum of the workforce, including segments that in the past were marginal, but are now becoming more dominant. Failing to do that will be costly and will prevent organizations from achieving full productivity.

(b) **Resource acquisition**: organizations with a favourable reputation for positive management of diversity (e.g. being in the *Fortune 100 Best Employers* list) will attract the most talented members of diverse groups.

(c) **Marketing**: organizations serve and produce for multicultural and diverse societies. A diverse workforce will have better insights and sensitivities to the needs of a diverse customer base.

(d) **Creativity**: a diverse workforce should enhance the level of creativity and innovation.

(e) **Problem solving**: a diverse workforce should produce high-quality decisions and solutions.

(f) **System flexibility**: the better management of diversity means more flexibility and faster and more efficient responsiveness to environmental changes.

Along similar lines, Cassell $(2001)^3$ argues that in general organizations are moving towards using the business case rather than the legal arguments in adopting alternative approaches to managing diversity. More specifically she added to the list of Cox and Blake the idea that the prospects of attracting ethical investors and government support are greater for organizations that practise positive management of diversity. The ideas presented by Cox and Blake have been echoed by many others, e.g. Hall and Parker $(1993),^4$ who focused on diversity as enhancing flexibility.

These arguments should help organizations not just to see the issue of managing diversity through the eyes of the legal adviser, making sure they comply with the law, but to value diversity as a source of strength and competitiveness. Combining ethical and moral perspectives with cost effectiveness and managerial best practice will result in recognition of the need to manage diversity for both strategic and pragmatic reasons.

Greenhaus *et al.* $(2000)^5$ present two schools of thoughts on why organizations should manage diversity. One approach recognizes that the world and the workplace are becoming increasingly diverse. This trend is inevitable, thus organizations must accept this new demographic reality, i.e. hire and develop the most talented individuals from varying backgrounds in an effective and fair manner. Diversity is a fact of life, here to stay (and expand), so let us live with it. The other approach goes further than seeing diversity as a necessity, and argues that diversity is inherently healthy and beneficial in its own right. This approach assumes that employees from different backgrounds will bring different strengths and perspectives, which, in turn, will enhance effectiveness.

In line with the first approach is the fact that certain changes in the composition of the workforce in Western societies are making the management of diversity even more acute. Kandola $(1995)^6$ listed three groups which have increased their representation in the workforce: first, women, with an increasing number entering the workforce (*see* below for elaboration), second, ethnic minorities, some of the increase due to immigration and some due to lack of parity in internal growth rates, and, third, older workers, as we witness the phenomenon of the ageing of the working population. Kandola argues that it is not merely the North American workforce that is experiencing these changes, but also Europe, including the UK. To Kandola's list we can add the issue of sexual orientation which, following societal changes that make people less reluctant to hide their sexual orientation, has become more prevalent in recent years.

Are the arguments presented in the second approach valid? Studies on diversity in top management teams (Williams, 1998; Thompson, 1999)[7] indicated that diversity leads to more effective decision-making processes and better organizational performance. This may be due to the process of sharing and gaining from a variety of perspectives and ideas. Promoting women and members of other disadvantaged groups into top managerial jobs is never simple, but can be done with the right attitude and managerial support. In the end, the outcomes for the organization will be positive, as found by Harel, Tzafrir and Baruch (2002)[8] (*see* later in this chapter for elaboration of this point).

Whether one adopts the first approach, the second, or both, the consequences are that diversity should be managed.

Are there risks?

Is diversity inherently good? Should we expect only positive outcomes from diversity? In fact there are some negative aspects of increasing diversity, and these are more severe if diversity is not introduced properly into the organizational culture. With no females in the workforce there would be no sexual harassment, and sexual harassment (or accusations of sexual harassment) is an unfortunate by-product of a mixed-gender workforce (Gruber and Bjorn, 1982; Gutek, Cohen and Konrad, 1990; Mansfield, Henderson, Vicary, Cohn and Young, 1991).[9] Other negative outcomes are a high rate of turnover, a lowered attachment of whites and males (Tsui, Egan and O'Reilly, 1992), and the findings that heterogeneous teams do not necessarily make better decisions (Jackson, Sessa, Cooper, Julin and Peyronnin, 1991).[10]

Another argument about the negative side of diversity focuses on attraction theory, and suggests that interpersonal similarity helps in communication and networking, and creates a social context for improved relationships, which diversity would hinder (Sessa, Jackson and Rapini, 1995).[11] Moreover, Sessa *et al.* cite several studies that indicate that minorities may have lower levels of cohesiveness, commitment and attachment.

Are the risks strong enough to discourage organizations from managing diversity? The answer is no. As clearly indicated, diversity is here to stay and expand, so trying to avoid it is a futile exercise. However, risk should be managed too, and awareness will help in prompting the setting of mechanisms to tackle such possible negative outcomes.

Managing diversity – releasing the hidden talent

Today's workforce is characterized by a growing level of diversity. In the past the majority of the workforce comprised white males, and the few females employed were almost exclusively in lower-level positions such as clerical and other types of support roles. The global trade in slaves created a significant segment of the labour market comprising people of a different ethnic background (most notably the blacks in the USA). Ethnic minorities were restricted to manual labour (in those countries where people of a different ethnic origin formed a considerable number of the workforce). Older people were presumed to be less productive (and with a large proportion of work then being manual, there might have been a kernel of truth in such an assumption). Non-conventional sexual orientations were well hidden in the closet.

Today we live in a society that is, on the one hand, more conscious of diversity, but on the other hand, much more litigious (Baruch, 2001).[12] This means, amongst other things, that people have learned to safeguard their rights. The American phrase, 'see you in court', means that an increasing emphasis is being put on being legally sound. Thus, one of the major impetuses for discussing the management of diversity is the possibility of discrimination and the means of preventing it in order to avoid litigation. The issue that should, however, be the major concern, and was only recognized in the last few decades is that of performance, as mentioned above. The effective use of the diverse competencies of a diverse workforce makes good business sense. As Thomas (1991)[13] sees it, managing diversity should take the form of a holistic approach to creating a corporate environment that allows a variety of people to reach their full potential in pursuit of organizational goals and targets.

Organizational initiatives for managing diversity

Thomas (1996,[14] cited by Kreitner, Kinicki and Burlens, 2002)[15] presents a framework of several interventions organizations may adopt to tackle and manage diversity in an effective manner. These are strategic approaches, which are translated into practices for dealing with diversity, some positive, others negative:

- *Include/exclude*: Following affirmative action programmes, organizations may try to increase or decrease the numbers of diverse employees at all levels.
- *Deny*: Deny that difference exist, thus ignoring any possible impact of demography. The search is for the best person for the job or post, thus the colour, gender, etc. of the candidate is irrelevant.
- *Assimilate*: The basic assumption is that all members of the apparently disadvantaged groups will learn to fit in and become like the dominant group. Adopt induction programmes and sets of policies to achieve a homogeneous workforce.
- *Suppress*: Quash and discourage differences, maintaining the status quo.
- *Isolate*: Maintain the current way of doing things by pushing diverse people onto the sidelines.
- *Tolerate*: Acknowledge the differences, but do not really value them. People of

diverse backgrounds are allowed in, but not really accepted. Live-and-let-live approach.

■ *Build relationships*: Assume that improved relationships will result in differences being overcome, thus working on shaping relationships amongst the various groups.

■ *Foster mutual adaptation*: People both recognize and accept differences, and agree that everyone is free to change, thus allowing the greatest accommodation of diversity.

Thomas's eight options are not all mutually exclusive, and hybrid or multiple approaches can be applied simultaneously within any specific organization. The preferred options in a 'best-practice' approach for managing diversity are *inclusion*, *building relationships* and *mutual adaptation*, the last being based on the most positive philosophy.

Arnold (1997)[16] added further possible organizational initiatives, as he labelled them:

■ Multicultural workshops designed to improve understanding and communication between cultural groups.

■ Multicultural 'core groups' which meet regularly to confront stereotypes and personal biases.

■ Support groups, mentoring and relationships and networks for women and cultural minorities (other groups can be added).

■ Advisory councils reporting to top management.

■ Rewarding executives on the basis of their record in developing members of targeted groups.

■ Fast-track development and special training opportunities for members of targeted groups.

In relation to these career practices, one has to remember that the first stage in managing diversity is recruiting a diverse workforce. Thus, specific attention to diversity should be reflected in the selection process, for both the performance and legal arguments. McMahan, Bell and Virick (1998)[17] argue that selection practices in organizations that value diversity might also work to create causal ambiguity. Such organizations would have systems in place to ensure their selection practices are non-discriminatory and continue their goals of increasing diversity. An analysis of such practices would include validating tests and performing job analyses to ensure that potential candidates were not unnecessarily and unjustifiably excluded (e.g., irrelevant height and weight requirements, which might exclude women or people of Asian origin). Interviewers would be diverse, including members of the population to which the pool of applicants belonged. Interviewers would be aware of potential biases that might exclude diverse workers or which might alienate diverse workers during recruitment and selection processes.

Organizations can facilitate mentoring relationships. These were proven to help not only the protégé, but also the mentor (usually male). Kanter (1977)[18] recognized that sponsoring and mentoring people of future potential helps them to gain power and respect. Spotting and nourishing future talent is a rewarding task, and organizations should make executives aware of it and encourage such practices (*see* Chapter 6 for more on mentoring).

Arnold mentions that there is a significant difference between learning to like or love diversity (which is difficult enough, in his words), and managing it. We need to start with awareness, move to appreciation, and end up with management of diversity, he argues. Thus, as McMahan *et al*. (1998) argue, valuing diversity is crucial. Valuing diversity refers to the desire to include and utilize the assets of workers from various groups as potential employees, rather than excluding or limiting contributions of any potential employee because of any factor related to diversity.

Organizational approaches to tackling discrimination

Many HR managers put an increasing emphasis on tackling all possible kinds of discrimination. Equal employment opportunity (EEO) issues are high on the agenda, especially in relation to the gender issue: women seem to suffer from the 'glass ceiling' effect, i.e. not being promoted above a certain managerial level (Morrison, White and Van Velsor, 1987).[19] According to Morrison *et al*., the glass ceiling is 'a transparent barrier, that kept women from rising above a certain level in corporations' (pp. 13 and 124). As indicated in Chapter 6, many programmes are meant to support the population discriminated against, sometimes even to create 'positive discrimination'. It is important, though, that such 'positive discrimination' does not imply abandonment of selection according to skills, competencies and suitability for the job. If there are two or more proper candidates, both qualified and well suited for the job, 'positive discrimination' should mean choosing from the less represented population (e.g. appointment of women to the board of directors). Otherwise 'positive discrimination' could result in choosing someone with lower skills and qualifications, reducing future prospects of success under the false banner of equality. Campbell and Moses (1986)[20] provide some interesting examples from the USA, and Ashburner (1991)[21] presents the UK case of women as an under-used resource. The above-mentioned are mainly gender-related cases, such as are presented by many scholars (*see*, for example, Pazy, 1986).[22]

Problems of discrimination exist for many groups, not just for women. Ethnic background, disability, age, and religious belief can prevent appropriate people from making their full contribution. For example, mass early retirements accepted by or imposed on people in their 50s might deprive organizations of a pool of talented and experienced people. Disabled people can be highly committed and productive when the disability does not affect the requirements of their role. Organizations which recognize these issues will benefit from pursuing different career management practices for particular populations with specific needs.

The prominence of special programmes for specific populations will increase in the 2000s for two main reasons. The first is the positive aspect, when organizations come to realize that practising discrimination, be it explicit or implicit, means underutilizing their most esteemed wealth-creating resource – their people. The second is the negative aspect, when organizations start emphasizing equal employment opportunity as part of the trend towards the 'political correct-ness' that is increasingly prevalent in all areas of life today. This will be reinforced also for the simple reason that with the passage of time, the labour market will become less white-male focused. By 2020, non-Hispanic whites will comprise less than 70 per cent of the US labour market (Judy and D'Amico, 1997).[23]

Special programmes are not necessarily concerned with discrimination. The case of dual-career couples brings up another issue, that of how to enable two people to develop side by side when both have a career. With the continuing growth in education and equality in employment we will see even more dual-career couples in the 2000s. The HR system must recognize this, especially where international relocations become necessary as part of career progress (Harvey, 1997).[24] The trend of globalization is expected to continue and managing expa-triates will be a crucial issue in the twenty-first century (*see* Chapter 7).

Beyond demographic factors

Due to the development of post-modern communities, employers have to manage an increasingly diverse workforce. This diversity is not limited to demo-graphic characteristics such as race, age and gender, but has many not so obvious facets. First; there are the attitudes of employees, in line with the concept pro-posed by Harrison *et al.* (1998),[25] of surface as opposed to deep-level diversity, and second, the diversity may relate to variables such as work arrangements (con-tingent as opposed to the core workforce) in the organizational context and social status in the social-level context. Research has shown that diversity affects group processes and performance (Chatman *et al.*, 1998).[26] While in this chapter I will focus mostly on personal characteristics as a source of diversity, other types of diversity exist, and will be discussed too.

The most obvious negative outcome of diversity is the possibility of people being discriminated against, not because of performance, attitudes, or other job-related factors, but because of an irrelevant personal background. It is important to realize that in both selection and career decisions the aim is to 'discriminate' – between the right people (who should be selected, promoted, etc.) and the wrong ones. The 'discrimination' that takes place should be undertaken accord-ing to fair and right criteria, and should comply with the law and with principles of management. If the 'discrimination' is based on irrelevant factors (e.g. gender, race, etc.) this is a real discrimination. One should also accept that sometimes it is reasonable and legal to discriminate on such grounds – for example when selecting an actor for the role of Othello, it is reasonable to prefer a black person. If the job requires physical activity, disabled people might not be sufficiently fit. A colour-blind person should not teach painting. But how about a male who wishes to work as a manicurist in a beauty salon for women? How about a woman wishing to become a driver of a Formula One racing car? Such people will probably be ridiculed. They will be different. But they may bring specific new qualities, that may become a source of competitive advantage.

What is a real and relevant difference and what is a stereotype?

A stereotype is 'a preconceived perception or image one has of another person based on that person's membership in a particular social group or category'

(Greenhaus *et al.*, 2000).[27] Some stereotypes can be positive; others are quite negative. Nevertheless organizational career decisions should not be based on stereotypes but on merit. When hiring a medical doctor, it should not matter if she is blonde (some people are influenced by the stereotype that suggests blonde females are not so wise; strangely enough, there is no such stereotype about blonde males).

Procedural justice and distributive justice

Procedural justice refers to the process by which norms are implemented. Distributive justice, on the other hand, refers to the actual outcomes of such procedures. Procedural justice can be viewed as the degree to which the rules and procedures specified by policies are properly followed in all cases under which they are applied (Milkovich and Newman, 1996).[28] In an organizational context procedural justice concerns the means (rather than the ends) of social justice (Furnham, 1997).[29] For example, 'pay procedures are more likely to be perceived as fair (1) if they are consistently applied to all employees, (2) if employee participation and/or representation is included, (3) if appeals procedures are available, and (4) if the data used are accurate' (Milkovich and Newman, 1996: 62). The underlying assumption is that employees will accept and comply with organizational policies and decisions if they are based on fair and just procedures.

Justice refers not just to being treated with dignity and respect, but also to being given adequate information regarding these procedures (Cropanzano and Greenberg, 1997).[30] Thus organizational career systems should ensure that the process is transparent. The manner in which an organizational action is carried out matters no less than its outcomes (Tyler and Bies 1990).[31] HRM practices, and in particular career-related decision processes, are highly relevant to the evaluation and acceptance of procedural justice, which engenders a culture of trust.

Procedural justice as reflected in HRM-related decision making has a strong effect on employees' attitudes and behaviours (Gilliland, 1994; Konovsky and Folger, 1987).[32] People need to know that a fair rule exists, and that it is applied to all. Then, of course, there is the issue of whether the rules and procedures are translated into actual fair distribution (distributive justice).

Question

> **Question 1**
> Think of ways in which the old system can pretend to apply rules justly, but refrain from doing so.
>
> **Question 2**
> Will people accept and believe such a system, or will they realize what is going on and resent the system or even quit because it fails to deliver?

The virtuous versus the vicious cycle of diversity

The starting point for the model presented in Figure 8.1 is the current labour market in most industrial societies. Many populations that once were not

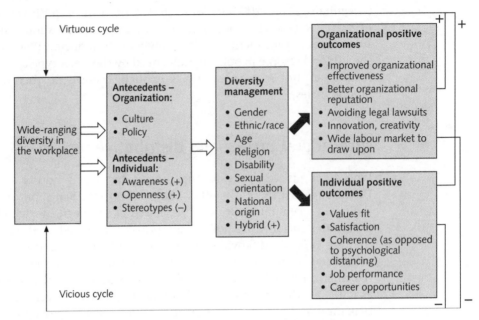

Figure 8.1 The virtuous versus the vicious cycle of diversity

represented in the workforce (people of different ethnic origin) or in the managerial workforce (women and people from deprived social classes) now have the opportunity to become equal partners. The question remains whether this right, though legally valid, is only on paper, or whether it is a reality, and if the latter, what is the effect of this reality for organizations and individual employees.

The first question to be considered is how far the wide diversity in the workforce is reflected in any specific workplace. Can we expect a similar distribution of diversity? What should be the reference level? For example, sometimes nation statistics should provide guidelines whereas in specific regions regional statistics should do so. For example, the representation of Roman Catholics in the management or organizations in Northern Ireland should be higher than that in Wales, as there are more Roman Catholics in Northern Ireland than in Wales. Similarly the expected percentage of Hispanics in the managerial workforce in San Antonio, Texas, should be higher than that in Seattle, Washington, whereas in Seattle one may expect to find more managers of Far Eastern national origin.

On the other hand, one can and should learn from industries where diversity has been proven to work effectively. Such is the case of women managers in the entertainment sector in the USA, as Ensher *et al.* (2002) report.[33] Different people bring different qualities, different perspectives and different inputs. This is what makes variety so beneficial, on the one hand, but also so challenging, on the other.

Following Harrison *et al.* (1998),[34] we can refer to visible as opposed to invisible diversity. Some types of diversity are clearly visible – e.g. colour of the skin, gender, others less so – e.g. religion, sexual orientation. In the latter cases it is up to the person whether or not to reveal their true identity. In a study that empirically tested deep-level and surface diversity, Harrison *et al.* (2002)[35] investigated the impact of time on both types of diversity. Their data supported the model presented in Figure 8.2, showing that, as time passes, integration reduces the impact of surface-level diversity (mostly demographic factors), but increases the relevance of deep-level diversity.

Clair *et al.* (2002)[36] discuss the types of strategies people use to either reveal or pass (i.e., hide their invisible differences) at work, the motives that lead people to reveal or pass, and the moderating effect of social and organizational context on the relationship between motives and strategies people use.

Building on social identity theory, Clair *et al.* (2002) identified several strategies for managing invisible, potentially stigmatized social identities at work. There are two basic strategic choices that individuals with potentially stigmatized social identities can make as they interact with someone at work: to hide (pass) or to reveal their invisible social identity. Within these two choices, there are a number of particular strategies that people may apply to pass or reveal their invisible difference during a workplace interaction. Passing is a category of identity management strategies, the outcome of which is to allow a person to be incorrectly classified by another person as someone without a discrediting or devalued social identity. Note that passing may also be unintentional. Individuals can rely on two different types of passing strategy: counterfeiting and evading. Counterfeiting is an active strategy of concealing part of the self to assume a false identity. An evading strategy results in passing because the individual evades all queries related to the invisible identity or social group membership in question.

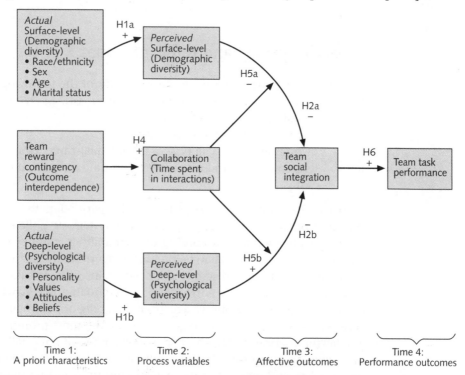

Figure 8.2 Intervening and interactive temporal mechanisms translating team surface- and deep-level diversity into social integration and performance

Source: D.A. Harrison *et al.* (2002) 'Time teams, and task performance: changing effects of surface and deep-level diversity on group functioning', *Academy of Management Journal*, 45(4), p. 1030.

While 'passing' is a category of strategies designed to conceal a potentially stigmatized identity or social identity group membership, revealing strategies are tactics designed to disclose to others an identity that would otherwise be invisible or unrecognizable. The three different revealing strategies Clair *et al.* propose are: signalling, normalizing and differentiating. Individuals who signal are attempting to disclose their hidden identity, but rather than explicitly 'going public' and fully disclosing their difference, they send messages, drop hints and give clues to those to whom they wish to disclose their true identity. Individuals employ a normalizing strategy by revealing their hidden, potentially stigmatized identity to others and then attempting to make their difference seem commonplace or ordinary, within the social norms of the organization, essentially denying that their identity matters. Lastly, differentiating means seeking to underscore difference, and this is sometimes done in an effort to change others' attitudes and behaviour.

The motives for choosing a strategy can be personal, instrumental or both. For example, instrumental motives for revealing may be to obtain social support, to obtain accommodation, to create awareness and to attempt creating social change. Of course, the organizational and cultural context will influence people's choice of a particular strategy.

Question	What strategy would you adopt if you felt you were different? Why? How would you practise your strategy?

Specific groups and relevant issues

This section examines specific groups in terms of the following factors:
(a)   Demographic factors – gender, ethnic origin, age (young; old), disability, sexual orientation, religion.
(b)   Presence of deep-level diversity.
(c)   Belonging to a special type of family: dual-career couples, single mothers.
(d)   Existence of hybrid diversity (combining more than one possible source of diversity).

At its narrowest, the management of diversity refers to the propensity of an organization to have an appropriate EEO system of policies and practices to ensure people are treated according to their abilities, competencies, contribution and performance, rather than being judged by irrelevant factors. Thus gender discrimination and racial discrimination come into the so-called management of diversity. This is indeed a narrow approach. Unfair and unlawful discrimination can have a variety of grounds: age, disability, religion, ethnicity, region of origin, class, sexual orientation, nepotism, to name the most prominent ones. There is also lawful discrimination when people of a different nationality face higher hurdles when applying for a job in a different country. With the rare exception of job searches within the European Community, countries actively discriminate against people of foreign nationality, refusing them employment unless they have a work permit (e.g. the US green card).

EXHIBIT 8.1	Meet our first ...

The presence in senior management positions of members of groups previously the object of discrimination is often the result of the efforts of pioneering people. Many of the women executives studied by Morrison *et al.*[37] were the first women to reach that rank in their organizations. The same is true in relation to the first black person in the job (Colin Powell as the first non-white Secretary of State in the USA), the first blind person (and to date, the performance of David Blunkett as a leading politician in the UK is an example that blindness does not prevent people from being able to lead, make tough decisions and be part of the government). In many cases, the presence of these pioneers paves the way for the next generation of a diverse workforce.

It remains the case, however, that such appointments are sometimes made for reasons of image or publicity or to comply with legal requirements. This means that there is a 'token woman' or 'token black' person on the Board. The acid test comes later: is that person followed by others? Thus, 'being there' as the first non-white-male in the top role imposes a heavy burden on that person, who is put under strong scrutiny, knowing that if they fail this will have a long-lasting impact for many future generations of non-white-males in the managerial ranks.

Gender variety

The human asset most cited as under-utilized in organizations is women, particularly at the management level (Betz, 1989).[38] Discrimination on many grounds is inherent in the culture of several societies and affects everyday working life in innumerable ways (Marshall, 1995).[39] Morrison *et al.* (1987)[40] argue that women face three principal factors that impose a greater challenge on their careers than on those of men: (a) the job itself, a challenge that every manager faces, of course, but on the top of that, (b) being a pioneer and (c) the family.

EXHIBIT 8.2	Some facts about women's participation in the UK labour market

The UK female level of employment is at record high levels. The number of women in employment has risen by 843 000 since 1990, while the number of men has increased by only 33 000. However, in the three years to 2000, the growth in employment was higher among men than among women. In Spring 2000 there were a record 12.5 million women (aged 16 and over) in employment in the UK.

The UK female employment rate is also at its highest ever level, at 69 per cent. There are regional differences: from 75 per cent in the South East to 58 per cent in Northern Ireland. Still, in all regions the male employment rate is higher than the female. The UK female employment rate is also higher than that of the European Union (EU), which stands at 53 per cent.

Women working full-time earned 82 per cent of the hourly earnings of male full-time employees in the UK in 2000. The gap is narrower than before, although it must be admitted that some of the decrease in the gap is due to the introduction of the minimum wage.

Exhibit 8.2 continued

Other features of women's participation in the labour market include: 88 per cent of jobs taken by women are in service industries – particularly public administration, education and health. Female employment is concentrated in non-manual occupations, in particular clerical, sales and personal/protective occupations.

Young women tend to make different educational choices to men and have their own beliefs and expectations about the experience of women in the labour market. Over half of all those who graduated with a first degree in 1999 were female. However there were gender differences in degree subject, one example being that approximately 15 000 men aged 18–24 obtained a first degree in engineering and technology, compared with around only 3000 women. Women in the under-35 age group are more likely than older women to leave their current organization in order to obtain more flexibility in working arrangements.

Source: www.womens-unit.gov.uk/research/factsheets/women_and_work.htm.

Women form some half of the population, but not half of the workforce. One positive trend is that women's participation in the workforce increased rapidly in the second half of the twentieth century, this trend is continuing and soon they may comprise an equal part. For two reasons it is difficult or impossible for women to make up exactly half of the labour force. First, in many countries women are forced or allowed to retire at an earlier age than men. Second, for biological reasons, many women do leave the workforce for a period to give birth and to care for their infants. Nevertheless, and to some extent affected by the greater involvement in recent years of fathers in caring for children, the trend is towards near-equality in terms of male and female participation in the labour force.

The negative aspect of this trend is that in terms of the pay gap between males and females and promotion to top positions, the movement towards equality is much slower. The pay gap is indeed decreasing (*see* Exhibit 8.2), but not at the same pace as labour market participation. Women still earn significantly less than males. In the UK the gap is around 80 per cent and in the USA 77 per cent (DOL, 2001).[41] Representation at the top is even less equal, but, again, there are some improvements. When Morrison *et al.* (1987) published their seminal book, *Breaking the Glass Ceiling*,[42] only 1.7 per cent of corporate officers of *Fortune 500* companies were women, and only one woman was a CEO. By 2001 the figures were rather different: women comprised 11.2 per cent of corporate officers of *Fortune 500* companies, and 3.8 per cent of the CEOs/Chairpersons (Catalyst, 2001).[43] While this represents a significant development, and in the right trend, the numbers are very small. Among the 'very big names', Carly Fiorina who leads the merged HP/Compaq company, is a prominent exception.

Still, the most widely studied issue in the management of diversity is women, especially with regard to equal employment opportunities (EEO). As we will see later, there are many other sources of diversity, some of which require a different management approach.

The Scandinavian countries led the way in introducing women as equal partners into the employment realm. Moen (1989)[44] explores how Sweden developed a new social model of gender equality at the end of the 1960s and in the 1970s. This model is not without its problems, and is responsible for the challenges of combining work and parenthood. Much of the trend towards gender equality was supported by legislation (Enquist, 1984),[45] and there is still considerable legal action to enable and encourage EEO in Western societies. Hull and Nelson (2000),[46] for example, explore three different theoretical models of gender differences in professional careers. They discovered, in line with other scholarly findings (cf. Hall-Taylor, 1997),[47] that differences in career path and achievements cannot be fully explained by career choice, and that there are constraints affecting women's development. Although more women start professional careers now than in the past, they begin in lower-prestige jobs than, and make slower career progress than, their male counterparts. A better picture is found where more diversity exists, such as in the civil service (Barnett, Baron and Stuart (2000).[48] However both the employment world (i.e. the labour market and employers' attitudes) and personal factors create and maintain the glass ceiling (Morrison, 1992; Davidson and Cooper, 1992).[49] Nevertheless diversity is not restricted to the issue of gender, as will be discussed later in this chapter.

Crow (1999)[50] regards equality legislation as the main external influence causing companies to comply and avoid penalties. She quotes Dickens (1994)[51] who distinguished, along the lines of the argument presented in this chapter between the 'compliance' argument and the 'organizational interest' argument, the former representing a reactive approach, with organizations making sure they comply with the law, and the latter the case of organizations realizing that diversity is good for business. For example, Bevan et al. (1999)[52] found that the business benefits of flexible employment practices include reduced casual sickness absence, improved retention, improved productivity and improved morale and commitment.

Recognition of the changing gender representation in managerial careers is evidenced by the fact that Levinson's (1978) book, *The Seasons of Man's Life*, was followed by Levinson and Levinson (1996) *The Seasons of Woman's Life*.[53] In the later book the authors differentiate between two female career streams: the 'homemaker' and the 'work career'. Their position is that, to address the issue of women's careers, one cannot avoid acknowledging the roles of woman as (sole) child-bearer and (principal) homemaker. One must accept that women have different career patterns from men. However, are women different from men at work? Many claim that there are no significant differences that are relevant to women's propensity to reach managerial and executive roles. Taking a different perspective, Hakim (2000)[54] asserts that only 20 per cent of women are 'work-centred', against 60 per cent of men.

The stereotype of women is that they are more caring and better in teamwork and at creating relationships than men. In certain roles these qualities are more important than others. However, in the tough current business environment, such qualities are not necessarily advantageous. It could be said that this argument is based on a stereotypical view of women; more studies are needed to identify if this is indeed the case for women in management.

Question

> **The Formula One story**
>
> Imagine that you are about to participate in a car race, and that all participants have quite similar cars, but some, including yours, need to have a pit-stop about half-way through the race. The other cars do not need to stop. What influence would that knowledge have on you?
>
> You may decide it is not worthwhile to race at all, with such different conditions. Alternatively, you may be highly motivated to be faster on the first leg, to reach the pit-stop as soon as you can.
>
> Now imagine that you have reached the pit-stop, and have experienced the hardships, the dangers, the risks and rough fights that characterize such a race. Now you have some time to think, and you are given a choice – to return to the race, or to take a different route. If you rejoin the race you return to the stress and competition, but your car is heavier with fuel and more difficult to steer, and you have lost much time in comparison with your competitors. The other route will give you a lot of satisfaction and you will earn appreciation from the crowd. Thus, although it is different from the route taken by Formula One winners, it does provide a good incentive. It is not hard to imagine that many will choose the alternative option.

Let us clarify the metaphor. The drivers that have to stop in the race are women. And during and following the break when they experience motherhood many realize that there are other incentives and different appreciations for people that are not in the 'fast lane' of the rat race of organizational life.

If this metaphor reflects reality, studies will show that young women develop faster than men in their early career stages, but after a time leave the race. There is some support for this argument – *see* Hakim, 1996, 2000,[55] and Simpson and Altman, 2000.[56]

While metaphors can clarify matters and provide clearer insights, they are not always perfect. One clear difference between Formula One racing and the rat race of organizations is that when cars stop at the pit-lane, they do so in order to receive (petrol, tyres), whereas women do it in order to give. Some may raise a moral question about the role of society in general in ensuring equity and fair play for all.

A similar metaphor was presented by Lyndon Johnson, the then American president, in 1965, when he compared the race between males and females to a 100-yard dash in which the legs of one of the participants are shackled together. In view of the fact that the other has a clear advantage, the race is then declared unfair. What is the appropriate course of action in such a situation – is removing the shackles enough? In a race the answer is clearly no. In the business world positive discrimination might produce some other injustice.

Initially it was felt that the way forward was to legislate to ensure equal terms of employment, with the hope that succeeding generations would overcome the old gap. However, thinking on equality issues moved on, and in the UK the Sex Discrimination Act 1975 helped to prevent gender-based discrimination (the Act was extended in 1986). Similarly, the Equal Pay Act (1970) was enacted to ensure equal pay for similar work. When it came into force many organizations tried to 'beat the system' by offering women only lower-level (and more poorly paid) jobs. Heavy fines, however, make it not worthwhile for companies to try to avoid the law.

EXHIBIT
8.3

Supporting women

The Center for Development and Population Activities (CEDPA) in Washington, DC aims to support women worldwide. In line with the idea that weaker groups deserve special support, the centre has for 24 years been running the Women in Management (WIM) programme with the aim of preparing women to lead development efforts. The results are impressive. Among the 5000 alumnae in 138 countries there are parliamentarians, ministers, NGO presidents and network coordinators. As women's roles in public life have expanded, these CEDPA alumnae have been at the forefront in identifying and addressing the critical issues that women face in the twenty-first century.

The programme helps women to develop personal and organizational strategies to bring about sustainable development in their countries. It covers the following topics:

- **Leadership** – how to cultivate a constituency and a committed team of staff members.
- **Visioning** – how to develop shared goals and garner support from the grassroots to policy makers.
- **Management** – techniques for effective resource management (including human, financial and other institutional resources).
- **Communication** – how to use strategic communication to educate, motivate and energize the public and institutions.
- **Donor relations** – how to engage donors in a long-term partnership; and
- **Participation** – methods to involve the community and other stakeholders in programme design.

Fletcher's (1999)[57] study of female design engineers has profound implications for attempts to change organizational culture. According to Fletcher, emotional intelligence and relational behaviour often, as she puts it, 'get disappeared' in practice. This is not because they are ineffective but because they are associated with the feminine or softer side of work. Even when they are in line with stated, formal organizational goals, these behaviours are viewed as inappropriate to the workplace because they collide with powerful, gender-linked images of good workers and successful organizations. Fletcher describes how this collision of gender and power often causes the very behaviour that organizations say they need to 'disappear' and undermines the possibility of radical change. She shows why the 'female advantage' does not seem to be advantaging females or organizations.

Women and entrepreneurship

Women are active in the business community, accounting for about one-third of business start-ups. In addition, one-third of businesses with a turnover of up to

£1 million are owned by women (Barclays, 2000).[58] Starting one's own business can be seen as 'an easy way to escape', although it only appears easy, as many entrepreneurs will testify.

Start-up as a career solution

AW was a broker in the City of London for 9 years. After working for Harlow-Butler, a financial broker, she and her husband decided it was time to raise a family. Less than two years after her first son was born, AW felt she needed the action of business life, but did not want to give up her family responsibilities. Her husband remained employed in another job in the city, the type she would have had if she had continued in her career. As a result, she decided to start her own small business, from home.

She opened Posh-Hair, a business importing hair accessories, and manages it all from the convenience of her home, close to London. After a shaky start she is beginning to see that the business should survive and grow while her family benefit from her being at home.

Earning money of her own gives her the sense of independence, as she found it hard to leave her career and become dependent on her husband's income. AW's advice for women in her situation is that taking care of a child is a huge responsibility, but it does not mean that you have to detach yourself from the business world.

The effectiveness argument

There is support for the effectiveness argument in a number of studies. Drawing on the literature of HRM, women in management and organizational effectiveness, Harel, Tzafrir and Baruch (2002)[59] suggested a model (*see* Figure 8.3) bringing these perspectives together into a single framework. Their model, based on an empirical study of 102 Israeli organizations, indicates a significant and positive association between high-quality HRM and fairness in promotion of women in organizations. Fairness in the promotion of women into managerial ranks was also found to be associated with higher organizational effectiveness.

Davidson and Burke (2002)[60] summarize other prominent research findings about women in management:

■ There has been progress in the number of women entering management, but the pace is slow, and attention to this issue is still needed.

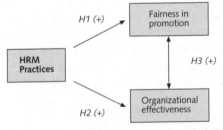

Figure 8.3 Model of fairness in promotion and organizational effectiveness

Source: Adapted from H.G. Harel, S. Tzafrir and Y. Baruch (2002) 'HRM Practices, Promotion of Women in Management, and Organizational Effectiveness: An Integrated Model', *International Journal of Human Resource Management*, in press.

- Managerial job segregation by gender persists (women are found in HR, public affairs, communication and law, but less in line management). One problem with such segregation is that these jobs rarely lead to executive-level positions.
- Hybrid diversity (in their case, women of ethnic minorities) is even harder to overcome.
- Affirmative action is important for making progress towards closing the gap, although it might create problems such as tokenism and backlash.
- A new trend towards lean and mean business management may contrast with the qualities women bring to the workplace. Being mostly in mid-level management, they will be more dispensable than men.
- Flexible and alternative work arrangements might be superficial mechanisms that in fact limit women's career prospects.
- Women still carry higher responsibility than men in their 'second shift' work at home.
- Organizational culture is mostly male culture, and this works against women.
- The best argument for women in management should be the business case of utilization of resources.

Thus organizations should promote a culture where women and other minorities can succeed.

Ethnicity

Gender variety comprises two groups only (males and females). Race and ethnicity produce a much richer variety, and in many countries the minorities comprise a combination of many different minorities. In the USA the major groups of ethnic minorities are the black people (called African-American for reasons of political correctness – white people are not called European-American), people of Asian origin – with Chinese, Indian and South-East Asian immigrants the source of this variety, Hispanic people (mostly from Mexico) and Native Americans. In the UK many immigrants came from the former British Empire, including many from India and Pakistan, but other places too. In Germany there is a growing community of Turkish-born immigrants. Other Western countries also have within their populations people of different ethnic origins.

In marketing and creative activities, ethnicity has to be taken into account. In many cases, people may put greater trust in people of the same origin, when they encounter them in business situations, e.g. representing companies in sales, negotiations and deal making. Moreover, consumer companies that target the whole population should be aware of the specific needs and tastes of various groups within the population. Ensuring that the teams that make decisions about products and markets are representative will make such targeting more effective. Such team members may also be a source of valuable (e.g. local) information.

Age

Age diversity in the workforce derives from the fact that those in work range in age from about 18 to 65, the formal retirement age in most countries. The two possible forms of age-related discrimination are that against young people and that against older people, with the latter gaining more attention from legislators and the media. The numbers of people of each age are easily identifiable, and trends are relatively simple to recognize.

There are several trends in relation to the age composition of people in the labour market. The age at entry has been rising as the proportion of school leavers who go on to university has increased, thus delaying their entry to the labour market (more than one-third of the current population in developed societies attend university, and the proportion will continue to grow). At the other end of the spectrum, people aged about 65 years are retiring from employment. Thus the main input for understanding age trends is the past birth rate. To take just one example, following the Second World War there was a large increase in births. People born in the late 1940s and the 1950s (termed the 'baby-boomers') entered the labour market in the 1960s, and these people are now approaching retirement. In contrast, in the following years the birth rate declined, and fewer people entered the labour market.

Developments in the age profile of workers have profound implications for the management of careers. Career structures that suited the traditional work attitudes of older generations do not suit the needs of more recent generations. Remuneration systems that reward seniority and tenure may prove too costly to maintain if there is a surplus of ageing employees in mid-level management, and might hamper a firm's competitiveness (Johnston, 1991).[61] Another apparent problem that may be no more than a stereotype is the tendency to perceive older people as reluctant to change, less creative, and with declining ability to undertake physical tasks. Some of these possible perceptions are invalid or irrelevant. Most older staff are not employed in manual labour, thus the expected reduction in physical ability is irrelevant for them. For the few who are so employed, their wider experience may compensate for their declining physical power.

In managerial as well as clerical jobs older personnel are likely to possess wide knowledge and experience, and may prove to be more loyal and committed than younger personnel – qualities that will benefit their employees. On the other hand, as we saw in Chapter 2, these qualities are not always required in a world of redundancies, restructuring and rightsizing.

Discrimination against young people may backfire too, as manifested in Exhibit 8.5. Such discrimination is problematic at the society level, as it might create a generation of people who will never enter the labour market.

EXHIBIT 8.5	**Too young, too inexperienced?**

FinCorp is a large, established and leading UK financial corporation. For generations they were known as a workplace that invested in their new talent, recruiting many graduates and training them as professionals in accounting, insurance, etc. In the mid-1990s they realized that there was a consistent trend, whereby young graduates who gained their first job with FinCorp tended to quit the company after some two to three years. They benefited from the investment and training provided, were able to put the name of FinCorp on their CVs, and were then happy to look elsewhere for jobs.

As a result, FinCorp decided to stop or reduce significantly their graduate recruitment and instead to hire people with a few years' experience. This way they would

Exhibit 8.5 continued

benefit from the investment that other companies put into their graduate recruits. But this also discriminated against young people entering the labour market.

The argument is clear, and to a certain extent the change in policy was effective. But what are the flaws in the argument?

First, FinCorp should have checked *why* those graduates were leaving them. Maybe their compensation scheme was inappropriate? Even if it is an employer who provides the training that makes an employee more valuable, the employer should recognize and reward that value. Maybe the roles offered to young managers were not challenging enough? Maybe they saw no future career prospects?

Second, by opting for this strategy, FinCorp would be able to recruit only people with a high tendency to quit their employers, i.e. less committed staff. This may have been FinCorp's intention, but not necessarily. With their ethos of being an established firm, they need a core of able and committed people who are well integrated into their culture. By leaving it to other firms to provide professional training for those who may become FinCorp's future managers, FinCorp also has no control over the culture they may absorb – and it may be a culture that is not appreciated in FinCorp.

When formulating their strategy and policies, organizations need to understand national-level trends. An ageing population, with falling participation rates amongst older workers, will adversely affect the labour market. The need to increase employment rates amongst older working-age women will become more and more important as employers face growing skills shortages.

The general ageing of the UK population will see the size of the 45–59 age category growing significantly. By 2010, 40 per cent of the UK workforce will be over 45 (www.womens-unit.gov.uk). If organizations continue to eliminate older people from their workforce, there will be fewer people to bear the burden of financing an increasing number of older people, not just those over 65 (a growing age group, as life expectancy improves), but also many aged 50–65. This burden may prove too great, or will require much higher taxation.

As against the negative stereotype, there is some empirical evidence suggesting that an age-diverse workforce brings reduced staff turnover and absenteeism, and improves motivation and commitment. Research also highlights the high level of communication and personal skills that older workers bring to the workplace and the commercial benefit gained by reflecting an age-diverse market (www.womens-unit.gov.uk).

One challenge, which is a national rather than a company-level issue, is how to retain within the labour market the huge number of people forced to take early retirement due to downsizing, preventing them from becoming an unproductive, declining and frustrated group. Moreover, many of these people need to work in those final ten years or so of their working life in order to secure a reasonable level of pension income, otherwise they will become a burden on their close family and community. In the UK in 2000, less than one-third of males over the age of 50 were employed, compared to 85 per cent in 1979 (Lamb, 2000).[62] The danger is that people forced to leave employment after a certain age will find it hard or practically impossible to rejoin the labour market. In some industries such as information technology being over 40 means 'old'. Not employing these people is a waste to both organizations and society.

On the other side of the coin there are young people who feel that they cannot get proper job offers because they are too young, although they may be well qualified and trained for the jobs they apply for.

One indirect impact of age on careers is that older workers may not hold the work attitudes and career perceptions an organization may expect its employees to hold. Attitudes are part of the 'deep' level of diversity mentioned at the start of this chapter.

Disability

By the end of the twentieth century there were 54 million disabled people in the US labour market, 50 per cent of whom were unemployed (Census, 1997).[63] The situation is quite similar in other Western societies. Due to past moral pressure, there are both legislative and government obligations on employers to recruit disabled people. The argument for doing so is not, however, merely ethical: disabled people prove to be highly loyal members of the workforce, with much lower turnover rates than others.

Physical disability

A physical disability is visible. Managing diversity based on physical disability should be simpler than managing other types of diversity. It is relatively easy to identify whether the physical problem would prevent, hinder or interfere with the performance of the job. If the answer is negative, people should not be discriminated against on the grounds of that disability. In fact, organizations may benefit from the stronger level of commitment of such people, who have been accepted in spite of their disability. One issue that can be relevant is whether future roles along the expected career path of the individual concerned would suffer from the specific disability. This might be a consideration, but the effects of physical disability are felt more in the realm of manual work than in managerial positions. The higher the level of managerial responsibility, the less the physical dimension matters.

Mental disability

There are plenty of jobs which people with learning difficulties are entirely capable of performing well. People with a mental disability are usually extremely well motivated, loyal and appreciative of their employers.

Other learning difficulties may not prevent people from taking on managerial roles (e.g. dyslexia, a problem of reading/writing that is not concerned with intelligence or ability to communicate).

One additional challenge for an organization employing people with any disability or difficulty is to facilitate their induction so that their colleagues and managers do not feel uneasy, and will accept them despite any possible difficulties. As stated above, both on moral grounds and from the business case argument, employing disabled people may be best practice.

Question

If you are disabled, would it be good for you to indicate this on your CV? The answer is not so simple. On the one hand, if the organization to which you are applying has a negative attitude towards disabled people it may be better not to mention it. If however the organization has a positive attitude, and in a large organization, it may be under regulatory pressure to recruit more disabled people than it does at present, so it may be to your advantage to mention it.

One simple answer is – if your disability would prevent you from performing in a certain job, just don't apply!

Religion

Religion can be a very highly emotionally charged issue. However, there are very few jobs or careers that require membership of a particular religion, and these are not found in business firms. In places like Northern Ireland, however, there is clear segregation between the communities, which is reflected also in the labour market and in the composition of the workforce in workplaces.

Sexual orientation

Sexual orientation can be an even more emotionally charged issue than religion, as many individuals object to people of non-conventional sexual orientation on moral grounds. Sound arguments may be presented for and against the relevance of sexual orientation for many jobs, but in the majority of jobs, sexual orientation would not have an impact on performance. No matter whether a person is an accountant or bricklayer, what they do in their private life remains their own business. Again, companies that will not recruit such people lose a wide pool of talent. The true number of non-heterosexual people is not clear, but the number known about is growing as more and more choose to come 'out of the closet'. Winfield and Spielman (1995)[64] reported that in the USA some 1.5 million households are identified as homosexual domestic partnerships.

Problems may arise for an organization that employs and promotes lesbians and homosexuals without knowing of their sexual orientation, but when it is revealed, it stops promoting these people. When people feel that they are forced to keep their true identity secret, their job satisfaction and commitment will deteriorate (Day and Schoenrade, 1995)[65] because of the stress and negative feelings that accompany the need to hide something of such importance from close colleagues. On the other hand, companies may make changes to their policies so that benefits usually provided only for the spouses of employees will be made available also to same-sex partners. Otherwise they might find themselves in court, as was the case with El Al, the Israeli airline, which was forced to provide free flights to partners of stewardesses.

Deep-level diversity

Deep-level diversity mainly comprises attitudes and personalities. Different attitudes lead to different work behaviours, as discussed in Chapter 1 (the Fishbein and Ajzen model – *see* Figure 1.4).[66] Beliefs influence attitudes, and thus organizations can and should train and educate people to value differences and to have beliefs based on facts rather than prejudice. When the various attitudes that exist in the community are reflected in the variety in an organization, the match between people and the organization, and between the organization and the environment, is greater.

People have different personality traits and factors. Cattell's 16PF model (discussed in Chapter 2), for example, shows 16 dimensions according to which people differ, and different roles require different personality profiles. For example, toughmindedness may be needed for a policeman whereas tendermindedness is more required from a social worker. However, the best negotiation team may be one that comprises people who can lead tough discussions, but also be tender and who can understand the other side's point of view.

Attitudes to careers have changed in recent years, and as a result the new generation have different views about employment. People with a traditional old-fashioned viewpoint may lament the death of *lifelong employment*. Others claim that this status never really existed, being merely a self-fulfilling illusion. The younger participants in today's labour markets (Generation X and those that have followed them) seem to be less interested in a lifelong job, and more interested in challenging and meaningful assignments for their self-development.

The X (or N) Generation have high level of corporate scepticism, even cynicism. To attract X-Generation people companies should be perceived as ethical, green and acting in the community interest (Tapscott, 1998).[67] Should companies treat employees as capital, and if so, what would be the reaction of the X-Generation knowledge workers?

Belonging to a special type of family

Dual-career couples

In the past the typical Western family comprised a father, a mother and two or three children. The mother would have children in her twenties, and would not work outside the home thereafter. Many changes in society mean that people today tend to work, not merely for money, but for interest and challenge. Women try to delay having children to avoid the damaging effect of a career break on their progress. Many choose not to have children or to have one or two at most. One of the most problematic issues in relation to dual-career couples is relocation. Whereas once this would have meant that the male would be moved to work in another place and the family would move too, now this requires that two people, with separate careers, have to move, or that one employer would have to accept an alternative working arrangement (e.g. telecommuting) for one of the partners, or to try to find a job for the partner in the new location, which may be in a different country (*see* Chapter 7). Career development now needs to take into consideration the whole family.

Single parents (mostly single mothers)

For social and political reasons governments do not wish single parents to drop out of the labour market. In the UK the government initiated programmes to help teenage mothers to return to education and enter the labour market. However, for these families, support mechanisms such as childcare facilities are essential. It has been found that married or cohabiting women are more likely than single women to be in employment. Employment rates are higher for women without children. For those with children, employment rates are much lower for lone mothers than for mothers who are married or cohabiting. However, employment growth in the three years to 2002 has been higher among lone mothers. Conversely, the employment rate for men is higher for those with children than for those without (www.womens-unit.gov.uk).

Birth-order diversity

Some studies have compared and contrasted people according to their birth order. First-born people were found to be more conscientious, conventional, defensive, responsible, but sometimes also more aggressive, whereas the last-born tend to be more dependent, lazy and spoilt. Middle-born people were identified as neglected, non-conforming, open-minded, rebellious and deep thinking (Nyman, 1994; Sulloway, 1995).[68] Companies may take such personality characteristics into account, especially if an association can be found between work role and one of these qualities. This consideration will not be relevant (but raises an intriguing question for the future) in China, where almost all the population will soon comprise people who are only children.

Hybrid diversity

Women may be discriminated against; black people may be discriminated against. What happens to black women? The glass ceiling becomes a concrete ceiling, according to some accounts (Bell and Nkomo, 2001).[69] Bell and Nkomo pointed out that it is not just colour and gender, but social class that determines and hinders career development for people who are different in more than one way from the dominant group of white males. Legislation usually refers to a single factor, as is the case with the UK's Sex Discrimination Act and the Race Discrimination Act, but not to more than one. Even when minorities are promoted, empirical evidence suggests that women are typically promoted into managerial jobs in the low-paid service sector, and this is especially true for non-white women (Bhavnani and Coyle, 2000).[70]

Of course dual diversity can take many forms – any combination of the diversity factors listed in this chapter. The hurdles are, then, doubled for people in a hybrid-diversity group. When exploring the issue of hybrid diversity, we find that the employment rate for ethnic minority women is 49 per cent, which is about 20 percentage points lower than the general UK female rate. Age has an impact too: the female employment rate ranges from 75 per cent for women aged 35–49 to 46 per cent for women aged 16–17. The female employment rate increases with the age of women until the 50–59 age group, where it falls to 64 per cent.

A cynic might suggest that there is a 'possible advantage' for a person with dual diversity, who may benefit from tokenism: for example, a black woman may be seen to serve as both a token woman and a token black in a managerial position.

Work arrangement diversity

Although not a 'people' diversity issue, alternative work arrangements, most of which were discussed earlier in this book, occur in several guises. It should be noted, however, that many of these arrangements are 'tailored' for the specific needs of unique populations, in particular women and parents. For example, many women, particularly those with young dependent children, prefer to work part-time. Part-time work and other flexible working arrangements represent an opportunity for employer and employee to satisfy their different needs.

The proportion of men who are part-time permanent employees (5 per cent) is much smaller than that of women (34 per cent). However, some 40 per cent of parents regard the opportunity to work part-time as essential in enabling women to return to work. Alternatives to part-time employment include formal job sharing and 'term-time' working, which are currently not commonly used.

Work and career breaks

There are more women than ever before returning to paid work soon after having children, with their own requirements for balancing work and family life. The proportion of women returning to work within a year after childbirth has increased dramatically – from 45 per cent in 1988 to 67 per cent in 1996.

It is in the interests of the nation to benefit from this segment of the workforce, and organizations may reap the benefits to their own advantage. A lack of flexible working arrangements plays a major role in influencing mothers' decisions to stay at home. A Women's Unit survey on mothers' reasons for not doing paid work found that reasons included the high cost of suitable childcare or that they couldn't find work with suitable hours (www.womens-unit.gov.uk). New legislation on requesting flexible working arrangements came into force in the UK in early 2003 which forces employers to apply flexibility at work, for example allowing flexi-time arrangements for parents.

Maternity is not the only reason that forces able people (usually women) to stay at home. Caring for elderly relatives has become a growing concern for many. The changing age profile of the population requires a change in work/life balance policies to include a focus on care for the elderly as well as on maternity leave and childcare. Around 14 per cent of all adults provide care, either to people living with them or to non-resident family members. Changes in demography mean that the proportion of dependants to carers will increase in future years.

Fourteen per cent of people are care-givers and this proportion is likely to increase. At the same time, there is also a popular belief that commitment to family responsibilities hinders the advancement of women in the workplace: 83 per cent of women believe that commitment to family responsibilities hinders women's advancement in the workplace (www.womens-unit.gov.uk). Nevertheless, since 1980, the proportion of mothers with children under the age of 5 who are in paid work has increased from 28 per cent to 53 per cent in 1999.

Organizational policies and their importance in managing diversity

The CAST model presented in Chapter 4 indicated that organizations should have clear policies for HRM and career issues. These policies translate the business philosophy and strategy into practice. When devising diversity policies organizations must incorporate both the legal issue (stemming from the *compliance* strategy) of EEO, and the business interest, which means getting the best out of the best people (stemming from the *valuing diversity* strategy). Such policies can include equal opportunity monitoring and fair procedures to ensure selection for recruitment into all levels of the organization (such as eliminating gender and age as selection criteria). A more proactive approach may be manifested, for example, in ensuring that there are no access problems for people with physical disabilities, setting recruitment targets for women, ethnic minorities, etc. Once these people are in the organization, similar policies should regulate and monitor selection for training and development and nomination and selection for promotion. A different set of policy directives should relate to relationships and the prevention of harassment on various grounds. At a further stage of policy development organizations can introduce steps to encourage, not just to enable, people of diverse backgrounds to apply and to work for the firm, and to promote wide mentoring programmes. Flexible work arrangements (teleworking, flexi-time, childcare facilities, job sharing, etc.) can be introduced.

Nelson and Quick (2003)[71] list five main benefits organizations can reap from diversity:

- The ability to attract and retain the best available human talent
- Enhancing marketing efforts
- Promoting creativity and innovation
- Improved problem solving
- Enhanced organizational flexibility

To balance the picture, Nelson and Quick also present five main challenges associated with diversity, factors which arise mostly because people are attracted to and feel comfortable with others like themselves:

- Resistance to change
- Lack of cohesiveness
- Communication problems
- Conflicts
- Decision making

In their book *Breaking the Glass Ceiling*, Morrison *et al.* (1987)[72] provided career advice that in my opinion is relevant not merely for women, but for members of any disadvantaged group. These are listed below, together with additional interpretation on how organizations can have a positive impact where relevant.

1 **Lesson 1 – Learn the ropes.** It is not enough to be good. One must understand the 'rules of the game' to survive and go forward. Being smart and working

hard are essential but not always sufficient. At a certain level it requires knowledge of the culture and becoming part of it, minimizing differences, and adjusting for what is acceptable behaviour. This can be done by observing, seeking feedback and interacting with executives. One needs not just to be smart (and sometimes to be careful not to be seen as 'too smart'), but to learn how to influence others. The organization can help a great deal by clarifying matters formally, and can encourage informal ways whereby people can get to learn how things are done. Another factor that sometimes may serve to the possible advantage of minority groups is their cheap cost. They often work harder and agree to be paid less than others. Managements seeking cost effectiveness thus will be less reluctant to give them a chance. For the organization it appears to be a simple factor, but it can get complicated, because the Adams theory of equity is still relevant, and after proving themselves successful, people might leave to work elsewhere where less prejudiced organizations will remunerate them according to their input, not their diverse background.

2 **Lesson 2: take control of your own career.** In line with what much of this book is about, people need to lead and navigate their own career. The guidelines Morrison *et al.* provide include:

- Go for the 'right' jobs, and do so early in the career, in particular line management roles. Learning which roles lead to the top is part of the first lesson above. Sometimes there are common career paths, sometimes one can learn from the history of former successful executives. Certain positions are clearly 'dead-ends'. Others open opportunities.
- Control your career in the best way you know (and no single way is the best).
- Ask for what you want. Clarify your aims, and don't let executives make stereotypical assumptions about you (e.g. that such a person would never agree to an overseas position).
- Avoid derailment traps: sometimes it is acceptable for management to want from you something that is not exactly what you want to do, as it may eventually lead you forward.

Organizations acknowledge that people need to manage their careers, but this does not mean that organizations should abandon their career system. They just need to change their role to one that is more supportive and consulting rather than directive and control based (Baruch, 2003).[73]

3 **Lesson 3: Build confidence.** Take calculated risks, build on your strengths and perform well. Listen to what others say, and amend approaches and behaviours that would otherwise cause you to clash with the system. Good bosses can make a difference by their guidance and advice. Expose yourself to other managers and learn their skills and qualities. You may realize that you do not have less competence than others. And lastly, sometimes engaging in outside activities helps in reassuring people about their competence and ability. Support networks are not restricted to the internal environment of an organization.

4 **Lesson 4 – Rely on others.** Learning and benefiting from others is a good career strategy. Mentoring relationships help immensely, and organizations

can and should promote the creation, maintenance and development of such relationships. Mentoring helps both the person who has a mentor, as well as the person who mentors others.

5 **Lesson 5 – Go for 'the bottom line'**. Being tough may be harder for women and minorities, but they must be tough, in order to get results. This needs to be conveyed by the organization. It would be a mistake for an organization to place minority managers only in support and peripheral roles.

6 **Lesson 6 – Integrate life and work**. This issue has special relevance for women and single parents (mostly women). It is a crucial factor, which might have negative outcomes if not dealt with, and organizations can do much, in terms of providing physical and psychological support mechanisms. Nevertheless, flexibility and alternative work arrangements should not cause people to be sidelined. For example, teleworkers might be 'out of sight' and therefore 'out of mind' (Baruch, 2001).[74]

To break or shatter the glass ceiling, Morrison *et al.* argue that one needs to develop credibility, advocacy and exploiting luck when it knocks on your door. On the other hand they warn against 'hitting the wall': sometimes people must realize their own limitations and find alternative work. The organization should be able to point out such limitations, to prevent people from feeling discriminated against, and help them find the right path, either within the organization, or outside it. However, if these limitations are elusive, it is up to the organization to make sure the value of people is released, by giving managerial support and utilizing the career system, and appointing people to roles that will be best for them and subsequently for the organization.

Summary

In this chapter we learned the nature of diversity, distinguished it from discrimination and identified the meaning of the management of diversity. We explored the expected benefits as well as the possible pitfalls of managing diversity, focusing on a wide variety of organizational initiatives. We discovered that diversity does not end with demography, and explored the issue of organizational justice and fairness.

Specific sources of diversity analysed included gender, ethnicity, age, disability, sexual orientation, religion, deep-level diversity, belonging to a special type of family and finally hybrid diversity, meaning more than a single diversity.

The chapter concluded with some advice on organizational policies and their importance in managing diversity.

Key terms

- Diversity
- Surface diversity
- Deep-level diversity

- Valuing diversity
- Discrimination
- EEO (Equal Employment Opportunity)
- Organizational initiatives
- Procedural justice
- Distributive justice
- Organizational diversity policies

DISCUSSION QUESTIONS

Diversity exercise

See Appendix 8.1.

Lessons and food for thought

1 *For HR managers*: Using the CAST concept, how would you develop practices, policies and strategies to tackle and manage diversity?
2 *For the HR consultant*: What would be your advice to HR managers in developing a comprehensive policy for managing diversity? How will your policy be influenced by the specific environment in which the organization operates?
3 *For the HR teacher*: In what way would you integrate new forms of diversity into existing career systems?
4 *For the Student*: Do you belong to any of the above listed diverse sub-groups? Have you experienced discrimination in the past – *see* the exercise in Appendix 8.1.

Review questions

1 What are the major impetuses for organizations to manage diversity?
2 In what ways does your university encourage students from diverse backgrounds to apply for places? What practices does the university apply to support people of diverse backgrounds during their studies? If you were suffering from a disability (e.g. dyslexia or impaired hearing), how would your university help you?

Critical thinking and ideas probing

Would you be ready to work in the same team with people who are...

- Of different gender?
- Much older than you?
- Of different ethnic origin?
- Disabled?
- Lesbian or homosexuals?

Would you be ready to be managed by people who are...

- Of different gender?
- Much older than you?
- Of different ethnic origin?
- Disabled?
- Lesbian or homosexuals?

Notes

[1] Harrison, D.A., Price, K.H. and Bell, M.P. (1998) 'Beyond Organizational Demography: Time and the Effects of Surface- Versus Deep-Level Diversity on Work Groups', *Academy of Management Journal*, 41, 96–107.

[2] Cox, T.H. and Blake, S. (1991) 'Managing cultural diversity: implications for organizational competitiveness', *Academy of Management Executive*, 5(3): 45–56.

[3] Cassell, C. (2001) 'Managing Diversity', in T. Redman and A. Wilkinson (eds) *Contemporary Human Resource Management*, Harlow, England: Prentice Hall, pp. 404–31.

[4] Hall, D.T. and Parker, V.A. (1993) 'The role of workplace flexibility in managing diversity', *Organizational Dynamics*, 22(1): 4–18.

[5] Greenhaus, J.H., Callanan, G.A. and Godshalk, V.M. (2000) *Career Management*, 3rd edn, Fort Worth, TX: the Dryden Press.

[6] Kandola, R. (1995) 'Managing diversity: new broom or old hat?', in C.L. Cooper and I.T. Robertson (eds) *International Review of Industrial and Organizational Psychology*, vol. 10, Chichester: Wiley.

[7] Williams, K.Y. (1998) 'Demography and diversity in organizations: review of 100 years of research', in B.M. Staw and L. L. Cummings (eds) *Research in Organizational Behavior*, Greenwich, CT: JAI Press, pp. 77–140; Thompson, W.R. (1999) 'Diversity among managers translates into profitability', *HRMagazine*, April, p. 10.

[8] Harel, H.G., Tzafrir, S. and Baruch, Y. (2002) 'HRM Practices, Promotion of Women in Management, and Organizational Effectiveness: An Integrated Model', *International Journal of Human Resource Management*, 14(2), 247–63.

[9] Gruber, J.E. and Bjorn, L. (1982) 'Blue-Collar Blues: The Sexual Harassment of Women Autoworkers', *Work and Occupations*, 9, 271–98; Gutek, B.A., Cohen, A.G. and Konrad, A.M. (1990) 'Predicting Social-Sexual Behavior at Work: A Contact Hypothesis', *Academy of Management Journal*, 33, 560–77; Mansfield, P.K., Koch, P.B., Henderson, J., Vicary, J.R., Cohn, M. and Young, E.W. (1991) 'The Job Climate for Women in Traditionally Male Blue-Collar Occupations', *Sex Roles*, 25, 63–79.

[10] Tsui, A.S., Egan, T.D. and O'Reilly III, C.A. (1992) 'Being Different: Relational Demography and Organizational Attachment', *Administrative Science Quarterly*, 37, 549–79; Jackson, S.E., Brett, J.F., Sessa, V.I., Cooper, D.M., Julin, J.A. and Peyronnin, K. (1991) 'Some Differences Make a Difference: Interpersonal Dissimilarity and Group Heterogeneity as Correlates of Recruitment, Promotion, and Turnover', *Journal of Applied Psychology*, 76, 675–89.

[11] Sessa, V.I., Jackson, S.E. and Rapini, D.T. (1995) 'Workforce diversity: the good, the bad and the reality', in G.R. Ferris, S.D. Rosen and D.T. Barnum (eds) *Handbook of Human Resource Management*, Cambridge, MA: Blackwell, pp. 263–81.

[12] Baruch, Y. (2001) 'The status of research on teleworking and an agenda for future research', *International Journal of Management Review*, 3(2), 113–29.

[13] Thomas, R.R. (1991) *Beyond Race and Gender*, NY: AMACOM.

[14] Thomas, R.R. (1996) *Redefining Diversity*, NY: AMACOM.

[15] Kreitner, R., Kinicki, A. and Burlens, M. (2002) *Organizational Behaviour*, 2nd European edn, London: McGraw Hill.

[16] Arnold, J. (1997) *Managing Careers into the 21st Century*, London: Paul Chapman.

[17] McMahan, G.C., Bell, M.P. and Virick, M. (1998) 'Strategic human resource management: employee involvement, diversity, and international issues', *Human Resource Management Review*, 8(3), 193–214.

[18] Kanter, R.M. (1977) *Men and Women of the Corporation*, NY: Basic Books.

[19] Morrison, A.M., White, R.P. and Veslor, E.V. (1987) *Breaking the Glass Ceiling*, Reading, MA: Addison-Wesley.

[20] Campbell, R.J. and Moses, J.L. (1986) 'Careers for organizational perspectives', in D.T. Hall & Assoc., *Career Development in Organizations*, San Francisco: Jossey-Bass.

[21] Ashburner, L. (1991) 'Men managers and women workers: women employees as an under used resource', *British Journal of Management*, 2, 3–16.

[22] Pazy, A. (1986) 'Sex differences in responsiveness to organizational career management', *Human Resource Management*, 26(5), 243–56.

[23] Judy, R.W. and D'Amico, C. (1997) *Workforce 2020*, Indianapolis, IN: Hudson Institute.

[24] Harvey, M. (1997) 'Dual-career expatriates: expectations, adjustment and satisfaction with international relocation', *Journal of International Business Studies*, 28(3), 627–58.

[25] *See* note 1 above.

[26] Chatman, J.A., Polzer, J.T., Barsade, S.G. and Neale, M.A. (1998) 'Being different yet feeling similar: the influence of demographic composition and organizational culture on work processes and outcomes', *Administrative Science Quarterly*, 43, 749–80.

[27] *See* note 5 above.

[28] Milkovich, T.G. and Newman, M.J. (1996) *Compensation*, 5th edn, Chicago, IL: Irwin.

[29] Furnham, A. (1997) *The Psychology of behaviour at work*, Hove, UK: The Psychology Press.

[30] Cropanzano, R. and Greenberg, J. (1997) 'Progress in organizational justice', in C.L. Cooper and I.T. Robertson (eds) *International Review of Industrial and Organizational Psychology*, NY: Wiley.

[31] Tyler, T.R. and Bies, R.J. (1990) 'Interpersonal aspects of procedural justice', in J.S. Carroll (ed.) *Applied Social Psychology in Business Settings*, Hillsdale, NJ: Lawrence Erlbaum.

[32] Gilliland, S.W. (1994) 'Effects of Procedural and Distributive Justice on Reactions to a Selection System', *Journal of Applied Psychology*, 79(5), 691–701; Konovsky, M. and Folger, R. (1994) 'Relative effects of procedural and distributive justice on employees attitudes', *Representative Research in Social Psychology*, 17(1), 15–24.

[33] Ensher, E.A., Murphy, S.E. and Sullivan, S.E. (2002) 'Reel women: Lessons from female TV executives on managing work and real life', *Academy of Management Executive*, 16(2), 106–21.

[34] *See* note 1 above.

[35] Harrison, D.A., Price, K.H., Gavin, J.H. and Florey, A.T. (2002) 'Time, teams, and task performance: changing effects of surface- and deep-level diversity on group functioning', *Academy of Management Journal*, 45(5), 1029–45.

[36] Clair, J.A., Beatty, J. and MacLean, T. (2002) *Out of Sight but Not Out of Mind: How People Manage Invisible Social Identities in the Workplace*, paper presented at the Academy of Management, August 2002, Denver, CO.

[37] *See* note 19 above.

[38] Betz, N.E. (1989) 'Self-realization in modern women', in E. Krau (ed.) *Self-Realization, Success and Adjustment*, NY: Praeger.

[39] Marshall, J. (1995) *Women Managers Moving on: Exploring Career and Life Choices*, London: International Thomson Publishing Europe.

[40] *See* note 19 above.

[41] DOL (2001) 'Usual weekly earning summary', *Labor Force Statistics from the Current Population Survey*, Washington DC: US Government, Department of Labor.

[42] *See* note 19 above.

[43] Catalyst (2001) *Catalyst Census of Women Corporate Officers and Top Earners*, NY: Catalyst.

[44] Moen, P. (1989) *Working Parents*, Madison, WI: University of Wisconsin Press.

[45] Enquist, P.O. (1984) 'The act of flying backward with dignity', *Daedalus*, 113(1), 61–74.

[46] Hull, K.E. and Nelson, R.L. (2000) 'Assimilation, choice or constraint? Testing theories of gender differences in the career of lawyers', *Social Forces*, 79(1), 229–64.

[47] Hall-Taylor, B. (1997) 'The construction of women's management skills and the marginalization of women in senior management', *Women in Management Review*, 12(7), 255–63.

[48] Barrett, W.P., Baron, J.N. and Stuart, T.E. (2000) 'Avenues of attainment: occupational demography and organizational careers in the California Civil Service', *American Journal of Sociology*, 106(1), 88–144.

[49] Morrison, A. (1992) *Shattering the Glass Ceiling*, Reading, MA: Addison-Wesley; Davidson, M. and Cooper, C. (1992) *Shattering the Glass Ceiling*, London: Paul Chapman.

[50] Crow, M. (1999) 'Achieving equality of opportunity?', in J. Leopold, L. Harris and T. Watson (eds) *Strategic Human Resourcing*, London: FT/Pitman, pp. 291–309.

[51] Dickens, L. (1994) 'Wasted resources? Equal opportunity in employment', in K. Sisson (ed.) *Personnel Management: A Comprehensive Guide to Theory and Practice in Britain*, Oxford: Blackwell, 253–96.

[52] Bevan, S., Dench, S, Tamkin P. and Cummings J. (1999) *Family-friendly employment: the business case*, DFEE Research brief No. 136.

[53] Levinson, D. (1978) *Seasons of Man's Life*, NY: Knopf; Levinson, D.J. and Levinson, J.D. (1996) *Seasons of a Woman's Life*, NY: Knopf.

[54] Hakim, C. (2000) *Work-Lifestyle Choices in the 21st Century: Preference Theory*, Oxford: OUP.

[55] Hakim, C. (1996) *Key Issues in Women's work: Female Heterogeneity and the Polarisation of Women's Employment*, London: Athlone Press; Hakim (2000), *see* note 54 above.

[56] Simpson, R. and Altman, Y. (2000) 'Young women managers: career progress and career success – evidence from the UK', *Journal of European Industrial Training*, 24(2/3/4), 190–8.

[57] Fletcher, J.K. (1999) *Disappearing Acts: Gender, Power, and Relational Practice at Work*, Boston, MA: MIT Press.

[58] Barclays (2000) *Women in Business – the Barriers Start to Fall*, London: Barclays Bank PLC.

[59] *See* note 8 above.

[60] Davidson, M.J. and Burke, R.J. (2000) 'Introduction', in M.J. Davidson and R.J. Burke (eds) *Women in management: current research issues*, London: Sage, vol. 2, pp. 5–6.

[61] Johnston, W.B. (1991) 'Global workforce 2000: the new world labor market', *Harvard Business Review*, 69, 115–27.

[62] Lamb, J. (2000) 'Age code needs legal backing', *People Management*, 16 March, p. 10.

[63] Census (1997) *Population Profile of the United States*, Washington DC: US Bureau of the Census, US Government Printing Office.

[64] Winfield, L. and Spielman, S. (1995) 'Straight talk about gays in the workplace: creating an inclusive, productive environment for everyone in your organization, New York: AMACOM.

[65] Day, N.E. and Schoenrade, P. (1995) 'Staying in the closet versus coming out: relationships between communication about sexual orientation and work attitudes', *Personnel Psychology*, 50, 147–63.

[66] Fishbein, M. and Ajzen, I. (1975) *Belief, attitude, intention and behavior: An Introduction to theory and research*, Reading, MA: Addison-Wesley.

[67] Tapscott, D. (1998) *Growing up Digital: The Rise of the Net Generation*, NY: McGraw-Hill.

[68] Nyman, L. (1994) 'The identification of birth order personality attributes', *The Journal of Psychology*, 129, 51–9; Sulloway, F.J. (1995) 'Birth order and evolutionary psychology: a meta-analytic overview', *Psychological Enquiry*, 6, 75–80.

[69] Bell, E.L.J.E. and Nkomo, S.M. (2001) *Our Separate Ways: Black and White Women and the Struggle for Professional Identity*, Cambridge, MA: Harvard Business Press.

[70] Bhavnani, R. and Coyle, A. (2000) 'Black and ethnic minority women managers in the UK – continuity or change?', in M.J. Davidson and R.J. Burke (eds) *Women in management: current research issues*, London: Sage, vol. 2, pp. 223–35.

[71] Nelson, D.L. and Quick, J.C. (2003) *Organizational Behavior: Foundations, Realities, and Challenges*, 4th edn, Mason, OH: Thomson-South-Western, p. 50.

[72] *See* note 19 above.

[73] Baruch Y. (2003) 'Career systems in transition, normative model of career practices', *Personnel Review*, in press.

[74] *See* note 12 above.

Appendix 8.1
Diversity exercise

An intriguing class exercise may comprise of comparing and contrasting individual and aggregate profiles of students' responses to questions 1 and 2. Question 3 can serve to stimulate a group discussion.

1. Did you encounter any discrimination *before* **your present studies**, e.g. did you perceive different attitudes towards you as compared with your **work colleagues** of other backgrounds?

	Gender	Race/ ethnicity	Disability	Religion	Age	Sexual orientation	Other
Not at all							
Very minor							
Minor							
Significant							
Very significant							

Please specify from whom (e.g. managers, peers, administrators . . .) and in what connection:

_____

2. Do you encounter any discrimination **as a student (relate to your present studies)**? For example, do you perceive different attitudes towards you as compared with your **class colleagues** of other backgrounds?

	Gender	Race/ ethnicity	Disability	Religion	Age	Sexual orientation	Other
Not at all							
Very minor							
Minor							
Significant							
Very significant							

Would you be able to specify from whom (e.g. academics, peers, administrators . . .) and in what connection:

_____

3. **Would you anticipate any discrimination** *after* you finish your present studies? Will it be stronger or milder than that before your studies, i.e. do you think that having a formal degree such as advanced degree in management can reduce or eliminate discrimination?

9 Conclusion: the future of career management

LEARNING OBJECTIVES

After reading this chapter you should be able to:

- Reflect on the role career system management will play in the future.

CHAPTER CONTENTS

- *Epilogue*
- *Back to basics*
- *Future trends*
- *Technology, e-business and careers*
- *Life or work career?*
- *Strategic career or career strategy?*
- *Lessons and challenges*
- *Notes*

Epilogue

It is widely accepted that the careers of today are quite different from traditional careers. The stable and linear career systems of the past have developed into a transitional, fluid type of system. This is true from both the individual and the organizational perspective. The process of destabilization was caused by macro-economic and social forces, as well as by workers themselves. On the one hand we have the boundaryless organization, indeed boundaryless society, with the breaking down of many traditional concepts, and the building of new concepts that are innovative but challenging. On the other hand we see the trend towards individualism, which started some time ago, and is still accelerating. People are becoming masters of their own destiny; they see the world as their oyster. Much of the change is due to novel ways by which career actors interpret and pursue emergent labour markets. Economic forces and the competitive nature of commerce forced organizations to make dramatic changes to the way they treat employees, and forced them to look for different ways of managing careers within and outside the organizational boundaries.

I hope that the book has provided an added value for students, as well as for practitioners and academic scholars interested in the subject area. The benefits stem from the book's broad scrutiny of the area of careers, as managed by organizations, including detailed analysis of practices and policies which must relate to the future rather than the past: in a time of change and confusion, managers need a relevant framework to guide them in managing people. People are most frequently cited as the most important asset of organizations, but managing this asset has never been clear, and with the breakdown of psychological contracts in the 1990s this task has become even tougher. I believe that this book, as well as providing the student with general and specific academic knowledge, offers readers an opportunity to re-think their own careers, perhaps to contemplate a career change or to re-shape their existing career plans.

Back to basics

The basic roles of HRM are to obtain and retain employees. These two roles remain the primary goal for HRM, just as they were in the past. However the nature of the activities that need to be undertaken in order to fulfil them has altered considerably. The 'obtain' element means finding the right person for organizational needs, the job, the career. The 'retain' is all about career management. Increasingly, it has become crucial to retain employees. When mergers occur the acquiring company 'buys' people. A typical example would be an IT specialist firm that leases its computers, rents its offices, outsources its services, and does not have even company cars. All the firm's assets, then, lie in the human capital and the brand name. Judged by these criteria, recent acquisitions would suggest that a price of a million dollars per person reflects the worth of a company. Thus, the most important element following an acquisition is to keep to the people.

But the nature of employment relationships has changed:

- From family organization to team and partnership (you cannot fire a family member, but you can fire a team member).
- From patronizing approach to freedom and autonomy, self-managed individuals and teams.
- From stability to dynamism and flexibility.
- From work-focused career to quality of life and search for work/life balance.

In search of excellence, organizations seek to become enabling, not controlling. They seek for the right promise to make to their employees (e.g. employability) in order to gain a competitive advantage, via creativity and innovation. The new psychological contracts form a different base for trust and commitment. Multiple commitments (such as commitment to the profession, the team, the self) emerge as substitutes for the traditional organizational commitment.

New careers seem to have new meanings and to serve new roles for people.[1] Nevertheless, in reality not all have changed, and there is a certain stability and continuity of development, not necessarily via step-changes. Most people still have a high internal need for work. The major roles work plays in people's lives remain similar to those of a few decades ago. While for many careers have changed or altered completely, and new professions have emerged, many old-style professions exist, as well as whole industrial sectors. Mundane work still makes up a large part of the job in many occupations, and companies apply the concept of division of labour to new innovative establishments (see, for example, call centres as modern sweatshops). Trust can be a powerful managerial tool via empowerment, but in many cases the so-called empowerment starts and ends with empty words. Even when changes do occur, they take time and the pace is slow, as the case of diversity in the workplace indicates (for women, who still experience a glass ceiling, ethnic minorities, older people, and others from diverse backgrounds who may suffer discrimination).

Future trends

From the perspective of sociology of vocations, the big question is – which new career options will be open to the generation cast out by the service industries? In the earlier mass movements of workers it was clear where the large majority would go: the farmers and tenant farmers moved to towns and cities and became production workers. Production workers who were cast out from the redundant factories moved to the service industries. Now fewer people are needed in the service industries, and the question is – where will they go?

The answer is problematic for two reasons. First, the process is still taking place, and as with forecasting the future, any suggestion is a risky guess. Second, it is clear that the answer will not be simple, but segmented. New industries emerge or develop further while mature labour markets may disappear. Amongst the possible opportunities that are emerging, three come to mind immediately: e-business, the leisure sector and tertiary education. The leisure sector arises since more people are working fewer hours (the number of working hours per week in Europe are continuing to decrease, getting below the threshold of 40 or 38 at the turn of the millennium), and many are not working (either because they have been made redundant or they are pensioners, with a longer life expectancy). Thus more facilities are needed in the leisure and entertainment industry. Fitness centres, restaurants, performing arts establishments and clubs flourish.

As for the education sector, while a university degree was rare in the early days of the twentieth century, by the end of that century one-third of young people in the relevant age group were students. It is expected that this proportion will increase to about half. Thus this sector (and associated industries) is rapidly growing.

Technology, e-business and careers

Technology, as has always been the case, influences not just a single occupation, but the whole labour market and society in general. The most significant technological developments influencing careers and employment are concerned with IT. However, the impact is not unidirectional. With continual growth in the number of jobs people whose work involves extensive use of IT, the skills required to conduct many jobs are *either* increasing *or* decreasing. Evidence suggests that more workers have experienced an increase than a decrease in skills as a result of digitization (Cascio, 2000).[2] What is becoming of great importance for future careers is the changing nature of the skills and competencies required, and in particular the role of intellectual capital. Intellectual capital is the knowledge, information, intellectual property and experience that can be put to use to create wealth and to enhance human welfare (Stewart, 1997).[3] Increasingly, intellectual capital dwells within humans' brains rather than within the system, making knowledge management a field of great importance. Human capital is the source of innovation and renewal, and its management is mediated via career management.

E-business makes a case for fast-growth service companies (while the production sectors took a more traditional approach to e-business at its start). Embarking on e-business means taking the risk that the operational changes that accompany it could jeopardize existing relationships with both environments – internal (employees) and external (customers). But on average, just a few years after the introduction of e-business, the early adopters are beginning to enjoy the significant operational benefits from their e-business commitment, and counting their employees and customers as their biggest supporters. The main benefactors, however, seem to be the shareholders. Companies expect to generate an increasing share of their revenue from e-business, while some businesses have been reluctant to disrupt their traditional ways of working. A word of caution is required too – careers in this dynamic but fragile business segment are just starting to be created, and there is no conventional model of an e-career. It will take some time for the emerging pattern of e-careers to take recognizable form.

To successfully navigate careers in the e-world people need different skills, the first of which is readiness for extensive change. For customers, the secret lies in their ability to adapt to the availability of new or existing products and services on the Internet. For employees it is that e-business entails a high degree of flexibility and willingness on the part of the people and HR management.

This latest technological development also creates new type of jobs and occupations. Web-page design is one such relatively new profession. Many industries are moving a major share of their business to the Internet, in particular sales of certain products such as flight tickets.

But it is not just sales that make good Internet business. Another prominent example is recruitment. Job advertising on the net has become commonplace, and more developments have occurred in online selection, including CV screening and other selection analysis. Table 9.1 presents the results of a recent student survey of the best and worst Internet websites for recruitment. Interestingly some sites were voted best and worst by different participants.

E-business does not start and end with highly prestigious, well-paid jobs. In addition to the IT, professional personnel and the like, the new e-business sector requires a new army of employees on call, many delivery people (the revival of the milkman?) – but this time delivering the latest book from Amazon.com or flight tickets from lastminute.com. These jobs are hardly intellectually stimulating, and form a core of mundane work in the new economy. Repetitive Strain

Table 9.1 Ranking of Internet recruitment websites by UK students

Best	*Worst*
www.workthing.com ★★★★★★★★★★★★	www.fish4jobs.co.uk ★★★★★★★★★
www.fish4.co.uk ★★★★★★★★★★	www.monster.co.uk ★★★★★★
www.monster.co.uk ★★★★★★★★	www.gisajob.com ★★★★
www.prospects.ac.uk ★★★★★★★★	www.gojobsite.co.uk ★★★★
www.totaljobs.com ★★★★★★★★	www.totaljobs.com ★★★★
www.milkround.co.uk ★★★★★	www.jobsearch.co.uk ★★★★
www.jobs.telegraph.co.uk ★★★★	www.doctorjob.com ★★★
www.jobs1.co.uk ★★★★	http://e-job.com ★★
www.jobsearch.co.uk ★★★★	www.dice.com/ ★★
www.thebigchoice.com/ ★★★★	www.jobtosuityou.co.uk ★★
www.gojob.co.uk ★★★★	www.jobs.telegraph.co.uk ★★
www.hobsons.com ★★★★	www.hobsons.com/ ★★
http://uk.careers.yahoo.com/ ★★	www.graduatelink.com ★★
www.gis-a-job.co.uk ★★	www.workthing.com/ ★★
www.topjobs.co.uk/ ★★	www.graduate-jobs.com ★★

Note: The sites listed received more than one vote as the *best* or *worst* job search site, with each ★ indicating one vote.

Injury (RSI) became quite common for people performing repetitive actions with their limbs (many people suffered wrist and finger problems from operating computers). In new workplaces such as call centres, where employees are required to respond to callers following a prescribed procedure and using the same words, people might suffer from what may be labelled Repetitive Brain Injury (RBI). If people are unable to break away from a rigid routine that calls for no intellectual effort, originality of thinking, or stimulating challenges, their minds become stultified. RBI is a metaphorical parallel of RSI. Similarly the approach to its cure should be a combination of mind activation and rest.

Life or working career?

The nature of career systems has also changed. Whereas in the past career systems largely involved planning and managing a relatively passive workforce, modern systems are different. The emphasis is on developmental processes, where the employee is expected and even encouraged to take an active role, while the organization play the role of facilitator or enabler. Career management is being transformed into a service designed to support managers, professionals and employees to create and re-create their development path. This can remove them from the organization, but neither side need lament this loss too much.

The organization is not expected to be altruistic and to retain all employees if they are not performing to the best of their ability, or if they are unable to achieve a required standard of performance. Moreover, even the best performers may find themselves out of a job due to a competitive market or for other reasons beyond the control of the organization. The implications for people management are the following trends:

From	To
Control and command system	Support and consult system
Organizational manpower planning	Individual career counselling
Managing careers	Developing people
Training for a qualification	Lifelong learning
Assigning jobs in succession	Coaching, mentoring, pointing out opportunities
Retirement with pension at 65	Various ways of employment ending, no age boundaries

Pfeffer (1998)[4] and Naisbitt and Aburdene (1990),[5] among others, refer to the creation of wealth via the human asset, a shift from financial capital, which was the core key to competitive advantage in the industrial society, to human capital, its concurrent replacement for the information age. Human capital is measured in terms of knowledge, and knowledge management is required from organizations. Sometimes the knowledge is embedded within the system, the technology, the procedures and regulations. This system of knowledge management somewhat neutralizes the human value. In other cases, the knowledge is embedded within people, forming human capital (and raising legal questions of intellectual properties). Knowledge held by individuals and their competencies become their career asset. The ability to learn is more valuable than formal qualification.

Strategic career or career strategy?

Writing on strategic management, Leavy (1996)[6] argues that 'strategy' as a field of study came into being only in the 1960s, and he goes further to claim that the strategy process cannot yet be fully understood in terms of any single framework. Rumlet *et al.* suggested that strategic management as a field of enquiry is firmly grounded in practice and exists because of the importance of its subject, not because of its historical coherence (Rumlet *et al.*, 1991).[7]

There is a striking similarity between the field of career studies and strategy. First, the study of careers as a specific research area started at about the same time. Moreover, as Arthur *et al.* (1989)[8] claim, the career area is not the 'property' of a single theoretical discipline. It is of interest to note that as in the area of strategy,[9] by the 1980s writing about careers had moved from a primary interest in growth to a focus on competitiveness and renewal.

Putting these strands together, strategic HRM emerged in the late 1980s and 1990s, and is continuing to develop. The strategic HRM approach was introduced by Devanna, Fombrun and Tichy (1981), continued with the work of Fombrun, Tichy and Devanna (1984) and Beer *et al.* (1984), and is still at the centre of current research (Salaman, 1992; Hendry, 1995; Tyson, 1995; Lundy and Cowling, 1996).[10] According to strategic HRM, the HR strategy should be developed alongside the general strategy of the organization, to acquire a cultural fit within the organization and with the outside environment. HR managers need to be involved in strategic decision-making processes and to link the HR policy and strategy with that of the organization. On the other hand, HRM is a profession which requires the knowledge of a wide range of theories and the skills to apply to a variety of practical programmes, activities and practices at the operational level (Storey, 1992).[11] Here the HR manager is faced with a question of balance between the practical aspect of the HRM roles and the need to be involved in strategic decision making at the organizational level (Baruch, 1998).[12]

New career models will emerge, and the only certainty will be the persistence of change. But the emergent theme in these changes is the growing role taken by individuals in directing and managing their careers.

Lessons and challenges

The new world of careers poses challenges to the traditional ways of thinking and perceiving careers. Let us look at a three-level analysis – individual, organization and society.

Individuals

Navigating uncertainties

If careers are journeys, the main role of the individual is to navigate their way through. The main challenges posed by future career navigating are growing uncertainty, the blurring of boundaries, the diminution of the roles organizations undertake and the lack of secure, stable employment.

In the past it was assumed that the organizational role was one of command and control. Now the person is in control. People should expect no job security, but ensure they have the capacity to acquire new employment should they be made redundant. They will gain employment via training, skills and competencies, and a proactive approach towards the labour market. A finger on the pulse is essential for knowledge of employability. On the other hand, it is acceptable to stay within one organization so long as career progress is being made (not necessarily upward progress, but such that increases competence).

The meaning of career success and measurement of it is not what it used to be. It is less about advancement in a hierarchy or gains in terms of formal power. Career success can be related to professionalism, employability and life/work balance. It is now less about money making (buying power), and more about the psychological aspects of satisfaction, recognition, esteem and self-actualization. The centrality of the work role acts as a moderator (Mannheim, Baruch and Tal, 1997).[13] Internal career success is no less important than external, and careers are looked at in the wider context of life. There are a variety of factors and issues that people may aim at in their career. While some will always strive to climb up hierarchies, others will create different challenges for themselves.

Organizations

Support, challenge, development, flexibility

The role of the organization in planning and management of careers has changed from command and control to the provision of support and guidance, as well as providing the map for the individual to navigate. Flexibility is a key concept. The flexible management of careers may take several forms. A diverse set of career practices exists, and they are directed at a diverse workforce. This diversity is not just demographic, but also relates to the type of contract under which people work (for example, there is a distinction between core people and peripheral employees). Introducing alternative work arrangements is an excellent example of what organizations can and should offer. Another form of flexibility may be introduced via the establishment of satellite firms. These can be supported by the core company, and with additional assistance from financial enterprises (e.g. venture capitalists), may be the object of a future management buy-out. In this way the people involved will gain control and will be able to build their future careers through positive contacts with their former employer.

While redundancies are not a way forward, companies that have no choice but to make people redundant should conduct the process very carefully. Using 'best practice' is advised, following guidelines suggested elsewhere, e.g. to make sure that all agree it was inevitable, it was the last action to be taken, it was conducted at all hierarchy levels, etc. (*See* Mishra, Spreitzer and Mishra, 1998, and Baruch and Hind, 1999, for examples of how to apply 'best practice'.)[14] To equip their employees properly with employability, the type of training that organizations invest in is important. Training improves the employability of unemployed, but should be labour market driven, not merely company specific, if organizations put the interests of employees first.

The wider context

Demography, globalization, technology, culture – convergence as against divergence

The composition of the population in industrial developed societies is changing. Two tendencies co-exist, which lead to an escalation of the same phenomenon. The birth rate is declining, and life expectancy is increasing. An alarming element in business life is the tendency to allow people to leave the active labour market even before normal retirement age. People leave organizations to take early retirement or are made redundant at the age of 55, 50 and lower. A crucial source of competence, experience and creative brainpower is being lost. As a result of the ageing of the population, some one-third of the population will be over 65 early in the twenty-first century. It is not surprising to hear voices questioning the logic (and the financial viability) of a system that forces people out of the workforce while they are still able to contribute. There are suggestions that the retirement age be raised to 70. This may be a new reality for many – but in contrast, many organizations encourage early retirement for people over 50. This places heavy burdens on pension funds, raises issues of quality of life, and increases the uncertainty and possible stress felt by the employed who watch the process, knowing that their turn will come soon.

Due to the low birth rate there are few options for replacement and ensuring growth. Many developed countries have to rely on cheap labour in the global market, and sometimes this creates sociological and cultural problems (such as those related to the Turkish community in Germany).

Globalization continues to flourish, but while there is much convergence in management systems and organizational practices, cultural differences have a strong influence and will continue to have an impact on how careers are managed and on the meaning of career and career success. More options for global careers by means of expatriation will develop, but, overall, global careers are not yet the norm, and will probably continue to be the exception in the near future. Similarly other phenomena such as virtual organizations and careers in the virtual world will be at the leading edge, but will be confined to a few rather than the majority of employees.

Furnham (2000)[15] tried to forecast what the world of work would look like in 2020. Such projections, as he himself admitted, might seem out of balance in terms of the time perspective. However there is no doubt first, that the world of work is changing, and second, that certain qualities are to stay with us, perhaps in a modified form. The pace of change is continuing to grow, and what is certain is that future careers will be dynamic and unpredictable.

'Expect the unexpected' should be the motto for individuals and organizations alike.

Notes

1   Arnold, J. (1997) *Managing Careers into the 21st Century*, London: Paul Chapman; Hall, D.T. (1996) *The Career is Dead – Long Live the Career*, San Francisco: Jossey-Bass.
2   Cascio, W.F. (2000) 'New Workplaces', in Jean M. Kummerow (ed.) *New Directions in Career Planning and the Workplace*, 2nd edn, Palo Alto, CA: Davies-Black Publishing.
3   Stewart, T.A. (1997) *Intellectual capital*, NY: Doubleday.
4   Pfeffer, J. (1998) *The Human Equation*, Boston: Harvard Business School Press.
5   Naisbitt, J. and Aburdene, P. (1990) *Megatrends 2000*, NY: Warner.
6   Leavy, B. (1996) *Key Processes in Strategy*, London: Thompson.
7   Rumlet, R.P., Schendel, D. and Teece, D.J. (1991) 'Strategic management and economics', *Strategic Management Journal*, 12S, 5–19.
8   Arthur, M.B., Hall, D.T. and Lawrence, B.S. (1989) 'Generating New Directions in Career Theory: The Case for a Transdisciplinary Approach', in M.B. Arthur, D.T. Hall and B.S. Lawrence (eds) *Handbook of Career Theory*, Cambridge: Cambridge University Press, pp. 7–25.
9   Leavy (1996), p. 2, *see* note 6.
10 Devanna, M.A., Fombrun, C.J. and Tichy, N.M. (1981) 'Human Resource Management: Strategic Perspective', *Organizational Dynamics*, 9(3), 51–67; Fombrun, C.J., Tichy, N.M. and Devanna, M.A. (1984) *Strategic Human Resource Management*, NY: John Wiley & Sons, pp. 19–31; Beer, M., Spector, B., Lawrence, P.R., Mill, Q.D. and Walton, R.E. (1984) *Managing Human Assets*, NY: The Free Press; Salaman, G. (1992) *Human Resource Strategies*, London: Sage; Hendry, C. (1995) *Human Resource Management, A strategic approach to employment*, Oxford: Butterworth-Heinemann; Tyson, S. (1995) *Human Resource Strategy*, London: Pitman; Lundy, O. and Cowling, A. (1996) *Strategic Human Resource Management*, London: Routledge.
11 Storey, J. (1992) *Developments in the Management of Human Resources*, Oxford: Blackwell.

[12] Baruch, Y. (1998) 'Walking the Tightrope: Strategic Issues for Human Resources', *Long Range Planning*, 31(3), 467–75.

[13] Mannheim, B., Baruch, Y. and Tal, J. (1997) 'Testing Alternative Models for Antecedents and Outcomes of Work Centrality and Job Satisfaction', *Human Relations*, 50(12), 1537–62.

[14] Mishra, K.E., Spreitzer, G.M. and Mishra, A.K. (1998) 'Preserving employee morale during downsizing', *Sloan Management Review*, Winter, 83–95; Baruch, Y. and Hind, P. (1999) 'Perpetual Motion in Organizations: Effective Management and the impact of the new psychological contracts on "Survivor Syndrome"', *European Journal of Work and Organizational Psychology*, 8(2), 295–306.

[15] Furnham, A. (2000) 'Work in 2020: prognostications about the world of work 20 years into the millennium', *Journal of Managerial Psychology*, 15(3), 242–54.

Company index

Author index

Subject index